Paranormal Prowlers: I'm Always With You

Tessa Marie Mauro

This book is based on true events, two sisters and a best friend, creating a paranormal investigating group and the results and evidence collected from their investigations.

For respect of some of our fellow investigators, some of the names (*) have been changed to protect their identities, as well as the deceased from my personal experiences, for the respect of their families and friends.

This book was written in 2016-2018

All rights reserved.

© Tessa Marie Mauro 2018

This book is dedicated to all the believers, fellow paranormal investigators, and to our loved ones that are no longer with us and waiting for us on the other side.

To see the pictures in this book in full color, you can find them, and many other pictures of mine on social media.

Instagram – officialparanormalprowlers
Facebook – Paranormal Prowlers
Twitter - @AuthorMauro

*To get updates about my worldwide paranormal talk show you can find me on Twitter @DJ_Prowla_KICH_*

Acknowledgements

Thank you to my phenomenal family for always supporting me and my passion for the Paranormal, I am forever grateful, I know some people whose families aren't so accepting of something that is so unknown.

Not only are you accepting, you always take time out of your Friday nights to listen to my paranormal talk show on the radio, watch ghost shows with me, happily hear (and ask) about my experiences and investigations. Hell, there's times when several of you have went out and conducted investigations alongside me.

Thank you dad. (Jerry) and mom (KimAnna) and my stepdad (Mike) for always being there for me and genuinely taking an interest in the mysterious world of the Paranormal and supporting me no matter what. You guys are my rock.

To my sisters, (Carly and Jenna) thank you for allowing me to be the weird sister, as a kid it sucked, but as an adult, it's pretty kick ass. Even though we argue sometimes because, hey, that's what siblings do, I couldn't ask for any better sisters.

Thank you, Jourdan Ortega for being my best friend, always being there for me, through the great times and the sad times, for helping me create what is now The Paranormal Prowlers. Not everyone can say they get to have conversations with their late Uncle.

Thank you to my Aunt Bridget for the pre-editing process of the book, I appreciate your time and effort. Thank you, Aunt Butch for allowing me to read the rough draft to you and helping me smooth some bits of the book out.

A HUGE thank you to my friend, author and paranormal investigator whose based out of the ever so beautiful Ireland, Kim O'Shea. At the time I didn't have an editor, and even though she's a super busy person, she graciously offered to edit my book for me and help me with self-publishing process!

Kim O'Shea is a phenomenal editor and I would recommend her to anybody who is thinking of writing a book. She's patient, she brings up good points and tips, and she is dedicated to make the to-be-author thrive and be successful!

Thank you to all the people I have met throughout the several years of investigating the Paranormal hot spots throughout the United States. I appreciate each of you and treasure the memories we've created together. Someday I'd love to go across the pond and investigate with all my friends who are lucky to live in such a beautiful place!

Thank you to the people who shared their paranormal experiences with me and allowed me to put them in this book:

*Carly Mauro, Ivan B, *Aunt Ms. Meribyrd, *Aunt Bridget, Sheila, Laurie, Rosalie, Nick, JC Salazar, Ken, John M, Angie E Velasquez, Jeanette Amlie, *Marianne, Aunt Ronda Mauro, M W Dolph, KimAnna, and Joe Musso.

I full heartedly enjoyed hearing your experiences and encounters. Some heartwarming, others mind blowing, all unique and special.

Thank you to the spirits who speak with me, show themselves to me and are there for me, for I am truly never alone in this world.

Thank you to everyone in my life. I appreciate each of you.

Contents

Chapter one 15
   Paranormal Experiences ....
Chapter two 32
   Words of a Medium ....
Chapter three 41
   Night Terrors ....
Chapter four 44
   Tales from another ....
Chapter five 91
   Paranormal Investigating ....
Chapter six 96
   Bachelor's Loop ....
   Creede, Colorado ....
Chapter seven 106
Chapter eight 131
   Rock Creek Cemetery ....
   Monte Vista, Colorado ....
Chapter nine 146
   Pioneer Cemetery ....
   Pueblo, Colorado ....
Chapter ten 158
   Moores Creek Battlefield ....
   Near Wilmington, North Carolina ....
Chapter eleven 162
   The Battle of Wyse Fork ....
   Kinston, North Carolina ....
Chapter twelve 165
   The Green Burial ....
   Saguache County, Penitente Canyon, ...

At Angel Rock, Colorado ....

Chapter thirteen 177

Chapter fourteen 185

    The Tutwiler Hotel ....

    Birmingham, Alabama ....

Chapter fifteen 191

    The Historic Windsor Hotel ....

    Del Norte, Colorado ....

Chapter sixteen 203

    Boot Hill Grave Yard ....

    Tombstone, Arizona ....

Chapter seventeen 214

    The Bird Cage Theatre ....

    Tombstone, Arizona ....

Chapter eighteen 223

    Big Nose Kate's Saloon ....

    Tombstone, Arizona ....

Chapter nineteen 227

    Watt and Tarbell Mortuary ....

    (Sisters Paranormal Investigations) ....

    Tombstone, Arizona ....

Chapter twenty 246

    Sheila's Copper Penny ....

    Jerome, Arizona ....

Chapter twenty-one 257

    Jerome Grand Hotel ....

    Jerome, Arizona ....

Chapter twenty-two 285

    Old Jerome Jail ....

    Jerome, Arizona ....

Chapter twenty-three 291

- Sedona Community Cemetery..
- Sedona, Arizona ....
- Chapter twenty-four 295
  - Waverly Hills Sanatorium ....
  - Louisville, Kentucky ....
- Chapter twenty-five 321
  - The Ouija Board sessions ....
  - Louisville, Kentucky ....
- Chapter twenty-six 331
  - Bernard's Mining Cabin,...
  - La Veta Pass, Colorado ....
- Chapter twenty-seven 340
  - Hose Company No. 3 Fire Museum ....
  - Pueblo, Colorado ....
- Chapter twenty-eight 355
  - Teller County Jail 'Outlaws & Law Men Jail Museum' .....
  - Cripple Creek, Colorado...
- Chapter twenty-nine 375
  - Investigating Sarah's home ....
  - Pueblo, Colorado ....
- Chapter thirty..382
  - The attachment and dealing with Red Sample ....

Table of Pictures

Figure 1 The Spirit approaches Jeanette Amlie 82
Figure 2 The Spirit gets a make-over 83
Figure 3 Picture of the orb 93
Figure 4 Close-up of the orb 94
Figure 5 Another close-up of the orb 94
Figure 6 Courtesy of Jourdan Ortega 112
Figure 7 Jourdan at her Uncle's grave 122
Figure 8 Picture of unknown object near the graves 136
Figure 9 Close-up of the unknown object 136
Figure 10 A face in the mist 139
Figure 11 Close-up of the face 139
Figure 12 Picture of noose with blue figure below 242
Figure 13 Sheila's picture of Dicus as a young man 248
Figure 14 Fire-fighter ghost silhouette 348
Figure 15 Red Sample's Grave 401

Introduction

By Tessa Marie Mauro

Ever since I was a young child, I always believed in ghosts. Always. I grew up with an open mind. As I write these words I am thirty-three years old. In my thirty-three years of life, I have had many different paranormal experiences. Communication from the other side from loved ones. Loved ones that I desperately missed. You will read about some of those experiences in the book itself.

Death seems to never be too far from my mind, my thoughts, my dreams … my heart. As a teen, my family and I spent some time in New Mexico, in a tiny mountain town, I was all too familiar with death and what it was, at a very tender age. For some reason, in New Mexico, the roads were very unforgiving. I consider them serial killers. You drive through those small towns and the sides of the roads are littered with crosses and memorials, the roads' victims. The place where they drew their last breath.

I had a couple close calls as a kid out there. One time my dad's friend, *Ashley, who worked for him at a Mineral Springs Resort, was going to Santa Fe, and she invited me along. My dad for some reason said no. We lived in a tiny, dirt-road town where, as a kid, there wasn't much to do. Santa Fe had the Plaza, cafes, the mall, the skatepark, and so much more. I was so mad he wouldn't let me go, I pouted the whole day.

Later, we noticed a large amount of action going on across the street from our house, which just so happened to be the volunteer fire department. Word got out that there was a horrific accident. One fatality. There was a cow involved, they swerved to miss the cow, and crashed. My dad's friend, my friend, someone I looked up to, was that fatality. Ashley was a wonderful person, who died too young. She was loving, and giving, and had a heart of gold.

Who knows, maybe if I went along that day, if my dad had said yes, maybe I would be gone as well. Perhaps I might have survived, it's impossible to say. After the shock of it all, once the tears dried up, I sat and thought, "Wow, my dad said no. If he said yes, what if…?" I can still hear her sweet voice, her laugh.

I also lost fellow students from school from car accidents, suicides, and even murder. Death stuns you. It shocks you. Death shakes you right to your core. Death is the only guarantee that we have in life. It doesn't matter if you are the inventor of beer, an Academy award winner, or a homeless person, we all die. That's one thing nobody can escape. Some pass on younger than others, but we all die.

My sister *Carly and I created Paranormal Prowlers back in 2011. It's a group of people, including my best friend Jourdan, that share the passion and belief of the paranormal. Our bond is strong. I cannot even fully describe the feeling that goes through me when we are investigating an area and hear the voices of the deceased. The EVP (Electronic Voice Phenomenon) of a man, so close, it's like he is standing right next to you, whispering in your ear.

As a team, while at an investigation site, we have important equipment that helps us get our results. To me, the digital recorder is the most important tool. It is so sensitive that it catches anything and everything, which is useful since, studies say, when a spirit speaks, their voice is two decibels below what the human ear can hear. I have personally found the digital recorder to be very useful and successful.

The other tools we use include, several different types of EMF meters (Electronic Magnetic Field), shadow and motion detectors, a digital camera, a spirit box, an Ovilus, the recorder and more. I will go into more detail about these items later in the book.

At an investigation we do what is called an EVP session. We do a few of these at different times throughout the investigation. An EVP session is when you use only the digital recorder and ask questions, with silence in between. You will be surprised what you can collect doing this. In EVP sessions my crew and I have been able to record, breathing, footsteps, disembodied sounds, whispering, crying, talking and much more. We also do sessions with the spirit box. With the digital recorder on, we use the spirit box, where it constantly sweeps through radio channels, which is supposed to help the spirits communicate easier.

Sometimes when watching paranormal shows, one might wonder, is it all true? Is any of it manipulated in some way? Is something added? If these shows don't have results then they don't have viewers, meaning they don't have ratings or a show. I am not saying that is the case, really, I'm not. I love those shows, and I fully enjoy watching them.

I believe what I see on those shows, for the most part, but the world is full of nonbelievers, close-minded people, debunkers and skeptics galore. Which is fine, if we were all the same, the world would be an excruciatingly boring place. However, I must ask, if there was a possibility that your deceased loved ones lived on through the soul, that they were there, looking over you, perhaps trying to communicate with you, believer or not, why not at least have an open mind?

I am not trying to encourage you to go out and start trying to communicate with the dead, I am lucky and have had no possessions or attachments, (at the time this was written, that was accurate, however a year after I had begun writing this book, a trip to Tombstone changed that and threw luck right out the window!) which can happen to people, and I heard it is really hard to get rid of an attachment. As a crew, while at investigation sites, we do an opening protection prayer and a closing prayer.

I have had many people that have passed, who were very close to me in life, communicate with me, through sound, smell, dreams, and more. I wouldn't trade these experiences for anything. It's raw. It's pure. It's life, and death. It's one of a kind, this book goes in to detail about the places we have investigated, the history behind these haunting sites and the results we have collected.

Unfortunately, for all we know, a spirit can be standing right next to us, screaming in our ear, only for us not to hear them. So, when I listen to these recordings, while I can make out many of the words, there are some that I listen to repeatedly but do not understand it at all.

The investigation at the site is just a part of it. I consider it the first half of the investigation. Long after we are gone from the site and back in our warm cozy homes, the investigation lives on. This is a perfect example; we record a five-minute EVP session. Five minutes, not long right? On the recorder I go to the slowest listening option possible, to really hear things, things that you cannot hear or easily miss when in regular play mode. Then there is endless rewinding, debunking, replaying, taking notes etc. A five-minute session can easily take thirty minutes or longer of listening, note taking and more.

Honestly, that's my favorite part. Investigations are so intense, I feel honored being a part of it. Sometimes, you leave an investigation, like a dog with his tail between his legs, feeling down, like you were unsuccessful. At home you listen and hear things that make your skin crawl, makes your heart jump and puts a smile on your face without you even noticing it.

Results you didn't know existed – like a Christmas present under the tree, or that oddly shaped birthday present that you're dying to know what's inside – that dog with the tail hidden between its legs, is suddenly shaking back and forth with such force its whole body is moving. That's how I feel when I hear those amazing raw results we collected from the investigation.

I want to be the first to say, we are not famous. All I can say is that what we do is real, raw, and honest. Every place we have gone to, to date, we have gotten results … as for that famous thing … who knows? Perhaps one day!

I hope you enjoy this book as much as we, as a team did, conducting these investigations, collecting the evidence and my creating this book for you. Please, grab a blanket, and a bowl of popcorn and read this book with an open mind.

Enjoy, my friends.

Prologue

The house hides deep within a secluded mountain, fog rolls through the trees, slowly making its way toward the house. Creaking. The wind, sounding like a lonely woman weeping. Disembodied footsteps on the upper floor.

The woman in bed, takes her reading glasses off, puts her novel down on her lap. Listening intently. She's home alone. Earlier that day, she arranged for her brother, who happened to be her roommate, to go on an overnight trip to a mutual friend's house. She looked forward to having the house to herself.

She regrets this decision. Listening. Yes, the footsteps are getting closer. She tiptoes to her safe, opens it, wincing at the noise of the click. She silently grabs her .22, loaded.

She walks to the bedroom door, quietly opening it. Slowly pokes her head out. Gun in one hand, in the other, her cell phone with 911 ready to go. She double checks all the windows and doors. All secured, locked, and untouched. Finally, she checks the security system. Nope, nothing.

She's not going crazy. She heard footsteps, or did she? As this thought races through her mind, she shakes, her skin surrendering to goosebumps. A cold spot? She walks to the heater. Yup, it's on.

She walks back to her room. Closes the door. She is suddenly overwhelmed by a scent. What is that? She can't seem to put her finger on it. So familiar, yet she cannot remember why. Shadows, dancing on the walls, intertwining with each other. Taunting her. The wind wailing again. She puts her head on the pillow. Closes her eyes.

Suddenly a thought creeps into her mind. Her eyes are now open wide. Her Grandma. That smell, her Grandma. Impossible. Her sweet Grandma has been gone for well over a decade. Dead. Went to take a nap, never woke up. No wonder she had trouble remembering the smell, she hadn't been around it in over ten years. How can this be? She was raised to believe there was no such thing as the boogeyman, ghosts, spirits, things that go bump in the night.

Think back. When you were a kid, you were probably told many things that weren't necessarily true. The Tooth Fairy. The Easter Bunny. Santa Clause, etc. Don't get me wrong, those things made childhood more adventurous. Why else would I be excited for my loose tooth to get painfully yanked out, so

I can receive a visit from the famous Tooth Fairy? You believed. They didn't exist. You don't believe in spirits, but what if they exist?

Let's face it. When you watch that scary movie, adrenaline runs through your body. You get the chills. You find yourself looking past your shoulder to reassure yourself that no one is there. Let me ask you a question, you don't see anybody there but ... what if someone is and you just can't see them?

Have you ever had someone in your life pass away? You love them. You miss them. You think about them. What if they were still around? Sure, they are physically gone, but spiritually they are there. Watching over you. Embracing you. I, myself have had so many experiences throughout my life, that I wholeheartedly believe that once the human body passes away, the soul lives on.

As a paranormal investigator, I have conducted countless investigations at several places and have collected different types of evidence. Sometimes you can have evidence of a spirit without even knowing you have it. Evidence we have collected includes; disembodied breathing, footsteps, noises, words, even burps, EVPs, direct intelligent answers to our questions, pictures of manifestations, orbs – not dust, friends, but actual orbs that have faces within them, phantom creatures, rainbow arches and so much more!

The evidence is overwhelming. The world is full of skeptics. Hell, I live with one, my boyfriend Justin is the biggest debunker out there. Unexplainable things would even happen to him and he would still debunk them.

Chapter one

Paranormal Experiences

~THE BLUE PROTECTOR~ (PUEBLO, COLORADO)

I graduated from high school in New Mexico. A place I hated and despised for several years, due to intense bullying from many of the children. What was their motive for the daily horrific bullying activities? Being Italian (or what they saw as white) and not being Hispanic, Spanish, or Mexican. Later, I did end up making some wonderful friends, but the bullying continued. So, it was no surprise that one week after graduation, I packed up all my belongings and moved back to Pueblo, Colorado.

Until I found an apartment of my own, I lived with my Grandma. We were roommates for two months and then I found an available apartment on O'Neal Avenue, just a couple blocks from my sweet Grandma's house.

Soon enough I made friends, but since I was bullied in all Middle school and a good part of high school, I felt I had to buy my friendships and buy them I did. Beer, booze, food, gifts, anything they wanted, I bought it for them. They were using me, and I was too stupid to see it or figure it out. Since I had my own pad, I was always hosting parties at my apartment.

If you know me, you know I always have a camera on me. Always taking pictures. Soon I started to notice that in these party pictures, a blue form would be present. If I were by myself, it was on my side, if it was a group picture, it would be behind me.

Being out on my own for the first time, and paying bills was foreign to me. When it came to "friends" I didn't mind spending money on them, but paying boring, lousy bills was quite the opposite. So, every time I left that apartment, I damned well made sure all electronics were off. I had this six-disc CD player system, the big huge bulky kind. I had it set up in my room. I would come home to find it on. Always. I would turn the power off, leave, only to find it on playing songs on my return. Then lights would be on when I knew they had been off earlier.

One of the parties I had quickly got out of hand. A case of CD's (including 3 Bone Thugs N Harmony CDs that were signed by them) got stolen. Hundreds of dollars' worth of music gone. This was before iTunes and I was devastated. I felt betrayed. Other things were stolen as well that night. I kicked the "friends" out and never saw them again.

I never saw that blue figure again either. I think that blue form, was a spirit looking after me while I was young and dumb and didn't know I was being used. I think this spirit did know. It was looking after me. Once those people were out of my life, so was the blue form.

~FOOTSTEPS FROM BEYOND THE GRAVE~ (MOUNTAIN VIEW, CALIFORNIA)

While I was living in California (2009-2012), I was deeply saddened to hear about the death of a friend back home in Colorado. He was so young. Early 20s. *Aaron and I worked together at my dad's Steakhouse. We became good friends and he became a regular when I had parties at my house.

Aaron was a big guy, he was very tall, had curly hair and loved football. He was such a friendly guy and his laugh and smile were certainly contagious. When I heard he died, I thought maybe it was a car accident or something of that sort. After I heard the cause of death – a heroin overdose – I was in utter shock.

I remember finding his obituary in my home town's local newspaper, The Pueblo Chieftain. We lived in a small apartment with the apartment above us vacant. My roommates were at work and it was just my boyfriend and I. My boyfriend, Justin, when bored, paces. Nonstop. Back and forth, back and forth, back and forth. I don't know if it's a nervous habit or just something to do.

He is doing this as I am trying to concentrate and read my dear friend's obit. I get impatient and kindly ask him to go in the kitchen to start making lunch for us – a pizza. He walks out, towards the kitchen. Our bedroom had a connecting bathroom to it, so I walk into the bathroom and sit down by the tub and start reading.

I'm probably in my third sentence of the obituary when I hear the pacing start up again. I try not to show my frustration and continue reading. Those footsteps, pacing, back and forth, back and forth, like going from one side of the room to the other. Repeatedly.

I can't take it anymore, and start complaining, "Geez, can you please stop that. I thought you were going to start lunch?" Yada, yada, yada.

All of a sudden, I hear another set of footsteps, coming from outside of my room, coming towards me. Justin walks in with a look of confusion on his face. "What? Were you just talking?" He asks.

Perplexed, I say, "Yes! I was talking to you!"

Turns out he was in the kitchen the whole time. I know I heard footsteps. So clearly. Then to hear another set of footprints. I cannot explain this. Here I am in the dumps, mourning my friend Aaron's death, reading his obituary when suddenly these footsteps are pacing the floor, just right outside the room I'm in.

Like I said, nobody lived above us, nobody else was home. I am sensitive when a loved one dies, and after all these years and countless deaths, Justin knows to leave me alone and give me my space. It was a perfect day that day, no wind, nothing like that. I would like to think, it was my friend Aaron there, comforting me in my time of sorrow.

~GRANDMA'S TOUCH~ (PUEBLO, COLORADO)

When my Grandma passed away, I was beyond devastated. We were very close, and her dying was a huge blow. I couldn't say Grandma and funeral in the same sentence without losing it completely. She was always there for me, and now she is gone. I can still feel her presence at times though.

A few days before her funeral, I was busy collecting as many pictures as I could and creating a beautiful collage dedicated to her. Not only was it dedicated to her, but it would be at her funeral, for all to see. I was staying at my dad's house. He had a date night with his girlfriend, so I wanted to make sure I was out of the house, so they could enjoy their dinner.

None of my friends could meet up with me because of jobs and prior plans. Last resort, Grandma's condo. Usually I would go there without hesitation, but now that she was gone, it seemed so weird to be there without her. I walk in the door and just feel the emptiness. All her possessions still in their designated spots.

I set up my cardboard, flowers, pictures, glue and tape on the living room floor and start to work on my collage. The silence is deafening. I feel like I am being watched. I suddenly am quite uneasy. I turn on the television, in hopes to change the mood. With 'Everybody Loves Raymond" as background noise, the uptight feeling slowly but surely melts away.

I am uncomfortable when it comes to staying the night here by myself. I don't know why. It was such a warm, lovely and welcoming place before. A place where many memories were created. A place where my Grandma spent countless hours in the kitchen making her famous Tortellini soup, or various baked goods. Grandma not being there is such a weird feeling. I kept half expecting her to walk in the door or something.

I kept the television on the whole time I was there to drown out the silence. When it was time to go to sleep, I decided to sleep on the couch in the living room not in the guest room or her bedroom, both of which had big enough beds to sleep three people.

While sleeping on the not so comfy couch, I kept waking up, getting blinded each time by the illuminating TV. I decide to turn it off and slowly fall asleep again. Something wakes me up. I hear what sounds like hushed whispering. I cannot make out the words, all I know is I absolutely heard whispering.

I get up to look around the house, I turn on the lights and double-check the front door and the back door. Both secure and locked. All by myself. I lay down and doze off again. I don't know how much time goes by, but I find myself awake again. I open my eyes. Something in the kitchen has my attention. There is a small light, almost like a lamp post attached to the wall, that is on. My Grandma used to leave it on overnight so if she had to wake up to get a cup of water she would be able to see. I know that light was off earlier, I turned it off myself after checking the place.

The light wasn't the only thing that caught my eye, there was a shadow figure standing by the light. Someone was standing there. I was by myself in this condo, yet plain as day, there this shadow figure was. I wasn't nervous or scared. I felt nothing. I simply closed my eyes, put the blanket over my face and stayed there till morning.

I would like to think that this shadow was my Grandma. She had called this comfy condo home for well over two decades. By the back door, just a few feet away from where I saw the figure standing, are concrete steps where she fell which resulted in her death. Life and death.

From time to time, I feel my Grandma. Sometimes I can smell her. A fresh clean welcoming laundry smell, Tide and Downy. Her sweet voice and laugh. I smile just thinking about them. Not a day goes by where I don't think about her. I know she is looking over me.

When I had that experience with what I think was her spirit, I was not in a good spot. I was depressed from losing her. I was feeling negative and had sadness and anger residing deep within me. The whispering and shadow may have been a way to let me know that I was not alone. She lived to be eighty-seven years old. She lived a good and long life, much longer than many people these days.

~BROTHERLY LOVE~ (SUNNYVALE, CALIFORNIA)

Even though we were not related through blood, Ryan was my brother. My youngest sister Carly and I adopted him as a brother when he and our middle sister, Jenna dated. His past was a sad one. He experienced many deaths of people near and dear to him, including both his parents.

When my car got totaled he insisted on trying to help me get a new one and continuously checked up on me. When Jenna and Ryan broke up, he would sometimes come over to my dad's house and hang out with me. He would bring Taco Bell and we would play Nintendo. Usually Mario Brothers.

He was such a great guy, and when I heard the news that he took his own life I was beside myself. I felt like I lost my brother. I still feel that way. He was way too young. When he shot himself, life was very stressful, and unfortunately, he did something permanent that couldn't be fixed.

I was just in Colorado visiting family for the holidays and had just come back to California a couple weeks earlier. Unfortunately, I didn't have the money or the availability to take off work, so I sadly stayed back as they put my adopted brother to rest. It killed me that I couldn't be there. When someone you care about dies, I always find it calming, comforting and therapeutic to be with those you love in such difficult times. Being 1,100 miles away from my family and friends, I felt so alone.

A couple weeks after Ryan's funeral, I was sitting on my bed in my tiny studio apartment, crying. In my hand, a photo of Ryan and I in a frame. I'm looking at it, crying, thinking about him. Still in complete shock of his absence. Off to

the side is my book charger that I use for work. It is silent. Unless it is in my hand and I am scanning something, it stays mute. Always.
Suddenly, as I sit there crying, the book scanner starts beeping continuously. I was confused why it would be doing this. I walk over to examine it. I cannot detect any reason why it would do that. At the same time my studio is overwhelmed with a smell. I recognize it immediately as Ryan.

I whole-heartedly believe my brother was there, looking over me. He saw I was distressed and knew I was deeply mourning him and I think he wanted me to know he is there and that I'm not alone. A few times since, I find myself in the presence of his smell. I will always have a place for my adopted brother in my heart.

~GRANDPA, GUARDIAN ANGEL OF GRANDDAUGHTER ~ (COLORADO)

Speaking of phantom smells, besides my adopted brother Ryan, I also from time to time have had the same experience with my Grandpa, my father's father. Like my Grandma, my Grandpa and I were very close and when he died I took it very hard.

Each Sunday for brunch, I would pick my Grandpa up to take him to my dad's Steakhouse, that in my opinion, had the best brunch in town. It was always the same thing, always the same routine. I would call him when I was on my way, honk when I arrived, he would come outside and wave. He would then come to my car window and say he had to feed the cat. To myself I would say, "Okay old man, why can't you feed your darn cat when I first call to let you know I am on the way." He then goes to feed his cat, probably uses the restroom, then comes out. It was our routine, time I got to spend with him. Just the two of us.

He was quite a spectacular man. He fought in the Second World War and Battle of the Bulge. I definitely feel and smell him around me sometimes and when I feel him, it's always a comforting and calming feeling.
I find it very comforting. Some people may feel weird, uneasy or uncomfortable if they were in my shoes. I embrace it. I find it an honor that through death, people I cared for very much while alive, now look over me. I wouldn't trade that for anything.

~CEDAR ALLEY, THE ALLEY OF PHANTOM SMELLS~ (DEL NORTE, COLORADO)

Since I'm on the topic about senses, I need to bring this up. I had this amazing apartment in Del Norte, it was my mom's building, but long ago it was the town's original Lumber yard. This apartment overlooks the small mountain town of Del Norte.

Many a times I would be sitting in the living room, along with my sister Carly and boyfriend Justin. It was our main hang out spot where we would eat, drink and watch movies. I cannot count the times I have had this occurrence take place. I would be sitting there, in my Grandma's recliner that I got after she passed away, watching TV (or reading a book), when suddenly I smell a woody, cedar type smell. This isn't just a hint of a scent, it's an in-your-face, the only thing you can smell type of scent.

I would even have Carly or Justin come over in front of where I was and see if they could smell this cedar smell. The smell was so strong you would think that it could be detected from across the room. I was confused when they could not smell this strong cedar scent.

To this day I am not too sure where this phantom smell comes from. As the building was a former lumber yard decades ago, could this smell be a residual haunting from a former lumber yard worker, or the lumber yard itself? It's almost like it's trapped.

A few times this happened, I had my EMF meter handy and I turned it on, it always spiked between 2-3. To date, I haven't experienced that cedar smell again. How one person can smell something so strongly to the point that their head is spinning, while others not the slightest whiff, is amazing to me.

~THE SCREAMING OUIJA~ (OJO CALIENTE, NEW MEXICO)

Back in the early 90s we lived in New Mexico, in a small town many have never even heard of. We didn't have many friends there, so when a little blond-haired girl, Christy, moved to town, my sisters and I were excited to make a new friend.

Christy lived in a house on a hill. My mom owned a little shop below the hill, so we often went to Christy's house to play. We were friends for quite a few years. Christy and I even went to a Becoming a Woman week ceremony in

Santa Fe with our mothers together. Throughout the years we have lost contact.

Thankfully for social media, her sweet mother, my dear friend, and I kept in touch on Facebook. I found out that Christy, in her early 30's, sadly passed away. I was taken aback. How devastating. I immediately thought about all the times we spent together. Memories flooding through me.

It made me wish that we would have stayed in each other's lives. Keeping in touch with old friends is not hard to do, but life gets in the way and you go on your own paths. We may have not talked in years, but I find myself thinking a lot about my childhood friend Christy.

Rewind back into the 90's. My sisters and I are at Christy's house. Somehow we got our little paws on a Ouija board, to this day, if I remember correctly, my sister Jenna had found one. We asked it some questions, and we got some answers. It was so long ago that I don't even remember what we asked or our results. I do remember her mom walking in the door and busting us. She was shocked that we were using this Ouija Board, took it from us and threw it in the fire.

I kid you not, that thing screamed. We all heard it with our own ears. Like the scream of a tormented woman. It was beyond eerie. As a child it was terrifying. As an adult I still get the chills as I recollect the memories of that day.

I had a discussion with Ouija board expert Robert Murch, who shared with me that he had been told this similar experience several times—the screaming when trying to destroy the Ouija. Another scary moment that we shared with Christy at a different time, we were at my house hanging out. We were sitting at the kitchen table. There sat a glass of water. This glass started moving by itself. No ice in it, no condensation. It started going in circles on the table, then with force, slid off the table onto the carpet floor.

We ran outside and ran up the street, to Christy's mom's boyfriend at the time, *Ken, who also is sadly no longer with us, and we told him what happened. He could see by the way we were acting that we weren't kidding around. Ken was a very spiritual person, he owned a rock and gem store and had many neat things to offer.

If I remember correctly, I believe he gave each of us a small rock for protection. In addition, he gave us a figurine, a magnificent figurine. It was an

Archangel. Wings high, holding a spear, standing on the devil himself while pointing the spear to his head. I was the oldest out of the bunch, so I held on to it for safe keeping.

Having possession of this item made me feel safe. When I moved around, state to state, it stayed with me. In fact, as I am writing these words, I stopped, just now, walked over to my desk and picked up the figurine. Two decades later, and I still have this Archangel by my side. I always considered it special; the purpose it held within itself, the secure protection, and also the man who gave it to us, a dear friend. *Ken passed away a few short years after from cancer.

Whenever I look at it I think of the paranormal encounters we had as kids together. Unique childhood memories. I think of protection. I think of Ken, and now I also think of Christy. May they both rest in peace.

~A VISIT FROM AN OLD FRIEND~ (PUEBLO, COLORADO)

Around 2002, I was working at my dad's Steakhouse, and became friends with a group of people that worked with me. One of those friends was Michael. We as a group were best of friends. We threw parties, either at my house, or sometimes his house.

Michael didn't have what we would call a normal childhood. We openly drank and smoked at his house without a care in the world. I won't go into detail about his life. He was a very private person and he allowed me to be part of that world. When our other friends were out doing their own thing, he would invite me to come over and we had some intense conversations. I really cared about him, he was one of my best friends and I will never forget the times we spent together. When he died, he was only in his late 20s. Even though we hadn't spoken in many years prior to his death, I felt a huge void when he died. It's hard to explain. Memories came to me like a speeding train.

When I heard he died, I felt nothing, then anger, then sadness and regret that we hadn't been friends or tried to mend the friendship. To this day I still mourn for Michael. In fact, I think he is with me … scratch that, I know he is with me. He is looking after me. At first, I thought it was an attachment but now I know he is just here to watch over me.

How do I know that it is Michael? I just do. I know that's not a good answer, especially for skeptics, but I feel his presence. I have also seen him a couple times. Clear as day. I have communicated with him through investigations numerous times and when I asked for a specific sign from him he gave it to me. I will explain more of this later when I talk about the investigations.

One day I was at home, his death fresh in my mind. I sat on a chair in the living room crying. I was home alone. The TV was on, I was watching a true crime show and I just couldn't wrap my brain around the thought that Michael was gone. I close my eyes as tears drop down my cheek. I say aloud, "Why can't I get you out of my head? Why can't I stop thinking about you?"

When I opened my eyes, he was sitting across from me on the couch. He was so close I could have touched him. He was sitting there, looking at me. He didn't say a single word. Just looked at me and as fast as he was there, he left. I will never forget that moment. Ever. That day, I saw Michael's full-bodied apparition.

This won't be the last time Michael is mentioned in this book. It's weird to say but, he is more a part of my life now, then he was the last few years of his life.

~GHOSTLY DREAMS~ (PUEBLO, COLORADO)

My friend *Peter was a Pueblo, Colorado guy … 100%. He lived in Pueblo his whole life, a family member became sick and he made the move out of state to be there to help. He always missed Pueblo. He knew he would move there again when things got better. He craved Pueblo. He missed his friends. His family. He missed Pueblo.

Many a time we would have conversations about his moving back and making plans to hang out and throw the biggest welcome back party out there. We always competed, especially when it came to beer bongs.

I was working at the Convention Center, when a mutual friend approached me and said he didn't know if it was true or not, but he heard through the grapevine that Peter was in a car accident. I had a full day of work ahead of me so, I put it on the back burner and went on with my day. The thought he may be hurt stuck with me in the back of my mind. My nerves played around with me that whole day. I tried staying positive, but all I could think about was Peter.

I get off work and start heading home, my phone starts ringing, it is raining hard. Unforgiving rain drops slam hard against my windshield, making it difficult for me to see. I pull over and answer the phone. My best friend and fellow paranormal investigator, Jourdan is on the other end, clearly upset. What I heard earlier at work was true. Peter was in a horrific car accident. There was one fatality. Peter was dead.

I was in shock. How can this be? He was so close to having enough money saved to move back to Pueblo. Back to his home. The only home he ever knew. He always knew when he went out of state that he would be back, I just don't think he thought it would be this way, to be buried.

I remember going to his funeral. I was an empty shell. I was numb. He was so damn young. Parents should not have to bury their children. I cannot imagine the pain they went through. I walk over to the open casket. So calm. So quiet. So unnatural. Peter was always so active, and here he is now, just lying there. I have to admit that I kind of expected him to jump out of that casket and yell, "Boo!" or something. He didn't. His death left a huge void in many people's lives. Including mine. Death is unforgiving.

One night I was sleeping—this was before his funeral—I am surrounded by what looks like clouds. I'm sitting on a bench when Peter approaches me. He sits next to me on the bench and clasps my hands. He looks in my eyes. My heart is racing, my head is pounding. I know he is dead, but here he is, here with me. He lets me know that he is okay. Not to be sad. He is in a better place. He let me know he came to me because he knew I would listen. He continued to tell me, "I know you will be okay, please, I'm concerned. Look after April D and *Darren."

I woke up with dried tears on my cheeks. I genuinely believe that spirits can come and communicate with the living through their dreams. This has happened a few times with me. Darren was a mutual friend, so that was easy enough for me, but at this point I had not yet met April, but only had heard about her from other people.

April Duran was one of Peters best friends. I don't know how I never met her before, but he had talked about her, so I knew her only from what he said. I knew how she looked because of pictures, but we never had chatted face to face.

That would soon change. I decided to make numerous copies of all the pictures of Peter I had collected throughout years of partying. I bought little photo albums and made one each for mutual friends, Jourdan, *Darren, April, and Peter's brother. I told April and *Darren about the dream. He came to me.

Sent a message, and I received that message and gave it to the people it involved.

April and I became friends, going to the cemetery to visit Peter. We would bring Mickeys, his favorite beer and drink in memory of him. We shared stories about Peter. April and I hadn't spoken in years. She and my best friend Jourdan are close friends as well, and recently we all got together and conducted an investigation. The results we got were great! (You'll read about that later on.)

Jourdan and I have had investigations at Peter's gravesite in the past, the last one we had, we caught Peter saying April's last name on audio. Class-A EVP, "Duran" clear as day. That's when I thought it would be a great thing to involve April in our next investigation.

Another dream I had of Peter, was eerie, scary and uncomfortable. I am outside and it is pitch black. I hear clinging noises up ahead of me. Like metal hitting the ground hard. I nervously walk toward the noise. As I get closer, I see a man, with an old shovel in his hands, sweat dripping off his face. Digging. Digging. Digging.

What is he digging? I creep up closer. He's not alone. A big object is off to his side. As I get closer, and my eyes adjust to the crude darkness, that big object turns into a casket. The bottom of the casket is full in form, but on top, the wood is decaying and gone. I peek my head above to look inside and see Peter lying there. The right side of his face is normal like how it looked at his funeral in the open casket. His left side is corroded with dirt, worms and maggots all over.

I wake up immediately, instantly cutting the dream off. I am covered in sweat. What the … The other dream he came to me, spoke to me. This dream was so different. I can't understand it. This dream was so incredibly graphic, so real. Peter has communicated with us in investigations, so you will hear more about Peter, and the results later as well.

~WENDY, THE FRIENDLY - AND VERY ACTIVE - GHOST (DEL NORTE, COLORADO)

When I lived in Del Norte, I worked at this fun store that had a cafe attached to it. One day, during closing hours, a photographer was there capturing pictures in the cafe. When developed, the photographer excitedly showed the owner. In the corner of the cafe stood a woman, in period clothing.

We called the woman Wendy. She was very active and not afraid to let us know that she was there watching us. From glasses flying off the shelves in the kitchen, to her opening the produce fridge doors in the store. A handful of times she even called out my sister's name, "Carly." For some reason, this spirit seems to have a connection with Carly and is very comfortable with her, Carly has shared some of the experiences she's had with Wendy. You'll read more about that later.

There have been countless times where I would be standing at the cash register, where I would be the only one around and suddenly the freezer would start opening and closing on its own. I would walk over to it and the door literally was opening and closing by itself. No way to explain that. No wind, and nobody around at all.

One time I heard loud banging and knocking, I notice it's at the front door. This was during opening hours and I had just checked the mail, so I knew that the door was unlocked. Again, I was the only person in the store at the time. I go to the door to open it, and it's locked! I unlocked the door to a not-so-happy owner. This has happened several times throughout the years. Unexplainable and quite frustrating.

Wendy has been a part of my life for many years. I don't know her real name or how she passed away, but she seems very at home in this unique store and the property that it sits on. She has been here for a long time. There are times when I would be in the store—cleaning, dusting or doing some type of other chore—only to feel like I'm not alone. Like I am being watched.

More recently, I was temporarily staying upstairs for a few months while working there, alone at night I'd lay in bed and while I didn't hear voices like Carly, I would hear footsteps, not creaks, coming up the stairs. I would also often get phantom smells late at night—sandalwood. Like the cedar smell, it was so overwhelming it was nauseating.

~SKEPTIC MEET DOPPELGANGER, DOPPELGANGER MEET SKEPTIC~ (DEL NORTE, COLORADO)

One evening before bed, Justin went outside to take our dog Midnight for his nightly potty walk. While he did this, I was sitting in bed with my iPad, watching the TV show, "The Haunting Of." Justin walks into the room after a few minutes of being gone and has a look of confusion on his face.

I pause my show, look up at him and ask, "What's wrong?"

He says, "Why didn't you wave back?"

Now it was my turn to be confused. I let him know that I was in bed the whole time.

He replies, "Really? I looked up at our bedroom window. I saw you standing there. So, I start waving, you don't move or react so, I continue to do this. Then you back up and I can't see you anymore."

Very interesting. Justin's eyes aren't the best at night so maybe when he looked up there and saw a woman standing there, he automatically assumed it was me. Even when this happens, this hardcore skeptic just brushes it off his shoulder. I know that it wasn't me. Nobody else was at the house at the time.

There have been times when I felt a presence at that apartment and I have been told by a medium that there is a spirit of a woman that resides there. That the apartment was the last place she was, before her untimely death. She chooses to be there because she is familiar with it. I believe that, this woman, is the person Jack saw when he was outside that night.

~SENDING A SIGN FROM THE GRAVE~ (PUEBLO, COLORADO)

One day I went to the cemetery to visit Michael. When I visit someone, I speak aloud to them, as if they are right there listening to me. I believe they are. I was discussing things going on in my life, this goes on for ten minutes or so. I then stop talking. Listening. I look behind me to see if someone is there. No, there isn't. I feel like I am not alone and start to get a little uneasy. I get goosebumps, and I kid you not, I feel someone brush against my arm. I ask Michael, "Michael, if you are here with me and can understand what I am saying, can you please give me a sign?"

Quickly when I finish that sentence the sprinkler closest to me goes off, getting me wet, then as quickly as it went on, it stopped. That was the only one out of all the sprinklers in that cemetery that went off. I remember looking at my phone at the time and it was some random number. Not like an even time for watering. (Like it would be on a timer or something.)

A couple weeks later Jourdan and I went back to do another session with Michael, and when Jourdan asks, "Did you send Tessa a message last time she was here?" In a voice that sounded close to Michaels we got the reply, "Yes." I felt a presence, got touched then experienced the sprinkler going off. It was quite an interesting feeling for sure.

~APPARITIONS BE THERE~ (DEL NORTE, COLORADO)

For the whole month of March back in 2016, I was hired to help close down a store. I was there by myself, day in and day out, often sleeping in the live-in space upstairs. This happens to be the same place where my sister Carly had her experiences with the spirit of a woman we affectionately named Wendy.

One day, it must have been the second week in, I was working. Cleaning, dusting, packaging things up, etc. All day I did this with no real events. Sure, when I was in the cafe I would hear voices in the store. I kept the lights on throughout the whole place. Day turns into night, and I am still in the cafe. I am standing in front of one of the tables and I look off to my right, where the doorway connecting and separating the store and cafe stands. There in front of me stands a woman, she was translucent, she was staring at me, by the front desk, as if she were a customer. I look away. For almost twenty years this business has been in operation.

There was rarely a time when people weren't here. As I look away, I think to myself, then remind myself, 'Wait. We're closed. We've been closed for months. Nobody should be here at all.' I look back and she was gone. I know what I saw. She was there. Wendy. Just to make sure, I walked around the whole store, calling out to nobody, checking the doors. Locked. I knew that, but I also like to debunk things, not everything is paranormal.

After major renovation was done to this anonymous site, Wendy appeared, and she has never left. We don't know what her real name is, how she died, or why she chose to stay here, but she is harmless and seems to just want people to know she is around. That she exists or used to exist.

The month that I stayed there, besides the apparition, which I only saw once, almost daily I heard walking, pacing, footsteps. While on investigations I am looking for that kind of stuff but after a long day of work and getting ready for another long day of work all I want to do is sleep. I would fall asleep to my music playing from my phone and in the background, footsteps coming up the stairs could be heard.

~TESLA AT LAFAYETTE CEMETERY~ (NEW ORLEANS, LOUISIANA)

New Orleans has been and always will be my favorite place on Earth. So much haunted history here, it's mind blowing. I used to go during part of the summers as a child. I would stay with my dear family friends, Mike and Tess, who is my amazing namesake!

Being named Tessa … you don't hear that name very often. You hear Tess, Tessie, and Theresa. Many people, including my boyfriend, call me Tess. So, you can imagine how confusing it got for all involved when Justin and I went to visit back in October of 2017 and Justin would suddenly say, "Hey Tess" and start talking. Naturally, both Tess and I would answer. Then he'd have to say, "Not this Tess but this one."

Well, earlier that day, I had mentioned that those who barely knew me or had just met me sometimes call me Theresa or even Tessla. So, Justin said, to make things less confusing, he'd start calling me Nicola. No way in hell I'd answer to that, so he started calling me Tesla, and it worked. Tess and Tesla were close enough where I naturally started answering.

Tess took us around several of the cemeteries that are close to her home. We used the recorder and the Ovilus to see if we can gather anything from these cities-of-the-dead trips.

At one point, the Ovilus says: SOLDIER. Justin is quick to point out that a WWII veteran's grave is just a few feet away. Walking around that cemetery we found several soldiers' headstones, including some Confederates'. I guess it could have been any of them!

We end up at one of my favorite cemeteries, Lafayette Cemetery No 1. This cemetery has been in several movies, including Double Jeopardy. As we walk in the cemetery I start to record a video. Justin the skeptic, was interested in my newest tool, thanks to my family, the Ovilus, and is holding it along with the recorder. Being a skeptic, and never interested in the paranormal I was more than delighted to let him conduct his own investigation.

I get lost and distracted with my video, and a few minutes later I look around to realize that Tess and Justin are gone. In fact, everyone had left that area. I end the video and start calling out to Tess and Justin. Moments later my phone rings. It's Justin, he shares his location with me and I start to make my way to him. As I walk around the corner, I see him standing about thirty or so feet away.

He waves me over and then suddenly looks down at the Ovilus. He is shocked to see what is on the screen. As I walk over he says, "It said Tesla!" No way! I look at the screen as TESLA is staring back at me. He goes on to explain that the several minutes he was exploring by himself, besides the words: SOUL and ME, which came through in the very beginning, no other words had come through. Then as soon as I came into view and he saw me, it said TESLA.

Now remember, all day he had been calling me that. He called me it in the cemeteries as well, including Lafayette. My mind was blown when I saw that word on the screen.

~HE CAN'T BREATHE~ (JACKSONVILLE, NORTH CAROLINA)

One night, back in January of 2017, my boyfriend and I were sound asleep. Our dog, Midnight, usually sleeps at the foot of our bed on the floor on his own doggy bed. Sometime in the night I wake up hearing my boyfriend say, in a loud whisper, "He can't breathe." Suddenly I hear a loud desperate sound coming from Midnight.

I jump out of bed, turn the overhead light on and run over to my pup. Justin gets up and is trying to help figure out what is wrong. I am petting Midnight and comforting him, he isn't choking on anything, we just couldn't figure out what the hell was wrong with him. A couple minutes later he is back to his old happy self again. To this day I am unsure of what the issue was.

After Justin and I climb back into bed, he says to me, "Good thing you heard him, I was sound asleep." Wait … what? I tell him, "No, you whispered to me that he couldn't breathe." In which he replies, "No. Tessa, I was sound asleep. I woke up when you turned the light on." Okay, so who exactly spoke to me that night? I'm a decently light sleeper. Usually I wake up to the smallest of sounds, but that night it wasn't my dogs desperate panting that got me up but the voice of a man. A man who I thought was my boyfriend but proved not to be.

Chapter two

Words of a Medium

One day I was at work, standing behind the counter, waiting for customers. A woman approaches me, I have never seen her before. It turns out she is a medium. The way she talked and acted, it was so genuine, so honest.

This woman *Erica, let me know that I had someone, a male, watching over me. A former friend of mine, Michael, had just passed away. He is the same person who manifested in front of me at my house. She continued to say that he was young when he died. His childhood was unfortunately a complicated one. She also mentioned that he had a drinking problem.

She was correct on all of those things. She then told me that he was in what looked like a forest (He loved the outdoors and nature), he had animals with him as protectors and companions. He was finding it hard to believe that he was dead and how he died.

Erica was on her way to a short vacation and had a long day of traveling ahead of her. We exchanged e-mails. I told her that someday when she has time I would love to do a session with her. I e-mailed her a couple times throughout the next couple months but with no response. I was bummed out that she wasn't writing back to me, after the encounter I had with her, I wanted more. I wanted to see what else she had to say about Michael.

When I was close to giving up, I made one last attempt to contact her. I was friendly enough, but I basically asked her to please acknowledge my e-mails and that if she is busy just to let me know and I will simply back off. I'm usually not persistent like that but the persistence finally paid off.

She wrote me back and we set up a time for me to call her and we finally had our session. I would like to share parts of that session with you. Before I do, I would just like to mention, I know not everybody believes in mediums. Hell, even some people who believe in spirits and paranormal activity don't believe in mediums.

I know the world is full of phonies who will say anything to make a quick buck. With what this woman told me, I believe she is one of the accurate ones. I rewrite these words in her notes that she sent to me from our session.

The Results

My archetype was the Anarchist. Archetypes have both a positive (light) side and a negative (more-dark) side. We need to learn from both the light and the shadow sides.

The light side of the Anarchist is wanting to create change, looking for new and fresh solutions and being determined to do and see things differently.

The shadow side of the Anarchist may have real trouble with authority, with obstacles, and being told no. Be careful to create, more than destroy or tear down.

My animal totem is the elk.

This animal has both strength and stamina. It is determined and sticks with its goals and plans. If the elk is indeed one of your animal totems, you need support from other people and do best when connected to people you care about. The elk paces his self for his long journey. He has energy and determination.

She spoke about Michael. Saying he is in a better place from when we last spoke and is safe and secure. He told her that he feels some shame, that he should have tried harder in life, often taking the easier route.

He struggled with unfinished projects, probably partied too much instead of pushing himself to grow. He feels regret for that. The culture in Colorado is often laid back. The low stress is good, but the lack of determination, of consistent and strong effort, the lack of will to achieve, grow and succeed does not feel as good in a life review. She shares that he also struggled with jobs.

A general note and lesson for myself, not from Michael, but from my guides; my job is to be the hero of my own story. I care for other people. That's a strength, but I have often let them get me off track, slowing me down and at times, holding me back. That old pattern needs to be gradually released and changed so that I can do the huge things I've come here to do.

My life has a much bigger purpose than picking up after people who keep falling down or even who keep throwing themselves to the ground. It is out of balance. I wish to be liked and accepted, which has often resulted in my being taken advantage of by those who are my "friends." Not balanced enough with some of my relationships, there's more take then give.

I must say about the above; I was being taken advantage of and I released those negative people from my life. I know now, the people I have in my life are real, honest, loyal and care for me. It is a very good feeling. At first, I was flaming mad, being used, but when I made the decision to kick these people to the curb, I felt relieved.

The medium continued to talk about a friend of mine, *Stella, who was brutally murdered. The details spoken are quite graphic, so I will not go there. The things Erica said seemed accurate to me.

I never had a session with a medium before, so I wasn't sure what to expect. The reading was a good one, I got some answers to questions I had. The last part was a shocker for me. Erica told me about my past life. Here are those interesting details.

Past Life

Greece. In Roman times. I was a male that lived to be 37 years old. My name was Gregory. I died in battle. I had been captured twice before as a soldier and had gotten away and rejoined my group, where I finally was killed in battle. I'm good at sneaking in and out and up.

I loved olives and olive oil. I was a tutor to a family with two young boys. I taught weaponry and Latin. I was fairly educated, although partly self-educated, for that time. I loved music, I played the flute. I was good at sports when I was young and my favorite thing about Roman culture, was the baths.

I still can love a soak in warm water, still enjoy the sun and its warmth, and that culture. It was a time of bettering myself beyond the circumstances into which I was born; of learning many new things; of not being afraid to try something new or do things in a new way. I had a playful and impish side to me as well as a serious side that prepared for battle and studied the Roman orators and oration.

Interesting stuff, right? Who would have thought? I'm not sure what I think about that. Anything is possible though.

Months later I had another session with another medium, unfortunately I don't have notes from that session, so I cannot go into major detail like I did with Erica. However, this session, she did mention Michael, my grandma, and a few other people. She was wrong about a lot of the stuff though. This session was my least favorite.

While the first session with Erica was over the phone, and this most recent session was in person, it was neat experiencing both techniques.

I have been told by yet another medium that a woman seems to be around me. She described this woman but I couldn't figure out who this woman is. She also told me that I tend to live in the past and not being present. I spend so much time thinking and mourning about the dead that I don't live in the moment and appreciate the living.

That is accurate. I am trying to change that. When someone dies, I try to remember every memory of them. I search for every picture I have of them. I dream of them and more. It's like once that person passes away they reside within me.

The most current session with a medium I had happened April 3, 2016. The Holistic Fair was in town, so my dad, his friend *Cass, Jourdan and I decided to go and check it out. Aura readers, fortune tellers, massage therapists, healing techniques, mediums, tarot card readers and more filled every space possible. A few days before I did my homework. I went on the site to see who would be there and I pin-pointed the mediums, wrote down their booth numbers and names, then researched them online.

When I got there, the mediums that I was interested in had a long list of people and always had someone in their seat. I circled them like a shark. No luck. I forgot about the other side of the fair. I walk over there and as I am passing a booth I look at this older woman in velvet-like purple and black dark-fairy-like get up. When I saw her, I didn't see a medium but more like a Tarot card, fortune-teller type, I was in search of mediums, so I continued on.

I stop at a booth and see that the woman here is among the names of mediums I would like to have a session with. She was with somebody, but it looked like the finishing stage of a session. I stayed close, so I could be next in line, but not close enough where I was listening in on their private session. Somehow, I got distracted—I think I saw my Aunt Bridget. When I came back the Medium was gone. I stood there and waited for her and was relieved when she came back a few moments later.

This Medium was a very friendly woman. I felt like we bonded immediately. Before the session started we talked for about fifteen minutes. I told her how I am a Paranormal Investigator and some of the sites we have been to, and she seemed genuinely interested. She wasn't being paid for this time of talking, she honestly wanted to know more and even admitted to being interested about trying it herself. I gave her some advice. It was great having that conversation.

*Beth Willings was kind enough to let me record the special session I had with her, so this is a word to word account of that session. Thank you Beth, for an amazing experience!

The Results (In Beth's words)

"Right off the bat I pick up a Guide that's with you all the time. I call it a Guide because she is with you all the time. She's an older lady, she's got some teeth missing. She is like a Shaman type lady I would say. She's got a drum with her, sometimes maybe you hear a drum in the distance. It's real faint. I'm saying maybe you can possibly hear it because of what you do."

(This next part is quite amazing, and honestly it shocked me, and you'll see why now.)

"I am getting a Michael with you." (As Beth is speaking these words at the end of it, an EVP is recorded saying, "Yes." Quite amazing! Even when I am not in an investigation I am getting results it seems!) She then asks me if I know a Michael, I must think hard, I admit that I have had so many people in my life pass away that yes, I do know some Michaels but cannot figure out who it is. She continues to describe him to me as he shows himself to her. She says, "I am seeing him as rather tall, dark headed, some tattoos on his arms."

As this is registering in my head I know immediately who this is. You have heard of Michael. You have read about him in this book, he was a big part of my life long ago. At one time, he was one of my best of friends. It was interesting because Michael is obviously not this young man's name. I won't share his real name in respect for his family and friends. However, Michael is the name I choose for him in this book and he told the medium that was his name knowing I would figure it out after the description was told to me.

One thing was off though. I told her how he had blond hair not dark hair. For a moment there is silence. Beth then looks at me and says, "Ah okay. So, I asked him if that's who it is, and I got a yes. I asked him why did you show me dark hair if you're blond? He said if she can change my name, I can change my hair color."

MIND BLOWN. That is so amazing. It confirms to me that Michael is with me often. I feel him around sometimes. The fact that she said Michael, and she said it matter of fact, not like trying to think of a name or guessing.

She continues, "He said he is with you much of the time. I know this sounds weird, but there's … he's telling me there are certain songs, certain lyrics to those songs, that you associate with him. He likes that. It makes him feel happy."

I tell her how that's accurate. How there are songs that make me think of him. Some of the songs are newer and came out after he died though, so he never heard them, not on this Earth anyway. She says, "When that happens it makes him happy, he's saying he does know the songs by the way. The new ones. There is a closeness between you two."

"He is a believer of the paranormal now, since he is going through this. He wants to show his other friends that he is still around." She then asked me if I am planning on going to Pennsylvania at some point. "He is bringing up Pennsylvania for some reason." He said when I am there, he will go there, that whatever pictures I am taking, he will be in one of them. I will be able to see him. That will be a gift for me from him.

"Are there people you still associate with, that know him?"

I reply to her that Jourdan who was just standing there with me knew him and was a former friend of his as well. Then of course there is mutual friends Sarah and Adam, a married couple, they will be in the book later. Michael said that when he shows up in that picture, to show them as proof, that after life exists. He said, 'I'm going to be your proof to these people that knew me. It will be Pennsylvania. Wherever you will be investigating, I will show up. I'll help you get that proof.'

"You have a Grandma with you too. I don't know what this is. It smells like cookies to me, but I don't want to say cookies … I keep smelling it. Not your average chocolate chip cookies. She is still baking. Watching over you. Sometimes she tries to send that smell to you. So that you can remember. She is around you. She says when you smell that, have a conversation with her."

Again, she nailed it. There are certain times when I am overwhelmed with a sweet, thick, delicious scent in the air and nothing is cooking or baking when I smell this. I can be sitting on the couch watching TV and this smell comes out of nowhere. This makes total sense to me and to know that this is my Grandma's way of stopping by and communicating with me, makes me smile!

She saw a guitar. She asks if I play. I don't, but my dad and sister both play, or used to anyways. She asks if my sister Carly is sick. I reply that I don't know because she was in Hawaii, but it happens to be her birthday the next day. Beth says she may have a little cold or a cough.

She even mentions this book. Saying not to stop writing. It will be a good seller, it will be successful. Keep telling people about the book, watch my connections, because somewhere around the line, of me talking to people about the book, someone will approach me and be very interested in wanting to publish this book. I won't have a problem finding the publisher. As of right now, I write this book, with no publisher in sight, but I plan to continue to share the book with people and pray for a publisher to grace me with their publishing presence soon.

Update:

Several months later, after I wrote these words, I became friends with author Steven David Lampley, he gave me amazing advice and showed me how to self-publish my book. While I didn't find a publisher like Beth mentioned, I did speak about my book like she said and did find connections, and I suppose I did find a publisher, inside myself.

Yet another update:

Through my talk show I met an amazing paranormal investigator /author/editor from Ireland named Kim O'Shea. She graciously offered to edit my book and help with the publishing!! I am so appreciative!! She did an amazing job! Anybody needing an editor should contact Kim.

Beth goes on:

"There is a dog in the spirit world that hangs around with you. It's a bigger dog. A German Shepard. I hate to say breeds because I'm not that good with them but I'm thinking German Shepard. This dog is with you because at times it kind of wards off things for you. He is a protector in the spirit world. There are times, might be moments where things are happening that are weird when suddenly the mood changes quickly. That dog is protecting you. Whatever it is, picks up on that and decides not to tackle this."

At this point, Jourdan shows up and takes a seat with us and joins in. On this day, it happens to be our dear friend Peter's birthday. We were planning to visit him later after the fair, so we wanted to see if she could communicate with him at all. Beth mentions that he is with someone who is like a sister to him. Jourdan and I think of April Duran right away.

Beth says he is with her much of the time watching over her; that they were very close. He is real protective over her. He is still around her a lot. Sometimes, she will notice things that move or are being misplaced. Trying to get her attention. He's around. Really watching out for her. Beth asks us is there someone that passed away in a car accident? We tell her that Peter was the only fatality in a car accident over a decade ago.

He tells Beth that no matter what the situation would have been, whether it was a car accident or something else, it was his time. "It was going to happen. I don't know if someone blames somebody or has resentment towards somebody. They have to let that anger about the situation go."

When Peter died in that fateful car accident, a friend of his, a girl who he really had a crush on and wanted more than just a friendship with, was with him when he passed away. She played on his feelings and knew he liked her and kind of played him along for some time.

She acted weird after he died and was very hateful to his friends when they tried to talk to her. Many of us were mad at her and felt she treated our deceased friend unfairly. I believe Beth was talking about this individual. I don't blame her for what happened to Peter, but I feel his life would have been better with her not in it. She hurt him, and her hurting him, hurt us as well.

At the end of the session, Jourdan got a special message from her beloved Uncle John, who we've done EVP sessions with before. Beth was hearing music and a ton of people and concerts. He loved music and Jourdan verified that. Beth said he is still loving the music and still around it and enjoys it. He plays music during our sessions sometimes for us.

Beth continues to say, she sees him standing at night in a room while someone is sleeping. "You walk in the door, and the bed is right there, right next to a window, and a dresser is right here … he kind of sits on the dresser and plays really light music. You probably can't hear it because obviously you're asleep, but if you were to record while you slept, you would hear it. Sometimes you might be very restless and cannot sleep." Jourdan verifies this. "He plays, what could be considered, a lullaby so you can sleep. He tries to soothe you."

Chapter three

Night Terrors

For as long as I can remember, I have had night terrors. I move uncontrollably while sleeping. I have these awful dreams where I wake up covered in sweat and with my heart racing. Something scares me, and I am not sure what it is.

I remember I had this recurring dream for many years as a child and into an adult. I still have these dreams but not as often thankfully. This dream involves snakes. Every type of snake you can possibly think of. Big ones, small ones, harmless ones, venomous ones, the most-deadly ones, the exotic ones.

These snakes would be everywhere. I couldn't escape them. They would be in all corners of the house; in the drawers, on the ground, on my feet, on my shoulders. I look up and they are on the fan, on the walls. Everywhere I look there are numerous snakes. I try to escape and go outside. These snakes are trying to wrap around me, biting at me, hissing, striking. It's quite a terrifying dream.

I finally manage to make it outside, only to find them all over the car, the ground, the railings, again everywhere! I'm crying. I'm scared and panicking. There is no escaping these slithering and hissing creatures.

When I finally wake up from this dream—this dream being so real and intense—I still think either, that this wasn't a dream at all and there are snakes in my room or, I am stuck in the dream and start to freak out tearing my room apart searching for the serpents. Justin wakes up to find me in a panic, out of bed searching for things. He says I mumble and am not making sense. Almost like I cannot find words to communicate with.

It's quite stressful. It used to happen a lot. Now it seems to have slowed down a huge amount. Thank goodness! Sometimes I will watch nature shows or those wildlife shows that have snakes on them. When that happens, much of the time I will have a dream about snakes. Not the recurring dream but different dreams. I wake up covered with sweat, my heart racing, but I know right away it was a dream and am able to fall back asleep rather quickly.

I ask myself why does this happen? How does this happen? I had a couple of experiences that weren't so good with snakes, as a child, in New Mexico. One involving an aggressive snake found in my room, that struck at us many times when trying to capture it so we can release it back outside. The other involved a friend grabbing a bull snake and knowing my fear threw it in my car, which then resulted it landing on my leg!

Those experiences happened when I was already having the dreams though. Maybe it intensified them and made me more paranoid. I think these are questions I may truly never know the answers to.

Snakes aside, I also have another experience that is quite troubling. Countless times I will be lying in bed, restless. I finally fall asleep, only to wake up a few moments later to hear what sounds like whispering from the corner of the room. I also see shadows hovering over me; dark figures without faces, inches from my face.

A few months back I woke up to see a face hovering next to mine. I sleep on my side, usually facing away from my boyfriend. So, when I saw this face of a man it really scared me. I freaked out and grabbed Justin. Again, I couldn't find the words to communicate with him, but I kept pointing and he could see I was clearly terrified. I finally was able to say, "Face! A man's head!" I don't know who this man was or what his floating head was doing in my room that night. This was NOT a dream.

It's unnerving to say the least. I also, at times, see a hand hanging over our bed. Unlike the snakes, I have no control over this and it happens quite often. I don't know if it's because I am a sensitive and communicate with spirits, or if they are comfortable to show themselves to me, or maybe, and hopefully not, they are taunting me.

I don't necessarily feel threatened, but it doesn't make me feel good either. When this happens, I end up staying awake for a long time. Sometimes, I wear a sleeping eye-mask. That usually works. A part of me likes to know if something is there, if it is something I should be worried about or be more careful around. Sleeping with that mask almost makes me feel blind, like a sitting duck, a target.

It has been suggested to me that I try to cleanse my house. Many of the investigations we conduct have been at cemeteries, battlefields, jails, brothels, hotels and so on. I try to stay away from houses. I did not used to feel that way, but that changed when we had an attachment occur at a person's house. It was a horrible experience.

I think of it this way; whoever this spirit is, doesn't seem to be threatening us. It's just active at night. With a skeptic on one side of the bed and my face mask on where I don't have to see it, I guess it's taken care of. Maybe it's a guardian.

There have been many times that I stare at my equipment and am so tempted to do an investigation in the house, but I stop myself. Things are calm here. I don't want to upset anything or stir anything up with doing an investigation or smudging. It helps in many cases but after the bad experience I had, I'd rather not and leave well enough alone.

Chapter four

Tales from another

This chapter is dedicated to my family, my friends, and fellow paranormal investigators that have had experiences of their own. These are their words, their experiences and encounters.

Things happened often at this store, where she temporarily lived upstairs, mind you, this was where I got phantom smells, heard footsteps coming up the stairs, and saw the apparition of a woman. Carly had so many incidents that she kept a journal about some of her experiences there.

In Carly's own words.

WENDY THE GHOST (DEL NORTE, COLORADO)

- I came back from the movies later. I walked through the sunroom into the kitchen taking an immediate left. A whiteish, translucent figure suddenly comes rushing at me! I terrifyingly turn around, then when I turned back and she's gone.

- I woke up to go to the bathroom, with my own eyes, I saw orbs at the bottom of the stairs by the coffee counter.

- I had two friends over, they went down to the bathroom. I come back to turn off the computer. I come back a while later to find the computer turned back on, a figure is sitting in the computer chair and I hear it say, "Carly."

- While in this building I have heard several sounds and screams. It's a very eerie feeling like someone is following me.

- While working in the cafe, I would sometimes notice the knob for the hot water on the espresso machine turning on by itself.

While Carly no longer lives there, she still often thinks back on the times she had with Wendy the friendly, active spirit.

This next experience was more recent at her then boyfriend at the time, *Randy's house.

HAUNTED (PUEBLO, COLORADO)

"I was at Randy's house, just hanging out and he said we could listen to Taylor Swift. You know how much I love Taylor Swift. We had the music going, just lying down and talking. We both go quiet. Randy feels a very realistic feeling of a hand take hold of his hand. Interlocking fingers (it was not mine). He lets it happen for about 5 minutes without telling me.

"Then I feel as if someone slammed their hand against the mattress behind me. Guess what song of Taylor's was playing when this was happening? 'Haunted.' It was crazy!"

PLAYING CARDS AT THE KONA KAI (PUEBLO, COLORADO)

Randy, Aunt Bridget and I went and hung out with Aunt Anne at the Kona Kai. We were playing cards in the atrium, the jungle area. Bridget had just left, so we're resuming our game of cards. A little earlier, a little girl and mother walk past us, going up to their room.

A few minutes later, I hear a noise, a voice. It was so close, like right in my ear. It was a man. It took me off guard. The others asked me if something was wrong. I told Aunt Anne and Randy that I heard a voice, Aunt Anne thought it was the little girl we had just seen, but I told her no, it was definitely a man that I had heard. I know what I heard. The voice in my ear, has happened to me before, while investigating with Tessa. It's happened to both of us multiple times.

End of Carly's experiences.

This experience is told by my friend Ivan B. Living in the Land of Enchantment, New Mexico. Many mysterious things happen there. From La Llorna to fireballs and UFOs, it truly is a hauntingly beautiful area.
In Ivan's own words. (New Mexico)

MYSTERIOUS VISITOR (EL RITO, NEW MEXICO)

"My dad's and my aunt's house is very haunted. I was about 13 years old when this all went down. The year was 2001. I would get on line and my dad would go visit my grandma.

"He would leave like at 8:30 and be back within the hour. He would visit on a daily basis. One of the nights, I was chilling in the living room on the computer when I started hearing footsteps. I didn't think nothing the first few times, but it kept getting louder and louder as days past.

"One day I had enough of it, so I thought to myself, it's my dad, so I called him out and didn't get any response. That went on for about two days. On the third night of hearing footsteps, it got quiet and I heard the fridge open and the cupboard open as well.

"This time I thought for sure it was my dad. I heard water pouring into a glass, and that's when I ran inside the kitchen to find the fridge open as well as the cupboard open, with water poured into the glass, because we always kept cold water in the fridge!

"I completely freaked out and fell to my knees and prayed. After that, I began to see fireballs all over town. Crazy shit. True story. To this day, my dad does not believe me. It seemed like the more I wanted to hear and see it, the more I would hear it."

End of Ivan's experience.

My Aunt *Ms. Meribyrd has had so many paranormal experiences she has experienced throughout her life, she could write her own book. We spent a day together, where, over some smothered (chilé) breakfast burritos in a local restaurant, she shared with me these intense experiences. Then she took me through the very haunted small town of Plaza, where many have practiced witchcraft.

As told by Aunt Ms. Meribyrd (San Luis Valley, Plaza Colorado)

HEAD START GHOSTS (MONTE VISTA, COLORADO)

"The girls at the Head Start, have had experiences there with the ghosts. There are two or three of them there. We hear noises all the time when we are in the classroom, like the door closing and opening."

- When I ask her if anyone has died there, her answer surprised me.

She replies, "Yeah, it used to be a nursing home at one point. It depends on what part of the building you are at. You hear different noises and stuff like that. It's quite interesting. The first time was weird because I didn't know what was going on. I knew the history of the place but I started hearing noises."

She laughs as she recalls the memory, "I kept looking around, now I know that they name them so now when I hear noises I just say something like, 'Hi, I'm okay, I know you are here just to check on me.' The students get freaked out sometimes though when they hear the noises. I just explain to them that it's one of the ghosts checking in."

"I always make sure the students don't leave alone. We all leave together. I have had some weird things happen there, so I prefer not to be by myself there. I was sitting there one night. I usually park under a big tree and you know how something can sometimes catch your peripheral vision? Well, something caught my eye and I turned to look and I saw a ... body passing by the window. I don't know if it was a man or a woman, it was too quick. I knew nobody was there. This was before I knew about the ghosts."

AMBULANCE BASE SPIRITS (MONTE VISTA, COLORADO)

"At the ambulance base we've had people who have actually seen a man standing by the Women's bathroom. They hear footsteps and stuff all the time. I've never heard anything there. I've been there by myself writing my reports and stuff and I myself have never heard anything.

"Occasionally I'll hear stuff, but I pay no attention to it. Like the doors on the ambulances will open and close by themselves. To me, it's just an echo of the previous shift. Almost residual because we have to go in to do our rechecks.

"A couple of the girls, *Maria was one who saw it, saw a man standing by the Women's bathroom when she came out of the office. It's creepy. I've never seen him. I know they have though."

HOLY REMAINS (OLD EL RITO, NEW MEXICO)

"As you're going towards Espanola, you start going out into the desert area on your left-hand side, you can see some old ruins. They used to be a church. We used to go down there when I was little. My dad, my grandpa and I would go and find arrowheads there. One time he and his friends were there. I don't remember how old I was. They were going through the church doors and one of them sunk!

"Anyway, they used to bury the priests inside the churches. When that door sunk they found a skeleton; the remains of one of the priests. They called CSP (Colorado State Patrol). It was one of the old priests that they buried there long ago. I was just a young girl, perhaps nine or ten, something like that.

"They took the body to either Santa Fe or Albuquerque to get checked. My dad always took me on some type of adventure, 'We gotta see this, we gotta check that out.' It was never a dull moment. 'Wanna get your license? Take me on this crazy drive without killing me.' Cliff on this side, embankment on the other. Windy road.

PREMONITIONS AND OUT-OF-BODY EXPERIENCES (SAN LUIS VALLEY, COLORADO)

"My friend *Cheryl and I were planning on going to a mutual friend of ours in Center. Cheryl was supposed to come and pick me up and we were supposed to go from here in Monte Vista to Center. Well, *Larry had come over to my house and we were talking and so anyhow, after talking he decided he wanted to come with us.

"So then, Cheryl calls me up and says, 'Hey, you need to come and pick me up.' She continues to say, 'I need to leave my mom the car.' I say, 'Okay. Not a problem.' Larry and I get ready and leave and go to Del Norte and it was by Organic Peddler. (The haunted store where Carly and I have had experiences.)

"We walk in and her mom looks at her so Cheryl told me to bring her my black skirt that I always liked and the blouse that went with it. When I asked her why, she replied, 'Because I wanna wear it.' So, I bring it to her and her mom looks at her and says, 'So, are you coming home tonight?' Cheryl says, 'I don't know. It depends on how deep the waters are.' Larry and I just looked at each other confused like, 'Uh … okay.' So, her mom looks at her and says, 'I'm not joking. Are you coming home tonight so I can leave the light on and unlock the door.' Cheryl turns around and looks at her and says, 'It depends on what train gets in the way.'

"What the hell is going on? She looks at us and says, 'Let's go.' Her mom is getting impatient and repeats herself, more sternly. 'Are you coming home tonight or are you staying at Ms. Meribyrd's?' Cheryl says, 'No. I am not coming home.' She said it so, matter-of-factly. Her tone of voice just changed. Her mom looked at her and said, 'You don't need to be so nasty. I was just asking you.'

"So, we leave it at that and head to the bar. You know me, I don't drink. She was adamant. She bought everybody a beer. She was adamant that I was going to drink a beer. I said, 'No! I don't drink!' She said, 'You are, tonight.' I look at the bartender and ask him to get me a Coke. Cheryl hands me the beer and takes away my coke. She says, 'You are going to drink.' I just looked at Larry, he says, 'Put that drink down and let's go dance.' He puts his beer down that she gave him. We go and dance.

"When we came back all the beer was gone. She drank it all. She was drinking like a fish out of water that night. We'd been there for a couple of hours, suddenly, she got a wild hair up her ass and wanted to leave the bar and go to the dance they had going in Monte. So, we get ready to leave, and Larry starts to get into my car.

"Cheryl grabs him and says, 'You're not going with us.' She points and says, 'You're going with them over there.' Everything was just happening so fast and it was weird, so I looked at Larry and said, 'Don't argue. Just go with *Marcy and them in the other car.'

"So, he went with them into the other car, while looking at me giving me a strange nervous look. I start driving, we get going. We got to Highway 112 and I turn my signal light on to turn right to come down the Highway 285. Cheryl is persistent and says, 'No! We need to go the other way. Through 3 east.' So, we start going toward 3 east and as we are going Marcy and Larry passed us up.

"I was good with that, I didn't have a problem with that. When we got to 4 north she tells me, 'You better pass them because Marcy is going to miss that turn.' So, I start passing her up and right as I start to get into my lane, I turned on the bright lights and there were black cows standing in the road.

"I tried to swerve to avoid hitting them and I hit the black cow that was in the middle of the road. I felt something hit me in the head and I remember myself saying, 'Dear Lord, help me.' You know when you pick up a baby, you scoop them up? I felt something scoop me up at the same time. I can see my seat belt lifting and I knew it was locked. I can see the seatbelt then next thing I knew, I was rolling on the pavement.

"I know people may think I'm crazy and stuff, but I had an out-of-body experience. I was dead. It was a pitch-black night. No stars. No moon. No nothing. I was seeing that everything was like…early morning—like it's just starting to get a little light. I could see where my car was at. I could see where Cheryl's body was at. I could see myself just floating away, I could see where my kids were. I could see my grandparents, and my mom and dad. They were all sleeping.

"Then I remember going back and I was watching my body. I was watching Larry. He was shaking me. It was such a peaceful, no pain feeling. I just wanted to keep going. So, I was seeing Larry, he was slapping me and stuff and the next thing I knew, I was in the most horrific pain that I'd ever felt. After this, I believe in it now. It was truly an eye opener. I never drank, I knew … it was an eye opener to me because of the way Cheryl was acting.

"She knew she was going to die. She knew, because she kept saying to her mom, 'I'm not coming home.' 'It depends on what gets in the way.' 'The water is too deep, the train.' It ended up being a cow that got in the way. She knew.

"Some people know stuff. Premonition. Cheryl was having that bizarre behavior. People react in different ways. I reacted by staying calm with her. Anybody else might have argued with her at any time but it totally took me back because I had never seen her act that way before. Talking to us that way. Nothing. I was completely shocked."

FRIENDLY UNSEEN HANDS (MONTE VISTA, COLORADO)

"Spirits communicate, they send signs. Occasionally, I will be feeling down, and I will smell your Grandpa's cologne. I know he is around. I think our bond started when, I tried calling him and there was no answer. The health and welfare checks. Calling the police and the sheriff to check on him. He kiddingly told Uncle Chuck, 'You better take good care of her, if not I'm stealing her from you.'

"I went to the nursing home and told them, 'You don't mess with him. You do everything that he asks, you jump. You don't question it.' The director, she turned around and told them, the nurses, 'Don't mess with her. You guys do everything, and make sure he has everything that he needs.' I told all the girls, 'You don't know when I'm going to show up.' After getting off work I would show up in the middle of the night. It would be anywhere from 11:30 pm to 2:30 am.

"After getting off work, before going home, that was the last thing I would do, check on Grandpa. First thing I would do in the morning after getting ready for work, I would go to check on him. So, they never really knew when I would come. I would always ask him, 'Are they treating you okay?'

"Right before he passed away I went and sat and chatted with him, asking if he was feeling okay. He looked at me and said, 'Oh yeah. I'm just tired. I think I'm going to take a nap. I'll let you know if I need anything.' I said, 'You do that. I'll come and check on you tonight.' I had only been at work for about forty-five minutes. One of the girls that was working with me was making some sandwiches for somebody and I was waiting on some customers and I felt a hand or something on my shoulder.

"I turned to look, and there was nothing, nobody. It was really weird. About thirty minutes later Uncle Chuck called me and said they called your mom and said that he had passed away. When I got to the nursing home, I had asked the girls what time he had passed away, and it was right around the time when that hand was on my shoulder. He was telling me good bye.

"I tell you, I know when he is around because I get a strong whiff of his cologne. He used to wear that one certain type of cologne."

MY GHOST (PLAZA HILL, COLORADO)

"My ghost. I was eighteen years old. It's been a long time now. So, I'm working at the hospital and nursing home in Del Norte as a professional 'ass wiper' back then. They had me on the graveyard shift. I was headed to work that night. I was going to work the 11-7 shift. I'm driving and have my music going and I start heading down Plaza Hill and all of a sudden out of nowhere comes a large owl.

"This owl hits my windshield—dead center. The wing span totally covered the windshield and I couldn't see anything! It just flew off and my windshield didn't break or anything. It should have The speed-limit back then was 75 miles per hour. So, I was going 75 miles an hour, it should've done some damage, but it didn't, at all. It was the middle of the night. I was too chicken-shit to stop and check. I was just grateful my windshield was okay.

"So, I get to work. They pulled me off the floor of the nursing home and put me to work in the hospital since they were short-handed. Forty-five minutes later we get an ambulance going to the emergency room. There was this old lady, *Dolores. They said they found her by the side of the road up there by Plaza Hill at Interstate 160. She had a broken leg. An obvious broken leg. So, we got her checked in and they did x-ray's. We put her in bed in a room.

"I was going in there and talking to her, making sure she was okay, seeing if she needed anything. I look at her and ask, 'How did it happen? The accident?' She says, 'You oughtta know. You hit me.' I was in total shock. I go, 'I didn't hit you! I didn't hit no lady!' She goes, 'You hit me.' We were arguing about this. Going back and forth. I told her, 'On my way from home going to work, I hit an owl right in that area, but I didn't hit no human!' She looks at me and says, 'You hit me.'

"She was Spanish speaking only, so in Spanish she was telling me this. I kept repeating myself, 'I didn't hit a human! It was an owl!' Then, the next morning I was heading back home, I stopped at the turn right there to go to Plaza. I walked in the field and I walked on the other side of the road. I walked up and down. Not a single feather. Nothing. You know? Nothing at all. You can see in the grass where there was an indentation of where something was lying.

"When I went back to work the next day, I talked to one of the EMTs who was on that ambulance call and I asked him, 'Where exactly did you find her?' We were talking and right where that indentation in the grass, that's where they found her. That was right around in that area, where I hit that owl.

"We became friends. We talked and stuff. I met her nieces and nephews, sons and daughters and all that. When she got out she wanted me to go with her, so I could help her settle into her house and stuff, so I did. We took her by ambulance, and I went and helped her settle in, and showed her family what to do and stuff. So, I became good friends with her.

"We were friends for maybe three or four years. One day she ended up with a hole in her leg. A through-and-through hole. She just kept telling me it was nothing. She ended up getting gangrene from the wound. She said that it was going to be the end of her. She wouldn't let anybody amputate it, even though it probably would have saved her life, but you never know because she was a really bad diabetic.

"That was what took her life. She passed away and I helped her family clean up her house and get it ready for sale. Going through her house and stuff, she had a ton of nice stuff. She had like a fake wall in a closet. There were just shelves there, so we opened it up and there were a bunch of black saints behind this fake wall.

"We also found a bunch of books, all in Spanish, 'The book of the Black Hand' black magic. In Spanish, it's called, 'Le Libra La Mano Negra'. It's about Black Magic and shit. She had another book that was, 'Como Cambiel Animal' how to change into an animal. We were sitting there looking at the book and I was amazed. It said they can change to cats and owls, dogs and rocks. You know, just all this shit. I tripped out.

"Once we found all that stuff and everything, once in a while, I would hear her say my name in the car or something. I would get in the car, and I have this habit, I would look around in the car before I get in and I know there's nothing there. So, I got in my car one night at work, getting ready to leave, I hear my name and it was Dolores' voice."

AN EERIE AMBULANCE RIDE (PLAZA, COLORADO)

"We're on an ambulance call. We get into Plaza, and the wiring and the lights start fading out, the radio goes out. This has never happened before. We were asked if we wanted another ambulance to go there and we told them no, that we would be okay. The lights were so dim that they really couldn't work on the patient.

"As soon as I got onto the highway, right at the turn off on Plaza and 160, my sirens started working, my lights went on to full bright, the flashing lights were on and the radio was working.

"The next day we brought the ambulance in to get a full check-up, and there was nothing wrong with it; no faulty wiring, no shortages, no nothing. There is a ton of witchcraft that goes on there. You know the San Luis Valley is the tip of the triangle. There are many weird things that go on here."

MUSIC FROM A FRIEND (MONTE VISTA, COLORADO)

"An elderly man was a really good friend of ours. When he passed away, that night at 2:30 in the morning, my jewelry music box started playing out of nowhere. The next day we found out he passed away. He had a heart attack at 2:30 in the morning while checking on some of his cows that were birthing." End of Aunt Meribyrd's experiences.

It is amazing my Aunt had all these bizarre experiences in her life. I learned a lot that day. After breakfast she took me to Plaza, I had never been there before but had passed that road hundreds of times. Plaza is where black magic and witchcraft was, or still is, practiced. Plaza is where the ambulance acted up, and where the most bizarre experience took place, Dolores, the animal transformer.

These next experiences are from my friend MW Dolph. He, like my Aunt, also lives in the Haunted San Luis Valley. He has had experiences also with animals as well. Here are his experiences, in his words.

A VISIT FROM GRANDMA (COLORADO)

"While staying over at a girlfriend's house, I was sleeping very well when suddenly I was awakened. The clock display read 4:00 am, at which time my girlfriend was startled and awakened, asking very seriously if I was okay. I said I was and seemingly, immediately, she fell asleep, I also fell asleep though it was for a short period of time.

"The next morning, I was working at my job when my mother called to inform me that my Grandmother was found that morning, passed away at an unknown time the night before."

THE POWER OF THE ALMIGHTY ZIMA (DENVER, COLORADO)

"My other experience that I found was enlightening, involved my cat ZimaZen. She was seventeen years old and had a nice big tumor on her chest and belly. I had to return home from a week of working in Denver to have her put to sleep. Two days after returning to work in Denver, I needed supplies. The boss said they were in the office which was across the street. I couldn't miss them. As I walked, I noticed the door curtain moved.

"When I entered, I saw a gray shaggy cat, that was very near to a twin to my ZimaZen. I picked it up. Gave it some attention. Then left for work with my supplies. I mentioned to the boss that I didn't let the cat out of the office. He said, 'What cat?' He then thanked me for telling him, so he could let it out before he went home. Two days later I ask if he let the cat out, he said he never saw a cat. So that's my Zima story!"

End of M. W. Dolph's experiences.

These next experiences are my Aunt Bridgett Bishop's experiences. Bridgett has always been a believer of the paranormal. I remember as kids hanging out at the Iron pool in New Mexico—back when my family owned a Mineral Springs Resort— looking for UFO's. She is a very open-minded individual and that's one of my favorite things about her. Throughout her life she has had countless experiences. These are just a couple of those experiences.

In Bridgett's words.

JUST A QUICK DIP (NEW MEXICO)

"Your dad and *Ron and a few other guys, they went in to the Springs after hours like around midnight or so. They went to go swimming. Back in 1983 they changed it. There used to be a big swimming pool outside where the bath house used to be when we were there. So anyways, this one summer day, the boys decided to go for a swim after hours.

"Do you remember how the mineral water wasn't clear? It was kind of murky. They are swimming, and diving. Well, cousin *Mark comes back up from the water after diving and says to the others, 'Geez! That was a weird thing! How did you touch me if you are all up there? How did you touch me, when I'm down here?' Anyways, it turns out that there were two bodies down there! "These two men snuck into the resort after closing. They were drunk, and they drowned."

(Not really a paranormal story but still very creepy and worthy of having in the book!)

THE HOTEL COLORADO (CRIPPLE CREEK, COLORADO)

"You know about the ghosts in Cripple Creek Colorado, right? Before there was a gambling town in Cripple Creek, there was a nice ghost town there. So, my friend *Lorena and I went up there back in 1996. There's a hotel on Main Street called The Hotel Colorado. Stevie Nicks wrote a song about The Hotel Colorado. We wanted to go check it out, see for ourselves what Stevie Nicks was writing and singing about.

"We go into the lobby, at that time, it was still quiet, not too many tourists. We go up these stairs to the second floor. We walk down this hallway and we notice all these lights are off, but we keep going. We see that they're doing construction and for some reason we were being nosey. We just wanted to see what they were building back there.

"So here we are just the two of us, walking down this dark hallway. It was quiet, there was nothing. It was late afternoon and the sun was setting. There were no lights in there because of the construction and they are working on the hotel in a certain wing. As we are walking down the hallway, I feel a 'swoosh' on my hand, I notice my ring that I was wearing is gone. My ring flew off my finger! It fell in the hallway, we looked for it, but we couldn't find it.

"Lorena saw it happen, and I felt it happen. We were looking all over. It was nowhere to be found. So, I walk ahead of Lorena and I see this doorway. I think to myself, 'How weird, the ring is just gone.' There is a room off to the side, so I go in that room. There's one of those old fainting couches. In the old days they were called 'fainting couches' because the women had to wear those tight corsets. Many times, when they had these corsets strung, they'd lose oxygen and faint.

"They were Victorian; they don't even make them anymore. They are very old-fashioned antiques. They are also called, 'settees'. So anyway, I walk into this room and there's a person lying on the settee. I'm like, 'Oh, hi … oops! How are you?' I think to myself, 'I better get out of here, being all nosey!' I go out. Lorena comes in, and when I turn around, the person is gone!"

Now, instead of Aunt Bridget and her friend Lorena staying at a hotel while in Cripple Creek, they stayed in a less crowded area (it was fourth of July weekend) they slept in a back of a truck in Mount Pisgah Cemetery by Brothel owner and prostitute Pearl DeVere's grave. She shares with me some history about this much-loved prostitute. This will be in the Brothels chapter.

TRANSFORMATIONS (COLORADO)

"So last weekend, there was an annual festival, Territory Days, that takes place in Old Colorado City, near Manitou. I asked your sister, Carly if she wanted to go with me this year, she said yes. So, we're driving on Interstate 25 from Pueblo heading towards Manitou. We were talking about my mother, your grandma.

"We're having all these great memories, then we listen to music. We're both quiet. Then I looked through the corner of my eye and Carly turned into Grandma! For about half a second, Grandma was there. I just saw it through my peripheral vision, but I know what I saw. She was there. I excitedly told Carly, 'Oh my God! Grandma was right here!' It was so cool! This was the last day of May I think."

End of Aunt Bridget's experiences.
The following experiences you will read come from another Aunt, Ronda Mauro. What's that in the Aunt department ... three? After spending the morning at Pioneer investigating, Ronda shares with me some of the paranormal incidents that she has dealt with in her life.

KNOCK! KNOCK! ANYONE HOME? (PUEBLO, COLORADO)

"I'm going to talk about a couple of my experiences about a house that my children and I lived in for a while. This house is off Sprague and Palmer. Right on the corner. Anyway, our very first experience in this house happened the very first day I had taken the kids to go see the house for the first time. I had went to go see it once and it met all the requirements for my housing voucher.

"It was within the price range. I could afford it and it was a real nice place. It was all refinished and remodeled. Brand new carpet, kitchen floors, cabinets, countertop, brand new everything. It had a huge bathroom and a half bathroom, four bedrooms; it was very spacious.

"Now, the way this house is designed, you go in the front door. This place used to be a grocery store, so you can imagine how they had to style it. It was a long house. To the right was the kitchen and right when you walk into the door it's a big living room. Straight ahead was a long hall where all the bedrooms were located. So, there were two bedrooms on the left and two on the right. At the very end of the house was a door that went into a storage type room—the whole end of the house. There was another door in that room that went outside. So before going outside you had to pass through two doors.

"So anyway, the kids are seeing it for the first time. *Jonathan decided he wanted to bring his best friend *Stella. They were both about fifteen years old. *May was about nine years old. We get to the house, I take them in and show them around. After seeing the house, Jonathan and May are loving it. There were a couple of spiders in the house; that being their only complaint.

"As we are getting ready to leave, I go around and turn off all the lights. All of a sudden, we're walking out and we hear this very loud BANG-BANG-BANG-BANG-BANG-BANG-BANG-BANG-BANG-BAM! Just this intense loud banging on the back door. It wasn't the back door that led to outside, you know, it was the back door going to the other room at the end of the house, the storage room. In order for someone to be knocking on that door, that would mean the back door would have to be open.

"So, they're banging on that door and I look at Jonathan and tell him, 'Go check it.' Then he says, 'No! You go check!' We go back and forth. Finally, I say, 'Fine. I'll go check it out.' I go and open the door and the back door was shut. There was nothing in that room. Absolutely nothing! The other door leading to the outside was locked. So how do you explain that? It was locked. Nobody could come in.

"So that was our first experience in that house. It really freaked the kids out. Neither Jonathan nor May want to move in after that happened. It met the requirements and it was affordable, so I told them, 'I don't care what's in this house, we're moving in!'"

*GREG AND THE DOPPELGANGER (PUEBLO, COLORADO)

"Another incident happened to Jonathan personally. I just found out about this a couple days ago. He claims he told me this before, but I don't remember. Jonathan was home with my youngest son *Emerson. It was just Jonathan and Emerson in the house. Emerson was in bed and Jonathan was in his room sleeping with the baby monitor close by.

"Jonathan says, all of a sudden, he hears the front door open and he heard *Greg, this idiot who was in my life at the time. He hears Greg yell at him, 'Jonathan! Get up! Get up!' He yells back to Greg, 'Okay fine, I'll get up!' Jonathan at the time, it was hard for him to get up, so he ends up staying in bed. A few minutes pass and Greg comes back and sticks his head in the door and angrily says, 'Jonathan, I said get up! Now! Get up, get up!' Jonathan finally rolls out of bed.

"He runs into the hallway, Greg isn't there. He runs into the living room. Greg wasn't in there either. He goes to the front door. Greg was always parked in this one certain spot and his truck wasn't there. There's no way he could have left that quickly, no way! So, whatever it was, it imitated Greg's voice."

A NOT SO HELPING HAND (PUEBLO, COLORADO)

"I heard another story from Greg. I feel that whatever was in this house was not good. There were some real bad entities in this house. Here is what Greg experienced. One night, we're in bed watching TV and about to go to sleep. The only light in the bedroom was coming from the glowing TV. Greg had gotten up to go to the kitchen to get something to drink.

"He was gone for like ten minutes! For someone who was just going to get a drink, he was gone for quite some time! Suddenly, he comes flying in the bedroom and he jumped in the bed and under the covers. Now this man always had to act macho. He's one of those macho men, but he had come flying in that room like a scared little boy, like a baby, and jumped under those covers. He pulled the covers to above his nose and he was shaking.

"His whole body was trembling! There was no doubt about it, this man was scared. Something happened that scared the shit out of this man! I asked him, 'What happened? What's going on? What's the matter with you?' It took him about ten to fifteen minutes to where he could talk. He was shaking so bad that his jaw was locked. He couldn't speak.

"Finally, when he was able to speak, he proceeded to tell me that he went into the kitchen to get something to drink. When he came back out he was walking by the TV in the living room, all of a sudden, the TV comes on all by itself. He stops and looks at the TV. He said that something black came out of that television, with hands and was reaching toward him.

"He told me this was the scariest thing that he'd ever seen in his life. Greg was paralyzed, he could not move! The man couldn't even scream! He said he'd never seen anything like that before in his entire life. After that, Greg didn't stay over at the house that much. He stayed at his mom's. He would occasionally stay over, and the nights that he did, he rarely slept and if he did, not comfortably."

SHUFFLING SHADOWS (PUEBLO, COLORADO)

"There was a period of time when I'd be in the house by myself and there were some really bad things going on in my life. Some real negative things that didn't start until I moved into that house. That house was evil. There were several times when I would be in the bathroom and if you shut the door in the main bathroom, which was right off the living room, there was a big … it almost seemed like the door was too big, it didn't quite fit the door frame. There was a ton of room between the floor and the bottom of the door. A large gap.

"Every time I'd shut the door and use the bathroom, I could see shadows going back and forth in front of the door. People walking. I would always hear so much commotion. That's what I hated the most because it happened all the time. Whether I was in the big bathroom or the little bathroom, it didn't matter. If I was in the bathroom and the door was shut it messed with me outside the door. You could hear it shuffling around.

"If I was in the bedroom, I could hear the drawers. You could constantly hear the door that would go out to the end of the house. That one room I was talking about—the storage room that went outside—well that first door going to the storage room had a rubber flap on the bottom of the door that would slide across the linoleum. You can hear the rubber sliding whenever somebody would open that door, there was no stopping it. No sneaking in.

"So anytime I was in my bedroom I would always hear that door, opening and closing, opening and closing. I would keep my door open and I can hear it at the end of the hall opening and closing. Open-shut. Open-shut. That was real constant. It was to the point where I didn't leave the doors open anymore. There was one specific time that they had messed with me so badly that I went running out of the bathroom, got two butcher knives and when Greg came into the house he found me sitting on the couch shaking violently.

"Shaking from fear. You know something is out there, but every time you open the door, it stops. It was so frustrating!"

MOB CONNECTIONS (PUEBLO, COLORADO)

Aunt Ronda shares the bloody history this former food market turned house hides.

"The history of the house ... after that first incident with the loud knocking on the door, after we moved in and got settled, I decided to go to the library and do some research on this house. I found out, at the time, the home was one hundred and two years old. It used to be a grocery store for a long time. It was a mini-mart. I guess way back in the 1950s and 1960s when the Mafia was here in Pueblo, and they were really bad, they ran the town.

"There was a big hit on several people at that grocery store. Back then, when there was a hit, not only that person would die. Sadly, several people died. The Mafia went in there with machine guns. Just tearing up people left and right, they left immediately afterwards, leaving nothing but dead bodies all over the place. They ended up killing everyone in that damn store!

"So, I did read that. Nothing else really stuck out to me. At one time it was a fish store, a rock store ... they sold rocks in there. That was the big thing though, that massacre that happened in the house, the Mafia Mob Slaughter."

When I ask her if she knows how many people perished in this attack, what she says next shocked and saddened me.

"I believe eighty-seven, if I remember correctly. Men, women and children. Jonathan and May told me they named a little girl spirit that was in the house. I think May had a personal experience with this girl in her room, but I cannot remember what the specific details are."

MOMMA'S TALE

"My mom has some strange stories from when she was a kid because they grew up in funeral homes that were turned into apartments. There were some real crazy things that went on there. My mom woke up one night to a lady sitting at the end of her bed. She was transparent, you could see through her momma said. She's sitting on the end of the bed at a vanity, she had real long hair.

"She's just sitting there brushing her hair, really slowly. Momma said she didn't have a brush in her hand, but you could see the hair going up as she was brushing it and momma shrieked. She was paralyzed, it scared her. She was only seven or eight years old. The lady stopped brushing her hair. She stopped as soon as momma made that noise. She stopped in mid-air and turned and looked at momma real slow.

"When she looked at momma … momma could see her eyes. Nothing but pure sadness. She said it was absolutely … like she had been crying for years and years. All of a sudden, she just went away. That was what my mom experienced. That is when she realized that there are spirits because she saw it with her own eyes."

End of Aunt Ronda's experiences.

The next experiences are from my friend Sheila, you'll read more about Sheila, and her store, 'Sheila's Copper Penny' which is located in Jerome, Arizona. Buckle up, it's about to get wild.

As told by Sheila.

BLACK OUT (MICHIGAN)

"Well, when I was ten years old I moved to Michigan, Northern Michigan. There was a house that in the late 1960s five people were murdered in that house. In 1983 I was ten years old when we moved into this house and I had quite a few experiences there. Friends would stay the night and we would have the light from the windows. The moonlight and the light from under the door in the hallway would go completely black.

"We would scream for my mother to help us get out of this and there wouldn't be nothing. They wouldn't hear us and we'd be like, 'We were screaming for a half hour, you didn't hear us?' My mom would say, 'No. Why are you so upset?' We would explain to her that something blacked out the whole light and sound from the room that we were in. This had happened numerous times."

NIGHTLY VISITOR

"The same room I mentioned earlier, my brother had an experience there as well. He was six years old, four years younger than me. Every night he said a man with a black top hat, red eyes, a red pen and a black coat would come up from the back of the door and write something on a tablet.

"Here's my little brother, coming home from kindergarten one day saying, 'Mom! I know what it is!' Confused, she replies, 'What are you talking about?' He says, 'We learned cursive today! He's writing my name on that tablet!' So, imagine as a teacher, dealing with young children … don't put them on pills, the answer isn't always ADD or ADHD. It might be spiritual activity in their lives!"

UNEXPLAINED SOUNDS (MICHIGAN)

"I grew up in a strict Christian family, bible based. Basically, television was our sin! We had no alcoholism or anything like that in the family. Anyway, we would hear children or footsteps running up and down the hallway and my father would say to us, 'Go to bed kids!' when we would already be in bed.

"Three feet of snow would be on the ground and we would hear horses dragging chains around and around the house. How can that be with three feet of snow?"

TO WHENCE THEY CAME (CALIFORNIA)

"One year later, we decided to move to California. Our grandparents warned us that there was a suicide in that house, in the bathroom. They would sometimes hear unexplained knocks in the house. Well, the first night I was there, I wake up in the middle of the night and I was pressed against the wall.

"A spirit voice told me at a young age, at eleven, 'The two spirits you brought with you have lesser power then him. He's going to send them back to where they came from.' His words were, 'to whence they came.' The bottom part of the bunk bed started to swirl and with this orange color mist, I saw these two figures that have plagued me every night, for quite a few years!

"A very skinny man, a black shadow man, and a very fat puffy man similar to Ghost Busters. At the time, that movie wasn't even out yet. They would come to my face, back and forth at night, making my lower jaw hurt. Ever since that one spirit casts those spirits to whence they came, I was never plagued by them again. My teeth never hurt again. That spirit really helped me.

"That house in California, I saw a pillar of fire. It was from the floor to the ceiling! It was crackling like fire and it moved around the whole room! It eventually moved into the dining room and went to the ceiling, then went away. It was very electric. The same spirit, I don't know if it was a spirit or something else in that home, showed me in a dream what the other side looked like.

"I saw creatures of all different shapes and sizes, good and bad, some aggressive, some were hiding. Putting fear into me. I was shown these creatures, which is quite odd, because it was showing me the other side of the veil, so to speak. I can't explain it."

THE MAN AT THE ELEVATOR (JEROME, ARIZONA)

"I've had experiences in Jerome as well. I saw something at the Jerome Grand Hotel. (You'll read more about this hotel in Chapter twenty-one) I saw a man with black hair and a V-neck dark brown shirt. At the time, I was an employee there, so I was helping people by an elevator. I was taking pictures for them in the area where a man named Claude Harvey was crushed by an elevator in the late 1920s.

"I tell the people that I need to go so I can help the man I had just walked by. The people saw the movement but didn't see anything else. I walked around the corner and there was nobody there. He couldn't have left, I would have seen him go down the hallway, there was no exit out the way where he had went. The elevator there is the authentic elevator from the 1920s."

EAST OF EDEN (JEROME, ARIZONA)

"Three summers ago, I worked at the Chamber of Commerce. (The building is just a few feet from where the store, Sheila's Copper Penny, is located.) While there, I had an unexplained strong, very strong, urge to read 'East of Eden' a book by John Steinbeck. Imagine myself being in a place that was, I would say like a sunroom, with plants. I strongly felt, 'It would be so great to read this book, I want to do this so badly!' It was very odd. So anyways, I read the book, loved the book.

"The following year, in November, I got a job at the Jerome Grand Hotel. Originally on the front desk but they kept pushing me to house-keeping because they liked the way I made the beds. They told me the initiation for the girls is to water the garden, so I go into the garden room and I felt so at peace there. It's a balcony that two rooms share, full of plants. It's called the Garden Room and you can rent it. Here I am watering the plants and what do I see?

"One of the rooms was still occupied with people inside, they had the door shut. On the table was East of Eden! Why I had the strong urge while in Jerome to read that book and seeing the book at the Garden Room? A very odd coincidence. Just very strange."

BREAK MY SPIRIT (CLARKSDALE, ARIZONA)

"I've had spirits show me things that are mean, almost to break my spirit. I cannot even explain it, to break a spirit ... my mother passed away in 2011. I've had dreams of seeing her in a casket, decomposed. I'll wake up asking, 'Why?' In Cottonwood, five years ago, I was at a bar. I don't go to bars anymore, I didn't go much anyway, just occasionally. Anyway, I'm in this bar called 'The Rock 'N Bee' and all of a sudden, I got real angry.

"I knew there was an angry spirit here. I was so angry! I wanted to kick somebody's butt. I hated everyone at that moment, I even hated my husband. This is before my mom died. I told my husband, 'We gotta go! I'm really angry. I'm not having fun. This sucks.' So, we went home. We live in a motor home. We have a king-sized bed modified to the back of this motor home.

"So, I'm lying there, not sleeping yet, just lying there and I see this black shadowy misty mass in the hallway and it goes up and over my head, WHOOSH! I turn my head to the left, it goes out the window and I see a black carriage being pulled by black horses. This is in lower Clarksdale and it goes down the road. That spirit, the black shadowy misty mass goes above my head and flies as fast as it can in to that carriage and runs away.

"I asked my husband, 'Am I dreaming yet? Am I sleeping yet?' After that happened, the anger was gone, no anger, no anxiety. I told my husband kiddingly, 'We can go back to the bar, the anger is gone.' We stayed home. It attached to me at that bar and I brought it back home with me."

THE GHOST HAS LEFT THE BUILDING (JEROME, ARIZONA)

"Also, here in Jerome next to the Spirit Room Bar, is the Conner Hotel. They have a nice gift shop there. In 2007 I was engaged, planning on getting married. I wanted to get a necklace from that gift shop. They have these nice upscale necklaces, they are so beautiful. I walked in there and I'm standing in the corner and it sounds like a glass shelf breaking. CRACK!

"The lady looks at me like, 'What did you break!' I explain to her, 'I'm sorry, it's nothing. It's a spirit, a spirit has entered this room.' Around me sometimes glass will break, glass will crack. I was hoping to hear it tonight, but I didn't want to say anything. I told the woman, 'When it leaves it will crack again.' She looked at me like I had three heads! I was like, 'You live in a known haunted town and you're looking at me like I'm crazy! Come on!' She didn't believe me. She shook her head and just went back to her book that she was reading.

"Two, maybe three minutes later, a very loud crack. She looks at me again with the same look, 'What did you break!' I looked at her and said, 'No! It's the spirit leaving. He's left now, he's gone.' She still didn't believe me."

A SPECIAL AGATE JUST FOR YOU (LAKE SUPERIOR, MICHIGAN)

"I took a trip back in 2011 to my high school reunion. My father and I, we grew up on the shore of Lake Superior. On Lake Superior we would pick agates all the time on the beach. We would pick agates and that's a fond memory I have of my father and I, picking agates and shells on the beach.

"In 2011 my dad had already passed away then. I had no idea the next weekend my mom would also pass away. I took this trip to Michigan. Here I am on the lake shore. I say, 'Dad, I really want to know if you're thinking about me. Even if it's just God Himself, just know that I know where I grew up and here I am again, I would love to find an agate.' I spent two days on that beach and I didn't find any agates. Not even one.

"It depends what time of year, what washes up. An agate is a rock that's clear with lines, some are red-orange, you can look through the rock. It's called Lake Superior Agate. People go agate hunting, and people can sell them. On the way back to the car, I'm walking on this muddy path. I look down and right in the middle of the path is a red agate shaped like a heart. I still have it. The spirit world can act in so many positive and negative ways."

End of Sheila's experiences.

My cousin, who I lived with for a while in a suburb in Denver, Colorado is a fellow paranormal investigator. I recently got to spend some much-needed time in the mountains off La Veta Pass in Colorado with him and his girlfriend. While enjoying the scenery by a camp fire, both my cousin Nick and his sweet girlfriend Laurie shared some experiences with me.

As told by Laurie.

WHIDBEY ISLAND (WASHINGTON STATE)

"Whidbey Island is in Washington State, which is north of Seattle. We had a cabin that's on the lake. It was the first house ever to be built on the lake. Countless times I would be staying there, I would be in the kitchen or sitting watching TV and the door would swing open by itself. Randomly. It happened several times."

NOT ALONE (VICTOR, COLORADO)

"We stayed at the Victor Hotel which is close to Cripple Creek. We stayed there last summer. This was my first real experience, when I first started believing in all this. I'm hard to convince. Nick was sitting out in the hallway. We were the only ones staying there for the night. Four floors and we are the only ones in the whole hotel! So, I walk into the bathroom, probably to do my hair.

"I walk back and sit on the bed. The hangers in the closet by the door there was like a wooden piece with like four different hangers, then actual hangers on it. All of a sudden, they started swinging back and forth! I was like, 'What the heck!' So, I walk into the hallway, Nick was sitting over by the elevators just looking at his phone. I tell him, 'Nick come here, right now!' I brought him in and told him what happened. It was so weird! As if someone walked by and messed with them!"

Nick and Laurie together tell me this experience.

FLICKER FOR CONFIRMATION (WHIDBEY ISLAND, WASHINGTON STATE)

"We were playing cards and Laurie's dad told us, 'Art, her Grandpa, always accused me of cheating.' As soon as he said that, the lights started flickering. Right when we were playing cards. This was Laurie's dad's father-in-law."

End of Laurie's experiences.

My cousin Rosalie is one of the sweetest people I know. She is such a loving and caring person. Our whole family is a tight-knit family. Rosalie shares the passion I have for the paranormal. She has had some experiences herself.

As told by Rosalie.

LONDON BRIDGES (ESTES PARK, COLORADO)

"Here is an experience from the Stanley Hotel in Estes Park. Nick had just gotten his driver's license—this was back in 2007. He had wanted to go to the Stanley Hotel. He loved it because he heard it was haunted. So, he convinced his sister *Maggie and myself to go. The three of us drove up there and we had a king bed. We all shared this bed. We were supposed to be in the most haunted room in that hotel.

"I was sleeping closest to the door, Maggie was in the middle, Nick on the other side. Every time there was a noise they would say, 'Mee-maw!' Every time they'd say that, I would jump out of bed, go to the door and look in the peep hole. I had to have done this, literally twenty times. Jump out of that bed and run. They wouldn't do it, so they made me do it!

"So, all of a sudden we hear this little girl singing, 'London Bridges.' I go to the peep hole and Tessa … I don't care if people think I'm crazy or what, I saw a little girl. She was about twelve years old. She had sort of auburn, reddish-brownish hair with a big braid. Like with people that have curly hair, it kind of sticks out from the braid a little bit. She had a green puff-sleeve blouse on with a little jumper.

"She was skipping past our room. I told Nick and Maggie what I saw. Nick jumped out of bed. I opened the door and she was gone. There were some people down the hallway. Nick went down the hallway and asked the people if they'd seen the girl. They said no. I don't like to tell this to anybody because they don't believe me. I know what I saw, nobody can take that away from me.

"It was amazing. Maggie started to cry, she was hysterical and wanted to go home. I had to convince her to stay. We were in a room that had an enclosed room and the windows rattled all night long. I kept getting up and it scared Maggie. There was no wind, no wind at all. I wrote all those experiences down, the experiences from that night at the Stanley.

"I have been back there one time and they have since remodeled that room. It's not the same. When we were there in 2007 we were able to creep around in the dark. You go there now, you can't do that anymore. It's just not the same anymore."

STRANGE HAPPENIN'S AT TRANS ALLEGHENY (WESTON, WEST VIRGINIA)

"Trans Allegheny Lunatic Asylum. There are so many … I can't even describe it. There are four floors. They are renovating part of it to make it look fancy with antiques. I prefer it to stay the way it is. I don't know if the spirits that are there, like that they are changing it. There is so much going on there. We had a guide that was so good that we asked for him a second time.

"This guide was so excited, he's obsessed with this Asylum. He's had many paranormal experiences there. I don't even know where to start. Many times, we'd be sitting on the floor in the dark waiting for something to happen, then we'd get up. Another couple was with us as well. It was pitch black, you can't even see your hands in front of your face.

"This one guy that was with us, along with his girlfriend said, 'I'm going to walk down that hall right now and you all watch me.' So, we all watch him, he has a flashlight and he's just walking along when, all of a sudden, a door slammed. It was so loud, it shook. I thought he was going to have a heart attack because it's where he was walking towards.

"That was one HUGE thing. Then when we listened to Nick's recorder we heard more things then what we heard with our ears. Civil War soldiers bunked on this one floor and they had a big kitchen, and we sat there for a while. I walked into the kitchen, it's quite big, it was about two blocks long. I went in there by myself and Nick kept saying, 'Mee-maw! Are you going to go in there by yourself?' I said, 'Yes! I'm not afraid!

"I kept being drawn to that place. We didn't hear anything then and then when we heard the recorder you can hear somebody walking with heavy boots. Big stride going BOOM-BOOM-BOOM-BOOM-BOOM! We caught that on recorder. There's a little girl there and her name is Lilly. There's a room that she has, there's toys and other things there for her.

"So, we went into her room, *Don, Nick, Maggie and me with our little flashlights. Nick was sitting in the middle of the floor and something nicked his leg. We couldn't tell what it was; there was stuff on the floor. We tried to replicate the sound and figured out that it might have been a crayon that was thrown at him.

"Whenever we see a penny, we think it's my mom. So, we went in there and there was no penny around, all of a sudden, a penny is found by Nick's leg.

Then on the recorder we heard a little girl, who we think to be Lilly, saying, 'Okay.' She had this sweet little voice. As clear as a bell. Her story, this Asylum housed some of the most vicious criminals, and the insane. They would kill each other and beat each other up.

"The guards or the care takers wouldn't even go because they were afraid of these guys. So many horrible things happened there. Killings, beatings, rapes, people getting hurt. Children were born there because these women would get pregnant by rape. Lilly is a product of that. They say she's looking for her mother. It's so incredibly sad.

"There was another woman, I think her name was Mary Ruth. Evidently, she was born at the asylum, and they put her into a foster home until she was eighteen. She ended up coming back and worked here for seventy-two years at that Asylum! Then they fixed a special room for her and she died when she was ninety-two years old. There are so many things going on there I can't even begin to tell you!

"Then they have these drawings of people. They had a doctor there that did lobotomies. There was a section for this. They actually stuck an ice pick in the frontal bone of your eye. Then they'd pound the ice pick in. There's also a morgue on the property. The property itself is twenty-six acres."

End of Rosalie's experiences.

Now this next person who will share his experiences is the reason my radio talk show even exists. He gave me this fabulous opportunity. He has had many experiences when it comes to the paranormal. Some, MIND BLOWING. As shared in JC Salazar's words.

JUDY THE FRIENDLY GHOST (PUEBLO, COLORADO)

"As a DJ I have experienced a couple different spiritual phenomena most dramatic at the Old Freed Middle School now known as Heroes Academy, and Aloha Gloria's Gentleman's Club … VERY STRONG PARANORMAL HOT SPOTS!

"At Aloha Gloria's she would tug on my shirt, throw CDs, and lower the volume controls on my mixing board. She would also make the room cold. Judy is very playful and will definitely let her presence be known. It's funny, if you are aware of who she is, she will NOT appear in visual form.

"She has manifested to many unsuspecting employees. She is said to be beautiful but what is the strangest thing to me is, as old as the building is, her story only began toward the early 1990's. She was an exotic dancer pulling tricks out of the club. She fell ill and went to the hospital and died there. I'm not sure why she stays at work of all places. Perhaps it's because it's where she found acceptance.

"Many have had experiences with Judy or at least she has been blamed for paranormal activity. This area was once a vein for bootleggers and a good old-fashioned detective agency on the upper floor where performers have experienced slamming lockers, etc. I as a DJ have always wanted to announce her to stage with her 'Money Set' see if she would appear and perform. I believe it would be the most spectacular show ever!"

HOSPITAL TUNNELS (PUEBLO, COLORADO)

"In Parkview Hospital on the bottom floor, close to the morgue, is a tunnel that leads from Parkview and across to the Mental Health Facility. I've had friends that were committed for youth crimes that swear to have seen multiple apparitions in that tunnel and it is open to the public!

"Also, I performed a bit of "Extremely Amateur" paranormal investigating at the state hospital museum and made contact with, what I later found out was the youngest daughter and mother of the original owner-head of the state hospital. My brother-in-law is a security officer at the state hospital and has experienced creepy feelings, etc. in the tunnels and abandoned buildings."

THE EXORCISM (PUEBLO, COLORADO)

"I was a pre-teen and there was a spectacular show on Christmas Eve. Nonetheless, I was always there because my father, prior to passing, was a preacher. A preacher was his true calling but he also worked as a meat specialist or butcher and this was his profession, which is how I saw the tunnel below Monte's. Not sure if the butchering he did for them was completely legal, but it was a cow.

"Anyway, the man came into the church through the main entrance on 4th Street. Nobody really noticed as he came in. Part way through the sermon, which was a guest sermon—revival sermon as they called them—he began to make his way down the center aisle. He was kind of dancing and shimmying.

"That kind of behavior wasn't completely off because it was a Pentecostal Church Holy Spirit and such a normal occurrence … until he reached the pulpit where he began hammering it with his fists and yelling obscenities at the guest pastor at which point the very small crowd of regulars began to chant something to the effect of the blood of Christ etc. …

"At which point, the yelling went from English obscenities to a live banter in a foreign language between the two men, which included anointing oil being splashed on the possessed gentleman.

"When this happened, he ended up writhing on the floor screaming in pain saying that he was burning as a white foam began to emerge from his mouth. I believe I will always remember the towel that was used to clean it from him and the floor which was white with a blue cross pattern, perhaps mostly because they kept the towel on a table in the basement and I had to pass it weekly to go to the bathroom.

"I am pretty sure they washed it but it still frightened me! To this day it still creeps me out going down there!"

THE HUMAN DUMMY

"Near the cemetery on Northern across from the grocery store is an apartment complex that was once an orphanage and has a church attached to it that I believe to be haunted. We held a haunted house production there and during a run-through, someone or something threw my cousin from the upper balcony to the floor below.

"Scared the hell out of us workers and the customers. Luckily, he fell on his back spread-eagled onto the rigging we were using to create walls and wasn't injured. Just really shaken up. He was up there to drop a dummy to scare the customers and he became the dummy. We were grown men mind you, in our mid-twenties."

End of JC's experiences.

My friend Ken has had several paranormal experiences throughout his life. As he put it, he is not shy about it. He even went on national TV and spoke about an orange orb that he saw. That will be explained more here in one of his experiences.

My friend Ken shared some interesting experiences with me for the book. As written by Ken.

BEAR (COLORADO)

"My experience involves a late Native American gentleman named 'Bear'. He came to me as a material bear while I was in the mountains. Others told me they have smelled his tobacco pipe in the mountains or in the house that he used to visit."

SACRED FEATHERS (COLORADO)

"We often see animals that act differently—that aren't normal. They stay around and just stare at us. Often, they come in the form of birds. I have talked to many people who claim that their late relatives or friends came to them as a hawk, eagle, owl or other bird.

"A book called 'Sacred Feathers' is about the paranormal experiences of many around America who have had that experience. They have come to me before as well.

"My late niece came to her mother before her mother passed away and left feathers. When I see a blue bird, I think of Susanna. A hummingbird, my mom. I have seen feathers by birds as well. They just drop them for me to use in ceremony. Friends have had this happen as well.

"Right before my mother died, over ten years ago, a horned owl was hooting outside my window, which is pretty rare. Then my mother died hours later. Kind of scary but awesome as well."

UNIDENTIFIED FLYING OBJECT (INDIAN HEAD PEAK, COLORADO)

"I spoke on national TV about a strange orange orb (UFO?) I saw by Indian Head Peak, just northwest of Del Norte. This was many years ago. It was at night and it was clearly not a plane, helicopter, meteorite or natural phenomena.

"There is an Indian Burial Ground there, so it could have been a spirit light. A friend who I hadn't seen in thirty years saw me on TV. He lives near Chicago,

Illinois. He emailed me asking about it and I told him I didn't know what it was, but it was awesome.

"It was a beautiful orange light hovering in the rocks. It was amazing, and it went national."

NOT ALONE (GETTYSBURG, PENNSYLVANIA)

"I just watched a show on TV last night called, 'Mysteries at the National Parks, the Haunted Battlefield.' It was about Gettysburg battle field. I was there many years ago by Little Round Top, where many Union and Confederate soldiers died in the 1860's during the Civil War.

"Thousands were killed, and some people have seen strange apparitions in the park, especially at night. Some were soldiers, but some were Native Americans, who battled there long before the Civil War.

"I never saw anything strange but felt someone was watching me while I walked in an area of rocky outcrops. I got an eerie feeling and the hair on my neck stood up. Scary but a wonderful experience. Go to Gettysburg if you ever get the chance. Beautiful and mysterious place.

End of Ken's experiences.

My friend John shares with me an experience he had a few years ago. These are in John's words.

ENERGY, ORBS AND A MEAN OLD LADY (DENVER, COLORADO)

"In December of 2008 I had my first and only (so far) ghost busting experience. My girlfriend at the time JS worked in Administration at one of Denver's hospitals. A co-worker of hers had related how much trouble they were having selling his relative's house.

"It had been on the market for a couple of years and there had been no interested parties. He thought it might be because the house was haunted. It was rumored that the deceased owner was a very mean, old woman. JS, long interested in the paranormal, offered to help.

"She recruited me to be a witness and technician with audio recording and photo equipment. Upon entering the house, there was an immediate feeling of dread. The air was thick with negative energy. I felt stifled. JS and the other people with us confirmed that they felt the same energy.

"We began to explore the house, moving from room to room. JS with the audio recorder and me making photographic images. At one point, JS said she felt the presence of a small child and bent over as if she were placing her hand on a child's head. I made an image of her doing that and then another immediately after she stood back up. When we looked at the images on the computer later, there was an unmistakable orb in the second photo, almost exactly the height where she had placed her hand to touch the energy she felt moments ago.

After touring the yard outside, we re-entered the house. Lighting a traditional Native American smudge stick, we again went room to room, directing smoke into every corner and crevice we could reach, with the intention of ridding the house of all dark energy.

"Afterwards, we all felt a sense of relief upon leaving the house. JS was told later that the house had sold within a few weeks of our ghost busting adventure."

End of John's experience.

My friend and fellow paranormal investigator, who has become part of the Paranormal Prowlers team in the middle of 2016 has some interesting experiences to share. These are in Angie E. Velasquez's words.

SAINT JAMES (CIMARRON, NEW MEXICO)

"It's called The Saint James Hotel and it's in Cimarron, New Mexico. Ghost Adventures did a show over there and other shows have also. Anyway, it's supposed to be one of the top most haunted hotels in the United States. They have room 18 that is padlocked shut and they refuse to let anyone in there and if they do, then they must sign a waiver, apparently.

"We stayed across the hall from 18. We stayed in the Mary Lambert room, we could hear steps coming down the hall and we were the only ones upstairs. In room 18 they had a gambler that was shot in the back entering his room and died right there on the threshold of the doorway going back into his room.

"So, they say that room is occupied, and they just leave it as occupied. They have a 'Don't Disturb' sign on the door. He's like the resident spirit. I think his name is TJ. When my husband and I first got there, they said we were the only ones upstairs.

"We were looking at the … they have these old photos and newspapers hanging on the walls, we were looking at them. Pretty much the whole upstairs was left untouched, it still looks the same, like it did back then. So, we went looking around. There was a communal bathroom up there because some of the rooms still don't have toilets.

"So anyway, the toilet in there sounded like it was running, so I went in there and jiggled the handle and when I came out I was looking at some of the artwork and I heard, 'Thank you' which I thought was comical.

"My husband was around the corner, so I walked a few steps and looked, and he was down at the end of the hall. It was kind of funny. So, after I got home I watched the Ghost Adventures episode when they were there, we had recorded it earlier. They also got an EVP of a voice saying, 'Thank you.'

"I had a disembodied voice saying it to me. Then I had an EVP from there. I sat outside of our door and I was talking to TJ. I got an EVP saying, 'Come here'. Then I got an EVP in our room before falling asleep and it was a really loud kind of a scream, 'Help me!'

"It's a really good place to go to—a lot of people have had experiences there. They have twenty-three bullet holes in the ceiling in the bar. Wyatt Earp and his family have stayed there before, while on their way to Tombstone. Doc Holliday and Jesse James, all the notorious people, they have stayed there.

"I almost forgot to mention this … my husband got very ill when we went to Cimarron, at the hotel. He started making fun of TJ the spirit. He walked by his room and said something sarcastic. After that he was quite ill the whole time we were there.

"About twenty minutes after leaving, he felt much better. So now, he believes. Now he knows you cannot talk to the spirits like that, you can't disrespect them. It is real."

SIX MINUTES IN A MURDER HOUSE (VILLISCA, IOWA)

"We just got back this summer from Villisca Axe Murder House. It was so awesome. I didn't stay the night, I wanted to, but they were already booked. From the time we knew we were coming, they had already been booked until the end of summer.

"However, I did get six minutes alone in there. I was downstairs and I was recording. I said, 'This was Lena and Ina's room'. Then I heard, 'Stupid'. It was calling me stupid! It was the middle of the day and I was only there for a few minutes, it was cool! I could only imagine what I could get at night and for a longer period of time!

"They have bells on everything—like the rocking chairs—so you can hear if something is moving. The door to the kids' room and the door to the attic area as well, open.

"I told the lady, the owner of the house, 'I would just kill just to stay the night here'. She said to me, 'Sweetie, come back next year or call me next year and I will make sure to get you in'. However, it's $428 a night ... but you can have up to ten people. So, if you get ten people chipping in, it's not too bad. I had the house all to myself for six minutes!"

ANGIE'S HERE (DEL NORTE, COLORADO)

"At the Windsor Hotel, I know you've heard of Maude. Other people believe there is more than just Maude here. I am starting to believe that too. We spent the night here two years ago. I went all over upstairs with my recorder and got nothing.

"So, I go downstairs into the event room, it was around Christmas time. I say in the recorder, 'Okay, I'm in the event room and if you're here then you know who I am'. Then you can hear a woman saying, 'Angie's here'. I have that on my phone, so you can listen to it".

(She let me hear the recording and, plain as day, you can hear a disembodied voice of what sounds like a woman saying, "Angie's here.")

THE PEACEFUL ORB (SOUTH FORK, COLORADO)

"So, my nephew was going through some difficult times and one night I was up late and crying and unable to sleep. I'm just lying there trying to sleep, and I can't. You know how when you're upset, and you have trouble falling asleep?

That's how I was. So, I'm lying there trying to go to sleep. So, I have this big tree thing at the end of my bed. I saw some light on the side of the tree. I looked over and there was a string of what looks like orbs.

"Some are brighter than others and there is nothing in our backyard that would cause light to come in through the window. We face the river so there is nothing—no houses, no road, no cars—nothing.

"So, I am looking at them for a moment and they just kind of fade off. I thought, Wow, I actually feel at peace. I told my husband about it and told him how this incident—it made me feel peaceful. Then I was able to fall right back asleep. Really weird.

"Another time I saw one come out of the same room, out of the wall, it kind of zig-zagged and then went back into the wall. I didn't want to sleep in there that night!"

SPOOKY SMOKE BREAK (SOUTH FORK, COLORADO)

"My son lost two best friends, it was horrible. He had a best friend and that best friend died then, shortly afterwards, the other best friend died. So now, it's hard for him to get too close to people now.

"So anyway, he was in the bathroom smoking and he coughed, he had the recorder going, and he got an EVP saying, 'What the fuck you thinking?' So that happened in my house … quite creepy!"

BURST OF SADNESS (DENVER, COLORADO)

"The Brown's Palace in Denver—we stayed there for three nights—and I believe it was the first morning that we were there. We got room service and as soon as they brought it in, my husband got out of the shower. He was in his robe. We had sat down to eat, and he just had this look that come over his face. I had never seen it on him before, it was really kind of weird. He then burst into tears and started talking about his brother who was deceased. Well, it was kind of weird that he would feel like that. He seems to be real sensitive. When we go places he will get real emotional, or he gets sick.

"The Brown's Palace is a really good one to go to. They say that there's a lady there who committed suicide. The top floor I think, there used to be apartments up there. She was kept in up there ... I cannot remember the story on it.

"I took a picture of him right before he burst into tears."

She pauses and turns on her phone and skims through some pictures and shows us a picture. There her husband is sitting at their hotel room table and has a big smile on his face. Looking at this picture it's shocking that just seconds later, with no incident, he is in tears!

"He was just eating his food and suddenly he got this look on his face and I was like, 'My God, what's wrong with him'. It was a real crazy look on his face.

"Such a look of disgust, then he just burst into tears! He knows, he has really become aware, that he is sensitive like that when we go to places that have something going on. He is actually getting into this stuff now. Not before, though. He was always the biggest skeptic. When I got my very first EVP, he got very excited. It was in our house. He knew!"

THE AWAKENING OF THE HOME (SOUTH FORK, COLORADO)

"Back in 2007, I started noticing weird things happening in the house. We had lived there, by that time, for eighteen years and never had a problem. NEVER. The whole time our kids were being raised nothing paranormal ever happened. In 2007 I noticed it started, I would lie down and when I would do that to rest in the middle of the day, I could hear what sounded like a cat.

"You know how a cat sounds like walking across the carpet? It's quiet enough, but you can hear it. Anyway, we didn't have any indoor animals at the time. It was weird, because it would always come and stalk the threshold of the bedroom door.

"I have heard it probably … half a dozen times before. One day, I actually heard it coming in past the door and I could just feel the electricity. I could feel it come on to the bed. It was on all fours around me and I could feel the energy and the electricity.

"When it came up to my face, I just closed my eyes. I was just frozen stiff. I was terrified. When it got to my ear, it sounded like a hissing sound. So, I jumped, and I ran outside. That's when it started getting pretty weird at my house.

"That never happened again—hearing it anyway—but my nephew who came to live with us … I think he brought what was there in the first place. By his own admission, he would make his own Ouija Boards. He is a dark person, dark poem kind of person.

"Well, he told me he heard what sounded like a cat jumping off the counter—you know the sound going off the counter and onto the floor—in the middle of the night. He said he heard that and he heard something running around. If I hadn't heard it for myself before, I would have thought maybe it was a pack-rat problem or something. So, that's how it got started. Then I would hear clinking sounds, like if you got two marbles and clinked them together. That's what it sounded like.

"It would happen on one side of the room, then quickly happen again on the opposite side of the room. It felt like two things trying to communicate. It's weird. It's quite creepy. No one I know has ever experienced anything like that before. I would try to fall asleep and I would be awakened as I tried to fall asleep with the clicking. So, I tried investigating it myself, seeing if it was night terrors or anything else. I tried to find an answer. I couldn't. It wouldn't matter what room I was in, I would go from room to room and it would just follow me.

"This never happened when my husband was awake. It would never make the sound when he was awake. When he is falling asleep, he will take a good deep breath, then I know he's drifting. That's when the clinking will start! So, I knew something was picking on me. I couldn't figure out what was going on.

"So, for four months I didn't hardly sleep. We fought a lot. It was constant fighting. He told me, 'Maybe you need to go see a psychiatrist because you're really starting to lose it and I don't think I can handle it. So, you need to stop with this crap, or I'm outta here'.

"It was kind of weird because that EVP I got in my room actually saved our marriage. He started understanding that there is something going on in this house—that it wasn't just all in my head. I told him I was going to put the recorder in my room and he got mad about that.

"I thought, I'm just going to let it run. So, I turned it on and I lay there. I got a sick feeling in my stomach. It was kind of funny because I turned, and the bed made a squeaky sound and I said, 'Just me' and I think they thought I said, 'Trust me' because there's a click-click, then an EVP of a voice asking, 'why?'

"It's a female. He knows there was nobody else in our house. My son said, 'Mom, there was something else there. The recording, it sounds like something on all fours is running up to you, hearing a man's voice, then the woman asks, 'Why?''

"So, I sent it to another paranormal group and they told me the same thing. Something running on all fours toward me, a man's voice, then the woman saying, 'Why?' Kind of creepy! My husband listened to it over and over and over. That's when he started believing."

End of Angie's experiences.
The following experience comes from my friend Jeanette. After Jeanette helped me get rid of my attachment (you will read about this at the end of the book—the last chapter) she spent some time telling me about The Blue Lady.

This is her experience in her own words.

THE BLUE LADY (SAN LUIS VALLEY, COLORADO)

"This spirit came to me through a spontaneous painting. I had been having fitful sleep and decided to do something radical that I had never done before. I got out a large sketch pad and paints and just started finger-painting without any intention other than to let this fitful energy to move through. What emerged, startled me to say the least. At first, I was quite distressed because I did not understand where the image came from or what it was.

"A couple days later I risked showing it to a friend who simply stated that it looked like I was channeling a spirit, which immediately resonated with me and set my mind a bit more at ease.

"I began to realize that it was a disembodied soul asking for assistance with forgiveness and healing. As I sat with him/her I began to hear a story of ambiguity and suffering. He had taken his own life after suffering for decades as a feminine spirit in a male body. Because of this act, he had been hanging in limbo and not able to move on.

"These were her words to me,

> I tried so hard, for so long, to pretend to be something and someone that others would accept as normal and perhaps even just a little bit lovable. I believed that I was evil and tried so hard not to reveal this deep, dark secret. Yet the harder I tried to cover up what was inside of me, the deeper my depression became. I did not know why I felt like I did … I did not know why I felt like a woman but looked like a man.

Figure 1 The Spirit approaches Jeanette Amlie

> Finally, I simply could not do it anymore. I did not want to die, but I had no will to live either. I could not see through my own fog of self-hatred enough to hear the answer to my prayers, so I answered them myself.

"Later that week on a New Moon, I brought the painting out into a sacred circle of women who had gathered to do a ceremony. We drummed and sang and prayed for her healing and release. We honored her as a woman. By the time we were finished, the image had softened in intensity and I no longer felt the heavy despondency … finally she was FREE!

"After a few days, I felt clear that it was time to help 'give her a make-over' as per her request. Of course, she totally wanted a glam look, but absolutely DID NOT want to be Pollyanna happified. She implored me to make sure she had defined eyebrows. We were both very happy with the sultry look … very fitting for her style. She had to understand that the scarf was the best I could do with her neck, given the circumstances.

Figure 2 The Spirit gets a make-over, not only the face, but the noose turns into a lovely scarf

"She was skeptical about the earrings, but humored me, and allowed me to try them anyway … and may I say that she LOVED them! We added just a touch of silver eye shadow to accent them too. Finally, we stood together in front of the mirror, admiring her new look and feeling a deep connection from the healing process. In the end we had a grand time and she was able to move on, no longer trapped in the trauma of her unfortunate ending. Finally, she was free to flit about the ethers in style! What an unexpected blessing this ended up being for both of us!"

Pictures painted and provided by Jeanette Amlie

End of Jeanette's experience.

While at my friend David's house, he planned a Ouija Board session and Seance. (You'll read more about the seance itself later on). Two of his friends came over to join in and one of them, *MariAnne shared an experience with me. This is in MariAnne's words.

DEATH BY THE PSYCHIC VAMPIRE (MICHIGAN)

"I had a friend that lived with us and her sister was torturing her in Michigan. She felt like her sister was trying to kill her. I thought she was over-exaggerating. I told her, 'If she's really being that mean to you, if you need to move back home, you can live with us'. So she moved back down here. We eat all organic. When she moved in, she was a big girl, she probably weighed 230 pounds. She moved in and ate all organic and she lost around 50 pounds from just living with us for a couple months.

"She was doing so much better, but her pacemaker was kind of crazy. She kept telling me that she was paranoid. She truly felt that somebody was trying to kill her. It was just random stuff. She was trying to get a new sleep machine and she ended up not signing one paper and the lady called the cops. She said my friend stole the machine. So, the cops came to my house looking for her. It was like ten feet of snow on the ground. It was crazy! Just stuff like that.

"She kept telling me about her paranoia, it was real weird. Then, all of a sudden, she was staying between mine and another friend *Harry's house. She died at Harry's house. I kept asking Harry, 'Did her parents even ask for a report?' He told me, 'No!' It was weird … it was crazy. I just felt like something happened to her. I wanted to know what happened. She was around thirty-five years old. She was young.

"So, I came over here—for a ouija session—and I wasn't expecting anything to go through me. I said something like, 'I felt like … it never sat right with me, what happened to her. It was wrong. It wasn't a natural death'. So, we did the seance and I was fucking hysterical, I was a bawling mess. They read my cards and the cousin said, 'Foul play' I was flipping out. She came through and talked to us. I have the paper still, (written results) I actually have it with me.

"I brought it with me because I thought it was part of her. She told us it was her sister that killed her because she's a psychic vampire. It really sucked. I knew it was her. I could feel her. My friend was a lesbian who smoked a ton of weed and who listened to Ozzy Osborne. For her funeral they dressed her up like a Grandma and they had all these fundraisers for weird random things. She was a weed supporter, she was in weed groups. They were singing

Gospel. I was like, 'She would have been ROCKING to Ozzy'. It was just gross.

"Get over yourself, your daughter was a lesbian. This was not her, and you didn't do this ... right! It was fucked up! I never asked if it was her, I just knew it was her. She died in April of 2015, and we did the seance during Halloween night. "

MariAnne then shows me the paper from that Halloween seance where her friend came through and communicated with her.

"I was in shock because when she was spelling out the name ... I lost it. I'm so over it. When I was in Michigan they kept bringing her name up. I said, 'If I see this bitch, it's going down. It's going to be bad'. I haven't seen her family since. PSYCHIC VAMPIRE! I didn't know there was such a thing. I looked it up one day. It was crazy. She told me she loved me forever. My sweet friend. In the seance the question was asked if Harry had something to do with her death and she got mad and said, 'No' She moved the piece really hard!

"The only reason it was asked was because she died at his house. She wanted me to tell Harry, so the next day I called him. I told him, 'Okay this is going to be really weird, I went to a seance last night ... ' She was sick but getting better. When she moved in with us she was really sick, but she had been getting better and better. She was doing so good that I thought she should get her pacemaker taken out because now, at this point, it's trying to kill her. I told her this. She said, 'Maybe I will'.

"She had a disease. Sort of like MS but I don't remember what the name is. I don't know why she had the pacemaker. She had some sort of heart formality. Harry needed help more than me. He was suicidal. He was fucked. After I told him about that night, everything got better for him. It was good. She was sending that, that's why she wanted me to tell him. She didn't want him to get worse, she wanted him to get better. It probably saved his life—her coming through in the seance. It was bad, he wouldn't leave the house, he was doped up on pills. He had a wreck and he didn't even know what county he was in. He didn't even know he left the county.

"He was acting psychotic. He kept going to the shrink. They kept loading him up on pills. He kept blacking out and not remembering things. Then there was *Josh. It was rough for me, real sad. I think Josh is angry, he seemed angry.

He talked about where he died, he told us who killed him, like he described tats and stuff. We think he was a police officer.

"He was with the canine unit, and when he died he was in an unmarked car. He wasn't in his car and he didn't have his dog with him. It was weird. It was a real hard and rough seance for sure. He said some Mexican Cartel killed him. He was so angry. He was a very angry nasty spirit. Nasty energy. "

End of MariAnne's experience.

My cousin Nick is also a paranormal investigator, who has become part of my paranormal team, and we conduct investigations together when time allows us to. Here are some of his experiences as told by him.

FOOTSTEPS AND LAUGHING AND LUNATIC ASYLUMS OH MY! (WESTON, WEST VIRGINIA)

"So, I originally found out about this place last October when I was out in West Virginia for a business trip. At this point, I hadn't moved out there yet. One of my coworkers told me about this place, Trans Alleghny Lunatic Asylum. I drove down there one day after work and they were doing thirty-minute flashlight tours. It's a half-historical tour, half-paranormal tour.

"They tell you the history of the place and it's a quick walk-through of only one floor. Even in that thirty minutes, we heard footsteps and we heard a little girl laughing. After that I was like, 'I got to come back here!' So, once Laurie and I moved out here we went on a two-hour tour from 10pm to midnight.

"Then just this last weekend, I went on the overnight tour with my Grandma, brother and sister. We had so many little things that were happening … I don't even know where to start. I guess where to start is on the fourth floor. Well, let me give you some history first. It was a mental hospital for the insane during the Civil War. So, the Civil War soldiers built the asylum. It's a big gothic-style asylum and the conditions there were so brutal.

"It was built to house 250 patients and I think by the 1920s, there were over 2,500 patients there. Murders, suicides, the whole nine. They did lobotomies there. So, the layout of the overnight tour; it was an eight-hour tour, there's four floors and we got two hours on each floor. The first fifteen to twenty minutes is the guide walking you around. Talking about the hot spots, 'this is what happened here, this is what happened there', then you get a little more than an hour and a half on each floor to roam around on your own. Conduct your own investigations.

"It's funny because we had ten people in our group and after twenty minutes on each floor, they'd just go outside and smoke cigarettes. It was basically us four and one couple. Just us six the entire night on our own. This place, this building, if you haven't seen it before, you really need to check it out. It's HUGE! Just the main building itself has nine acres of floor space.

"The fourth floor was the alcohol and addiction rehab center. We are sitting in the middle of the fourth-floor hallway, this couple had the spirit box. They were doing a session and we were sitting down with them. The guy *Carl was walking down the hallway and his girlfriend (or wife) whatever she was, she says, 'If you want him to stop, make a loud noise'. Nothing happened, he was continuing to walk. He got to the middle hallway, turned back and started walking back towards us.

"As he turned, the door right behind him slammed shut—like it was so loud it shook the entire floor. It startled all of us. We went down there, nobody was there. No wind, nothing at all. It slammed hard. Then on the fourth floor we constantly heard footsteps, creaks and all sorts of different noises.

"Then, on the first floor was Lilly's room. A little girl that was in the children's ward. The story behind Lilly, she was born here, and she roams the hallways looking for her mom. She tugs on women's dresses. We were sitting in her room where there are a bunch of toys, balls, and other things that people bring her. We are sitting there in the pitch-black dark with the spirit box going. They ask, 'Lilly are you here?' All of a sudden, a penny gets thrown at me.

"It bounces twice and hits my shoe. The woman with us gets the penny and throws it across the room and says, 'Here Lilly. If you are here with us, throw the penny back over here'. Nothing happened. Then suddenly, on the spirit box there's a deep voice—obviously not a little girl—the voice says, 'Why?' So, we're like freaking out. The guy in the group says, 'Who was that who just asked *why* on the spirit box?' Nothing comes through the spirit box but when I went back to review the digital recorder, right after Carl asked who it was, you can hear a little girl say something. I couldn't make out what she said.

"It's a distinct little girl's voice. It was a full sentence, I just cannot make out the words. Then about fifteen minutes later we were leaving that room and heading back towards the breakroom so we can go to the next floor. Carl asks his girlfriend if she wants to walk down the hallway and right after he asks her, that same little girl's voice says, 'Yeah'. Sweet little voice, with excitement in her voice. As soon as I heard that it, sent chills down my back.

"There were only six of us in the group. We're all adults, no children and it was obviously a little girl's voice. Pretty crazy. That was the most concrete evidence that we got all night. We had a couple people in the group that saw a little shadow figure through a doorway. I didn't see it personally but throughout the night there were a bunch of noises and little shadows.

"It was definitely worth it. I really want to go back at some point. The money that they get from the tours, they use the money for the building—to keep it standing. Restorations. At least the money goes towards a good cause. I'd gladly spend the money to go on another over-night tour. They also have the option where you can pay $150 a person and get the whole asylum to yourself. A private ghost hunt. It's an awesome option!

"At one point they were going to tear the Asylum down. I think they wanted to turn it into a Walmart or a Casino. Then, they put it on the National Historic Landmark Registry, so now it's protected forever! Laurie and I went one time to the Asylum. They have a forensics' building in the back where they had the criminally insane patients, people that plead insanity. The absolute worst.

"We went back there, we didn't have any experiences, but our tour guide said that when she went back there to practice her speech of the history for the tour she was back there, and she got pushed up against the wall and was being choked. She could not breathe because she was being choked, she ran out of the building."

THE LONE PINE INN (OLD LA VETA PASS, COLORADO)

"So, in old La Veta Pass, before the main highway was constructed, the main road used to go just south of where it is now. There used to be an old train depot up there, there was also a church, a school house, it was kind of like a small town. There was a little … I guess you can say it was a bed and breakfast. It was called 'The Lone Pine Inn.' My Grandma worked there when she was a teenager.

"She would do house-keeping type stuff, she spent her summers up there. It says 'no trespassing' but some of our relatives own it, so we can still go in there and open it up. You can still see the old dance floor, the ball room and the kitchen. You can go upstairs and see … there's some creepy rooms there. I think that would be a good place to go to, or at least have potential to have some sort of activity.

"It'd be weird for my Grandma to go in because she hasn't been in there since she was a teen. They're actually trying to tear it down. They want to tear it down so it's not a liability. They haven't done it yet. To me it's kind of like tearing down the Riviera in Las Vegas. Tearing down a piece of history."

HOTEL COLORADO AND THE PHANTOM COUGHER (GLENWOOD SPRINGS, COLORADO)

"The Hotel Colorado in Glenwood Springs is an infamous hotel. Both Laurie and I heard someone scratching and coughing in the room next to us, repeatedly. We went to the hot springs and came back, and it was still going on. A loud raspy cough. You go to the room next door, not only is it not occupied but it is actually boarded-up. It's a boarded-up area, it's not even a room. The next room is way far over. It was weird! That place is definitely haunted!"

End of Nick's experiences.

Joe is a paranormal investigator in my hometown and has had several experiences when it comes to the paranormal. Here is one about attachments, you can read the rest of them in my upcoming book. Stay tuned.

JOE'S ATTACHMENT (PUEBLO, COLORADO)

My friend and fellow paranormal investigator Joe Musso shared a few haunting experiences with me. Here is one about an attachment he dealt with. In Joe's own words:

"At the time I was going through a divorce and going through other issues. I was having problems with my back. My guard was down, which was bad for me, it was my fault. It was fully my fault that I let it attach to me. With this one though, it was more like, 'what can I do to freak you out' versus anything against me. My son was living with me, I think he was fourteen then.

"It was testing me. Sitting in a chair, you can feel it behind you, like breathing on your neck. My son would be sitting there doing his homework and he would come up to me and say, "Dad, I feel like someone is there and I can feel breathing on my neck." Literally, I could feel a breath going in and out. It kind of went after him more than it did me. He would go in to take a shower, and the lights would go off in the bathroom. Things like that.

"It didn't do anything to physically harm us, but it was there, and it was not a happy camper, let's just put it that way! That was basically when I realized what was going on...I finally got back to myself again and stood up and got my home back again. If there was even a creak in the house, I would say something. I took back what was mine. After about a week of doing that, it stopped. We had no problems at all. It was more a freaky thing than a, 'I'm gonna get you.'

Chapter five

Paranormal Investigating

Why did I become a Paranormal Investigator? Like I said earlier, I have believed in spirits my whole life. I have had experiences throughout my life that I have no other choice but to believe. I've always watched the ghost investigating shows with curiosity, an open mind and amazement. I wanted to do what they did, craved what they did. Not being on TV, but the investigation itself, getting results, hearing the voices, communicating with the dead, catching orbs, not dust but genuine true orbs, and manifestations on film and more.

It all started several years ago when my boyfriend bought me my first fancy digital camera. When I say it all started, I mean the investigations, not my belief, fascination or experiences and encounters with the paranormal. As a baby, my mother says that we would be driving past graveyards and I would yell from my baby seat, 'graveyard! graveyard! Me Go! ME GO! ME WALK!"

My mom was shocked. How does a two-year-old know what a graveyard is? Anyway, my best friend Jourdan and her boyfriend at the time, *Tanner, came to visit me for my birthday. At the time I lived in Del Norte and she lived in Pueblo, so they drove the two-and-a-half-hour drive. I planned to take them to a small old mining town that was close by called, Creede.

This place is one of my favorite places. You go through the small town itself, and once you hit the dirt road it's all mining history from there. They have an underground fire department which is quite amazing and a mining museum. I like to take the tour then go on Bachelor's Loop. You can see the river down below, the mountains are magical, and the mines are so beautiful and historical, I try to close my eyes and go back to the 1800s when it was booming.

Anyway, we arrive to the small mountain town of Creede. We walk through the museum and quickly after that we head to Bachelor's Loop. We spend time at Commodore Mine—the most photographed mine there. With our backs to the mine, we are also enjoying the scenery of the river down below and the mountain that stood proud and tall in front of us. I start taking pictures of the Mine and the view, then I take one of Tanner who is taking in the scenery.

I think nothing of it but later on, this one picture ends up being very important and you will see why real soon. We jump in the car and head up Bachelor's Loop. Next stop is Amethyst Mine. This is an area where four young miners died in a fire. In that area is a large barn and next door to that barn is a collapsed cabin. We start exploring the area. I had been there a couple dozen times at least but every time I find myself more amazed, stunned and in total awe of the haunting beauty and deadly secrets these mines hold. It's like the spirits of the miners are there watching us and every move we make.

Jourdan and I walk in the doorway of the collapsed cabin and Tanner starts taking pictures of us. It's kind of a creepy place. In archives I cannot find anywhere, what this collapsed cabin served as. I try to close my eyes and imagine what it could have been. Maybe a home for the miners? For the miners' spouses? A safe place for their mining equipment? We wander on and do the rest of the Loop.

I must say if you are ever in the area, I recommend taking a drive on Bachelor's Loop. Jam-packed with history, the mines are amazing. You can even dig on the hills by Amethyst Mine, where you just might dig up, yup, you guessed it, Amethyst! Justin, Carly and myself have been there several times and have dug up some beautiful amethyst. Also, on one of the stops is the towns historic graveyard that some of the notorious thugs are buried in and much more!

Later at my house, we are watching a movie and about to get ready for bed. Jourdan approaches me with her phone and starts showing me pictures of us in the collapsed cabin. Many of them have orbs in them. I pull out my camera and find that mine also have orbs in them. They aren't dust particles. I know what that looks like and have experienced that.

I wake up the next day and hang out with Jourdan and Tanner before they have to head back home to Pueblo. After they leave I mention to Carly about the orbs in the pictures. She is on her way out the door to work and before she leaves she tells me to look closely at the orbs in the pictures. Faces may be in them.

Stupid me! DUH! Yes, I have heard of faces being in orbs, but didn't think about it. I had the day off and had nothing else to do, so I start going through my pictures, one-by-one. The first one that has an orb in it is the picture I took of Tanner, while at Commodore Mine. It's a decent size orb, with the mountains behind it, and the river rushing harshly below it. It has pastel rainbow type colors in it.

I zoom in, the camera Justin got me has a 35 zoom, so I get in close to this orb. To my amazement, on top of the orb, turning the photo upside down I see two eyes looking at me, with high cheek bones. I am BEWILDERED. Excitement rushes through my veins. A face! Several thoughts run through my mind, who is this? Is he a miner? How did he die? When did he die? What's his name? Did he have a family? What year did he die?

When Carly gets home from work I show her the picture, by this time I zoomed in on the orb itself and posted it on social media. She sees the face and, in addition, points out another face to me. The face is much more detailed then half-face I saw. It's in the middle of the orb, it's a man, with curly hair, eyes looking up to the sky, cheeks, and a strong chin.

Justin kidded around with me saying it was Tesla, because it looked sort of like Nicola Tesla. This picture amazes me to this day. No, I didn't manipulate it, I did not add anything to it, nor have I tampered with it. I don't have the computer savvy to do that. The faces are so clear.

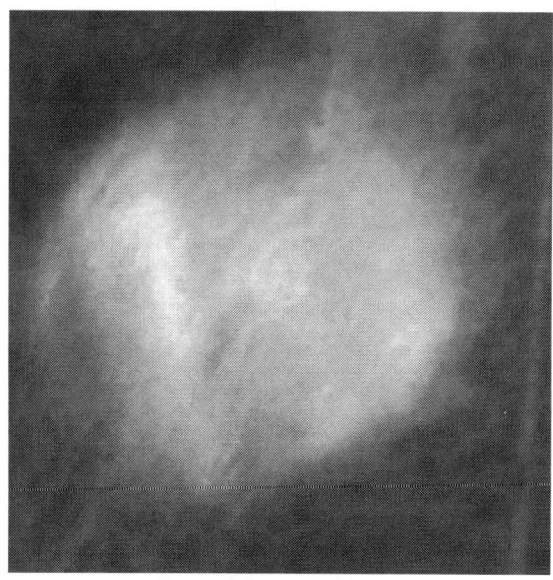

Figure 3 Picture of the orb

Figure 4 Close-up of the orb

Figure 5 Another close-up of the orb

The camera I have, I just adore it. With it, I have captured orbs, manifestations and more. Another important tool to have while investigating. Anyway, I got so caught up with this picture that I need to talk about the other pictures. At Amethyst Mine where the collapsed cabin is, those are definitely orbs.

In one picture I took of Jourdan, there is a bluish figure standing behind her. In the pictures Tanner took of both of us, there are orbs in them, In one picture we are standing in the doorway and on my shoulder you can clearly see what looks like a ferret. It looks like this phantom ferret is biting me. I felt no pressure on my shoulder nor weight. In another picture there are orbs surrounding our heads.

In yet another picture, Jourdan is further into the cabin and I am still at the doorway looking towards her. My lanyard, the part with the keys is in my pocket, where the rest of the lanyard is hanging down against my leg. It is seen in many pictures just lying there. In this particular picture, the lanyard is slanted, lifted in mid-air. At the opposite side of the lanyard is an orb.

Looking at these pictures, I was quite amazed. Adrenaline fully rushed through me. The crave I felt to investigate overwhelmed me. I had to do it. I went online and bought the items I needed to start off with, a spirit box, a digital recorder, and an EMF meter. I would buy more later but I was so excited to do this as quickly as possible.

Where to go? Investigation spots were endless. Cemeteries, homes, mines, etc. Of course, since I got such overwhelming evidence caught on film, I thought it would be awesome for our first investigation to be at Bachelor's Loop.

I hold credit to Tanner for taking those pictures and for being in the picture with the faces in it. Again, I don't know why I took that picture. He was standing there and had never been there before, I was just trying to capture the moment I suppose.

I also hold credit to Jourdan, she has an open mind just like me, and noticed things in her pictures which brought attention to me to check mine, sure I would have noticed them but not as quickly as I did. I believe the orbs were there with the two of us, because we both believe and perhaps we might have even been in their home.

Credit needs to be given to my sister Carly for suggesting the searching for faces. Again, I might have thought of it later on, much later on. When I saw those faces I was like a kid at a candy store, or to better describe me, me in my favorite place ever, New Orleans.

As I write this book, I continue to conduct investigations that will be added to the book. Just yesterday Justin and I went to Moore's Creek National Battlefield. The history behind this battle is quite amazing. That will be a chapter all in itself.

The following chapters are the results and experiences we've had through our investigations. I will talk about the place itself and the history it holds, then the evidence we got.

Chapter six

Bachelor's Loop, Creede, Colorado

A little history lesson ...

Bachelor's Loop is nestled deep in the mountains in a small mountain town called Creede in Colorado. In 1889, a gentleman by the name of Nicholas Creede was passing through the area. He stopped one day for lunch and he discovered what became, the Holy Moses Mine. Almost overnight, his camp became a large tent city. In the summer of 1890, amazingly, the tiny town grew by about 300 people a day.

I have been to this sweet, small mountain town more times than I can count, and it stuns me that by 1892 there were more than 10,000 people living in the area. Among those people were Calamity Jane Canary, Bob Ford—who was the side kick and killer of Jesse James—Poker Alice, Lawman Bat Masterson, and a con man named Soapy Smith. These people and more all came running to Creede when the Amethyst Vein was discovered.

The Amethyst Vein was an average 4 to 10 foot-wide vein of ore that was consistently delivering up to 200 ounces of silver per ton of rock. Amazingly, in some places the Vein was up to 100 feet wide, some of the outcroppings and boulders would deliver up to 1,500 ounces of silver per ton!

Bachelor's Loop was established, conveniently, along the major roads through the area that tied the mines and settlements together. We know this as Bachelor's Loop.

In 1892, the mining town had yielded one million dollars' worth of silver ore per month. Unfortunately for the miners, in 1893 the Congress enacted the Silver Act and the price of silver dramatically dropped from $1.29 per ounce to a measly half a dollar. HUGE difference. With the Silver Act in effect, Creede almost shut down. Thankfully the loyal townspeople pulled together and came through.

Thank goodness for that. Creede, with the history seeping from it, is one of my all-time favorite places. In 1939, a whopping 500,000 ounces of silver was still shipping from the generous mines each week. By the year 1966, the number plummeted to 150,000 ounces PER YEAR. Amazingly, the last producing mine was Bulldog Mine which ended in 1985. I find it quite impressive that the Creede mines operated continuously from 1890 to 1985.

What's even more IMPRESSIVE are the total production numbers:

Silver ~ 58 million troy ounces
Gold ~ 150 thousand ounces
Lead ~ 112 thousand metric tons
Zinc ~ 34 thousand metric tons
Copper ~ 2 million metric tons

Creede to me is an extremely magical place. It has such a huge feel of history to it. The town itself is so sweet, with its small cozy store fronts, mom and pop shops, local goods and more. I can just close my eyes and picture horse drawn carriages filling the streets.

Once you're off the paved road and hit dirt, you are in the Mining District. It feels as if you are going back in to time, back in the 1800s, again I close my eyes and can hear the residual sounds of the miners hard at work. I have also recorded those sounds while on investigations—extracting minerals from the earth. Of course, Creede being a boom-mining community back then, the town has seen its share of mining accidents and untimely deaths of miners.

Remember that picture I took, with the faces in the orb at Commodore Mine? Well, after that, I started to search deep within the internet archives and found all Colorado Miners' deaths. I dug in deeper and with squinted eyes, found the Miners who died at the mines on Bachelor's Loop. It took a long time and patience and about 100 pages of the smallest writing you can find.

I was trying to see if I can find any pictures of these miners but, back in the 1800s it was quite different then our present day. I thought it would be awesome if I could match one of their faces with the faces in the orb. So, who exactly are those men trapped in that orb? The mystery continues.

Commodore Mine has racked up a few deaths—at least seven that are documented. Amethyst Mine has four documented deaths, all on one fateful day, August 24, 1894. The news articles report about a fire that the miners perished in, but in the archives, the cause of death is, "Fall of skip".

Bachelor's Loop continues to amaze me with its rugged beauty of the jagged mountains and hillsides. The water rushing rapidly through the mountain between the road and mountain. Stuck in time. The ruins of these amazingly generous mines, the widow makers. On the hillsides you can still see the tracks with decaying mine carts. Rundown now, but they were a big part of the mining world. A truly, hauntingly-beautiful, mining town.

In the Denver Library Archives, I found the following information on these miners:

-Fred Ames died on November 5,1893 in Last Chance Mine, crushed by bucket.
-Frederick Ames died on November 5,1893 in Last Chance Mine, skip jumped track.
-Samuel N. Birdsey died May 27,1966 in an unknown mine, fell from raise.
-Floyd E. Brown died July 26,1967 in an unknown mine, struck by a disintegrated wheel.
-Ernest R. Carter died May 20,1971 in an unknown mine, fell down Winze.
-Joseph D. Casey died February 15,1967 in an unknown mine, crushed by loader frame.
-Thomas Cressale died August 24,1894 in Amethyst Mine, fall of skip (maybe fire).
-Henry Dold died June 20,1893 in Mammoth Mine, fall of bucket.
-Dacy Duncan died October 10,1899 in Cole Mine, he fell from roof or back of drift.
-E. G. Eloin died March 10,1899 in Commodore Mine, explosion while cutting capping fuse.
-Hugh Fay died August 24,1894 in Amethyst Mine, fall of skip (maybe fire).
-Leland A. Flaugh died January 30,1969 in an unknown mine, crushed between door and motor.
-L. C. Fowler died June 6,1899 in Commodore Mine, fell to lower tunnel level.
-William Haeberle died October 10,1899 in Cole Mine, large quantity of dirt and vein matter.
-F. J. Hess died March 10,1899 in Commodore Mine, explosion while cutting cape fuse.
-William C. Jackson died March 7,1969 in an unknown mine, buried by mud and rock.
-Charles E. Lloyd died December 5,1899 in Commodore Mine, fell from ladder.
-George Bruce Manning died October 13,1942 in Creede Mine, caught between cable and drum.

-R. McDonald died August 4, 1894 in Amethyst Mine, fall of skip (maybe fire).
-Jacob S. Miller died March 3, 1899 in Commodore Mine, fell down incline.
-Ray Morgan died September 21, 1917 in an unknown mine, fall of rock.
-Dee H. Palmer died November 5, 1969 in an unknown mine, buried by ground fall.
-Charles Proctor died August 24, 1894 in Amethyst Mine, fall of skip. (Maybe fire).
-Phillip Ragen died March 7, 1917 in an unknown mine, by blast.
-John Sona died March 10, 1899 in Commodore Mine, explosion while cutting fuse.
-William H. Swinehart died December 29, 1951 in Creede Mine, crushed by falling rock.
-John Albert Ward died February 6, 1937 in an unknown mine, caught between cars and chute.
-Robert Watson died March 10, 1899 in Commodore Mine, explosion while capping fuse.
-Ruben Wesander died September 26, 1947 in Creede Mine, explosives.
-Samuel Writman died April 28, 1898 in Ridge Mine, fell backward.

These men, these miners, all died while mining in these Colorado mines. May each of them rest in peace.

I just want to note that as you read through these chapters about the investigations, there is a lot going on, getting ready for an investigation, setting up and the testing of equipment, several questions asked that go unanswered, debunking and much more. I don't go through all that in these chapters, I am just simply giving you some of the results we've collected.

October 31, 2014, The Investigation

Conducted by Tessa and Carly Mauro, Justin, *Kyle and *Melanie on October 31 in 2014. For being late October in the mountains of Colorado, I was surprised at how well the weather was cooperating and staying slightly on the warmer side. Seeing that the weather was so nice and that it was Halloween, we found it to be quite appropriate to go over the hill and through the windy roads to do some investigating.

By the time the others got out of work and driving the 40-minute drive, the investigation started around 7:05 pm. Kyle and Melanie hadn't been in the area in quite some time, so I thought we would first start out at Amethyst

Mine, the Mine where four men met their untimely deaths and where the abandoned skeletons of the barn and collapsed cabin stand.

We caught many EVP's (Electronic Voice Phenomenon), disembodied noises, intelligent answers to our questions and more. Throughout the investigation an unexplained loud clinking noise was recorded on audio eight different times. There are many ways a spirit can communicate, one of them is through sound.

Results and evidence collected

Every investigation, we start with an opening protection prayer. Even if you are not religious, seriously it's very quick, and it couldn't hurt doing so.

Quickly into the investigation, on recording we catch a man moaning and shortly after a woman moans as well. Hope we aren't interrupting anything here. I just need to note that we are up in the mountains, away from the town, no one lives up in the mine area and no one was around that night when we were there. When we hear noises with our ears we debunk it immediately. These moans went unheard by us.

During the investigation, the recorder caught unexplained loud, labored breathing. At the end of the breathing we captured an EVP of a man saying, "Home." Moments later, a woman is recorded crying, off in the distance, again unheard by us.

At one point, a sound is caught, an all too familiar sound, put your hands together and rub. Like what one would do to warm their hands. This was repeatedly done for several seconds. We all had gloves on and we weren't responsible for this sound.

Shortly after this an EVP from, who I believe to be, a woman is recorded. She says, "Coal … The coal … Coal." Exhale. "Coal." At first, when I came upon this treasure, I thought perhaps she was saying "cold" but listening closer, and slowing down the audio, it is clear that this spirit was saying, "Coal."

I cannot say how excited I was when I heard this! What a treat! It was all the same voice, what I believe to be a woman, but I could be wrong. I also need to say, this was happening before the spirit box was even turned on.

At one point, Justin stumbles, he almost falls but catches himself. I remind him that I didn't bring flashlights for nothing, use them! After I finish my sentence, an EVP of a man's disembodied voice is recorded saying, "Yeah." I'm glad someone was agreeing with me! Justin, who's holding the spirit box, turns it on and starts sweeping through channels.

Spirit Box Session

Me: What's your name?

Man: Me.
Unexplained static. Unheard by ears but captured on recorder.

Voice: Go Far.

Justin then says that he is going to switch over the spirit box.

Man: Why? (Followed by a disembodied laugh).

A few minutes go by with no further voices. Justin turns it off for now. We are still at Amethyst Mine and during an EVP Session, I ask, "What's your name?" What my recorder caught next was amazing. A man gives this EVP; "McDonald." Days later after listening to the audio, I looked through my notes, searched the miners' names, and right there was R. McDonald. He was one of the unfortunate men who died at Amethyst Mine due to a fire.

Unbelievable! Not only did we catch a name of a miner who actually died here but quickly after that EVP, a different voice was caught. This voice was that of a man as well and was on the scratchy side. This scratchy voice said, "You were brave." Is this a fellow miner telling his miner brother that he was brave until the very end? Or, perhaps this scratchy voice also fell victim to the fire. Remember, R McDonald and four other men, Charles Proctor, Hugh Fay, Thomas Cressale and an unknown miner, died in that fire. Maybe Charles, Hugh, Thomas or the other miner were there as well.

My sister Carly asks, "Did you used to live here?" A few seconds later a man is recorded giving this EVP; "My house."

We spend some time exploring the old collapsed cabin, where we got many of these EVP's, then we make our way to the old barn, just a few feet away from the cabin. At the time, we did not have the spirit box going, just the digital recorder is on. I ask, "How many people died here?" While I didn't get an answer to that about a moment later we got an EVP of a man saying, "Help." Than a few seconds later, he repeated himself, "Help."

As we are standing in the old barn, a burp-like-sound is caught on the recorder. Unnoticed or unheard by us. Burps happen in life folks, it's natural, and at times, shall I dare say it … fun. Burps are fun! While on investigation if we burp, sneeze, cough, whatever sounds we make, we debunk it and say it immediately, so later on, when I go through all the audio and evidence, I know exactly what it is that I am listening to.

In the barn we notice feces everywhere. So, the inner child of both Melanie and myself starts to show as we play a game of guessing what poop it could be. We forget that the recorder is on and start guessing. Melanie says, "Elk." A man is recorded saying, "No." She says something else and again the same man is caught on recorder, once again, disagreeing with her. "No." I ask if any spirits here around us are victims of a mining accident. An EVP is recorded of a man responding, "Enough." This is followed by loud muffled breathing.

Around this time, a woman started coming through. We got several EVPs from her. She said, "Let us." Than a moment after that she said, "Hello?" I walk outside of the barn and take pictures. I detect an orb around the corner of the old collapsed cabin. As I let the others know that I caught an orb on camera, the woman speaks once again, "Let's plead." Her voice is louder and much closer than when she spoke earlier. This is followed by a loud screech-like sound.

My sister asks, "What's today?" Being that it was Halloween, how badass would that have been to get an EVP of a spirit saying, "Um duh, Halloween." Instead a woman, who I believe to be the same one who has been speaking, is recorded saying, "Be quiet." Was this woman telling us to be quiet or was she possibly warning another spirit to not talk to us and to be quiet. Many possibilities indeed.

Then the recorder captures a man and a woman. The man speaks unintelligible words, followed by the woman, it sounds like she is possibly responding to him. Her words are also unintelligible and she sounds very sad. Did we capture the conversation of a deceased man and woman speaking to one another? Perhaps he was a miner and she was his wife.

The crew and me walk down to the river, not too far from the barn and cabin. As we are walking, the woman, who's been throwing EVPs our way the past several minutes, says, "House." Now I am unsure what this means. There are several different things it could be. It may be the cabin we were in earlier or across the dirt road from the farm and cabin is a small hill where a tiny one room cabin is. Maybe she was referring to that. Again, I think miner's wife ... a widow?

My flashlight starts to malfunction. It is fairly new and expensive and I put fresh new batteries in before that night's investigation yet, here it is, starting to flicker. Draining away quickly. This is followed by an unexplained pop-like sound unheard by us.

We spend some time down by the river then, make our way back to the cabin and barn. A woman, a different one, is recorded giving this EVP, "This way." Seconds later, she repeats herself, "This way." Then about half a minute later a different voice, this one croak-like is caught on the recorder telling us to, "Hurry up." We make our way up the small hill towards the small cabin that I mentioned earlier. As we climb up the hill, a man is recorded saying, "Hide."

Interesting enough. I start to describe about how last week when I was here, I took a picture of the small abandoned one room cabin up the hill. In the picture was a face of a man in the window. Was this the man? We are now in front of the small cabin and start talking amongst ourselves. We start hearing sounds—rustling in the trees. Even though we cannot debunk it and identify the sound, I cannot prove this to be the paranormal. It is unexplained, but it could easily have been an animal. So that's what I assume it was.

My recorder captures this interesting moment, at least two men, possibly more, speaking in unison, saying what sounds like, "Woah, up!" Is this possibly a residual haunting of miners, possibly still mining here at Amethyst Mine?

As we start to make the small descent down the hill, I start to not-so-gracefully slide. I debunk the sounds I'm making with annoyance, saying, "Sliding." After I say this, a man sounding rather confused, is recorded asking me, "How are you sliding?"

We get into our cars, Kyle and Melanie in their truck and Carly, Justin and me in my 4runner. We make our way up and down the rocky, windy dirt roads. We say goodbye to Amethyst Mine and make the short drive to Commodore Mine. We had driven past this mine earlier to get to Amethyst Mine.

I have the recorder still on, all other equipment is off so not to get any false readings with the EMF meters in the car. As we drive we go over a large bump in the road, the 4runner makes creak sounds. I debunk these sounds then, shortly after, we stop the cars—we have arrived at Commodore Mine.

We get there before Kyle and Melanie. We decide to wait in the car for them, as it is getting a bit more on the chilly side.

As we sit there, my recorder captures what sounds like a woman screaming. We did not hear this, and no one else is around us.

As Kyle and Melanie pull up, I say to Justin and Carly how I was disappointed that we didn't get any EMF spikes at Amethyst Mine. After I say this, a man is recorded saying my name, but instead of Tessa, it sounded more like, "Tay-sa." This is not the first, nor the last time that my name is said by a spirit during an investigation.

We get out of the car and start to walk around and immediately the KII EMF starts fluctuating between 2 and 3. This is just a couple minutes after I showed my disappointment of it not spiking at the other mine. Now remember, at least seven men were killed here. Possibly more. As we are walking, Kyle, Justin and Melanie are recorded talking to one another in the background. Suddenly, an unexplained growl is recorded. I don't think this is a living creature. We didn't hear this growl when it occurred.

Carly stands in front of Commodore Mine, the most photographed mine at Bachelor's Loop, and asks, "Can you tell us what your names are? I am sure there are more than just one of you." An EVP is recorded, responding, "Several."

I join in Carly's EVP session and ask, "How many people died here?" Quite a few seconds go by with nothing but silence, then a disembodied voice of a man says, "Nine." Now, as mentioned earlier, seven documented deaths occurred here, however, many miners died in unknown mines, so the number can possibly be higher, like NINE.

I ask, "Did you die here?" A man says, "Uh-huh." This was very close, as if right in front of the recorder. Carly asks, "Were you raised here?" We get a somewhat creepy response. A man gives us this eerie EVP, "Buried here." A few seconds later, the same man says, what sounds like, "Yearn."

The weather starts to get colder and at a rapid pace so, we turn off the equipment and start slowly heading back to our vehicles. As we walk we listen as Kyle tells us the story of a woman who lived in Monte Vista in the 1800s and had monkeys as pets who ended up killing her and now she is known to haunt her house. If it weren't on private property I would be there in a heartbeat.

Paranormal investigators or not, I really do recommend coming to this small cozy historic town and spending the day there. If you were to come, just a handy helpful tip, don't come in the winter. Many of the cute local stores are closed-down for the season and Bachelor's Loop is cordoned off. Summer is a perfect time, being way up in the mountains, it's not too hot and the weather is just right, and if you're lucky you might be greeted by some of the ghostly miners.

Chapter seven

Empress Cemetery, Pueblo, Colorado

Pueblo will always be home to me. Many of my family and most of my friends live there. It's the home of war heroes. I did create a fictional name for this cemetery—since it is still an active one—I didn't want to ruffle any feathers. Now this particular cemetery is only about half a mile from my dad's house. About ten years ago, after a friend of mine, Peter, died unexpectedly in a car accident, I would ride my bike to this cemetery almost every day. To pay my respects to him. To visit him. To mourn him.

Then another friend, Michael, died and is also at this cemetery. I now live away from Pueblo but I visit often and when I do I always make sure to make time to visit, making time for those who are no longer with us. This cemetery is larger than it looks. From the road it looks rather small but, drive through it and it seems never-ending. I've seen much larger—the cities of the dead in New Orleans—now that's never-ending.

We have conducted many investigations here. Discreetly, of course. If there is a funeral in process or mourners paying respects to their loved ones, then we stop what we are doing. We don't mean any ill intentions, disrespect, or harm while doing these investigations. There are usually two or three of us and we only visit family members and friends of ours that have passed away.

Instead of doing several different chapters about the same place, I will make it just one large chapter with all the Empress investigations. There's not much history I can find about this cemetery.

November 10, 2014, The investigation ...

Our first investigation in this cemetery was conducted by Jourdan, her then boyfriend Tanner, and myself on November 10, 2014. It started off as a warm enough day but as we started the investigation the weather grew colder. We eventually cut the investigation short because it was starting to get unbearable. If it wasn't cold enough, the wind started picking up. That's one bad thing about Colorado weather. It can be gorgeous and perfect weather one moment, then the next, it can turn cold and wet.

What was creepy to me, a man in a black car seemed to be almost stalking us, or so it felt like stalking. We didn't bring huge fancy equipment whatsoever. We brought hand-held devices that day. When we go to an open cemetery that still does burials, that's all we bring. So, when we are there sitting at a site in the cemetery, it looks like we are visiting. Which we are, it's just being recorded and they're talking back to us.

So, this guy is in his car, he drives by very slowly, eyes on us. He stops. My skin crawls and not because it's cold. Something doesn't feel right. So, I tell Jourdan and Tanner to turn off the equipment, we do so, and wait for the nosy guy to leave. He circles around and a few minutes later he is back. I felt like a baby defenseless gazelle in Africa, drinking water from the watering hole, and the man in the black car, a crocodile submerged in the water waiting to make his move.

After we saw him a third time, I had just about enough of the cold and wind and my patience was wearing thin with the unknown man, so we left.

Results and evidence collected ...

Jourdan, Tanner and myself get to the cemetery, park and hop out of the car and make our way to where Peter is buried. As we get there, we stop and before we can say anything or greet Peter, the digital recorder picks up an EVP from a woman. She says, "My hands ... mine ... mine!" As this is happening, it also sounds like as if someone is grasping at the recorder.

This was not Jourdan's voice, nor mine, and nobody else was currently in the area we were in. We always make sure no one is around while conducting our visitation/investigation. Then, shortly after this, a woman is recorded breathing quite rapidly. I start to talk, Jourdan says something in the back ground responding to me and as this occurs the woman can still be heard breathing. Going unheard by us.

I ask Peter, "Can you tell us any of our names?" Several seconds go by, then a man is caught on recorder saying, "Yes." This is very faint. I ask this because, besides Tanner, Peter goes way back with Jourdan and me. We've all been friends for several years.

I must say that this is the main reason why I have the play mode on the slowest setting, on regular play mode you would miss so much. Starting off doing this at the beginning, I would listen to the recordings on regular mode and only slow it down if something caught my attention. Now I definitely listen to it on slow and am catching so much more then I could have imagined.

It is at this point that the black car with the creepy man in it makes his first appearance. I get an uneasy feeling but ignore it. He parks the car and stares at us. Not like an employee of the cemetery, curious to what we are doing, for we are just sitting there with our easy-to-hide equipment. We look like visitors, so why would this creep just be staring at us. After a couple long moments, the car pulls out and heads deeper within the cemetery property.

Suddenly what sounds like a duo, a man and a woman are caught on the recorder. The man saying, "Hop pop a pop." In a musical tonal voice, and after he says this, the woman says, "Ah la la la." Interesting. Sometimes things just don't make sense at an investigation.

Jourdan and I encourage Peter to speak with us. We tell him to come to the colorful lights that is illuminated on our equipment. We remain silent for a moment and while this is happening a man gives us this EVP, "Your eyes." We ask a few questions, with no results. Than a couple minutes later, who I believe to be the same man, says either, "Look it" or "Looking." Followed by a deep exhale.

Jourdan asks, "Do you like jokes? If so I have a lot of jokes I can tell you." A man is recorded saying, "Yes." Tanner, who's been more silent and just an observer cracks a joke, saying that Jourdan's jokes aren't funny. We all laugh. My laugh kind of lingers and as I stop I make a growl sound. I do that sometimes just randomly. I'm weird. What's even more weird is that as I end my growl you can hear a man growling as well. This is a very deep growl. An aggressive growl. Much different than my wimpy sarcastic growl. This was hardcore. It was eerie.

Jourdan asks, "Has anyone died here at the cemetery?" We get a creepy EVP of a disembodied voice responding, "Two." Now I am not sure if that is true or accurate. It can even mean someone came to visit and died later that day elsewhere or something or maybe people have died on this property. It could have happened before it became a burial ground.

Unintelligible whispering is recorded. That happens from time to time. You know something is there. You can hear it, you can feel it, but unfortunately you cannot always understand what they are trying to tell you. I can't even start to say how frustrating it is that I cannot understand some of these words being spoken to us. I rack my brain. I rewind endless times and really try to hear and understand what's being said. I will continue to try to listen to these and get more answers.

The nosy man in the black car is back. He is starting to get on my nerves. Get out and visit somebody if you are here to do so. Don't just be a creeper. After this happens a couple more times, we decide we've had enough. We turn off most of the equipment but leave the recorder on and we start to slowly make our way back to the car.

We get into the car and try to warm up. Before I turn off the recorder, I say, "All right, we're leaving now." Shortly after this, a growl is recorded. Not as creepy as the growl that we caught while visiting Peter but still a growl nonetheless.

As we sit in the car and try to get warm, we get an EVP of probably one of the creepiest things I have ever heard. It's an EVP of a man in a very panicked voice and he is screaming bloody murder, "OH MY GOD … .AHHHH!!" as if that's not scary enough, right after that are two very loud boom noises, possibly gun shots.

That was all EVP and since we listened on regular mode we didn't catch any of these things you're reading now. We caught a growl and that was it. I thought this very unsuccessful and a dead investigation until I listened to it in the slowest option. When I heard that man, adrenaline went through my body, I got chills, as I do now reliving it. I really believe we heard a murder victim in a residual haunting. Re-living his panic and terror and getting shot. I cannot even imagine. It was so sad. Heart-breaking.

End of investigation.

May 6, 2015, The Investigation ...

This investigation was conducted by Jourdan Ortega and Tessa Mauro. A day before this investigation Jourdan and I talked and thought we would go to the cemetery and search for her Uncle John. She knew the vicinity of where he was but, it was a large area by the Singing Tower. We looked around but were unsuccessful.

The next day, May 6, 2015, we had planned to go to one of our favorite spots for lunch, just off Northern Avenue and very close to the cemetery. Before that though, I headed to the cemetery and went to the office and asked where John was buried. With a map in hand, I head to the area and find it immediately. Feeling good that I could surprise Jourdan with the direct location, I head to lunch. I show her the map and let her know I have the equipment, so we plan to eat and then head over after lunch for a session with her Uncle.

Since we are there, we plan to also do sessions with Michael and Peter. So, this will be a number of sessions throughout the cemetery on the same day. We finish lunch and drive to the cemetery. Depending on where you are in Colorado, May can be a real cold month, but Pueblo is a warmer area so. it was a really great day.

Results and evidence ...
Session one John Wayne Blunn

Since this is Jourdan's uncle—someone she was very close to—we decide she should be the one doing most of the questioning. So, she takes control of the spirit box and the digital recorder. Most of the responses we received were from the same voice of a man. When it's a different man I will say, "Another man."

So, we are sitting on the grass, each at a side of the headstone. As we sit, a loud thud-like sound is recorded. Unheard by us, and no one else was around. It sounded as if super close to the recorder. Then shortly after, a pop-like sound is recorded. These are recorded several times throughout the investigations. It's like the perfect pop sound and it always goes unheard by us. I have no idea what it is.

Several years ago, when I was just starting to investigate a seasoned paranormal investigator told me about this pop sound—that he had experienced them too. He asked if I had recorded any, at the time I had not, but when I started getting them I knew that's what he was talking about.

A man is recorded saying this, "Lost." Jourdan asks, "Hey Uncle John, can you hear me talking to you?" A few seconds go by and the same man gives another EVP, "Yes." Jourdan tells her beloved Uncle John Wayne, "I'd like to visit you more often." We stay quiet for a while and the same man, who we believe to be John is recorded saying, "Please." This followed by another EVP but by a different man, "Always."

We turn on the spirit box and it starts sweeping. Jourdan mentions to her Uncle that we drove by his old house on Denver Street earlier today and as she says this the recorder records a very loud static. This static is unheard by us and not coming from the spirit box. When the static finally dies down, a man can be heard speaking. Thanks to the static the words he speaks are unintelligible.

A man's voice comes through the spirit box and says, "Bones." Jourdan tells John that the beautiful sunflowers that he once loved so much, the sunflowers that he cared for in front of his house, were no longer there. The man comes through the spirit box once again, asks, "Why?"

Jourdan asks her Uncle if he can play music for us. Several times when we are visiting John Wayne Blunn, we have asked him to play music and most of the times he does just that. Sometimes it is a second of old music on the spirit box or caught as an EVP on the recorder, going unheard by us till we listen to it later. In life he loved music so much and I feel that in death he loves it possibly even more. So anyway, after she asks him to play music for us, a woman's voice comes through the spirit box and says quite clearly, "Not it."

Then, a faint voice of a man, who we feel may be the same man who was speaking earlier, says through the spirit box, "Me." Then two seconds later music comes through for like half a second. It's almost like the spirit of the woman was like, "I'm not playing any music for you." Then the man swoops through and gives us what we asked for. Sweet music to our ears. Now it may not be the music of our choice or what we listen to, but we believe it to be music that John sends our way, so we love it!

I say, "John, your niece misses you so much, she talks about you a lot." The recorder captures an EVP of the man saying, "Awe." I mention to him how I wish I could have met him, that he seems like such an awesome person. The man replies, "Yes."

Jourdan says, "Hey Uncle John, can you tell me which sister of yours is my mom?" The spirit box remains silent but the recorder captures a phenomenal EVP, an EVP that validates who we are speaking to. It's one word, but one hell of a word. The man says, "Merritt." Now this is not Jourdan's mom's first name, however it is her LAST NAME! How incredible! This followed by unexplained and unintelligible whispering.

Figure 6 Courtesy of Jourdan Ortega

Jourdan asks him if Grandma ever comes to visit him and a disembodied voice of a man comes through the spirit box saying, "Yes." Jourdan than points to the Singing Tower that is not too terribly far from where John is buried and asks if he enjoys listening to the music. The same man comes through the spirit box again repeating himself, "Yes."

We turn the spirit box off as we are about to leave this part of the cemetery and head over to where our friend Michael is buried. Jourdan, who loves picking flowers and making crowns out of them, puts the flower crown she had made earlier that day for him, in front of his headstone and says, "Hey Uncle John, I brought you a flower crown that I made earlier. I hope you like it." Right after she says this, an exhale of a man is recorded, followed by loud breathing, then static.

Jourdan says, "We're going to say bye for now, we have a couple other people to visit here. Bye Uncle John." Right before we turn the equipment off, the man is recorded saying, "Bye." I must say it was quite exciting that we were communicating with her Uncle. It was a great feeling. Reunited in a way. I think he truly is one of Jourdan's angels, looking after her.

Right before the completion of this book, John Wayne's sister, Jourdan's mother Robin (Roberta) Merritt sadly and unexpectedly passed away. I am sure John Wayne Blunn greeted his sister Robin with open arms and now they are reunited and looking over Jourdan together.

In loving memory of Robin Merritt.

Session two Michael
Mini EVP session

Although the spirit box is off, the usually excruciatingly clear digital recorder records a static interference, almost like a distant robot speaking. In fact, it stays very slight and distant through much of the EVP session. I start to talk about how when I was visiting last time, just a few days earlier, I asked for a sign and the sprinkler right next to me went off. None of the others, just the one that was right next to me, and only for a couple seconds before turning off again. The recorder catches what sounds like a muffled laugh. Followed by what sounds like a man breathing. It's neither Jourdan nor myself.

We hear loud knocking sounds in the distance, probably towards the road, Jourdan notes that and I kiddingly ask, "Is that you?" and almost as if responding to that question, a static robotic-like voice comes through, speaking unintelligible words. Jourdan and I try to persuade Michael to speak to us, that we are there to listen and that we deeply miss him. I say, "Come to this red light (on the recorder) so we can hear you." Seconds later we catch this EVP of a man saying calmly, "No, no, no."

Session three Michael

In this session we communicated with a man whose voice slightly resembled Michael's. We also had a very disembodied raspy voice come through too and unfortunately, when it spoke, we couldn't understand it most of the time. We turn the spirit box on. I ask, "Michael, can you say either of our names?" That raspy voice is recorded, saying an unintelligible word. Then a disembodied voice of a man comes through the spirit box and asks, "What?" This followed by that unexplained pop noise.

I ask, "Is there anything you want to say at all?" Shortly after I ask this, a creepy disembodied sound comes through the spirit box, almost what sounds like a distressed animal. A man that sounds kind of similar to Michael is recorded giving us this EVP, "Dog." Interesting. I think he was responding to the noise that we just heard.

Jourdan asks Michael if he ever hangs out with mutual friend Peter, who is also buried at this cemetery, "No" is spoken by a man through the spirit box. The voice that sounds like Michael, (I'll refer to him as 'the man' throughout the rest of this session) says, "Slip." Now this doesn't make sense to us but, it was his voice. So special. A moment later that disembodied voice is recorded speaking again, and again, the words are unintelligible.

I mention to Michael that his brother is going down a dangerous path, a path filled with drugs and bad people, I ask him if he is aware of this. The man's voice comes through the spirit box saying, "Yes." This is followed by an EVP of the same man saying, "Bad." Jourdan says, "Last time Tessa was here, she asked for a sign. Did you give her one?" The man gives this EVP and says, "Yup." A few seconds later this is repeated again by the man, "Yup" only this time, it's through the spirit box. Jourdan asks excitedly, "Did you just say yup?" Seconds later an unexplained sound is recorded. The noise sounds like, what I would describe as a DJ turning tables.

I say, "I appreciate that. We all miss you, and I feel your presence around a lot." We catch an EVP of the man, sounding like he is standing right by our side whispering, what sounds like, "Take." (More like Taaaaaake) I say, "I wish we could have all still been friends." The man says, "Now." This is followed by what sounds like rap music. Michael absolutely loved rap music. Especially Eminem.

To me that is very accurate. We hadn't spoken in quite a few years. In fact, I harvested not very friendly feelings about him for a long time. When he died, I feel like I have changed. Those feelings, now regret, and I have grown. It is weird to say but, in death, I am much closer to him now. So, when he said, "Now" I do believe he felt the same way and was saying so then, as if to show that it's truly him, rap music afterward.

Jourdan asks, "Is there something you want to say to us? Anything at all?" The man says, "You bet." This is followed by the unexplained pop noise. About a moment after he says, 'You bet' He then says, "Fucked." Then for about five seconds, weird unexplained beep noises are recorded. This is not coming from any of our equipment.

I say, "Can you give us a sign that you are here? You gave me a sign before, can you do it again?" Several seconds go by and the man gives this EVP saying, "Yes." The next few entries are possibly the sign we were asking for. Numerous sounds and interference as you will read.

The weird beeping noise comes through again. A disembodied voice says an unintelligible word through the spirit box. Two unexplained pops are recorded. Than a loud static comes through, unheard by us but caught on the digital recorder. Finally, the man is recorded saying, "Yes?" Well ... yes Michael, thank you.

I say, "*Adam Braston (a mutual friend) misses you and talks about you often." When I'm finished talking, an unexplained sound is recorded—what sounds like someone's hands trying to grab at the recorder that is in my hand. I just want to say that when I am holding equipment, especially the recorder, I am very careful and stay still so as not to get any false readings or evidence.

The man is recorded saying what sounds like, "Box." This is followed by a sound—what sounds like to me as though someone is vigorously grabbing at the recorder. The man than repeats himself, "Box." The noises are recorded again, as if someone is grasping the equipment. At the end of the noises, the man says, "Me." I asked Adam's wife, Sarah, if she knew of such a box. Maybe it was a box full of his stuff or a box he made or something. At first, she couldn't think of anything then, she told me that Michael might be referring to Adam's tackle box, that she thinks has some of Michael's stuff along with his fishing stuff.

I ask, "Michael, can you say either of our names?" Several seconds go by and suddenly we get this amazing EVP of the man whispering repeatedly, "Say it, say it, say it, say it." Then silence. His voice is then captured saying, "*Braston." This is the last name of a mutual friend, that I mentioned earlier. They were like brothers and were very close. While he didn't say Jourdan or Tessa, what he said, proves to us that we are indeed speaking and communicating with Michael! He didn't say the first name, which is kind of a name you hear a lot, but he said his last name. No way it's anybody but Michael.

Jourdan asks, "Do you remember when we were all friends and we would all hang out?" The man responds saying, "Ever." I say, "Those were some good times we all had together, huh?" After this question is asked there is some static and at the same time a man is recorded breathing. This is followed by a disembodied voice coming through the spirit box saying, "Yes."

I ask, "Is there something you want to say to us before we leave Michael?" The man comes through the spirit box saying, "Yes." Jourdan asks, "Is that a yes?" The man comes through again and says, "Maybe." Then a disembodied voice says, "Yes." Jourdan says, "We're going to go visit Peter. We'll tell him you say hi okay?" A few seconds after she says this, a voice comes through the spirit box saying, "Stop."

Jourdan asks me, "Did he just say, 'Stop' Why would he say that?" Before I can even answer the man answers her by coming through the spirit box saying, "Yeah." I say, "Okay we'll be back some other time. We miss you." We catch an EVP of the man saying, "Wait." I say, "We'll talk to you later. Can you say bye to us?" Right before I turn off the recorder we get a very clear EVP, "See ya."

Session four Peter
Mini EVP session

An unexplained pop sound is recorded, and some say that this can either be a sign that a spirit is trying to communicate with the living or trying to manifest itself. This has happened to me many places, indoors and outdoors at many different areas.

I look down at my friend's headstone, and I say, "Peter, you left us way too soon and unexpectedly." Immediately after saying that this EVP is recorded of a male saying, what sounds like, "Yes." Though more drawn out like, "Yeeeeeesss." This is followed by another pop noise. On what was a particularly warm day, Jourdan suddenly gets very cold and gets goosebumps.

I ask, "Is there a message you'd like us to give to someone?" For a few seconds nothing but the sounds of birds chirping behind us, then we catch a recording of a disembodied voice speaking an unintelligible word. It almost sounds like as if someone is way too close to a microphone and trying to talk. More unexplained noises are recorded—what reminds me of the sounds you'd hear from a video game—then a bing-like-sound, then an enthusiastic voice saying, "Yes!"

Session five Peter
Final session

Immediately as we turn the spirit box on we start getting action. Again, I have to say, we missed all this the first few times listening to the session. It wasn't until I put the slowest listening option on that I heard these hidden messages. If it weren't for that, this would all be easily skipped over.

Jourdan turns the spirit box on. Suddenly, a huge gust of wind comes through and what sounds like a "Noooo." is recorded. The voice sounds familiar to me. At an earlier date, when we were here, and we saw the creepy man in the car and recorded that EVP growl. The voice saying, "Noooo" sounded just like that. We were close to the same area when we caught that growl, so it possibly may be the same spirit.

The sound of what sounds like someone playing a chord on a guitar comes through the spirit box. Jourdan asks, "Peter, did you just play some music for us?" A few seconds later, we get a reply saying, "Yes." Amazing! Jourdan asks, "Do you have something to tell us buddy?" Music of a guitar comes through AGAIN and we get a response in a singing voice saying, "Yes." Right after this, "Yes" is repeated by the male but this time not in a singing voice.

Jourdan says to Peter, "I listen to Atmosphere a lot, and it makes me think of you. I know you used to love them." The male comes through the spirit box and says, "Yes." Then very clearly says, "God." Peter listened to Atmosphere all the time, and one of the songs is called, "God Loves Ugly" not only a song but also the name of one of the duo's many albums. He could have very well been referring to this. Again, amazing!

I look at Jourdan and smile and I kiddingly ask, "Did you ever kiss one of us at one of my parties?" Years back, while in my basement at one of my parties, Jourdan and Peter shared a kiss. An EVP whisper is recorded saying, "Shhhh!" followed by an unintelligible word.

Jourdan kids around saying, "I remember when you gave me that kiss, sugar!" The man comes through the spirit box saying, quite clearly, "Hot." Jourdan asks, "Do you remember when you let me dress you in Tessa's clothing?" A disembodied voice says, "Yes." Jourdan says, "I still have pictures of that, you know." After she says this, we get an amazing EVP, sounding so close as if whispering in our ears saying, "Tessa ... dress." Followed by unexplained heavy breathing.

This is amazing and very accurate. At my house we were having a party and Peter being more than slightly drunk allowed Jourdan and I to put him in a dress of mine. It was a black dress with flowers. So, when we got that EVP saying Tessa ... dress, you cannot get more accurate than that.

I just want to note that we visit three people at this cemetery. John Wayne, Michael and Peter. We have gotten the validation we needed and wanted that we were indeed communicating with these specific souls. John Wayne told us the last name of Jourdan's mom, his sister. Michael told us the last name of a mutual friend, and Peter is sharing a memory we created well over a DECADE ago!

When it comes to asking Peter about this funny incident, these are some of the results we got, mind you, after asking a question it usually takes several seconds to get an answer, if you get one at all.

I ask Peter if he remembers what he wore that night at my house. The man gives us this EVP, "Yes." Seconds later, a different voice comes through, saying, "No." This can possibly be the growler! The spirit box, which has been on, but had been silent, besides the sweeping of channels, blurts out a burst of what sounds like guitar sounds. Jourdan asks, "Are you here Peter?" The man is recorded saying excitedly, "Run!" Then yet another man gives us this EVP, "Mill."

Now this is just speculation, but perhaps the EVP "Run" was someone's way saying possibly the growler was around. The growling voice is very deep and dark and gives me the chills each time I hear it. Very negative. As for "Mill" Pueblo has a Steel Mill located across town, maybe a former steel mill worker is buried there, or died at the Mill. Our friend Michael, for a short while, worked at the Mill.

After no response with the spirit box, Jourdan asks again, "Peter, are you here with us?" A disembodied voice comes through the spirit box and says, "Yes … Ain't I?"

What happens next really wasn't supposed to be part of the investigation. Peter and I moved from Pueblo around the same time. Both of us missed the place called Home. We talked every night on Myspace, back when it was Myspace and not Facebook. We always said when he moved back in to the state, we would throw a huge party, all you can eat Taco Bell, and all the beer and booze one could imagine. We always challenged each other when it came to the mighty beer bong. So, this part here I'm really just kidding around, like we used to.

I joke around saying, "I bet if you were here right now, I'd still beat you at the beer bong." The man is recorded saying, "Guess." Jourdan asks, "What do you think about that?" Several seconds go by of just silence, then a man comes through the spirit box and says, "Never." Then an EVP of the man saying, "No." Repeats himself on the spirit box, "No." Then as if to challenge me, he says, "Do it."

Jourdan asked, "Do you know that we try to come visit you often?" A disembodied voice comes through the spirit box and says, "Yes." Then close to a minute later, my name is whispered in an EVP by a man, "Tessa." Jourdan asks Peter if he has seen Michael, that he is buried here too. "No" comes through the spirit box. We asked Michael earlier and he too said, "No." Jourdan starts to talk and as she does a woman starts to speak as well. Her words are unintelligible. Again, no one is around. No mourners, no visitors, no funerals, nothing. If we heard a woman speaking in the distance, we would have debunked it.

Jourdan says, "You and Michael should hang out sometime," the man agrees, saying through the spirit box, "Yup." Jourdan says, "So you won't be so lonely." The man comes through the spirit box again, repeating himself, "Yup." I ask, "Is there anything you want to tell us before we head out?" A disembodied voice is recorded saying an unintelligible word. Then, the man says what sounds like, "Michael."

As Jourdan and I sit there at our friend's headstone, Jourdan gets an idea to ask about the flowers. Someone brought an assortment of flowers for him. Many different types of flowers, each kind being a different color. Jourdan asks, "What color are these roses on your grave?" About ten seconds goes by, then we catch an EVP saying, "Red." Then through the spirit box he repeats it, "Red."

I ask, "Peter, there was a certain fast food chain, that you absolutely loved. Can you tell us the name of this place?" A disembodied voice is recorded speaking an unintelligible word. Then, shortly after this an EVP, what sounds like a faint, "Taco" is recorded.

Peter loved Taco Bell. Jourdan looks at me and verifies and mouths the words, "Taco Bell?" I nod. Jourdan says, "Can you finish my sentence? Yo Quiero Taco …?" A whisper is recorded saying, "Stop." Then an EVP of the man saying, "Word." Jourdan repeats herself, "Yo quiero Taco …"

As I listen to the audio, I hear loud heavy breathing, followed by a disembodied voice saying what sounds like, "Do it." Jourdan says one last time, "Yo quiero Taco … Bell! Come on Peter!" The disembodied voice is recorded saying, "Say it, say it." The man comes through the spirit box and says, "Neon." Perhaps he is talking about the lit-up signs that Taco Bell has in front of their chains.

Jourdan asks, "Do you like the flowers that are here on your grave?" The man says via the spirit box, "Yeah." Jourdan asks, "Do you know who put the flowers there?" Seconds later the disembodied voice says, "Yes … yes."

We get this interesting EVP, "Ghosts." It's very drawn out, "Ghooosts." Jourdan asks, "Do you know who I was hanging out with last night?" Several seconds go by and finally an EVP, an amazing EVP, another verification that we are indeed speaking to our dearly departed friend Peter. He says, "Duran." This is amazing. The night before Jourdan was hanging out with April, whose last name happens to be, hello … Duran! This was a Class A EVP, crystal clear, in the male voice that happened to sound slightly like our buddy, Peter!

End of visits/sessions for the day.

Listening to our friend Peter speak to us, was amazing. Him and April Duran were best friends, so when he said Duran, it blew my mind. In the dream of him I mentioned earlier, this is the April he was talking about. He told me to watch over her, and I did. When he died we grew a strong bond. We stopped hanging out a long time ago, went on to different friends.

When I heard "Duran" from our dear Peter, I really felt a connection, it's like all those negative feelings went away. I felt it was crucial for her to go with Jourdan and I to the cemetery and do a couple sessions with Peter since he mentioned her. Jourdan discussed it with her and the three of us got together one slightly chilly day in December. You'll read about those details a little later on.

August 12, 2015
The Investigation

This investigation was conducted by Jourdan Ortega and Tessa Mauro. Every investigation we have conducted, to date, we have collected amazing evidence. Every time we come to visit Jourdan's Uncle I always leave happy because he always seems to communicate with us—especially Jourdan. Not many people can say they get to talk to a loved one who is gone and that they actually answer back!

Results and evidence collected
John Wayne

The spirit box is turned on and just a few seconds later the disembodied voice of a man comes through saying, "Hey." Jourdan says, "Hello, Uncle John, it's Jourdan here." A very raspy breathing is recorded. Jourdan asks, "Do you have something to say?" A very faint and distant disembodied voice replies, "No." An unexplained whistling sound is recorded then a disembodied voice of a man says, "No." This followed by yet another whistle. Jourdan says, "You're not really coming through." A man's voice comes through the spirit box and says, "Now?" A woman comes through saying, "Free."

After hearing a several of different voices, I ask, "Who are we talking to?" A woman whispers an EVP of two unintelligible words. A man, through the spirit box says, "Me." Jourdan asks, "Do you not want to talk to us?" Heavy breathing is recorded, then a disembodied voice of a man says, "Not really." Another man comes through the spirit box and says, "Hello."

Disembodied music comes through, sounding like very old music. I say, "We just heard music. We know you enjoyed music a lot, can you play music for us again?" A man says, "Sing." Then amazingly, the same old disembodied music comes through the spirit box again. This is followed by a pop-like-sound. Then what sounds like a man singing, very faint and distant.

As we sit there talking to Jourdan's Uncle, one of Jourdan's friends drives by and stops to talk to us for a minute. The recorder catches all three of our voices, but another voice comes through, saying what sounds like a whole sentence. After listening many times, it sounds like the voice is saying, "Going to take you to the office." Not too positive, but that's what it sounded like. Unsure what that means! A voice comes through the spirit box that sounds like our friend Michael, who is buried remotely close to where we are says, "Good morning."

What happens next is pretty awesome, Jourdan asks, "Did you get what I put on your grave for you last time I was here?" Seconds later we get an EVP of a man saying, "Crown.". If you recall, the last time we visited him, Jourdan made a flower crown and put it on his headstone. Amazing! "Crown" being an EVP, coming through the recorder itself, not the spirit box, we didn't hear that right away, so I ask, "Can you tell her what that was?" The same voice repeats, "Crown." Then a very loud crunch is recorded. The best description I can give about this noise is as if someone grabbed an apple and biting into it for the first time. Very loud. Crunch. This goes unheard by us.

The chewing sounds go on for quite a few seconds, and no, we never ever eat during investigations. An unexplainable beeping noise is recorded. I debunk this as not being any of our equipment. After we ask several questions with no responses from the recorder and no EMF spikes, Jourdan says, "All right, you don't have to talk to us right now if you don't want to." A few seconds later we catch this EVP of a man saying, "All right."

An unexplainable noise is recorded. I cannot even begin to explain what this noise was, I will try though, but the words don't give it justice. The noise had a slight echo to it. An alien like purring noise, very loud right at the digital recorders microphone. Jourdan says, "Okay, we're going to let you go for now." We get an EVP of the man saying, "Okay."

Figure 7 Jourdan at her Uncle's grave

December 21, 2015
The Investigation

This investigation was conducted by Jourdan Ortega, April Duran and Tessa Mauro. Earlier I talked about how we were going to try to get April Duran to join us in an investigation with mutual friend Peter, seeing as we got a recording of an EVP of Peter saying April's last name I was very excited to see what results we would get now that she was there with us. It was a mild winter day, slightly cold but not overwhelming like it can be this time of year here.

Results and evidence collected
Session one EVP session, Peter

This EVP session was real neat, and it seemed to be only the one male that was speaking to us. While much of it, for this session, was unintelligible we were able to tell that it was the same voice responding back to us.

April asks, "Peter are you around here right now?" During what was a calm day, a huge gust of wind comes out of nowhere. Then it leaves as quick as it came. Then a disembodied voice of a male comes through making a noise. Jourdan asks, "Hey Peter, did you go with April and I to the Atmosphere show at Red Rocks last year?" The male speaks, what sounds like three words, all unfortunately unintelligible. This is than followed by what sounds like the same male singing in the background.

Since Peter has mentioned my name in the past, and April's last name, I ask, "Peter can you say any of our names?" The male whispers but I cannot understand what he is saying. Irritating! I know it takes a lot of energy to speak even one small word, so it always saddens me when I can't understand them. I try my best and will continue to do so.

Jourdan asks, "Who put this nice wreath here for you?" As the wind picks up the male speaks an unintelligible word. Jourdan receives a text on her phone. Her text alert is a song from Atmosphere, Peter's favorite. After the music stops a disembodied laugh is recorded.

Session two EVP session, Peter

April says, "Okay Peter, tell me who plays this song." We get an EVP of the male responding, whispering, "Okay." April turns her phone volume up and has an Atmosphere song playing. She has it playing for about a good minute. At one point, Slug sings, "Love an angel but he's got to take a chance." Right after this verse, unexplained whispering of a man is recorded, but since the music is on and the volume is up, there's no way to know what the voice was saying. Unintelligible words. Later Slug sings, "Already knew the deal." Another EVP whisper of the male, this time we understood this one word, saying, "Loss." As April turns the music off, loud heavy breathing is recorded.

I just like to note that when we investigate and are recording, I always remind people to be as quiet as humanly possible, so not to taint any evidence. So, all the heavy breathing we have caught on recordings is not from us. It is unexplainable. It is, what I believe to be, paranormal.

I ask, "Can you tell us who that was?" The male, very faintly says what sounds like, "Slug." Atmosphere is a band, two men, are in. One, being the rapper, whose name is Sean Daley, but who goes by the name Slug. So that answer was indeed extremely accurate. I ask, "Peter, do you remember last time we were here, and Jourdan mentioned that whenever she listens to Atmosphere it makes her think of you?" A quick burst of static comes through the recorder, unheard by us, then an EVP of the male saying, "Yes." I continue, "A few seconds after she said that, you said, 'God.' Is Atmosphere God to you?" Jourdan chimes in, "Or were you talking about, 'God Loves Ugly' the album, or the song?" Again, the heavy breathing is recorded. Seconds later we get an EVP of the male saying, "God."

In my hand I have three pictures of the night I mentioned earlier when we dressed him in one of my dresses. I hand a picture each to Jourdan and April, keeping one for myself. "I brought pictures today. We are each holding one, can you tell us what any of them are?" Immediately after asking this, there's a quick static interference then an unexplained thump noise.

Jourdan asks, "Who is with you in the picture that I'm holding?" An unexplainable wheezing sound is recorded. Then after that, what sounds like the male saying, "It's *Jacob." Now, Peter was not the only one to drunkenly parade around in my clothing. In the photo, Peter was wearing a black dress and standing with him was his friend, Jacob wearing a bikini top. They both were making funny faces. It's a real hilarious picture! They had so much fun that night. It's neat that he said Jacob's name.

More wheezing sounds are recorded.

Session three, Peter

Jourdan asks, "What's your last name?" Yet again we get a verification that this is Peter. We get an EVP of the male saying, "*Santo." Then a few seconds later, this is repeated but really light and faint saying, "Santo." This is followed by a disembodied voice making a noise, possibly a moan or a groan. Just for the record, the name he said, twice, was his last name. Love when that happens! It really is enlightening going to this cemetery. I feel so at home here, so welcomed. It really is a visit/investigation.

I say, "Somebody is here with us that wasn't here last time, you even mentioned her name. Who is with us?" A male whispers what sounds like, "Ahh." This is followed by an unintelligible word coming through the spirit box. I say, "You just said something, we'll rewind it later and listen to it then." The male gives us this awesome EVP, saying, "Rewind it." Six unexplainable footsteps are recorded. We are all sitting and have been this whole time, it sounds as if the footsteps are walking around us. Very close. This is followed by heavy breathing.

Jourdan asks, "Would you be able to play us a song?" The male says, "Yep." A disembodied music comes through. I ask, "Peter, April has a tattoo dedicated to you, can you tell us what it says or what it is?" An EVP is recorded. The man whispering what sounds like, "Sad. Memory." Jourdan asks, "How many of us are here visiting you today?" The man comes through the spirit box saying, "Three."

I ask, "We played a song for you earlier, can you tell us who sang it or the name of the song?" We get an EVP saying, "Yes, _____." The second word is unfortunately unintelligible. April asks, "What color car did you used to have?" A different man comes through, saying what sounds like, "Violet."

As we sit here talking to Peter, several cars pass by us, heading to the opposite side of the cemetery for a funeral. Again, I must mention, when we come here all we bring are small hand-held things so people have no clue what we are doing. We debunk the cars. Jourdan says, "There's a ton of cars over here right now. Can you tell us why?" Several seconds go by then a very faint disembodied voice is recorded saying what sounds like, "Death ... death!" Then another man comes through the spirit box also saying, "Death." Amazing!

Session four, Peter

Jourdan starts singing an Atmosphere song. I ask Peter, "Jourdan was just singing. What was she singing?" We get an EVP of the man asking, "Who is it?" Than a different man comes through, he sounds like he possibly can be our friend Michael, who is buried not too far from where Peter is, saying, "Tessa." This is followed by an unexplained heavy exhale. I say, "So, the last few months while you were in Texas and you were planning to come back, we were talking a lot on Myspace." I pause, and before continuing, this EVP is recorded, "Yessss." I continue "What were we supposed to do together when you got back into town?" The male comes through the spirit box and says what sounds like, "Beer." A woman comes through asking, "Get down?" I say to Jourdan and April, "That was a woman, I think." The woman who just said, 'get down' comes through the spirit box and says, "Yes."

So, the responses to that question were beer and get down. Two responses from two different sources. Beer is accurate, get down, not so much. I mentioned it earlier, but what we planned on doing when he got back in to town was to have a beer bong competition. I kid around saying, "Last time we were here I mentioned something about kicking your butt at beer bong and we got a couple responses back. You didn't like that." A quick gust of wind comes through and shortly after the wind the male comes through the spirit box and says, "Shit."

Final session, session five EVP

This session was about three minutes long, but we only got one result. This was a very interesting result because we got an EVP, then a woman came to visit a grave next to us, so we then just started talking to Peter and telling stories about Peter while being recorded. The recorder, looking like a phone in the hand. We get an EVP of the male, who we believe to be our friend Peter saying, "Turn it off." Possibly warning us a mourner was headed our way.

April 3, 2016
The investigation

This investigation was conducted by Jourdan Ortega and Tessa Mauro. Before arriving at the cemetery, we had spent a couple hours at the Holistic Fair where I had a special session with an amazing Medium, Beth. You read about that session in the Medium Chapter. She was so dead-on accurate on so many things.

She mentioned Peter, Michael, and Jourdan's uncle John. Today is Peter's birthday. It's hard to believe he has been gone for ten years. Since we communicated with Peter through Beth, and it was his birthday we wanted to definitely visit him.

Results and evidence collected
Session one Peter, mini session

Jourdan asks, "Earlier today did you have a lady come talk to us representing you? What was her name?" We receive an EVP, "Willing." Unsure what that means. Maybe he found someone who was willing to speak for him. We turn the spirit box on. I ask Jourdan to repeat the question she just asked now that the spirit box is on. Before she can ask the question, a man's voice comes through the spirit box saying, "Yes." Jourdan repeats herself, "Did you have a woman contact you representing us earlier today? What's her name?" No answer, just a loud exhale from a man.

Almost a minute goes by with no voices coming through, then a man comes through saying, "Beer." After this a voice that sounds similar to Peter says, "What's up?" Another man comes through the spirit box and says, "Hear." Followed by static interference. The voice dubbed Peter comes through saying in an incredibly clear voice, "Son." Peter comes through and says his name, "Peter." We turn off the spirit box.

I say, "We got so many voices coming through, very intense. Can we get some EVP's?" As I am speaking, in the middle of my sentence a man comes through giving us this EVP, "Hear me?"

I ask, "One of the things the medium said was that there is someone who is like a sister to you, that you watch over her and are very protective over her." A voice comes through in an EVP saying what sounds like, "Yes." I continue,

"Can you tell us who that person is?" We ask a couple more questions with no results.

Session two, Peter

We turn the spirit box on and Jourdan asks, "So, how old would you be today Peter?" Quite a few seconds go by with nothing but the sound of the sweeping of the channels, then we get a very faint EVP saying, "Twenty-nine." There's a pause, with several seconds in between then the same voice starts whispering, but these are unintelligible words.

We continue to ask questions and after quite a bit of silence to a couple unanswered questions, we turn the spirit box off. I ask, "Can you tell us the color of flowers that are on your grave?" Immediately after I ask that question static comes through. This static is very loud, but unheard by us. The static is then followed by a man exhaling and the pop sound.

Session three, Peter, Mini EVP session

We decided for our final session of the day with Peter, we would stay quiet. So, I tell him, "Say anything you want to us, what your feelings are about your birthday, who you miss, any messages for anybody, anything. Speak up." From the second I finish speaking until the end of the session, the only sounds heard is the light wind in the background. No voices, no words, no breathing, nothing. Just wind. Even though we got no EVP's in this last session, we did get some minor EMF spikes. The Mel Meter was reading at 0.6. Then it fluctuated between 0.5-0.6, then 0.1-0.3, then back to 0.5-0.6 again. As we left Peter, it went to 0.8. No high spikes mind you, but the whole day we were there it remained at 0.

Session four, Michael

As I was for Peter, I was excited to visit Michael. The medium said he was there with me and approached me about him and described Michael to a T. Even using his alias for the book, Michael. To this day, I am still utterly amazed by this! As Jourdan and I get to where Michael is, the Mel Meter spikes to 0.6.

I ask, "Is there anything you would like to tell us?" For a few seconds all that can be heard is wind. Suddenly a disembodied voice is heard saying what sounds like, "No fair." Jourdan turns the spirit box on to see if we can catch Michael that way. There have been several times where his voice had come through, not only as an EVP through the digital recorder but also through the spirit box itself.

I say, "Okay, we are here with Michael." Immediately after I finish talking, a man's voice comes through the spirit box and replies, "Yes." Followed by the unexplained pop noise.

I continue, "Today, I spoke to a woman—a medium—and you had a lot to do with the conversation." A disembodied male voice comes through the spirit box, making a noise or speaking an unintelligible word. Then several seconds later, the disembodied voice says two more unintelligible words.

The spirit box suddenly gets very much louder as it sweeps through channels. Not noticeable by us but listening to it later, there is a definite difference. I've never encountered this before. It stayed like this for quite a few seconds. Much louder, mixed with static.

Jourdan reads the EMF meter being at 0.8. I repeat Jourdan as the EMF is rising. "Okay now at 0.9." A man's voice that sounds like Michael comes through saying, "Yes." As mentioned before, throughout our many sessions with Michael, we have recorded this voice many times. I tell Jourdan, "His voice just came through." Before she can continue to speak, an EVP is recorded in a hushed whisper saying, "Yeah."

I ask, "Can you talk to us? You just came through." An unexplained pop noise is recorded, I continue, "Or what sounded like you. Can you say something?" An exhale is recorded. I say, "I told the medium that we weren't—," I'm cut off when a male comes through the spirit box saying what sounds like, "No."

I continue, "We weren't friends for a long time and that," as I pause, a voice comes through saying, "It hurts." I keep talking, "We're closer in death then when you were alive. Does that make sense to you?" Rap music comes through the spirit box, he sure loved his rap music.

The voice that sounds like Michael says, "Do it." Then an unexplained flick like noise is recorded. As if someone walked up to my recorder that's in my hand and flicked at the speaker. Very loud.

Session five, Michael, EVP session

Jourdan is holding the Mel Meter and lets me know that it went to 1.0, stayed for a while then back to 0. As this is happening an unintelligible word from a man is recorded.

I ask, "Is there anything you would like to say to us? Anything at all? Whether it's telling somebody something, like a message for somebody? Even if we don't talk to that person, we will tell them. Is there anything?" A whisper is recorded saying what sounds like, "Tessa." I continue on, "Your brothers, or—" an unexplained exhale is recorded. I continue, "Or anybody at all? Me or Jourdan?" Right after that last part, we get an EVP saying, "Yes!" This is followed by a disembodied cry.

The EMF makes an alert sound. Jourdan made it go off, so I debunk this. I laugh and say, "Jourdan playing with the EMF." A voice comes through giving us this EVP, "Yes", almost sounding child-like.

Jourdan reads the meter, "0.8" while she tests out the meter to make sure it makes alert noises, the readings of the electromagnetic field meter and thermometer automatically do their own thing. I ask, "Are you around us sometimes?" A quick reply, an EVP, "Yes." I continue, "Watching over us?" An unexplained static interference is recorded.

Throughout the years, we have been to this cemetery countless times. There are so many investigations that we have conducted here, that I have not yet listened to. With having my radio show and trying to complete this book, I stay pretty busy, but I can't wait to hear what more the spirits of Empress Cemetery have to say. Just waiting for me to hear it.

Chapter eight

Rock Creek Cemetery
Monte Vista, Colorado

A little history lesson ...

Rock Creek is a sweet little cemetery in the mountains of the small town, Monte Vista. A former coworker, Kyle, told me about this cemetery and how he and his friends experienced something there. He had already done the investigation at the Mines in Creede with us.

This is a remote, small cemetery. It has sage growing there, and the scene, being nestled in the mountains, away from the city, is just beautiful. "Old Baldy" the mountain standing guard in the far distance. Many of this town's earliest settlers are laid to rest here. Around 1870, emigrants with wagons and all their belongings started making their way over the treacherous Colorado passes to settle here.

Over 155 of those people are buried here. If you are there and see white stones with lambs on them, that usually means a child is buried there. One such family was unfortunate to have four white children's stones. Larger stones topped with carved emblems are family plots.

When you head this way, you can see markers on the highway and the dirt road itself to direct you to the cemetery. In fact, a man named Z.C. Eagle, who had settled in the area with his family back in 1887, had erected those markers in the spots you see there today. He also tried to locate as many graves as he could, the nameless ones, and try to put names to the people there. What an outstanding citizen!

The oldest marked grave is that of a five-day old baby boy named Lewis. Baby Lewis died October 7, 1874. Over forty different pioneer families are buried here. Many of their descendants still live in Monte Vista to this day.

December 5, 2014
The Investigation

This investigation was conducted by Tessa and Carly Mauro, Kyle, and Melanie. Approaching this cemetery, you can tell it's soaked in history. It was a slightly chilly night in December, armed with our equipment we were ready to get in there.

When we got there, we had our flashlights but the moon was close to being full and illuminated the whole area for us so we didn't even use our flashlights. Amazingly, a few nights later we went back and it was pitch black where even our flashlights weren't much help.

The results we collected were amazing. We had EVP's, photographic evidence, including orbs, and even what looks like a spirit manifestation. We also had communication by sound. Not just any sound but a very specific sound.

Results and evidence collected

We start off standing by our vehicles close to the cemetery gate. I start the investigation with an Open Protection Prayer. I say, "We come to this cemetery with the utmost respect." As I speak, a woman is recorded whispering this EVP, that sounds like, "Yes," followed by six unexplained knock-like sounds. These knocks are loud and while the recorder catches the sounds, it goes unheard by us. Then we get an EVP from the same woman saying what sounds like, "Look over" followed by the unexplained knocking sounds again.

At this point we are still not even in the cemetery but at the entrance, so right now all we have on is the digital recorder. The spirit box, at this point, is off. I continue, "We please ask that nobody follow us home, positive or negative." Right after I say that, we get yet another EVP from again the same woman, whispering these eerie words, "I will." I say, "We are going in to the cemetery now." We get an EVP from the woman whose spirit seems to be joining our investigation saying, "Yes." This is followed by unexplainable static.

Carly turns the spirit box on, it's making its regular sounds as it sweeps through the frequencies. I must say, I am very impressed that just a few minutes into this investigation we have already collected four EVP's from the same woman, unexplainable sounds like the knocking sounds and unexplained static. Very awesome!

Kyle starts to tell us about an experience him and friends had here. His friend's car and his were parked right about where ours are now, right by the cemetery gate at one of the corners. About 50 feet from where we were standing. He starts:

"We were right over there, just hanging out." As he pauses, an unexplained pop noise is recorded. He continues, "We were just there in my friend's car, where my truck is right now. Our other friend was parked on the other side to the left. We had our windows down and were having a cigarette and talking. My friend's car was a standard and he had his car in neutral with the emergency brake on. His car started getting pushed." Again, Kyle pauses and this time an unexplained purr like noise is recorded.

Kyle says, "He thought it was us getting out of our car and pushing him. It got pushed so hard you could see the skid marks." Carly gasps, interrupting Kyle, she tells us that she heard a man whisper in her ear. Listening to the audio, it did not catch a man's voice at that time. Carly, like me, is a sensitive so there have been times where she will hear the disembodied voice of a man or a woman with her own ears. A disembodied voice of a man comes through the spirit box responding to Carly saying, "So what?"

Kyle goes on, "So, he pulled up and flipped around and came back this way to put his headlights on. We sat there for about five minutes just staring we were in complete shock." What Kyle says next is very important because we ourselves as a team experience it numerous times in this investigation. Kyle finishes his experience by saying, "After that happened, we heard a continuous metal-on-metal clank like noise, like … 'Dink' coming from over this way." He points to the opposite side of the cemetery from where we are standing. "We heard this unexplained noise until we left." Then the look of shock comes on his face like disbelief and he says, "It left skid marks."

We make our way to the gate, we fumble with the chain, it's not locked or anything it just had the chain keeping the gate closed. The sound of the heavy chain dropping to the ground and the gate opens, it had a very creepy creaky noise to it, the noise reminded me of the type of noise you would hear in an old scary movie. We step foot into the cemetery. We are officially in Rock Creek Cemetery.

Kyle tells us he wants to take us to a certain spot, so Carly and I follow him. Kyle and Melanie recently got a baby puppy. They didn't want to leave it home alone, so Melanie stayed in the truck with the pup. We stop by a group of headstones. Kyle points and says, "The noises we were hearing sounded like they originated from this area. It was close ... we distinctively remember because of this fenced in area."

We ask a few questions with no responses. Carly asks, "How many of you are here with us right now?" A disembodied voice of what sounds like a young woman comes through the spirit box saying, "Me." We all show excitement, because this is the first thing we heard with our own ears in this investigation. Since I don't listen to the audio until later we didn't know we had EVP's so when we heard "Me" we were ecstatic.

Carly mentions that before "me" was said, she heard something else, but it wasn't recorded. I tell the spirits to come to the lights on our equipment and Carly joins in, "Speak into it so we can hear you." A woman is caught on recorder, exhaling quite loudly, as if right in front and way too close to the recorder.

I ask, "How many of you are here with us?" A few seconds go by, then a man comes through the spirit box and says what sounds like, "Both." I ask, "How did you die?" The man who spoke earlier says what sounds like either, "Come home" or "Go home." Followed by a disembodied noise. Kyle asks, "Are you a kid?" An unexplained sound is recorded. It sounded like a door swinging in the wind, creaking.

The KII Meter fluctuates between 2 and 3. Carly asks, "Do you know where we are right now? Can you tell us the name?" After several seconds, a very distant, faint voice comes through saying, "Yes." In regular play mode it is unheard and even in the slowest setting it could easily be missed. What is amazing about this is, right after this, Carly immediately says excitedly, "He said yes!" Listening a few times to this investigation it was missed. Now only on the slowest setting did I hear it. We thought it wasn't recorded. She heard it perfectly with her own ears, but Kyle and I heard nothing, and it was recorded. Amazing!

Carly asks happily, "Where are we then?" Kyle gasps, "Did you hear that?" I start to respond when Kyle says, "Again! Again!" We start making our way closer to where the noises are coming from. The noise Kyle told us about earlier has started. I will refer to this mysterious metal on metal noise as, 'The noise.' The pop sound is recorded, of course, always going unheard by us.

Carly asks, "Is that you making all that noise?" I chime in, "Are you trying to get our attention?" A man comes through the spirit box saying what sounds like, "Maybe." This is immediately followed by the noise, which is heard by us and caught on recorder again. We stand there silent for a moment, nothing but silence. I ask, "Can you make that noise again for us please?" A few seconds pass by then the noise is heard by us and recorded once again. I say, "We're not here to hurt you." The noise is heard by us and recorded again. We all gasp. Kyle admits how he is kind of freaked out by this.

I think aloud, "What can that noise be?" A man gives us this EVP, "Me." Kyle takes control of the digital recorder while I start to take pictures throughout the cemetery. I remind Kyle and Carly, "If you see, hear, feel or smell something, start taking pictures, you can possibly catch something on film." A few seconds after I say this we get an EVP of a disembodied voice saying, "Not me." Emphasis on me, like, 'Meeeee.' This is followed by heavy breathing. The noise is heard by us again and caught on recorder.

We stay quiet for a while then as we ask questions, we hear the noise. Kyle makes the good observation that the noise happens when we are asking questions or taking pictures. I start to talk when a woman comes through the spirit box saying what sounds like, "Stop." I take pictures and in one of the pictures I detect an orb hovering over a grave. I ask, "How long have you been here?" A disembodied voice of a man says via the spirit box, "Help."

Kyle hears the noise again, not recorded. Carly says she is going to take some pictures, as she finishes her sentence the man who just said, "Help" is recorded saying it again, "Help." This is coming through the spirit box, the same man's voice, however it's so low, that we missed this unfortunately. I say, "So I feel you are trying to communicate with us. You've been talking to us. Can you say something else? What's your name?" An unexplained deep inhale is recorded followed by an exhale.

Kyle suggests that we should drive to the other side of the cemetery towards the noise. As he is speaking, the noise is recorded, but unlike the other times, where we heard it, this time, the sound goes unheard by us. How interesting. Kyle is just saying to us that we should go across to where the sound is originating from and the sound is then recorded, but we don't hear it this time. I take a picture of some graves that are a short distance ahead of us. I look at the picture and am in awe. I show the crew the picture I just took. It's hard to find the words to try to describe the picture.

Figure 8 Picture of unknown object near the graves

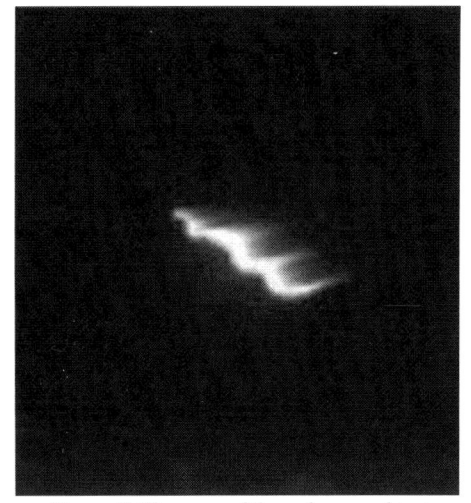

Figure 9 Close-up of the unknown object

It looks like an illuminated wave, to me it looks like a woman, side profile floating. You can't see details of a face or anything like that, but I strongly feel this to be a woman. Now, in the past, I have seen full bodied apparitions, in-your-face style, where there's no doubt what it is. This I am simply saying what I THINK it is. I wasn't using flash, it was a full blown full moon that night, no flash was necessary. I didn't see it with my own eyes 'til I took the picture.

I debunk the sounds of our clicking cameras by saying, "We are taking pictures." A woman, possibly the one from the very beginning of the investigation is recorded giving us this EVP, "Yeah." Kyle and I are talking about the mysterious noise, and how we are hearing the noise a lot. I say, "It sounds like it's coming from the other side of the cemetery." Several seconds later the same woman is caught on recorder, once again responding to us, "Yeah."

Carly asks, "If it's not you making that noise, can you tell us who it is?" As Carly finishes talking the same woman says, "Yes." Then there's a pause of about 10 seconds or so then "Yes" is repeated, but as if closer. Then a man comes through the spirit box saying, what sounds like, "Who are you right here?" but not positive. I ask, "Can you tell us who it is?" We get an EVP of the same woman saying, "Yeah!"

Kyle gets an unsettling feeling and suddenly says we should leave. Carly agrees. I have never left an investigation early and strongly disagree, wanting to stay, but I'm being outnumbered so I say okay. Not wanting to end the investigation early I ask Kyle if it would be okay if we drove to the opposite side of the cemetery. He had mixed feelings part of him wanted to, the other not so much.

One thing about Kyle, we worked together at my mom's cafe. We had fun working together and got along, for the most part, awesomely. Kyle was a skeptic. He was sort of open to the idea that there may be something else out there but hadn't really had the paranormal proof he needed to full-heartedly be a believer.

Many people are like that, some never get that proof, while others get more than they asked for. I think with the voices we collected and the metal on metal sound that showed itself to us when we'd asked questions … well, I think that was the proof for him, and he may have felt uneasy because it was all so foreign to him. I'm glad he had these experiences and is a believer now.

Kyle, still feeling uneasy says, "It's almost like it knew that I knew something. Do you know what I mean?" We get an EVP of a man answering Kyle saying, "Yes, I do."

We slowly start making our way towards our vehicles. I am talking as we walk, "We're heading back to our cars now. Possibly will drive over to the other side." The woman is recorded saying, "Listen to me." A few seconds go by and she repeats herself, "Listen to me." This is followed by the noise. This goes unheard by us.

We reach the gate and open it, loudly creaking. I ask, "Before we leave, is there anything you'd like to tell us?" A whisper is recorded, speaking unintelligible words. As Kyle is fumbling with the chain to secure the gate, we get an EVP of a voice whispering, "Stop." Unexplained rapid heavy breathing from what sounds like a female is recorded. This is neither Carly or myself, and Melanie had been in the truck the whole time. The woman says what sounds like, "My eyes."

Once we get back to our cars, we finally all agree to take a drive to the other side of the cemetery. Carly suggests we all go in one vehicle instead two. I agree and jump into the back bed of Kyle's truck. He offers we can sit in the back, his girlfriend Melanie and their puppy are in the front. Carly and I prefer the truck bed, so we get situated and keep on recording. After driving on the dirt road surrounding the cemetery, and going over bumps and dips in the road, we arrive at the spot. We get out of the truck. The noise is heard by us and recorded. Kyle and I excitedly say in unison, "I heard it!" I walk up ahead and point, "I think it's coming from this area." We get an EVP of a voice saying what sounds like, "Whaaaat?"

An unexplainable sound is recorded, what sounds as if someone threw something at us. Like a rock being thrown. We all hear it and start to look around. Carly asks, "What was that noise? Can you tell us?" A woman is recorded speaking, unintelligible word. We all heard it with our own ears. However, we couldn't understand what she had said.

Melanie gets out of the truck and joins us for a few minutes. We tell her about the sounds we heard and the voices we had heard as well. Carly asks, "Is that you making that noise?" We get an EVP of a whisper saying, "Yes." Like earlier in the investigation, Carly immediately hears this spirits response. She excitedly says, "It said yes!" Again, it was so far and faint it could have easily been missed or skipped over. It's amazing that my sister heard this clear as a bell two times that night!

I ask, "Can you tell us your name?" We get an EVP of what sounds like the woman saying, "No." After a couple minutes of us just walking around the area the noise came from, Kyle asks us, "Did you hear that?" He says he heard talking. It wasn't recorded. Carly asks, "What did you say? Can you repeat that?" The noise is heard by us and recorded. As I start to say something to Melanie, an EVP of a woman is recorded whispering what sounds like, "Share it. Sing."

The noise is recorded but this time it goes unheard by us.

Carly asks, "There is an animal here with us right now. Can you tell us what it is?" Several seconds go by, then suddenly a voice comes through the spirit box of a woman or possibly a child, saying, "Puppy." It sounds more like "Pup-eee." This is indeed accurate, as Melanie, at that time, was outside with us and she was holding her puppy.

I turn the camera on and start taking pictures. While in this area, I take several pictures. In one of those pictures by the barbed wire right in front of a double headstone is a black mass-like mist, in it is a face. I believe when I took this picture, I caught a spirit manifesting itself in front of us.

Figure 10 A face in the mist

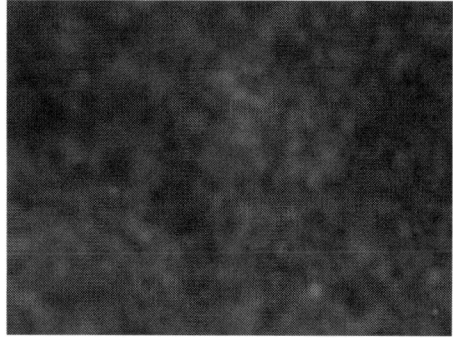

Figure 11 Close-up of the face

Stare long and hard at this picture. The longer you look at it, the more you see. Quite an amazing picture.

We catch an EVP of a voice speaking unintelligible words at the beginning though at the end it says what sounds like, "Fear the wolf." This is followed by the noise. The same voice that just spoke then is recorded saying, "The wolf." Carly asks, "Can you make that noise again for us please?" The noise is recorded but we don't hear it.

I look off to my side and see that there is an opening in the barbed wire fence, right by the area where the manifestation was caught on film. I go back in the cemetery and look around in the area where the noise came from. Trying to debunk the noise. There was not a single thing, clue or answer to what the noise was or where it came from. I stand in front of a double headstone and ask, "Is this your grave? Is your last name *Gonzalez?" Almost immediately after I ask this question, we get an EVP of a man whispering "*Gonzalez."

Carly asks, "How old are you?" Chimes go off in the background. I locate the chimes, which are hung above a young child's headstone. I gently push the chimes so they can make a noise. Kyle, Carly and I all agree that they were not the noise they had heard throughout the investigation. It was in the same general area where the chimes were, but it was a completely different sound.

Carly looks up in the sky and says, "It looks like it may snow sometime soon. Do you like snow?" At disembodied voice replies via the spirit box, "Yeah." Kyle tells me, "Hey that headstone you're in front of, I knew those people very well. They were good friends." As Kyle finishes talking, three pop sounds are recorded. Carly asks, "We have Kyle here with us. We know you were friends. You remember Kyle, right?" An unexplained sound is recorded, almost sounds like someone mumbling, followed by a voice saying in an EVP "Yes."

After hearing the sweet sound of the child's chime dancing gently in the wind, Carly says, "It's a chime." A disembodied voice says, "I know." An unexplained noise is recorded, sounding like a baby noise. We hear an animal like noise in the distance, Carly is nervous and voices her concern that she wants to leave. We start to make our way back to the truck. I kid around saying, "Ghost cow." A woman is recorded saying what sounds like, "Bitch."

We get into the truck. I take pictures and debunk them when I see hundreds of dust particles, what look like mini orbs. Kyle puts his window down and tells us before he drops us off at our car that he's going to drive around the whole cemetery. Carly asks, "What was that animal noise? Was it you?" A man is recorded saying in the distance, what sounds like, "Me." Carly asks, "We're almost back to the car." A woman is recorded saying in a hushed whisper, "Yes."

We arrive at the car and stand around talking. Carly and I thank our friend Kyle for introducing us to this special, unique cemetery. The experience we had here was a good one for us all. When I first discussed the paranormal with Kyle he was sort of a skeptic, but he was open to the possibility, he had the experience before with his friends but hearing the voices of the dead communicate with us not only through their voices but using noise as a communication tool as well was an eye opener for him. I haven't seen Kyle for a while, we lost touch. I hope he never forgets that night.

December 12, 2014
The Investigation

This investigation was conducted by Carly and Tessa Mauro, *Tim and his son *Carl. Tim has been a paranormal investigator for many years. I first heard about him from Ken F, a mutual friend who knew we were doing investigations. One day, while at work, Tim called me and we had a great discussion sharing some of our experiences.

He lived a few hours away but was planning on traveling through my town. Carly and I met with Tim and his son Carl, at the cafe we worked at, which happens to be haunted. A few moments later Ken F showed up as well. We shared audio recordings with one another, more experiences and photos. It was like a little paranormal meeting. This is my type of setting. I was soaking it all in!

I was telling them about the things we experienced at Rock Creek, Tim said he usually doesn't investigate cemeteries. We talked about other places here in Del Norte. There is one infamous place, people from Del Norte will know the place I speak about, even with the false name, *Atella House. This house has been on many haunting and ghost shows. It has a demonic energy to it. People have been driven out. Tim even shared how one unfortunate person had an attachment from that house for years. I cannot even imagine. The one and only attachment I had lasted a little over a month and I thought I was going insane! To have an attachment for years? Forget about it!

After talking, it was decided that we would go with Tim and his son and drive around. He made some phone calls because he has connections to the Atella

House but he got no automatic replies, so we drove past it. Just looking at this place gave me the goosebumps. How does a house get so damned evil?

I knew the San Luis Valley (SLV) had tons of haunted history to it, but Tim told me a lot that I had no clue about. He said that in my town alone, there have been many cases of Incubus and Succubus hauntings. One woman even getting orgasms from it, another quickly moving away after her experience.

For those who are unaware of what incubus and succubus are, the incubus is a malevolent spirit, some consider demonic, this is male form and has sex with women. More like rape. The succubus, is thought to appear in men's dreams, seducing them, and having sex with them. I have heard of this and it is scary. I am not afraid of spirits and ghosts, but I never want to have an experience with this.

After driving around for a while it was decided, even though he wasn't into the cemeteries, we'd go to Rock Creek. Now this particular evening, just a few nights after we had last gone, it was different. It was a lot colder, it was windy at times, and it was very dark. No moon would be helping us on this investigation tonight. We get there and get the equipment ready. Earlier that evening, I had bought a Mel EMF meter from Tim, I was excited to try that bad boy out.

Tim had been investigating for well over a decade, maybe even closer to two decades, so I was excited to see him in the field. We were hoping to learn some things, and we did. First thing I noticed from Tim, he doesn't use the spirit box. While it's not my favorite tool, I personally enjoy using the spirit box. Since Tim didn't use spirit boxes we conducted this investigation without the spirit box, so everything we got in this investigation were EVP's. At the very end before leaving I did turn on the spirit box.

Results and evidence collected

We start the investigation off with an opening protection prayer. I say, "We do come in peace and with full utmost respect." As I pause, unexplained laughing is recorded. I finish the protection prayer after Tim adds a couple things. Carly is holding and keeping an eye on the Mel Meter and lets us know that it is reading at 0.2. I am fumbling with the chain and as this is happening, the sound of a woman moaning is recorded. We enter the cemetery grounds.

An unexplained noise is recorded—what sounds like a woman yelping or possibly weeping. Carly and I try to find the spot Kyle showed us a few nights earlier, where the noises were coming from. With no full moon to guide our way it took a little longer to find the location in the dark night. A couple minutes later we are finally in the general area. I ask, "How did you die?" We get this eerie EVP from a woman saying, what sounds like, "Hem the lines. Kill. Yes." This is followed by static.

I let the spirits know that the group understands it takes energy to talk and that we appreciate them talking to us. I also mention that if talking is too difficult, maybe communicate through sounds like they did last time? An unexplainable pop sound is recorded.

Tim asks, "Do you want to go to the other side?" A disembodied voice of a man asks, "How?" Once again unexplainable static is recorded. Carly takes note that the chimes from the little child's grave we heard last time are making noise. Tim asks Carly if we have any hits on the EMF meter. It is currently at a 0. Quickly then, we get an EVP chuckle from a man, "Heh heh." We make our way to the chimes, and an unexplained sound is recorded. I can only explain it as what a weak and desperate child would sound like gasping for air. A very saddening sound for sure.

I say, "We're here for you, we came back so we can talk to you." As I pause an EVP of a woman is recorded saying what sounds like, "Yes," followed by an unexplainable pop sound. Carly alerts us that the EMF meter is reading at 2.2, a few seconds later it spiked to 2.6. A few minutes later, a man with some type of accent, possibly speaking in a different language, gives us this interesting EVP. This is what it sounds like, "Gurro go kisch … kisch." (He rolled the r's in Gurro)

After looking online, I found that Gurro is a Scottish village in the Italian Alps. A commune in the Province of Verbano-Cusio-Ossola, which is in the Italian region Piedmont. When I looked up Kisch, the only thing I found was an author who wrote his books in German, a man named Egon Kisch or there is always Kitsch which is something considered to be in poor taste. Who knows!

The child's chimes are ringing, what sounds like a younger woman is recorded saying in an echo-like voice, "Tessa." As I said before, this isn't the first time nor is it the last time my name is said by a spirit during an investigation.

I lead the others to the spot where the mist was caught in a picture I took just a few days earlier. It is also the same location where Kyle's two friends, a married couple, are buried. This is also the same area when I asked if their last name was Gonzalez and I got an EVP of a voice saying, "Gonzalez." I stand in front of the double headstone and say, "Gonzalez. We come in peace. We were here earlier with your friend Kyle." We get this EVP whisper saying, "Yes." Followed by static interference. I continue, "Would you like to tell us something?" An unexplainable static is recorded with beep like noises.

I ask, "Would you like us to relay a message to your friend Kyle?" An unexplained noise is recorded. The noise sounds like as if someone scraping their fingernail against the digital recorder. Followed by THE noise. The noise was recorded, but it goes unheard by us.

We are back at the child's grave with the chimes. I ask, "Sweetie, how old were you when you died?" What sounds like a child breathing is recorded, this is followed by a purr like sound. The same woman who said my name earlier repeats herself, "Tessa."

I ask Carly to hold my equipment so I can take off my gloves. As I am in the process of doing this, we get this EVP of a woman whispering, "Get it off!" This is followed by two unexplained pop sounds that are recorded. I then hear THE noise—nobody else hears it and it is not caught on recorder.

It starts to get a bit on the colder side and Tim and his son, who live about two hours away, need to call it a night so they can travel home. So, I mention how I want to turn the spirit box on before we leave and a woman is recorded saying, "Yes." I turn the spirit box on and I ask, "Can you tell us what your name is?" A man comes through the spirit box and says, "Owen" Tim asks, "Owen, do you want us to go away?" Owen comes through again and says, "Yup." Respecting the man's wishes, we start to slowly make our way in the dark, back towards the car.

I ask, "Can you tell us how many of us are here?" We catch this EVP saying, "Too much."

The Mel Meter starts making noises. This is followed by static interference. The EMF reading is a 0.4. Tim asks Carly if she touched the antenna, she has not. The antenna is touched to test it, and it is a different noise. Tim mentions that the EMF while it spiked, hasn't made any noises this whole time, making us think that a spirit or spirits are trying to tell us something or trying to get our attention before we leave.

I ask, "Is there something you are trying to tell us before we head out for the night?" Seconds later, a man whispers this EVP saying, "No." Followed about ten seconds later, by another, "No." The second 'no' is louder, closer. Same voice.

I hear a man speak as I start to talk, "It just said something as I was finishing my sentence." Nothing was caught on the recorder though. Then we get an EVP from a woman sounding as if she is mocking or copying me saying, "It just said s— " I ask, "Are you there? Are you trying to tell us something?" A woman is recorded saying very faintly what sounds like, "Yes."

Carly asks, "Do you still want us to leave?" An EVP is recorded of a voice saying, "Yeah." Then a man who I believe to be Owen says, "Must."
We end the investigation and head back to the truck. We listen to our findings as we warm up in the truck. Again, here is a perfect example why it is so important to listen to the audio on the slow setting. We listened to it on regular play mode and missed several of the EVP's we caught and much more.

Carly and I had a great time doing some investigating and driving around checking out haunted locations with Tim and Carl. If you ever find yourself in the small mountain town of Monte Vista, I recommend checking out this tiny mountain cemetery. Not too far from the drive-thru theatre.

Chapter nine

Pioneer Cemetery
Pueblo, Colorado

This old historical cemetery is the oldest burial ground in Pueblo. With lush green trees, historic plaques, memorial benches and much more, it's a very welcoming place. This cemetery has an amazing assortment of burials here including, families, children, pioneers, senators, war heroes, teachers, Law men and many more.

Pioneer was established in 1870. Unmarked and unrecorded grave-sites are scattered along this property among the hundreds of burials here. The infamous flood of 1921 destroyed the City Cemetery records for this particular cemetery.

For many years there have been countless reports of paranormal activity that has been reported throughout this old cemetery. People have experienced a black mist, which can be a spirit trying to manifest itself to you. Other eerie things people have witnessed are cold spots, odors, temperature changes, orbs caught on film and more. Paranormal investigators have caught EVP's, EMF spikes, photographic evidence, and other types of evidence.

To date, Pioneer Cemetery is one of the most active sites we have investigated. I tried the spirit box before entering the grounds and there was no talking, nothing at all. We walk into the grounds and there was so much action that even when we tried to talk we were getting cut off.

January 14, 2015
The Investigation

This investigation was conducted by Jourdan Ortega, Tessa and Carly Mauro. The evidence we collected in our sessions at this amazing cemetery were, to say the least, quite exhilarating. We communicated with men, women, a baby, a child and more. We got EVP's, picture evidence, intelligent answers to our questions, had a spirit of a man call us not-so-nice names and much more. This is a definite hot spot for investigations. Hearing about this cemetery, the things people have experienced here, I was expecting some paranormal action but not nearly as much as we got.

When we arrived at this cemetery, I tested out the equipment. Fresh batteries in everything. The spirit box was dead and unfortunately, I didn't have my back pack with me that held batteries and flashlights. Why I didn't have it on me, I don't know … I usually have it with me. First and last time that happens. So, we go to a gas station and buy batteries for the spirit box. Pioneer cemetery was so active it totally drained the spirit box after the investigation. To this day, the spirit box has a shorter battery life span. Now after using it, I take the batteries out. I never had this problem until I went to Pioneer Cemetery.

There are so many disembodied sounds, unexplained pops, cries, moans, unintelligible words, EVPs, one-word answers and more. To listen to all of this can be exhausting at times, especially when listening to it for long periods. I swear after a few hours of this, I have to give my ears, mind and soul a break and turn on the TV only to hear the voices still ringing in my head.

We heard tons of this with help of the spirit box and with our own ears, however, when in a session, we don't stop recording, rewind and listen to a voice we just heard to see what it said. Sometimes we understand it when it is said, sometimes we don't. When at home listening to the evidence, the whisper of an EVP gives me chills every time. I get so pumped up hearing this!

Results and evidence collected
Session one

Immediately as the investigation starts, an unexplained pop noise is recorded. The spirit box is turned on. We are standing by a tree when I spot an adorable woodpecker. I ask Jourdan and Carly, "Where did it go?" A disembodied voice of a man comes through the spirit box saying, "Quick." A disembodied voice of a woman is recorded giving this EVP, saying, what sounds like, "Tessa." I ask, "Are you buried here?" Very old music comes through, followed by an unexplained thump-like noise. Seconds later, a man is recorded saying, "Help" the man is then recorded breathing heavily.

A woman is caught speaking an unintelligible word. I ask, "What's your name?" A woman is recorded faintly saying, "Marie." Jourdan, Carly and I head to a statue. A pioneer family, a man a woman and their children. As we make our way toward the statue, three unexplainable loud pops are recorded, this goes on for about three seconds.

I ask, "Can you tell us the name of this statue that's in front of us?" The pop sound is recorded followed by an EVP of a man saying, "Anne." Jourdan lets us know that the Mel EMF meter she is holding is at 2.9. I repeat the question, "Can you tell us the name?" An unexplained deep labored exhale is recorded. A loud thump-like noise is recorded followed by a man talking a panic-stricken voice, speaking an unintelligible word.

After hearing a man a couple times, Carly asks, "What are you trying to tell us?" A disembodied voice of what sounds like an older woman says, "His." Jourdan asks, "What's your name?" A man says an unintelligible word, followed by what sounds like a man gasping for air. I say to Jourdan and Carly, "I'm turning on my camera real quick." As I am turning my camera on, we get this EVP of a woman saying, "Not yet." Jourdan asks us, "Should we walk by some graves?" Before Carly or I reply, a woman gives us this EVP asking, "Really? Really?"

An unexplainable noise is recorded, what sounds like unseen hands grasping at the digital recorder. After the sound, we receive an EVP of a young child saying in an easy-to-miss whisper, "Hello." Pronounced like, "Hay-Lo." I ask, "How did you die?" We get an EVP of what sounds like the same child who just spoke saying, "Not telling you." Quite the childlike response. This EVP is then followed by what sounds like a small child breathing excitedly. The Mel Meter makes an alert noise.

Jourdan starts to talk, and as she does so, at the same time, a man is recorded talking. Unintelligible words. Two unexplainable loud knocks are recorded, followed by a woman saying, "I did." Then a man is recorded saying, "Did." I ask, "How long have you been here?" The same child speaks again, giving us this sad EVP, "A long time." A man speaks through the spirit box saying, "Walk."

I ask, "Can you say that again?" to the man we just heard. An unexplainable pop noise is recorded. Then a child is recorded, what sounds like breathing. I ask, "You just said something, can you repeat that please?" A man says what sounds like, "Empty." An unexplainable noise is recorded. I can only describe this noise as if someone had an aluminum bat and hitting a ball really hard.

Disembodied music comes through, to me it sounds like old circus music. Jourdan alerts us that the EMF is at 0.6. Shortly after the spike an EVP of a woman moaning is recorded.

A woman is recorded, what sounds like breathing, followed by an, "Ahh." I hear this with my own ears and say, "Guys, a woman just said something. I just heard a woman. Can you tell us what your name is?" A woman is recorded breathing heavily. Then says, "Beth." The breathing was an EVP, but "Beth" came through the spirit box and we heard that as it was said.

What sounds like a man whistling is recorded, EVP. Followed by a gasp-like sound. The man then says, "Come out." A man is recorded giving us two EVPs, "Fuck." Then several seconds later, he is recorded saying what sounds like, "Leave me alone." Now I just want to say that if this was said through the spirit box, we would have respected this man and his words and went to another location, but I didn't hear this until after the fact.

I ask, "When did you die?" An EVP is recorded of a whisper, that sounds like, "The house." A disembodied voice of a man says, "March sixth." We then get an EVP of the same man saying, "Kill." Is this man trying to say he was killed on March the sixth? Next time I go to this cemetery I want to see if I can find a burial that dates March sixth, too bad I have no year!

We get this interesting EVP, "You'd be crazy. How do I get out of here?" Followed by an unexplained shuffle noise. The EMF spikes to 0.4 and as we enter a small family gated area, the EMF starts making alert noises. We receive an EVP from a child saying what sounds like, "Look around." A woman comes through the spirit box and says, "What?" I say, "We're in this private family area, it looks that way anyway." A disembodied voice gives us this EVP, "Yes, it does."

I read from a headstone, "Ethel Marie Reyes died in 1898. Is that you, is that your name?" A disembodied voice comes through the spirit box and says what sounds like, "Rey." A woman is recorded speaking unintelligible words. Then a man says, "Rey." A few seconds later the same man says, "Reyes." Amazing! The disembodied voice of a woman comes through the spirit box saying what sounds like, "Hit."

I ask, "Is your name Ethel?" An unexplainable noise is recorded, what sounds like shuffling and clap noises. An EVP is recorded. A whisper from a woman, saying, "Diane." Followed by very loud and raspy breathing which is recorded for a good five seconds. I ask, "When did you die?" An exasperated exhale is recorded.

We start to talk about how many of these people died young. It was much harder surviving back in the early 1800s than it is today. As we talk, an unexplained pop noise is recorded. Then more unexplained deep breathing, from what sounds like a man, is caught on the recorder. Now one may read this and think, well breathing … it's one of them. No. This breathing is different. It's loud, it's labored, it's exasperated, we don't go on investigations and spend our time breathing loudly into the mic. That's what it sounds like, that someone is way too close, their mouth practically on the recorder and breathing.

An unexplainable sound, that sounds like a woman weeping is recorded. Jourdan asks, "Can you tell us whose grave we're standing over?" A deep breath is recorded, then a very faint, very distant EVP, "Mine." Followed by an unexplainable crash like noise. A man says, what sounds like, "Mary." While standing there talking, Jourdan looks down and notices a very small, partially sunken tombstone.

It's only protruding a few inches. It's one of the many unmarked graves here. Jourdan bends down and points the EMF toward the grave. The EMF starts beeping continuously at the unmarked grave. She takes it away and puts in other areas and it is silent. Anytime it comes slightly close to this particular grave it alerts us.

I ask, "Can you tell us whose grave this is?" We get an EVP of a possible child, saying, "Stop." Followed by a man saying, "Yeah." The EMF makes alert noises again. This is followed by what sounds like a woman sobbing mixed with pant-like breathing sounds. As this is happening, a child breathing is also caught on the recorder. It seems a woman and child are together.

Ahead of the sunken unmarked grave is a much taller family grave. A man named Thomas and his son Thomas Jr who died shortly after his father, at just one year old caught our attention. Carly asks, "What is your name? Is it Thomas?" An unexplained deep breath coming from a man is recorded, then we receive this EVP from a man, what sounds like, "You." An unexplained baby gurgling noise comes through the spirit box.

I excitedly say, "That sounded like a baby … we know that there is a baby buried here, a one year old. Was that a baby we just heard?" Carly, thinking we just heard Thomas Jr, adds, "Your name was Thomas too." An unexplained pop noise is recorded, then we get this EVP of a man saying, "No, it's not." He sounded so close, as if he were stand right at our side and talking right in our ear. Amazing!

Session two

After this man gives us this EVP another unexplained pop noise is recorded. I say, "We are still in the family," as I pause to find the appropriate word, a man gives this EVP saying what sounds like, "Lot?"

A woman speaks. Giving us this amazing and sad EVP. The first part is unintelligible, but the last part she says, "I missed my kids." Followed by an unexplained weeping-like sound. Then an unexplained sound, what sounds like something being thrown in our direction is recorded. I swear this cemetery is so active we were getting so many damn EVP's. It felt like Christmas. No kidding. Yet another unexplained sound is recorded. This one quite eerie. It sounds like a child yelping. This did not come through the spirit box but was caught on recorder, though I heard it with my own ears. Immediately after this I say, "I just heard a kid!"

Carly says, "So Thomas, you were talking to us earlier." A man whispers this EVP, "No." Carly says, "Your son died a few months after you did." The same man says, "So what?" Clearly this is not Thomas Sr. An unexplained sound is recorded. I can only describe it as an old-fashioned car horn sound. Carly asks Thomas, "What are your feelings about your son dying?" For a couple seconds, a man is recording breathing quite heavily. A man says, "It's hard."

We start reading off names at the graves and ask if anyone is there. A man comes through the spirit box saying, "Lilly." Another man comes through saying, "Gary." I ask, "Is there anything else you want to say to us before we leave?" A man comes through saying, "Yeah." Then another man very clearly says, "No." As we leave the site we start to discuss the amazing amount of action we have gotten so far from this historic cemetery. As we continue to walk, what sounds like a child makes an exhale noise is recorded, then a man says what sounds like, "Walk." Followed by an unexplained pop noise.

We stop at a different area of the cemetery and I say, "Can you tell us what your name is?" A man says. via the spirit box, what sounds like, "Jeff." Then another man says, "Red." Then amazingly, a woman says, "Mary." So, we got three direct intelligent responses to our question.

A bird lands on a tree next to us and starts screeching, I kiddingly say, "Shush" to the bird. A man comes through the spirit box and says, "Quiet."

Jourdan and Carly find this comical and start busting up laughing. Jourdan says, "That man just told you to be quiet!" I personally think that he was agreeing with me and shushing our feathered friend. Either way, I agree, it is funny.

I look across the street and say to Jourdan and Carly, "Look over there, another cemetery and what looks like a school." Jourdan replies, "That's where babies and children are buried." I then ask, "Can you tell us what's across the street from us?" A man says, "School." Which is indeed accurate. In fact, this was the school Jourdan attended as a child.

A woman is recorded saying what sounds like, "Eve." A man with what sounds like a Hispanic accent says, "Tess." Then a man repeats what the woman said just a few seconds earlier, "Eve". I am talking about how we appreciate all the responses we are receiving, considering how hard it is to sometimes communicate. Again, the man says, "Eve." I remind the spirits, "We come in peace and respect." A man says through the spirit box, "All right."

Jourdan asks, "Is George here?" A man is recorded whispering, "Yessss." Several seconds after the man speaks, we get what sounds like a woman, giving us this amazing EVP, "I'm talking to you ... Jesus." I ask, "Can you tell us what your last name is?" Loud unexplained thump-like noises are recorded. Similar to drums, not like Rock N Roll drums, but what Indians might use. A voice comes through the spirit box answering my question, "Never." Jourdan and I say in unison, "Never?" I ask, "You don't want to tell us what your name is?" We get an EVP, "No."

I ask, "Can you tell us what your first name is?" A woman says what sounds like, "Helen." Shortly after a man says, "Mauve." After this a woman comes through saying, "Debbie." Then a woman says through the spirit box quite clearly, "Beth." We are very excited and show it. We just heard Beth for the second time. I wonder aloud if this is the same Beth that we spoke to earlier, Jourdan thinks it might be a different woman.

As Jourdan, Carly and I are talking about this, a man comes through saying in a very faint, distant, easy-to-miss voice, "You guessed." We stop at a family plot area and I start reading out the names of the people buried there. "Elsie

… Angie … Melvin … Albert." As I stop, a child is recorded saying either, "Sherry" or "Sharing."

I ask, "Are you afraid of us?" Apparently, a man didn't like being asked that question because a man comes through in a very clear voice giving us this crystal-clear EVP, saying "Slut." A man comes through saying either, "Ed' or "Ted." Then a woman is recorded saying, "Headache." Jourdan asks, "Can you tell us how many of us are here?" A man's voice comes through the spirit box saying, "Three."

I ask, "How did you die?" Several seconds go by where nothing but silence and the occasional bird chirp is recorded, then in a very faint and distant voice, a man whispers this EVP, saying, "Hang." This is followed by an unexplained pop noise. Carly asks, "How old were you when you died?" A disembodied voice says what sounds like, "Six." This is followed by a woman whispering, "Suzie." A girl speaks unintelligible words. Followed by a loud unexplained crash-like sound. Can this possibly be a mother and her child, who died at the tender age of six? It's all speculation and guesses. I will go back and try to find out more.

A man comes through the spirit box and says, "Tessa." Jourdan introduces herself, "I'm Jourdan." We stay silent for a few seconds to see if any voices come through the spirit box, nothing. I ask, "Can you say Jourdan?" A man speaks an unintelligible word through the spirit box. Then we get quite the inappropriate EVP response from a not so very happy spirit of a man, saying, "Fuck you!"

Carly asks, "Do you like music?" Immediately after asking about music, very old music pours out of the spirit box. Carly likes asking this question, and she seems to get results each time she asks it. We continue to move on to another section of this old cemetery. While walking, the recorder catches what sounds like a young girl speaking unfortunately, these words are unintelligible. A woman comes through the spirit box asking, "Really?" Perhaps she was responding to the child-like voice who gave us the EVP.

Carly asks, "Want to play some more music for us?" Seconds later, Carly says matter of fact, "No." This was not caught on our recorder, nor did Jourdan nor I hear it but Carly did, and this has happened to her, and myself as well, in past investigations. Carly asks, "Do you want us to leave your area?" We get an EVP from a man saying, "Yes." A man comes through the spirit box saying, "Yup." Followed by an unexplained pop noise. I repeat the question,

"Well, do you want us gone?" A very faint woman's voice comes through saying, "Yes." Then a man, possibly one who spoke earlier says, "Yes."

Not hearing these replies, all yes, we decide to leave anyways. I notice an old marble looking grave, broken and lying on the ground. "Let's go over there." As we make our way to the fallen grave, we get this EVP of a man yelling, "Pull out!" When I heard it, it reminded me of what one would hear from an old war movie.

Carly asks, "Is there anything you want to tell us before we leave?" An EVP of either a woman or a child is recorded saying, "Yes." There are kids walking past us talking, as I debunk this noise a whisper EVP is recorded saying, "Yes." Jourdan asks, "Can you tell us the name of the grave that we are standing at right now?" Yet another EVP is recorded whispering, "Yes." Then a man comes through the spirit box saying, "No."

Carly tells us, "It said something!" Then the same man who just said, 'no' comes through again and says, "Not it" this is followed by an unexplained sound, that sounds like someone rubbing two sticks together. A few seconds go by and a man comes through the spirit box saying what sounds like, "Help." We start walking through the cemetery and see a woman walking her dogs, I ask if the spirits knew what type of animal was there. No response, but in the past, I have received intelligent answers to that question.

I ask, "Do you like dogs?" A disembodied voice says, "No." Jourdan asks, "We came to visit you guys today … Can you tell us your name?" We got a few responses to this question. Here are the names that came through the spirit box; -Lars -Jason -Ed, then "Jason" is repeated. This is then followed by a loud raspy wheeze like sound.

I notice the woman's dog going to the bathroom and the woman bends down pretending to pick up the mess but doesn't. I let it be known that is one of my pet peeves. As I am talking about it, a man comes through saying, "Worse." Jourdan alerts us that the EMF meter is at 0.2. Seconds later, we get an EVP of a disembodied voice repeating Jourdan, "0.2" A woman comes through the spirit box saying quite clearly, "Mom." I ask, "What did you say?" A man says, "Dennis." Then a woman comes through and says, "Hurry."

Session three

As the crew walks around, I say, "A ton of people are buried here." We get an EVP of a man saying, "Yeah." A woman says, "Andy." Then a different woman speaks, saying quite clearly, "Tied." I say, "I heard there have been black mists reportedly seen here. Can you try to manifest yourself for us?" A man comes through the spirit box saying, "Really?" A different man says, "Okay." I turn the camera on to start taking pictures and record a video. Carly says, "She is going to take some pictures to try to see if she can catch a manifestation." A man comes through the spirit box whispering, "Fuck you."

We walk and stop in front of a grave that has the letter G on it and that's all, no dates, no name, nothing, just a G. Jourdan looks down at the plain headstone and says, "G? Don't know what it means." After she says this, we get a clear EVP from a man saying, "Ghost." Of course, we didn't hear this till after the fact.

We move on to a family lot. I read, "Schultz. Wilson. Lieberman." A man whispers in a raspy like voice this EVP, "Yes." I ask, "Can you tell us any of the names that are buried here on this lot?" A woman comes through the spirit box saying, "Mom!" Remember earlier a woman came through, also saying mom.

A man says what sounds like, "Here." Jourdan asks, "Is the Schultz family here with us?" An EVP of a man is recorded asking, "See it?" I see a small white object by the middle headstone. I walk up to it, point and I ask, "Can you tell me what I am standing right next to?" We get this amazing EVP from a man, a direct intelligent answer to our question, "Golf ball." Very low, quiet and in a whisper. Very easy-to-miss. That's exactly what it was. A family member must have put it there. How awesome! After the EVP, unexplained heavy breathing is recorded. An unexplained pop is then recorded.

We are still in the same area and disembodied music comes through the spirit box. A man comes through after the music and says, "Sing." We get an EVP from a child who sounds sad and in a panic-like voice is recorded saying, "Mommy!" I say, "We understand it takes a ton of energy to do something so if you cannot, we understand." A woman gives us this interesting EVP, whispering, "Homeless." A man comes through the spirit box saying, "Rick." A few seconds go by and the same man repeats the name, "Rick."

Jourdan looks at one of the headstones and asks, "Could this be Harry?" A man comes through the spirit box and says, "Yes." Quickly afterwards, "Yes" is repeated in an EVP. Jourdan lets us know it is 2:00, she has prior plans, so we start to slowly make our way towards the car, walking past countless graves. Some of whose owners we had just communicated with. As we walk, you can hear the crunching of leaves under our feet, and a gentle breeze passes by. Those are all sounds heard by us, but what goes unheard by our ears is a sound similar to a grunting pig.

We start to talk amongst one another about all the spirits we had communicated with. The rest of our walk back is quiet and uneventful. A couple unexplained pop noises. We got to the car and ended the investigation.

May 6, 2015
The investigation

This investigation was conducted by Jourdan Ortega and Tessa Mauro. Since we had several results at this historic cemetery we definitely thought it would be great to come back. May in Pueblo Colorado is perfect weather. Not cold, not too hot, and there was no wind that day.

Session one EVP session

Session one was quite uneventful. It only lasted about two minutes, we asked a few questions, got no results. All we got was a little unexplained pop.

Session two

Last time we came here we visited a man and his son, Thomas and Thomas, Jr. So, we thought we would come back to visit them again, since I believe we talked to both of them. I ask, "Can you talk to us? What's your name?" A man says what sounds like, "Coming south." That one I didn't understand, kind of made no sense but what happens next are numerous intelligent direct responses to our question. Names that came through the spirit box - Seth - Keith - Carl, all said by men. Then a woman comes through saying, "Me." I ask, "Can you repeat that?" The woman who just said, 'me' asks, "Who?"

Jourdan asks, "Tom, are you here with us?" A disembodied voice of a man says, "Free." I ask, "How did you die?" A man comes through saying, "War." Then a disembodied voice comes through saying what sounds like, "Noose." I ask, "We are hearing numerous voices coming through the spirit box. Can you specify to us who's talking?" Within about ten seconds, we get several responses. A voice comes through saying, "Me." A man says what sounds like, "Troy." Then another man says, "Bush." A deep exhale is recorded then followed by a man saying, "Ethel." The spirit box is turned off.

I say, "Is there anything you want to say to us? We're leaving this area now but know we will come back and visit you." An EVP of a woman is recorded saying, "Who? Me?" Followed by an unexplained noise of what sounds like a chain rattling.

Session three EVP Session

Like session one, nothing really came of this session. At the very end right before we ended this session a man is recorded giving an exasperated exhale. Obviously not hearing this, we ended it at that point. Bummer, I wonder if we kept recording if the man who exhaled would have spoken to us.

Session four

Another slow session, which is okay. A man came through the spirit box saying, "Hi" to us, that was about it. We headed out for the day and promised to come back. I guess now is a good time to mention this, since it just happened. Every investigation we have been lucky and have received generous amounts of evidence. However, there are many a times when there are no voices coming through, no answers to our questions, numerous pictures taken of nothing, and so on.

You may read this book and think, "Geez, every time they ask any questions they get a response of some kind." Well, what I am doing is just giving the results. These investigations are much longer and I don't want to bore you with stuff that have no results to it. Several questions go unanswered. There is a lot of dead air and just the typical sounds that come from a spirit box. I go through countless hours of audio, pictures taken, and other types of evidence.

Chapter ten

Moores Creek Battlefield, Near Wilmington, North Carolina

This battle could easily be one of the shortest battles of all time. Some say it lasted no longer then ten minutes. In reality, I think the time was about thirty minutes. This battle left many men wounded and thirty-one men lost their lives. The Moores Creek Battle was fought between the Loyalists and the Patriots.

The battle happened on a small bridge. The Loyalists, didn't expect such a large number of Patriots and were not fully prepared for what was to happen. Before the Loyalists arrived, the Patriots removed the planks from the bridge then smeared the remains of the bridge in lard making it quite difficult for the men.

The Loyalists, then had to slowly go across the bridge single file, making them far more vulnerable and very easy targets. This was quite an amazing battle. To learn more, look it up on line, or better yet, if you are in North Carolina and have yourself some time and want to learn something new, check out a battlefield. Go visit some time. I really recommend it. Inside is a short film to watch, then a small museum and a fun gift shop, then go outside and take the self-tour!

January 14, 2016
The investigation

This investigation was conducted by Tessa Mauro with her skeptic boyfriend Justin as an observer. It was a beautiful day in North Carolina and the weather was thankfully on the warmer side for being in January. After watching the video and checking out the museum, we walked outside and were happy to see we were the only ones there at that time.

I wanted to learn the history about this area but also, I wanted to try to do some mini sessions as well. We stood on the bridge where the battle took place, where countless men were injured and where thirty-one men met their fate.

I closed my eyes and tried to go back in time, back to February 27, 1776. Blood everywhere. Men are hurt, suffering, bleeding, in excruciating pain, and dying. Others fighting for their lives. Yelling, screaming, taking cover, firing their weapons. Who would survive and walk away from this and who would be unfortunate enough to breathe their last breath there? Since I was sort of solo on this investigation, I decided to do mini sessions, that's why these sessions are so short!

Session one EVP Session

I ask a handful of questions and am greeted with nothing but silence. I ask, "What side were you on?" Justin then adds, "Loyalists or Patriots?" An unexplained whistling sound is recorded and goes unheard by us. A few seconds go by and then the whistling is recorded again. Remember, no one else was around, we had the place to ourselves and Justin and I sure weren't whistling.

An unexplained foreign beep-like sound is recorded, followed by another strange sound as if one's hands are grasping for the recorder. I ask, "Can you tell us what your name is?" After this question is asked, while we didn't receive any intelligent answers to that question, a series of pops was caught on the recorder. I counted four pops. We of course, did not hear this. Again, the pop noise is another form of communication. I am not sure what it means.

Session two

Not much was recorded in this short session but while on the bridge a man is recorded breathing. Justin at the time was on the opposite side of the bridge waiting for me. That breathing did not come from me.

Session three

After we get over the Moores Creek Bridge, I stop, and I ask, "Is anybody here with us?" A man is recorded giving this EVP, saying, "Michael." As the man speaks, Justin starts to say something, and I regrettably snap at him and he walks away. As he walks away, I receive an EVP from a man saying, "Don't go." Then several seconds later, a woman is recorded speaking unintelligible words. You can hear the panic in her voice.

Session four

I ask, "Were you a Loyalist or a Patriot?" In the middle of my question, right after I say, 'Loyalist' we receive this EVP, very faint and distant, a whisper, "Yes."

As we start walking, we receive an EVP from a man saying, "You, come here." I ask, "What was your name?" Another man comes through saying, "Vic." An unexplained hiss-like noise is recorded. Then an EVP of a woman is recorded crying, "Help!" Seconds go by and the woman repeats herself, "Hel-Hel-Help!"

A faint echo-like voice is in the background whispering unintelligible words. It went unheard by myself and the whispering actually continued on until I stopped the recorder! The same voice spoke over numerous sweeping channels, I just wish I could understand what was being said!

Session five, The bridge

I am walking on the bridge and about to turn on the spirit box, when an EVP of a man is recorded saying, "Come here. Don't do it." The spirit box is turned on. I ask, "What's your name?" A man says, "Michael." Then a few seconds later, the same voice repeats itself, "Michael." Remember in session three, when I asked if anyone was there with us, we received an EVP of a man saying, "Michael." Seems like he followed us.

I ask, "Did you die in this battle?" Surprisingly, a woman comes through the spirit box saying, "Yes." Her voice was sad and panic-stricken. Who knows, perhaps she lost her husband, father, son, or brother to this battle. This is followed by a recorded unexplained pop.

Session six and Session seven

Again, not much action in these sessions, a series of questions answered with really no responses. A couple of times, heavy breathing from what sounded like a man was recorded. After Session seven, we head over to the burial and memorial of the Patriot who died, Private John Grady.

Session eight, Patriot memorial

The spirit box is turned on and sweeping through channels. I ask, "John Grady, can you say anything to us?" For the next several seconds, there is absolutely nothing. No EVP's, no static, no voices, nothing.

I read the memorial, "It says you fell bravely, fighting for your country. The first martyr and cause of freedom for North Carolina." A burst of wind passes through, and as quickly as it came, it was gone. Suddenly, this amazing EVP from a man is recorded, "You'll never run, you'll never know." After waiting a while longer and getting no spirit box results, I turn it off and I ask, "John Grady, can you tell me what you were? A patriot or a loyalist?" While I didn't receive an answer, a series of unexplained pops are recorded, as usual, unheard by us. Seven pops to be exact.

The final session, session nine
Monument of women

I say, "We are at the end of our tour," as I pause, we receive an EVP of what sounds like a woman whispering, "Yes." I continue, "We are at the Monument of Women. I was wondering if any heroic women are here with us right now?" I read, "Mary Slocomb, wife of Lt. Slocomb, riding alone at night, sixty-five miles to succor the wounded on this battle field. Her heroism places her very high on the pages of history."

At the beginning as I start talking, between Mary and Slocomb, a woman speaks unintelligible words, very faintly. Then, after I'm done reading what sounds like a woman breathing is recorded. I ask, "Mary are you here?" An unexplained whistle-like noise is recorded. I ask, "Are you with me right now Mary? I feel like I'm not alone." I get an EVP of a man sounding like he's speaking under his breath, "Who are you?"

I really enjoyed Moores Creek. We were so lucky to be the only ones there when we visited this battlefield. If you are near Wilmington, I recommend visiting, we learned a lot.

Chapter eleven

The Battle of Wyse Fork, Kinston, North Carolina

On March 7,1865 the Battle of Wyse Fork took place in Kinston, North Carolina. It ended on March 10,1865 with a victory for the Union. If you ever find yourself in Lenore County in North Carolina, go to the visitors' center, pick up a map and enjoy the driving tour. See where the battle was fought and where the Confederates lost. For more history on this battle between the Union and the Confederates, please go on-line.

January 25, 2016
The investigation

This investigation was conducted by Tessa Mauro. In Colorado, January is usually a much cooler month. In North Carolina, when I saw how cooperative the weather was, we decided to go check out some battlefields. North Carolina has plenty of them. Bentonville, Kinston, Moore's Creek, and Fort Macon to name just a few. We previously had gone to and enjoyed Moore's Creek so we were excited to see more. This day would be Battle of Wyse Fork.

Justin and I, knowing it was a driving tour decided that instead of keeping our dog cooped up in the house all day we would bring him along. Justin's mom and her dog joined us for the tour. Between Justin being a skeptic and the dogs I found myself sneaking away to conduct these investigations, so I wouldn't have any type of disturbance or manipulation of any kind. Some of the stops we made were by the roadside like some of the other sessions you've read about, some of these are also short.

Session One

A little information about this spot; nine-hundred Union troops were captured here, along with Union artillery, making this the most significant success of the Confederates during this battle. This battle was the second largest Civil War battle in North Carolina. Casualties: Union 1,101 and Confederates 1,500.

It's amazing how much civil war history lies right here in the state of North Carolina. People will go for a nice walk and find a musket ball. To this very day things are still being discovered here.

I walk off a short distance for some privacy and decide to conduct a little EVP session.

Mini EVP session

Me: Are there any Union Soldiers here with us?

Man: Yes.

Man: Put it up here.

Another man: Put it back.

Me: What's your name?

Man: Michael.

Michael. There's that name again. Last Chapter, while at Moore's Creek, we had a man introduce himself as Michael. I also have a deceased friend named Michael who is with me much of the time. Can this be my former friend or is this a soldier? I also asked what type of weapons they used for this battle and a man said, what sounds like, "Berts-Ah." I have no clue what that means.

Session two

I move on from the Union and try to ask some questions to the Confederates. I turn the spirit box on. Every question I ask goes unanswered. After several questions and no voices coming through the spirit box or no EVP's recorded, I turn the spirit box off. I say, "We just passed a three-story white house that served as the hospital back while this battle took place. Did you, or someone you know, die there?" No answers but three loud thump-like sounds were recorded going unheard by us.

I mention to Justin that I am going to walk off again to try another EVP session. His response is recorded. In addition to Justin's response, another man is recorded as well. The man says, "Okay" but more separated like, "Oh-Kay."

I ask, "If anyone is here with me, can you please talk to me? Speak right here into the device (recorder) that I'm holding." The man who said, 'Okay' is recorded giving this EVP, "I am." This is then followed by an unexplained pop.

Session three

A little history lesson about the site we are at right now; again I am finding this information in the pamphlet for the driving tour.

This site where we are about to conduct session three is where the Confederates line angled southwest. Across the road, past the line of trees, was an area that witnessed heavy battle. Evidenced by thousands of mini-balls, canon ball projectiles and every kind of artifact one could imagine. The grounds were saturated with lead.

I turn the spirit box on and after asking a few questions with no results, I turn it off and start a mini EVP session. Again, these are short because many times I am by the road, or too many disruptions. I ask, "Did you die in result from the Battle of Wyse Fork?" Several seconds go by, then a man gives this interesting EVP, "You'll see."

Many a time, I am on the site of an investigation and will suddenly feel a strong presence. This happens at this battle site and I try to encourage any spirits to come and speak to me by saying, "I have this recorder in my hand that will help me be able to hear you. Can you speak to me?" I receive an EVP from a man, possibly the same man who just spoke earlier saying, 'You'll see' and he says, "No."

Many men died during this battle, fighting for what they believed in, and paid the ultimate sacrifice. Whenever I am on a battle field I always feel strong intense energy there, trying hard to imagine what took place, but cannot even come close. This is a driving tour, so there are no necessary hours, come when you want to and do some investigating.

Chapter twelve

The Green Burial:
Angel Rock in Penitente Canyon
Saguache County, Colorado

I can't speak for the entire state of Colorado, but for Saguache County I can say my Grandpa *Chuck is the first LEGAL "Green Burial." Before he passed away, it was agreed upon that he be buried at my mother's ranch up in the beautiful Colorado Mountains. He was sick and unfortunately, he wasn't getting any better. He had diseases that were rapidly taking over his body and killing him.

In the state of Colorado, if you plan on doing a Green Burial, if the deceased is not getting embalmed, you have twenty-four hours from the time of death to bury the person. That's right, you have one full day from time of death till burial. When someone is buried, you must bury them six feet deep right? Surprisingly, my mother was told, no, that's incorrect. Legally, you only have to bury the body two feet down. They buried my Grandpa six feet anyway.

My mom told me her "Green" experience as I recorded her, so this is a word for word account. Here we go:

> Carly needed a regular twin bed that we had, so that day, we didn't know Grandpa was going to die that day of course, so we put the bed in the back of the truck and drove. It happened to be Carly's birthday. So, we drove to Alamosa. We had just brought up the twin bed and put it in her dorm and then took the cot out. We were putting the cot in the back of the truck when we got the call that Grandpa had passed away.
>
> Now, we had already done all the paper work, and it was in his file at the hospital where he was staying. It was an Elderly care place, like an assisted living, if you will. We stopped at the store, bought a beautiful cotton quilt and a dozen red roses. Then went to where Grandpa was, we had planned on going anyway to visit him. We were only fifteen minutes from seeing him when he passed, unfortunately.

So anyway, when we showed up, they had already tidied him up, I wanted to change his socks. There was something about it … I wanted to put socks on him, he was bare feet. Grandpa had diabetes, so with the diabetes, his feet and legs and calves were always swollen and purple. Very heavy, so heavy that he couldn't even walk in the end.

I went to lift his one leg, thinking that I'm really going to have to wrestle with it a little bit you know? It went up as light as a feather, it went up just so easily. I was able to put his sock on. I was like, 'My gosh! He's as light as a feather!' Then I just put that leg down, I lifted up that other leg and same thing so easy in the air. I was so amazed.

So, I wrapped him up in the quilt, and then put a rose in his hand, his hands were on his chest, and I put a rose in his hand. Then everybody in the place, they all wheeled him out, he was in his bed. They all wheeled him out there with us. We slid him, it was perfect because we had that cot from Carly's dorm in the back of the bed. *Mickey (my Stepdad), had straightened up the back of the bed, and then we were able to put him in the back of the truck bed.

We drove to the Town Clerk's home, the last thing I needed, we had already had all the paper work filled out … they actually gave us a death certificate early, which they never release. It was totally filled out, the town clerk told me to fill it out early and also, we needed a letter stating that dad wanted to be buried up on the property. At the time he was in and out of a coma. This was earlier, a couple weeks before, I said, 'What happens, you know, if my dad passes before I get his signature on here?' She goes, 'Well, you better hurry.' Later on, I found out that the family can make that decision for the person.

However, at the time, of course we had to wait a few days for Grandpa to be in his conscious state because he had already said he wanted to be buried there but I had to get his signature, which we got. It was in the file. The only other thing we needed was the Doctor's signature and the time of death then, the Town Clerk, we needed her signature.

I asked her, 'What happens if my dad passes away on a weekend or after hours?' She was so kind and gave me her personal phone number and home address and she said, 'You can come to my house.' Which is such a beautiful thing about small towns. So, after we picked up Grandpa, we drove to her house. I don't think she realized it, but dad was in the back of the truck!

I went in and sat down with her, filled out the papers, signed them, and then said, 'He died in Rio Grande County but is being buried in Saguache County, so I actually had to involve both counties. I am going to have to register his death in Saguache County tomorrow. I also have to GPS the grave, so they know exactly where it was.' So, down the road if anyone else ends up owning the property that they know that there is a legal burial on the property.

She signed the papers. On the way, we called a few family members that were in town like Cousin *Perry. Of course, Uncle *Chuck and Aunt *Meribyrd already knew, they were driving behind ... following us. Cousin Perry joined in and started following us, we called *Stephen and *Carol, they joined us. It seemed that a ton of cars ended up on the road with us, following us up here. Like a little procession. It just happened that way, we were calling them, and they were jumping in their cars and meeting us on the road. (They all knew time was critical!)

At this point I interrupt her to ask her something that was bouncing around in my head. Which is, when someone dies, and you are doing a green burial, instead of the funeral people—the ambulance or mortician—transporting the body themselves to the site of the burial, the family can take over the body and drive it themselves?

She replies.

"Yeah, see I think, they don't really know how to handle stuff like that. I acted like we knew what we were doing, and they kind of went along with it.

It's so unusual, that there's really no real protocol for that, if they don't have the book or instructions so, if somebody acts like, 'I'm taking the body.' I mean we had the papers signed, everything was in order. They knew it was going to happen when it did. We didn't know the legalities, if there was such a thing, I just don't know.

So anyways, we all met up at the ranch. *Bart was staying up here at the time, so he had the hole dug, he had the tiki torches. Three tiki torches behind the grave site and three solar lamps in front so nobody would get burned. We pulled the truck up to the house, and everybody met up there. Stephen brought a really old, really nice bottle of

> Whiskey. So, we all met here at the house. There were a few that didn't join the procession but came shortly after. Grandpa Chuck would always have the TV on, watching sports of course. So, I brought in a boom box, along with Dean Martin's love songs, which he absolutely loved.

I need to interrupt this and tell you something amazing just happened. So here I am listening to the recorder of my mom telling me this amazing experience about my Grandpa Chuck, her father, and two things happened. The first was when she mentioned Stephen bringing Whiskey; in the background a man can be heard as my mom is speaking. I cannot understand what he was saying, but after talking, whistling is also recorded.

The second thing, which just blew me away; my mom says, "Dean Martin's love songs, which he loved." Right after she says that, we receive an amazing EVP crystal clear from who I completely believe is my Grandpa saying, "I did." So close, he might as well have been standing right by my mom's side and speaking in the phone himself! Amazing!

My mom continues:

> So, when I would go see him, I would turn off the TV and would turn Dean Martin on. So, we took the boom box from his room with the Dean Martin love songs and brought it up here. We put it in the back of the truck and then Mickey slowly drove the truck over to the gravesite which is probably about an acre away. So, he drove slowly and we all walked behind it with Dean Martin's love songs playing.
>
> We got to the gravesite. You had e-mailed a letter to me for Grandpa, because you weren't able to be there.

I wanted to be there so badly, but at the time, I was in Northern California, and with less than 24 hours-notice, it was impossible for me to get there in time.

> There must have been ten of us because I had given dad a rose in his hand, everybody who was here got a rose and after I read your letter, what we did, we took Grandpa out of the truck and lowered him into the ground. Mickey and I carried him down there.
>
> It was interesting, he wasn't heavy at all, it was so easy. It didn't take much energy, I don't know, it's interesting. When they talk about dead

weight, it's not like your trying to move a big bag of potatoes, it was just very easy to maneuver him. There was a slope going down to the grave, we used the back hoe so we can walk down there.

We walked down and laid him down, tucked him in to the quilt, uncovered his face so we can give him a kiss and say good bye, Mike and I. We brought down Baby and Scooby, his dogs, so that they could say goodbye. Then we went up top, covered him up nicely, went up top. Stephen suggested, 'Maybe we should give him a shot of this Whiskey.' I say, 'No, you know what, Dad gave up drinking a few years earlier, I don't think I want to change that right now.'

So anyway, I read your letter, after I read your letter, I put the letter down there with him and tucked a rose down there for you. Then, we kind of went around, Uncle Chuck said some words, then he tucked his rose, then I said some words and tucked my rose in. We went around and everybody said something and put a rose in or said something quietly and put a rose in, but everybody there did a little something for him.

Then we took a bale of hay. Half of it was laid underneath him, we had already made a nice bed there before lowering him in, so we weren't just putting him in the cold earth. It was a comfy, fluffy, warm, straw bed. Then we put the other half and fluffed it on top of him, so it wasn't like this heavy earth would go on top of him. It made me feel better. Then your Uncle Chuck took the first shovel-full and put it in, then I did and then we kind of went in a circle, taking turns.

We kept filling up the grave until it was full, then we moved the tiki torches from behind it and put it right on top of it, gathered rocks that were there at the time and did a circle around it. We came over to the house and got a bonfire going, got the bottle of Whiskey, Grandpa … I used to know exactly when he died, I think it was 3 or 4 in the afternoon. We had him buried 8 that evening. So, within four or five hours of his death we had him buried.

We grabbed that bottle of Whiskey, lit the bonfire and we talked; stories about Grandpa till two in the morning. Everybody was there talking. So that was the burial, that was the deal. Basically, everybody there, we must have done something right because out of the ten or eleven people that were there, eight of them asked if they can be buried up there too in the same way!

I asked her how much it cost her to do this green burial for my Grandpa, her father, the answer surprised me. She replies:

> In the end which is interesting, it cost $85. That included the death certificate and the quilt that he was wrapped in AND the roses. In these days, you cannot get away from a burial for less than eight to ten grand.

As mentioned earlier, when my Grandpa died I was unfortunately stuck in California. Having to bury him in twenty-four hours, it was impossible for me to make it. Later that summer, most of the family were there for a family reunion so we were able to have a little memorial there for all to join. It was neat. We each had picked a beautiful crystal, quartz, or other neat rock. Some spoke, as we did, we put the rock down. I even made like a pamphlet, those that you are handed when you attend a funeral.

The Investigation
December 22, 2015

This investigation was conducted by my mom, Carly and Tessa Mauro. I guess when I do investigations for my grandpa and loved ones visited at cemeteries, it's more like a recorded visitation, with the deceased responding.

Carly and I were at my mom's and stepdad's ranch, where Grandpa Chuck happens to be buried. We were going for a walk, visiting all the animals on the property—which is a lot. After the walk, we went to go visit Grandpa. I had brought along the spirit box and the recorder because earlier I had asked my mom if she would be interested in doing a session and she was. She was curious to see the results we'd receive.

Being that it was December, and we were in the cold Colorado Mountains, we decided to do shorter sessions. There were blue skies with some clouds, but boy was it chilly. We also stopped sooner than we would have because my stepdad and his friend started construction on a project.

Results and evidence collected
Session one

For about the first minute all that really is heard is a light wind passing by us.

I first start off by explaining to my mom that when she asks a question to wait a considerable amount of seconds. Like me, I ask a question and will wait for about twenty seconds or sometimes longer. I can spew out dozens of words in seconds; that's not the case with spirits. It takes a lot of energy to speak and I always acknowledge that and thank them. While doing these visitations/investigations with my Grandpa Chuck, we didn't get many EVP's. While we did get a few, I believe he was more a communicator via sound.

Mom first starts off by asking, "How are you doing Pompano?" Immediately after asking this a man is recorded exhaling. The only people here are my mom, sister, and myself. That exhale came from a man and very close to the recorder. We never hold the recorder close to our faces. After several seconds, my mom asks another question, "Are you reunited with your mom, dad, brother, and sister?" While we do not receive an EVP, we do catch on recording, chew-like sounds.

Session two

We get some unexpected visitors and I don't mean the spiritual kind. I mean the furry kind that demand attention and might possibly drool on you while doing so. We take a moment to gather the herd of my mother's loyal furry pups and send them on their way up the hill to the cabin. Treats my friends. Always offer treats.

Carly asks, "Hey Grandpa Chuck, do you know … do you remember what day you died?" No voices, but an unexplained static is recorded, unheard by us. She asks this question because, as mentioned earlier, he passed away on her birthday. What first was a day of happiness and celebration quickly turned into a day of mourning and depression.

She told me she doesn't even feel like celebrating her birthday anymore because she will always know he died on her birthday. I told her that he was sick, his body full of disease, he was in a lot of pain, and not himself anymore. I told her that on her birthday he thought it was time not to be in pain anymore. I told her that she should still celebrate her birthday and mourn the death of grandpa the day before or the day after her birthday.

Even, me myself, when the day before his death and her birthday approach, I do a memorial online for him and I save the next day for my sweet sister. It is sad that he passed away on her birthday but he is no longer in pain. She has since celebrated her birthday again ... thankfully.

I ask Grandpa, "Can you say any of our names?" While we don't receive an EVP, several small things take place and are recorded after I ask that question. First static interference, just a quick burst, then one of those unexplained pop sounds. This is followed by more static finally ending with a deep exhale. All of these things went unheard by us.

Our mom asks, "Pompano, who's buried by your sides?" Again, no voices but static. It's clear when we talk amongst ourselves or are in the middle of asking a question, but boy when it is his turn to answer, the static shows up. Before my Grandpa died he had two small dogs. He loved them very much and when he died my mom kept them with her and her sweet brood of ranch animals at the ranch. They passed away, I think, within a year of my Grandpa's passing. My mom buried Scooby on one side and when Baby died, she buried her on his other side.

Mom asks, "Are you hanging around watching over us?" We receive an EVP of a man, who I believe to be my Grandpa saying, "Most days." This is followed by a pop.

It was interesting, that when we asked questions, in response, we were getting static. This happened to us at Rock Creek Cemetery. We asked questions and we had the metal on metal noise responding back to us. One of the ways to communicate is through noise.

Session three

My Grandpas, on both maternal and paternal sides, were avid golfers. My mom put one of his old golf clubs on top of his grave. I pick it up and ask, "Grandpa, can you tell me what I'm holding right now?" Soon after I ask this my recorder catches an EVP of the man who spoke earlier in session two and he says two words. The first word is "Golf" the second word is unintelligible. This is followed by a short breath and ends with a clank-like-sound. All unheard by us.

I tell him that one of my mom's new rescue dogs looks a lot like his beloved Chihuahua, Baby. Unexplained sounds are recorded, which sound like chewing. Now honestly, this can either be Baby herself, who is buried on site with my Grandpa; it can be my Grandpa; or something else altogether. The man gives this EVP, "Yes." I continue on, "Can you tell us the name of your dog?" Yet another EVP from the same man is recorded. He says, "Head home." Unsure what that means. Now, this is my mother's property, maybe he is saying he is done talking for the day and it's time for us to retire and walk up the road back to the home—head home. Just speculation.

My mom was always there for my Grandpa, especially in his later years. My Uncle Chuck, Aunt Meribyrd, and my mom were fortunate enough to live very close to him in his last remaining years, so they were always checking up on him and so on. My mom always wished that she and her father could have been closer and have had a normal father/daughter relationship, but he was gone much of the time.

She asks him, in a kind of kidding way, "Who was your favorite child?" Immediately after asking this question, several different, small things happened and were caught on the recorder. What was a decent day at the beginning of our investigation/visitation, soon became dark. A bright lightening volt shows itself in the distance followed by a loud clap of thunder. Got to love Mother Nature. We laugh and I kid around saying, "Geez mom, I think that's his way of saying it sure wasn't you!" A few pops are then recorded. I counted four.

Then, for several seconds, heavy breathing from a man is recorded. This breather is very close to the recorder—something I learned the hard way, several years back, never to do. The recorder capturing every breath, and finally, ending with an exasperated exhale.

I ask my Grandpa if he has had any regrets in his life and a loud static is recorded. Loud enough where you'd hear it from an adjoining room. This goes on for a few seconds and as the static stops the man's voice is heard saying, "Would." Once again, the recorder catches a man breathing, quite loudly and very close. A pop is recorded soon after.

End of investigation.

February 29, 2016 (Leap year)
The investigation

This investigation was conducted by Tessa Mauro and her mom. After spending the morning tending to and visiting all the ranch animals, my mom and I thought it would be a good time to go visit Grandpa and see if we could reach out to him again. It seems to have been quite a mild winter, at least for February and March. We go down to the site where he is and notice we have a parade of my mom's beloved animals following us. This includes goats, geese, chickens, dogs, cats, and one of her mini ponies.

We reach Grandpa's grave. Mom decides to bring the dogs up to the cabin and close them in, so they don't interrupt us. The others follow with promise of treats and I am left alone. I decide to stay down with Grandpa as she does this. The first three sessions I am alone, on the fourth, my mom is back.

Results and Evidence Collected
Session one EVP Session

I ask, "Is there anything you'd like to say to me?" No responses. In the background what can be heard are the farm animals. Geese squawking at each other, roosters making their annoying cock-a-doodle-doo sounds, echoing through the canyons.

I say, "Grandpa if you want to let me know that you're here but don't have enough power or strength to talk," as I pause a man is recorded taking a breath. I continue, "Walk up to me, and this thing that's on my knee, touch it. The—" Again a man is recorded breathing. I keep talking, "—Antenna like this." Another breath from the man is recorded.

Session two

As I sit alone talking to my Grandpa, I think of the memories I have with him and I feel a presence. I ask him, "Grandpa Chuck, are you here with me right now?" No EVP response but two unexplained pops are recorded. The Mel EMF reads the temperature outside at being 49 degrees. Not bad for winter in the mountains of Colorado. I repeat my question, "Are you with me Grandpa?"

No pops this time, instead breathing from a man is recorded. I ask a few more questions with no responses. I sit in silence just enjoying being with my Grandpa. As this is taking place unexplained footsteps are recorded. I am sitting on a short tree-stump-turned-seat, not moving at all, and my mom has yet to come back down. There are no animals around, just me.

As I sit, I notice it's silent. No sounds from the animals, which is rare, no wind or breeze, no nothing. I say aloud to myself, "Silence." Right before I say this an unexplained pop is recorded and right after I say this another pop is recorded. After asking a few more questions with no results, I end the session.

Session three, EVP session

I say, "Okay Grandpa, I want to ask a series of questions and then I will be silent and let you talk, or breath, whatever you want to do. If I don't respond right away, that means I haven't heard it yet, but when I listen later I will hear it okay? So, do you miss me? Do you miss my mom? Do you wish you were still here? Are you reunited with family and friends? With your dogs?" As I pause in between questions, an unexplained bang-like noise is recorded. As I continue, "Any regrets in life?" An EVP of a man faintly saying, "Yes" is recorded.

It stays rather silent for about a minute or so, then a pop sound is recorded, this is followed by an EVP of possibly the same man saying, "Don't cry." Then a deep breath is recorded. I see my mom walking down the hill towards me, so I end this session, so that when she gets here we can start a fresh session.

Session four

As we start session four, I begin to speak and as I do this, a disembodied voice is caught on recorder saying, "Stop. Stop." My mom asks, "Pompano, how are you doing?" An EVP is recorded but it's a hushed whisper, as if one is speaking under their breath, so not to be heard. My mom asks a handful of questions and no further results are recorded in this session.

Session five

For this session we turn the spirit box on. I look down at the Mel EMF and notice that the temp is now up to 56 degrees, when I first started it was 49 degrees, it's definitely warming up! Mom asks, "Are you with your mom and dad?" An EVP is recorded of the same man who's been speaking, and he says, "No." As we sit here talking to my Grandfather, footsteps are recorded. Again, we are both sitting on tree-stumps-turned-chairs, no one else is around, at least nothing living.

My mom asks if she can hold the Mel meter, when I was holding it the temp was 56.0 and immediately when I handed it to her it went down to 47. She, not knowing the immediate change, says, "Let me know you're here dad, so I know if I should even come to visit you." I let her know the change, suggesting that he is letting us know, her getting a cold spot. Yes mom, definitely go visit him.

Session six, EVP session, final session

Mom asks, "Pompano, are you having fun with your dogs, Scooby and Baby?" Quickly after she asks this, a disembodied purr-like noise is recorded. I instruct my mom to touch a certain object that is lying on top of his grave. She picks it up and I ask, "Grandpa, what is my mom touching right now? What is she holding? Can you tell us?"

Several seconds go by then a disembodied voice of a man gives this EVP, "Golf club." Absolutely amazing! That is exactly what she is holding. Remember in another investigation, on another day, I asked the same thing as I was holding the very same golf club and he too answered that question.

I start to talk about golf and an unexplained purr-like noise is recorded. I ask, as the purring is still going, "Do you remember that at all?" The purr continues, then an EVP is recorded, "Somebody" whatever did the purring continued, as the EVP, 'somebody' was recorded. We didn't hear the purring, none of my mom's animals were in the area this took place.

While dogs usually do not purr and it's more the feline that does so, I myself have borne witness to a dog purring. When my boyfriend Justin scratches my dog's ear just right, he sure does purr like a cat. So, this is possible that the purring we caught on audio could easily have been one of my Grandpa's dogs Baby or Scooby, for they are buried here as well.

Chapter thirteen

The Sloss Furnaces, Birmingham, Alabama

This historic landmark has been on a few paranormal TV series like 'Ghost Adventures' and one of my personal favorites, 'Ghost Asylum.' This location has always piqued my interest. It is reported that the Birmingham Police stay quite busy with the Sloss Furnaces establishment, having over 100 recorded reports of paranormal and unexplainable activity that has happened there. I always wanted to go and check it out when I was traveling through and found by chance that the Sloss Furnaces happened to be less than three miles from my hotel, I knew I had to go.

The problem? I had a ten-hour drive ahead of me that day. They didn't open till 10 a.m. Usually I'd be on the road by around 6 a.m. I had to really tug at the idea. I'm this close and I might not be able to enjoy this amazing place. I slept on it and woke up energized, excited, and not caring if I have a late start to my traveling plans. I am going to Sloss Furnaces today.

I was so excited that instead of staying at the hotel—The Tutwiler Hotel, also a haunted location, also in the book—and relaxing in my room till close to 10 am, I was anxious, and not wanting to be in traffic, I drove the short drive to Sloss and waited for them to open in a parking lot across the street. I called Justin and even though I woke him up he was kind enough to stay on the phone and keep me company as I patiently waited for Sloss to open.

When you first pull into the gates of Sloss Furnaces you take a left and follow the small road. You see the back of the furnaces and it is quite an extraordinary sight. There's parking so you can pull over and snap a few pictures of the area. You continue to the parking lot and you must sign-in at the desk before walking around. They hand you an info booklet. While there, check out the little museum there, it's free, and you learn a lot too.

The gift shop is fun also. I found some neat souvenirs, including awesome things made of cast iron by employees who work at Sloss—a piece of history I'm proud to say I own. I walked around and watched some of the workers. It was awesome, they were so passionate at what they were doing. To be able to work at a place like this must be so rewarding!

A little history about the place:

> (I would just like to note that what you are about to read, regarding the history, I am re-writing bits and pieces from the booklet they gave me and the book I bought in the gift shop.)

In the early 1860s, James Withers Sloss, realizing the need for expansion of southern rail lines, became active in the railroad construction. During this post-Civil War period, Sloss not only promoted the expansion of southern rail lines but he became one of the chief proponents of Alabama's post-war industrial development, most notably the area around present day Birmingham.

During the 1880s, as pig iron production in Alabama rose from 68,995 to 706,629 gross tons, no fewer than nineteen blast furnaces would be built in Jefferson County alone. The second of these furnaces would be built by James Withers Sloss. Construction of Sloss's new furnace began in June 1881, when ground was broken on a fifty-acre site that had been donated by the Elyton Land Company.

Harry Hargreaves, a European born engineer, was in charge of construction. Hargreaves had been a pupil of Thomas Whitwell, a British inventor who had designed the stoves that would supply the hot-air blast for the new furnace.

Sixty feet high and eighteen feet in a diameter, Sloss's new Whitwell stoves were the first of their type ever built in Birmingham and were comparable to similar equipment used in the North. Birmingham industrialists were impressed that much of the machinery used by Sloss's new furnace would be manufactured in the South.

This machinery included two blowing engines and ten boilers. Although the enormous boilers were too complex to be built in Birmingham, they were made in the South. Walton & Company, located in Louisville, completed the task in time for the opening in 1882. After only its first year of operations, Sloss Furnace Company had sold 24,000 tons of iron. At the 1883 Louisville Exposition, the company won a bronze medal for "Best Pig Iron."

James W. Sloss not only exported his iron, but he managed to supply large amounts for local agricultural purposes. The majority of Sloss pig iron, however, ended up in Cincinnati, Louisville, St. Louis, Nashville, Chicago,

Detroit and Cleveland. Pig iron costs in Northern plants averaged $18.30 per ton in 1884 while pig iron in the South could be produced for $10-$11 a ton.

This is just a mere fraction of what is in the book, there is so much more information and history to learn about. I recommend anybody who is in the area (Birmingham, Alabama) to please take time to visit this spectacular landmark. Take a self-guided tour—I love those—go at your own pace, chat with the people there—they are so friendly and very knowledgeable—run into a ghost or two. Whether you are there for a history lesson, for the paranormal, a national historic landmark lover, or all the above, this place is a must-go!

In the Self-Guided tour booklet, you learn about all the equipment like the boilers, the hot blast stoves, the pig castor and so much more!

February 27, 2016
The investigation

I was watching some of the workers on site and how they were using the cast iron and one of the workers, a sweet woman, walked up to me when she saw me watching and greeted me, I told her I was a paranormal investigator and while I was here to enjoy a tour, I was also trying to see if I can get any results here at this famous well known haunted landmark. She told me to go to the Boilers. The one right in front of us, was responsible for men's deaths. She continued to tell me that their remains are still in the boiler including the iron they died trying to retrieve.

It was just a few minutes after opening their gates to the public and many people were already there—so much for the early bird thing. I didn't want to be overly obvious with a ton of equipment, so I left everything in the car except for my digital recorder. I also had my phone and camera. Knowing what I know now, I'm wishing I would have brought the rest of the equipment. I didn't spend much time at the Boilers because there was music on in the back ground where the employees were and background chatter.

I stayed and enjoyed the area, then continued on. I walked up to a man who had helped me earlier on and asked where I should go if I were interested in the paranormal. He mentioned the Tunnel and pointed me in the right direction. I crossed my fingers, hoping nobody else was in the tunnel and I made my way down the path and off to my right I hear dripping and I look and there is what I assume to be the tunnel. It is very dark, sprayed in graffiti are the words, "Watch your head" I make my way down, wishing I had a flashlight. While many people were at Sloss enjoying the landmark, I had the tunnel to myself. Yes! Just what I was hoping for!

I use my camera's flash to try to make my way down the steps leading to the tunnel. It's so dark the pictures turn out hazy and creepy. I hear constant dripping of water and hope I don't step into a puddle. As I make my way down the steps, all while 'watching my head', I notice lights in the tunnel. Even though it's dark going in, there is light at the end of the tunnel! I have to say the tunnel was my favorite. I got amazing results down there. While I was in the South, it was obviously a warm day and the tunnel was warm. I ran into a major cold spot and while this was happening I received one of the best EVP's I have ever collected.

I cannot begin to say what this place means to me, by the time I left I was ecstatic. I was so happy that I decided to stay and not leave earlier that morning, for I know, I would have majorly regretted that decision. I plan on going back sometime in the future.

Results and evidence collected

Before I started, I walked over to Boiler One, imagining men working high above and falling to their deaths. I turn on the recorder and start talking and almost immediately a strange sounding unexplained breathing is recorded. I'm explaining since there is music and people talking in the background I will head to another area on the Sloss Furnaces' grounds. I do ask if someone is with me and I receive an EVP, "Yes."

I just want to note, that since I do not have the spirit box with me, all the words spoken are EVPs and I do not hear them until later on. I hope you enjoy this chapter as much as I enjoyed this experience.

As I am heading towards the tunnel, I am recording. I say session three even though the last recordings, including this one, are only a few seconds, hence why I am not counting them as sessions, but as it records, and I am walking, I say, "Session three." As I pause, I receive an EVP of a man whispering, "What do you want?" I continue, "I'm heading over to the tunnels." The same man says, "Stop." As I continue walking a strange breathing is recorded. Amazing!

Session one, Tunnel

As I am in the tunnel, I look around and say aloud to myself, "This place is pretty creepy." An EVP of a hushed, unintelligible whisper is recorded. I turn on my camera to take pictures, as I am doing this, a faint voice, which almost sounds like the voice who spoke to me earlier says, "Don't go." I say, "Since we are down here, you will really have to speak up." As I pause, an EVP is recorded of a man saying, "No."

I ask a few other questions such as 'Did you work here at Sloss Furnaces?' 'Did you die here?' 'How did you die?' 'What was your name?' with no answers or responses. When I was introducing myself as a paranormal investigator words were spoken, unintelligible words. Then at the end of this session footsteps were recorded but I was standing in place, and nobody else was down in the tunnel with me, or so I thought.

Session two, Tunnel

I say, "I would love to get an EVP from you." Unexplained breathing is recorded. I continue, "If you're talking and I'm not responding," as I pause, I receive an EVP saying what sounds like, "I … Hate." I continue, "When I listen to this afterward, I will hear you. So, tell me anything you'd like to say." The voice replies giving this EVP, "Okay."

I ask, "Is there anything you'd like to say?" I receive this eerie EVP from what sounds like the same voice, instructing me, or possibly warning me, "Turn around and run." As I am standing in silence, surrounded by dripping water suddenly a hushed voice says, "No." Then unexplained breathing close by is recorded, suddenly my recorder is overwhelmed by the loud sound of static, of course this goes unheard by me, it always does.

I receive a series of short EVPs, "Okay." A few seconds later, "I'm okay." A couple more seconds go by, "Okay." Then shortly after that, "I'm okay." An unexplained sound is recorded, what I can only describe as someone having trouble breathing and gasping for air. I ask, "What is your name?" Again, I receive a series of EVPs. The first being, "Ghosts." Then I receive an EVP of a man saying an unintelligible word, what sounds like, "Herimogi" (Hear-ah-moe-gee) but I am not sure, I can be wrong, not sure what this means. Possibly a last name or a nickname? A few seconds go by, then I receive this interesting EVP, "I'm a ghost." Several seconds pass by then what sounds like the same voice is recorded repeating himself, "I'm a ghost."

This whole session is amazing but what happens next stayed with me my entire trip back home to Colorado. I ask, "How did you die?" I get this sad EVP, of a man saying, "Wrong place" then the voice gets fainter, it's easy to miss, but what sounds like, "at the wrong time." As this is happening, I experience a cold spot, and in response to that cold spot, I say, "Woah!" Another EVP is recorded, "Ghosts." Silence for a few seconds. I continue, "It got really cold all of a sudden when it wasn't earlier." I am in the South, during the summer, in a tunnel that is warm, so the cold spot was pretty damn noticeable.

While this was happening, besides my recorder being on, I had my phone recording a video so one can see how the tunnel looked—the creepiness, the water dripping, the darkness—the video doesn't do it justice. When I was down there it was eerily calming to me. I didn't want to leave. It's almost as if something or someone was holding me back. There were a few times where I would start to leave, then I'd look back and find myself walking back down there.

Since I felt a cold spot—not knowing about the EVP—once I was out of the tunnel after the sessions, I listened to the phone recording and after I asked the question, 'How did you die?' a voice is heard, followed by me announcing a cold spot. When I heard the voice on the phone, I prayed that the digital recorder caught that voice and I can get a better audio of what it said, and it did.

This tunnel is a hot spot, or as I experienced, a cold spot, for spirits, especially EVP, electronic voice phenomena, activity. Like this one, "Ghosts. Ghosts … Ghosts." They sure were quick to tell me ghosts were down there. Then what almost sounds like a woman but unsure, "Ghoooooosts." Followed by a moan and then a series of 'Go' is spoken. "Go." A few seconds go by then, "Don't be afraid." This is followed by the EVP, "Go, go, go." A few seconds later a more urgent, "Go!"

I ask, "How did you die?" I receive this EVP, "Big Alice." Big Alice. When I heard this, it didn't mean anything to me, I had no clue what it meant. My first thought was an angry wife or a girlfriend. I looked on line to see if that had any meaning at Sloss Furnaces, and boy I was surprised. This is what I found while researching Big Alice:

Big Alice is the highest furnace at Sloss. There are at least 60 known deaths at Sloss. They say forty-seven of them are linked to an evil sadistic man named James Robert Wormwood, nick-named "Slag." Wormwood was a plant manager, from 1886 until the time of his death in 1899, word is that he fell off the catwalk and straight into molten ore.

Sounds like justice to me. He liked to manhandle and push around other men to their untimely deaths, like I said, justice.

I must say, I love when I get an EVP of something that might, at first, not make sense but after doing research it all comes together. Big Alice baby.

Session three, Tunnel

After session two, before I could start session three, I heard a voice coming from the darker part of the tunnel. Again, I was by myself in the tunnel this whole time. If other people came down, I would have left so not to taint any evidence.

I start, "Unfortunately this wasn't recording," an EVP of a whisper, "Oh." Followed by an exasperated breath. I continue, "but I heard what sounded like a voice. Coming from back over here." As I stop talking, I receive an EVP from a spirit who I believe has been down here the whole time saying what sounds like, "How did you know?" Two unexplained thump-like noises are recorded followed by a disembodied cry.

Session four, Tunnel

Again, I hear something while the recorder is off. I ask, "I just heard something again, is somebody here with me?" An EVP of a man whispering what sounds like, "Yeah" is recorded. As I stand in silence, trying to see if I receive any EVPs, this man speaks giving me this EVP, "Wait." He speaks this slowly, so it sounds more like, "Waaaaittt." Unexplained shuffling sounds are recorded, followed by this EVP of the same man saying, "Wait here."

I say, "This place is absolutely amazing." As I pause, I receive this EVP, "What!" As if in shock that someone would find such a dark wet place to be 'amazing.' As I leave the tunnel unexplained breathing is recorded. In the distance a train can be heard.

Session five, Boilers

Three girls were singing in the Boiler area, so I just recorded without talking and waited for them to finish singing. A few times in this short period unexplained breathing was recorded. The girls and other visitors were a short distance from where I was, so the breathing wasn't from them nor myself. When there is silence I say, "If there is someone here with me, I'd really like it if you talked to me." I receive an EVP of a spirit asking, "Why?" I say, "I'm sorry that you died here." The same voice gives me another EVP saying, "It's okay." I continue to speak, "It must have been really scary." Again, I get a reply, "Yessss." This is followed by loud unexplained breathing from a man recorded.

The girls start singing again and more people are coming so I try to find a more secluded area, but without having much luck. As I am searching for another area to go to, an unexplained pop noise is recorded. I say aloud to myself, "I can see how someone can easily fall to their deaths here." A man is recorded, breathing, almost like a wheeze.

Since I had a long drive ahead of me, I forced myself to stop doing sessions and drag myself to my car. I really didn't want to leave. It's like an unseen entity was trying to make me stay … just like how I didn't want to leave the tunnel. With all the results I got without all my equipment there, can you imagine what I would have received if I used all the equipment? I really do plan on going back to Sloss Furnaces sometime, and you should go too.

Chapter fourteen

The Tutwiler Hotel, Birmingham, Alabama

A little history ...

This beautiful hotel opened back in 1914. In fact, when I was staying there back in late February one of the hotel employees told me it was close to the 102nd anniversary for the hotel. The hotel was known for hosting high profile events including a press conference for Charles Lindbergh.

Speaking to a few of the employees, who were very friendly and full of knowledge about this historical hotel, I learned about a spirit, thought to be a man, who knocks on doors of the rooms of hotel guests. The hotel is also thought to be haunted by Major Tutwiler himself! In 1986 Tutwiler bought the hotel and started a complete renovation of the building. That my friends, is when paranormal activity started happening. That's known to happen. Renovating a structure of any type seems to do that. I have seen that and have personally experienced it at other places as well.

The investigation
February 26, 2016

A couple of years ago for Christmas, for one of my presents, my little sister Carly had given me a book, of haunted places you can visit—a state-by-state guide. I love it. It's very handy and convenient to have. When I was traveling from North Carolina to Colorado, I had planned on going through Kentucky but when Justin had looked the night before my travels, it seems that Kentucky had recently gotten a lot of snowfall. Snow. Last thing I wanted to deal with before my 1,920 mile drive back.

I decided to go a different route, which included Birmingham, Alabama. Birmingham was my destination for the first night. While I had picked a few things from the book that I would have liked to have seen in Louisville, Kentucky—like the Waverly Hills Sanatorium—I looked at the book and noticed Tutwiler hotel, which was one of the hotels I was considering staying at. Seeing the hotel in the book kind of sealed the deal for me.

It was a little more expensive then I would have liked it to be, but I stayed, and it was worth it, the hotel people were friendly and accommodating. The hotel itself was absolutely beautiful and within its walls spirits roamed, and history seeped out. When I arrived, I spoke with a woman at the counter and she was quite friendly. In fact, I came down a couple times just to chat with her, when she wasn't busy with guests and check-ins'.

After we had my room sorted and I was walking away, I thought about going back and asking about the spirits of this hotel. I turned around to walk back to the desk, but the woman was gone. A man, who I found out was the hotel manager, was there. I asked him about ghosts and telling him I wanted to do some paranormal investigating. He told me, "You want a room on the sixth floor then." I reply that I had already been checked in. He replies, "Let me see the card." I hand over the hotel card, he takes a quick look, "Oh no, this won't do. Let me change that for you." With a few taps on the keyboard I was soon upgraded to the sixth floor for some paranormal action.

It was interesting. It seemed like during sessions here, I would look at the recorder thinking it would just be a minute or two and be shocked when it was six minutes. It seemed like time didn't matter here. Also, when I walked into the elevator to go downstairs to have dinner, something happened. This is hard to explain. I was in the elevator, I already made a few trips in the elevator that evening but this ride was different. It seemed to have stopped or been stuck. For at least one minute there was no sound, no movement, nothing.

I didn't panic. I stayed quiet. I pushed a button and that seemed to do the trick. The elevator was moving again and that was that. Suddenly, I start to feel very light headed and very dizzy. At that moment I almost felt like I was in a drunken stupor. I couldn't walk a straight line and I had to grab the railing in fear that I may fall. It was very interesting to me. I was driving all day, so I did not have a drop of alcohol in my system. I couldn't figure out what was happening. When the doors open to the lobby, I walk to the desk, feeling better, then it hits me again, but just for a moment.

This has never happened to me before and thankfully it hasn't happened since. I don't know if this was paranormal or something else, but I feel I had to share this weird experience.

As for the knocker ghost, I did hear knocks. Unfortunately, every time I heard knocks I was in the bathroom. I heard knocks while using the bathroom, I heard knocks while I was in the shower also. If I was in the room itself I would have been able to answer the door to see if a person was there, or something else. Sadly, I have to debunk these knocks, though they could have been paranormal, but I am not 100% sure since I couldn't check it myself.

Results and evidence collected
Session one, Room 604,

One thing I liked about this hotel, besides the history of course, was that I didn't hear other hotel guests every few minutes. I tell you, I was in New Orleans a couple months back and wow, I heard every single thing from my neighbors. EVERY. SINGLE. THING.

I sit on the floor and get comfortable. With the recorder on the table by the bed, I ask, "Hi, my name is Tessa. Can you tell me what your name is?" A pop sound is recorded. Really, I don't know what these pop sounds are, but I get them often and again, never hearing it until after I listen to the recording. The pop is followed by a disembodied moan.

I ask, "How did you die?" The recorder caught a woman speaking two unintelligible words. As I sit in silence a man is recorded breathing heavily, sounding like he's very close to the recorder. This is then followed by another pop. I ask a few more questions, with no results and say, "I'm going to end session one now." A raspy whisper is recorded saying, "No." Sounding like it's speaking under its breath.

Session two, EVP session

I feel a presence in the room and start a mini EVP session. I grab the Mel EMF meter and turn it on and situate it. I then tell the spirits what this tool is used for and demonstrate that it won't hurt them but will show me that they are there. I then sit there and wait in silence. While the Meter sees no action at the moment, my recorder does capture a clink-like-sound.

This sound reminds me of wine glasses gently touching each other, like one does to salute or cheers. This is then followed by muffled breathing, which sounds like a woman.

Session three, EVP session

At first, as I was listening to the recording, a man is heard talking, after a few seconds, my voice pours through the speaker debunking this, there are people talking down the hallway.

In these investigations, there is a ton of debunking going on. I found out the hard way earlier on when we just started doing this. Someone was breathing heavily then whispered something to themselves. Listening to it later on, it took me quite a while to figure out that it was a living person and not something paranormal. In the end I would've had to debunk it anyway if I couldn't have figured it out.

Something that is not shown here in the investigations, again, boring details, are the debunks. Walking, coughing, sneezing, laughing, stumbling, etc. Now if someone speaks, they speak loudly, so there is no doubt who is talking. Coughing, the cougher will say, "Jourdan cough." The sneezer will say, "Carley sneeze". You get the idea. Anyway, you learn from your mistakes, or at least try to. If there's a noise in the background that we hear with our own ears, we say what it is, because if we don't and I listen to it later, it jots down as something paranormal when it is not at all.

It's very important, as you can see, the man talking in the hall was debunked immediately. It's been a couple months since that visit in Alabama so when I heard that voice just now I got excited thinking EVP, and that debunk helped.

Back to the investigation ...

Since there is talking in the background from the people in the hall, so not to taint my evidence, I kindly ask, "There are people in the hall talking, can you come right up to this recorder and speak as loud as you can, so I can hear you?" An unexplained noise is recorded. What sounds like a ding or a foreign like beep.

The EMF reads at 1.0, I ask, "Is that you?" A few seconds later the EMF makes an alert beep noise. I suggest, "If you really want to see many neat colors, come and touch this antenna." Almost immediately after I say this, the EMF lights up and makes a series of the alert beep like noises.

Session four, EVP session

I ask a variety of questions with no EVP's recorded. However, unexplained breathing was caught quite a few times, from who I believe to be a woman or possibly a child.

Session five, EVP session

Right before this session started the EMF read at 5.0 I say, "The EMF is at 5.0." the same voice who I believe to be the breather gives this EVP saying, "Yes." I say, "I was just wondering," as I pause breathing is recorded. The more I hear it the more I think it is a child. I continue, "if you can please," again before I speak little chewing sounds are recorded. As if chewing on something right by the recorder. I continue, "make a sound for me, anything at all."

I am talking about ways these spirits can let me know they are there, I ask for spikes on the EMF, to talk to me, to turn the lights off, and as I walk over to turn the light off, breathing is recorded. You hear a click, that's me turning the light off, a couple seconds later a grunt is recorded. This doesn't sound like it's coming from the woman (or child) who's been here the whole time with me. It felt kind of dark and negative.

What happens next is quite interesting. After the grunt, which I believe to be male, the breather starts breathing quickly and says what sounds like, "Mommy, hold me, hold me, hold me, lights." Almost frightened. Am I dealing with a sweet child spirit who's possibly afraid of the dark? Or is this child afraid of the grunter?

I say, "Okay, I'm going to turn the lights back on." I stand up, a click, the lights are now back on, as they are turning on, an EVP is recorded, "Yes!" The breather starts breathing, so close it's as if it's right next to the recorder. Almost what sounds like a sigh of relief. My footsteps are recorded coming from the opposite side of the room, the equipment is laying on the bed, not in my hand as it usually is.

Session six, EVP session, Final session

I ask, "Who are you?" Unexplained, yet familiar to me now, breathing is recorded. I walk over to a corner, close to where the bed is located, my Mel EMF Meter goes to 0.6 and makes an alert sound, and an unexplained sound is recorded. To me it sounds like someone swallowing something, like a gulp sound. The breather is caught on the recording once again. The EMF goes off again. I put it closer to the lamp, alarm clock, basically that whole area to see if that's what is triggering the meter, none of those items are the source.

I wanted to be totally sure that this lamp, or other items weren't the reason why my EMF was reacting, so I pulled out a second EMF. I rarely use this one because of the fact that it doesn't make noises, so one has to constantly watch it to see if the colors light up instead of investigating, but this KII is a good tool to have as a back-up. I try it out and I can verify that both the Mel and the KII did not react to this lamp. So that means the Mel was reacting to something else—perhaps the breather who has been here the whole time with me.

The Mel starts going off again. I turn on my camera to see if I can get some photographic evidence. As I am doing this, the breather is recorded breathing. I take a picture, immediately after, an unexplained pop noise is recorded. An unexplained thump-like noise is recorded, and the breather is very close to the recorder now, which is lying on the bed in the middle of the room. Clicks of my camera as I take pictures are recorded and heard all over the room as I walk around, yet the breathing is right near the equipment on the bed.

I am back at the equipment and the breathing stops. Shortly after, a disembodied light yelp-like noise is recorded. I walk into the bathroom and the breather is recorded. The EMF suddenly spikes to 5.0. I ask a few more questions but with no further results or responses.

Chapter fifteen

The Historic Windsor Hotel, Del Norte, Colorado

The owner of this amazing hotel is a family friend of mine. I have known him for many years, and when my mom had her store in town, he would often come in for some coffee and to visit. My sister Carly was leaving for a temporary nanny job in Italy for three months. I wanted to do something special for her as a going-away present, so I asked the owner how much it would be to stay in one of the rooms. He knew this was a present for Carly and since we are friends, he gave us a generous deal.

He reserved the room for us that is known to get the most paranormal results. I was so excited. The hard part was keeping my mouth shut and not spoiling the surprise for my sister. I knew she would be just as excited as I was about our stay at this historical, haunted hotel. We went there the night that the dining room was closed so Justin was a sweetie and brought us some food from Peace of Art Cafe.

We ate. I look out our hotel window and the view is perfect. Downstairs, they have an awesome courtyard. Sure, it's a nice courtyard but what makes it so unique is the stone building, kind of broken down. Its presence is amazing. It saw a lot of death back in its days of operation. Back in the 1800s it served as the towns mortuary.

The people would go to the cemetery and dig a certain number of graves during warm season because when the harsh Colorado winter would come, the ground was frozen solid. They'd dig graves hoping that would be enough till after winter is gone. Sometimes it was enough, while other times they found themselves with bodies that had no place to be buried.

You have to remember that this dates back to the 1800s. Mortuaries back then didn't have what mortuaries today have, refrigeration. How did they keep the deceased until they could be properly buried? They would go to the Rio Grande River that ran through town and would get huge chunks of ice and keep the bodies on ice until spring came and the ground thawed.

That may be one reason why this historic hotel is haunted. The other reason is a specific ghost—a woman named Maude Heinz. She committed suicide at the hotel back in 1906, over one hundred years ago. She was a lover of music and enjoyed playing the piano and violin. Maude was engaged to a man who lived in New Mexico, a freight brakeman named V.W Parker.

Before Maude came along, he was engaged to a woman who lived about thirty minutes away from the hotel, two towns over, named Gertrude Walker. Soon after the end of that engagement, Maude and V.W started seeing each other. After becoming engaged V.W and Gertrude ran into each other and the realization set in for both of them, the love was very much still there. They rekindled their love and yet again became engaged.

Maude was devastated to say the least and understandably so. She just lost the man she thought she would spend the rest of her life with. According to archives, Maude took the train in from Alamosa, the town where Gertrude lived, and checked herself into the Windsor Hotel. She checked in under an alias, Violet Tierri, from Columbus Ohio.

She sat down and wrote letters to her father, Charles Heinz, who lived in Creede (Where the Bachelor's Loop and the mines are) and to the man who broke her heart—her would-be-husband V.W Parker. She mailed the letters, she then proceeded to Weiss Mercantile that was conveniently located across the street. She bought a 38-caliber revolver along with a box of bullets.

She interrupted the store clerk when he started to show her how to take the revolver apart for cleaning saying, "I know as much about guns as you do." She then went back to her hotel room and used that gun to kill herself. She would endure no more heartbreaks from that moment on.

Charles, her father was absolutely heartbroken. He wanted answers. His daughter was dead. This shouldn't be. He found V.W. After talking to the man who broke his daughters heart, he left town with his daughter's body and brought her back to Creede. You can find a more detailed and fuller story about Maude and Windsor's history online. I also want to note that the owner himself told me that he himself has never experienced any haunting whatsoever but he has had guests approach him sharing their own haunting experiences here.

Besides Maude and whatever other spirits that may reside here, this hotel is full of history. (I found the following info on the Windsor's own home page)

The Windsor is one of Colorado's oldest hotels, being established in 1874, three years after the town was founded.

That in itself is amazing, this hotel has been here almost as long as the town itself!

Del Norte was a booming mining and ranching location in the last quarter of the 1800s. The Windsor became the main social and commercial center of the area and remained a regional gathering spot for well over a hundred years! In the 1970s the Windsor was well into major disrepair and it stayed that way until 1993 when a wrecking ball was at the curb.

At the last minute, before it was to be torn down, the Windsor was saved by a local benefactor and his wife. The story is an amazing one, find out more about this historical landmark online, or even better, stay the night at this place, just passing through and don't have time to stay? Have a meal there. Have a drink at the bar. If you're lucky you can stop and talk to the owner himself. He's a great guy and can tell you more about this amazing place.

December 14, 2014
The investigation

This investigation was conducted by Carly and Tessa Mauro. Carly was very excited when I told her we'd be staying at the Windsor. Living in town, we could see the Windsor right across the street from where we lived. Literally a stone's throw away. Both Carly and I had to work that day but had early shifts and got off decently early.

We conducted our investigations in our hotel room—Room 209 and at the town's original ice house, the mortuary. There are many sessions in this chapter. We stayed a whole night, so we did as many as we could. Some are mini sessions, while others are longer. Next time we are here, with the owner's permission, we plan on going into the actual mortuary itself.

Results and evidence collected
Session one, Room 209

I ask, "Is there somebody here with us right now?" Several seconds go by with nothing but silence and then a woman is recorded giving this EVP, "Yes." Carly asks, "Are you a woman?" Unexplained breathing is recorded, this goes on for a few seconds. The KII Meter and the Mel Meter, both EMF meters, are sitting on the middle of the bed, the KII just spiked up to 3. Earlier we tested the bed to make sure there wasn't anything on, in or around it to make the EMF's go off. The Mel is fluctuating between .4 and .5. I ask, "Can you do something to let us know you're here?" An EVP is recorded, a whisper, "Like what?"

Session two

Immediately after Carly and I ended session one, we both felt a cold spot take over part of the room. I want to remind you, this was in December, and like all other Colorado hotels, the heat was on in the room and it was warm this whole time.

We turn the spirit box on. I say, "Okay, both Carly and myself both felt a burst of cold air pass through both of us." What sounds like a woman is caught on the recorder, whispering this EVP, "Us." I ask, "Is there something you'd like to tell us?" The woman replies in this EVP, "No" but more drawn out, "Nooo." I ask, "Did you die in this hotel?" An unexplained deep breath is recorded, followed by a pop sound. Then about ten seconds later another pop sound is recorded.

A woman's voice comes through the spirit box, making a distressed shriek-like noise. This is then followed by an unexplained disembodied sound on the recorder, which sounds like a woman making a muffled sound.

The Mel EMF starts making an alert noise letting us know it's getting a spike. Think of it this way, if I were to grab the antenna with my hand or touch it, the meter would light up and make loud noises. This happens with humans as well as if a spirit or any type of paranormal activity were nearby or touching it.

The KII which is still on the bed spikes to 2.

Session three

Immediately after session two was over, the Mel Meter started making alert sounds and I heard what sounded like a woman's voice. I checked and there was nobody in the halls. Being in December, the hotel didn't have many guests at that time. We turn the spirit box on.

Unexplained breathing from what I believe to be a woman or child is recorded, I ask, "Is there anything you want to tell us?" Immediately after I ask that question we receive an EVP from a woman saying, "Yes." Static comes through the recorder, this of course goes unheard by us. An unexplained sound is recorded. What it would sound like is if someone was on a respirator breathing in.

Session four

For this session, we thought we would leave the equipment on in the room while we went to explore the mortuary. We were going to do a session later and just wanted to check it out first, before we did so. We are not here for this session so there are no questions asked. Let's see what happens.

I am putting the time frame in, so you can see how long in between there was just silence, and when something happened. So, for example, one minute and ten seconds will be written down as 1.10.

I am talking to any spirits that may be in the room, explaining that Carly and myself will be leaving but to talk or do anything so we know they are there. I say, "We will have the camera recording a video and the digital recorder on as well, okay?" An EVP is recorded, of a hushed whisper saying, "Yes."

We turn the spirit box on. Carly goes out of the room and into the hall way, closing the door to see if our equipment can be heard in the hall. It cannot. An unexplained sound is recorded. Again, it sounds as if someone is breathing through a respirator—something a hospital would have. Very mechanical, very labored breathing almost forced.

Camera is turned on, situated, and zoomed in and is recording. Following this an unexplained growl-like sound is recorded. The KII EMF on the bed spikes at 0.2. I position the shadow detector motion sensor and turn it on. I say, "We are leaving now for a little while." A disembodied sound is recorded followed by an EVP, "Yes."

Once we have all the equipment on and positioned, we start to head for the door. A man is caught on recorder saying what sounds like, "Get out." Then as we are leaving, he repeats himself, "Get out."

- 2.28 We are out of the room, the door closing behind us.

- 2.38 An unexplained noise is recorded, what sounds like a woman moaning.

- 2.53 The Mel EMF beeps.

-3.39 Unexplained static.

- 4.0 A disembodied voice comes through, almost sounding like it's in the direction toward the window saying, "Hi." Very child-like.

- 5.09 A series of pop-like noises are recorded, what sounds like as if someone has gum in their mouth and is making bubbles, or just making noises with mouth. Times - 5.9, 5.11, 5.13, 5.14, 5.16, 5.20, 5.29, 5.41, 5.58, 6.04

- 7.04 An EVP of what sounds like a woman saying, "Go on." Then at 7.07 what sounds like a baby noise is recorded.

- 7.32 Unexplained static is recorded.

- 8.52 Disembodied voice of a man speaking unintelligible words on the spirit box.

8.58 The Mel EMF beeps.

- 9.12 The Mel EMF beeps.

9.51 Unexplained static is recorded.

- 10.28 The Mel EMF makes yet another alert beep sound.

11.11 The Mel EMF makes another beep.

12.39 A woman is recorded making a sound, "Hmmm."

12.41 Unexplained static is recorded.

-13.14 Unexplained exhales coming from a man. Very close to the recorder.

17.55 Unexplained static is recorded.

18.12 The door opens, and Carly and I enter.

18.18 A man inhales.

Session five
The old Mortuary, AKA The Icehouse

I ask Carly for the time and as she replies, an EVP whisper says, "Go on." We hear a rustling sound, look around and find the furry culprit, an adorable cat. We turn the spirit box on. As I start to explain how they would use chunks of ice from the river to store bodies till burial, we get an EVP of a man saying, "Ice." Incredible.

I say, "There's an animal here with us. Can you tell us what it is?" Seconds later, we get an EVP of a man saying, "Course." I ask, "Were you stuck in the mortuary for a while?" An EVP of a man is recorded as he says, "Uh-huh" As this is happening, the Mel Meter spikes at 0.4, while the KII EMF starts to fluctuate between 2 and 3.

As I am attempting to take pictures with my camera—which by the way has brand new fresh batteries—it starts to malfunction. Turning off quickly then back on. This happens many times and it occurs when I am trying to shoot in a specific area. Can I explain this? No. Is it paranormal? It's a possibility, but really, I just don't know.

Carly asks, "What's your name?" The spirit box which had been silent up to this point comes to life as a man's voice comes through saying, "Mark." As this is happening, the Mel EMF starts making noises. I ask, "Are you trying to tell us you are here by making that noise?" Seconds later the recorder receives an EVP, "Yes." The Mel then goes silent. This is followed by a pop sound.

Carly talks about how she enjoys seeing the different colors appear on the EMF, an EVP of a man is recorded saying, "I know." A man comes through the spirit box and says, what sounds like, "Help a little." Then a few seconds later, the same man comes through the spirit box saying, "Help." I ask, "What is your name?" A man gives this EVP, "Alex." I then ask, "How many of you are here with us?" Several seconds go by, we then receive this eerie EVP from a woman saying, "Ten."

Being that it is December and it is night time. I suggest to Carly that we head back inside to warm up and start investigating in our hotel room. The KII spikes and a man comes through the spirit box saying, "Don't go." Carly asks,

"Are you here right now?" An EVP is recorded of a voice excitedly saying, "Yes!"

Session six

We are now in our warm hotel room, we get situated and I ask, "Can you tell us your name?" A man comes through the spirit box saying, "Lake Cohen." Another man comes through the spirit box saying, "Big Al." This is followed by an EVP of an exasperated breath, "Ahhh." We ask a handful of questions with no voices coming through the spirit box and no EVP's caught on recorder.

Session seven

As we start this session, I ask, "Can you make a sound for us, like a tapping sound, or a knock?" While we didn't get a tap or a knock, an unexplained pop is recorded.

I ask, "Is there something you would like to tell us?" A man comes through the spirit box and says, "Yes." Carly excitedly asks, "Did you just say yes?" An unexplained static is recorded. I ask, "How many of you are here with us right now?" A man comes through the spirit box saying, what sounds like, "Us." Carly asks, "Can you tell us any of our names?" A man comes through the spirit box saying, "No." This is followed by unexplained static.

Carly asks, "Do you mind that this is a hotel now?" In quite an enthusiastic voice a man comes through the spirit box saying, "Yes!" After this an unexplained breathing of a man is caught on recording, and real close. Now sometimes we ask silly questions, or what some might think … dare I say it … stupid questions. However, they aren't stupid when we get intelligent direct responses such as this. I ask, "Can you say Tessa?" A few seconds go by then a woman comes through the spirit box saying, "Tessa."

I ask, "Did you spend any time in the mortuary?" A man comes through the spirit box saying, "Yes." Then a few seconds later he repeats himself, "Yes." Again, unexplained static is recorded. It seems we ask a question, get an answer, then it's followed by static. We never hear the static. An EVP of a man breathing quite loudly as if right in front of the recorder! Unexplained static is recorded yet again a few seconds later, then again, the same man is recorded breathing loudly, this goes on for fifteen seconds—the breathing and the static.

I start to talk to Carly, as I do this, the same man starts breathing again. I say, "We're about to end this session now, do you want to say anything before we end it?" A voice comes through the spirit box saying what sounds like, "Help." Unexplained music is recorded, this is followed by more static.

Session eight

I ask, "Can you tell us your name?" An EVP of a quivering voice, shaky, "So, move us." An unexplained pop sound is caught on recorder followed by a man breathing loudly. I say, "I heard this is Maude's room." An EVP is recorded, "Whatever." A man speaks through the spirit box saying, "Bed." Unsure if he is talking about our equipment that is lying on the bed, or something completely different.

I say, "You just said something. Can you say it again?" The same man comes through the spirit box saying, "Yes." Then amazingly he repeats himself saying, "Bed." That's so awesome.

Session nine

Carly asks, "This is Carly. I will be asking you some questions." An EVP of what sounds like a young woman saying, "Nice." This response is followed yet again, by unexplained static. Carly asks, "Do you know what building this is?" A man speaks through the spirit box, "Yes." Carly says to me, "It sounds like he just said yes." An EVP of a man whispering, "Yes." Carly says, "Can you tell me what it is?" The same man speaks through the spirit box saying, "House."

Carly asks, "Were you in the mortuary?" The same man yet again speaks through the spirit box saying, "Yes." He repeats himself, "Yes." Carly asks, "Can you make a noise for us please?" An EVP of the man saying, "Yes." Followed by a man breathing, unexplained. When asked if Maude is in the room with us, two unexplained pops are recorded.

Session ten

As soon as we start this session, unexplained static is recorded. A few seconds go by when suddenly an EVP of a woman saying what sounds like, "Come on" is recorded. This is then followed a few seconds later by unexplained old music.

I ask, "How long have you been here?" A disembodied voice of a man comes through the spirit box saying what sounds like, "Maude." While this is not an answer to the question I just asked, the name Maude has been connected to this old hotel since she took her own life here over one hundred and eleven years ago. Maybe he is letting us know Maude is close by, or perhaps he is telling us he has been here as long as Maude? Who knows?

Session eleven

Unexplained sounds are recorded, I can only describe it like old-school video game sounds. Carly asks, "Can anyone say one of our names?" A woman comes through the spirit box and says, "Yes." Carly asks, "Is there a woman here with us?" Crying sounds of a woman start to come out of the spirit box. Carly asks, "What's your name?" A man speaks from the spirit box saying, "Oz." Then a few seconds later, the same voice repeats, "Oz."

Carly says, "If you want to talk to us, you can come to this light on the recorder and speak so we can hear you." Immediately following this, an unexplained loud repeated breathing as if the mouth is right on the recorder piece is recorded. A child comes through the spirit box saying, "Dad."

Session twelve

An EVP from a woman or possibly a child saying, "Oh no, don't go." Carly looks at the TV and asks, "Do you like changing the channels?" A disembodied voice comes through the spirit box saying, "Yes." We receive an EVP from a man asking us, "Where you going?" I ask, "Do you know what room number we are in right now?" A woman moaning is recorded.

Now, after listening to this very oh so short session, we get two EVP's. One being, "Oh no, don't go." The other is, "Where you going?" We have not made any announcement or comment that we are leaving any time soon. It makes me wonder if these two EVPs were directed at another spirit.

Session thirteen

I ask, "How did you die?" We get a sad EVP from a child saying, "Fever." This is followed by unexplained static. We get an EVP of a woman saying,

"Hat." Now I was wearing a baseball hat. I don't know if she was talking about that or something else. This was followed by a pop sound. I ask, "What's outside our bedroom window?" A man comes through the spirit box and says, "Death." Another man also comes through the spirit box saying, "Tears."

I would say those are both accurate. Being the morgue, yes definitely death would be a quite appropriate answer, and I assume sometimes the family would be there to pick up the body or come to identify the dead, say good bye or something, and I'm sure its seen its fair share of tears. This session ends with static.

Session fourteen

I start off by saying, "The floor is yours, is there something you would like to tell us? A message for someone? Anything at all?" No voices come through the spirit box, and a little static comes through. A disembodied voice comes through the spirit box saying, what sounds like, "Help." Carly asks, "Do you like to look out the window?" An unexplained sound from a woman is recorded. Then a woman comes through the spirit box and says, "Yes." This is followed by yet again, more static.

Session fifteen

We ask a few questions and no sounds, static, spirit box voices or EVPs are recorded. Quite uneventful.

Session sixteen

A disembodied voice yelps, "Help us" through the spirit box. An unexplained pop is recorded. I ask, "Have you ever heard of a woman named Maude?" An EVP, sort of with an echo says, "I'm here."

Session seventeen, final session

Carly asks, "Do you know what room number we're in?" An unexplained light thump-like noise is recorded. Carly asks, "Do you like to watch the TV?" An EVP is recorded of a disembodied voice saying, "Yeah." A man is recorded giving us this interesting EVP, "Pisses me off." This is then followed by unexplained raspy breathing. I ask, "What ethnicity are you?" An

EVP of a woman whispering, "Anglo." Then what sounds like an older person, I think a woman, gives us this EVP, "Bones."

I investigated the Windsor several months later with my friend Angie Velasquez and in under two hours investigating the Ice House, she received nine EVPs, I have yet to hear what my recorder caught.

Chapter sixteen

Boot Hill Grave Yard, Tombstone, Arizona

When I was a teen my mom gave me a pamphlet about this historical cemetery. It gave info about all the people buried there and how they died. Many shootings, stabbings, murders, suicides, sickness, hangings, lynching's and more. Throughout the years I must have read that pamphlet a dozen times at least! I love those old western cowboy outlaw towns. For as long as I can remember I have wanted to go to Tombstone.

Back in the nineteenth century, Boot Hill was a common name for cemeteries with the remains of gunfighters, cowboys, outlaws, who died with their boots on mostly in a violent type way. Some of these bad boys are Billy Clanton, Frank McLaury and Tom McLaury, who were killed by the Earp brothers and Doc Holliday during the thirty second famous gun fight at the O.K. Corral. Also, the men responsible for the Bisbee massacre, Dan Dowd, Red Sample, Tex Howard, Bill DeLaney and Dan Kelly. Without my knowing it at the time, I get an attachment from one of these murderous men.

This graveyard has over 200 recorded burials here. Some unknowns. Immigrants were also buried here but without record, so the number is far higher than 200. The cemetery closed in the later months of 1886 when a newer cemetery opened in town. After 1886 they buried a few other people, but that was it. When you walk through the gift shop doors (which then gives you access to the grave yard) a sign greets you, "No guns please, graveyard full."

Back in June of 2016 my Grandma was having surgery. She lives in Tucson, about ninety miles from Tombstone. My mother and I traveled from Colorado, so we could be there for the surgery and to help afterwards. My Grandma is a Rockstar and kicked that surgeries butt! One of these days, I decided to take a solo trip to Tombstone. When I went my first stop was Boot Hill. I was so excited I could hardly contain myself. For years I have been wanting to come here and that moment has finally arrived.

Now, when we went to Arizona I didn't really think I would be going to investigate so I only brought a couple tools—just in case. My recorder and one of my EMF meters. That's it. So, all the evidence recorded are EVPs. I didn't have my spirit box with me this trip.

Me and my itinerary mind, came up with a list full of places to go to; Boot Hill, Big Nose Kate's Saloon, O.K Corral, Birdcage Theatre etc.! When I first rolled up to this old graveyard, it was around 100 degrees. I walked around the gift shop for a bit then paid the entry fee and went out into the heat, pamphlet in hand. I noticed people coming out and going in just as quickly as they arrived.

There was no way I would leave quickly like that. I stayed for close to three hours and I visited each-and-every grave, unknowns and all. By the end I was quite delirious, as the temp was about 110 and quickly rising. At the Bisbee Five (massacre) I was quite rude, which I had never done before—and I have spoken to murderers before, so I don't know what happened there. I blame the intense Arizona heat.

It is here in front of these five murderers that I got my first (and I pray my last) attachment. It was horrible, I thought I was having a heart attack. This is a chapter all in itself, and how I got rid of the attachment is in that chapter as well. Talk about intense. If you remember, in the beginning of the book I mentioned how I've never had attachments before. Well, that's changed. That's the crazy thing about this book, things change, and I have no idea how it will end. There are investigations that will be in here that haven't even been conducted yet.

June 18, 2016
The investigation

This investigation was conducted by Me, Myself and I. All the Tombstone investigations were solo jobs, with the recorder and Mel as my companions. The hot Arizona summer sweltering heat couldn't … wouldn't stop me. I was on a mission. Unique tombstones like Stinging Lizard shot by Cherokee and more. I always enjoy going to cemeteries, they are each unique and special in their own way.

To date, Boot Hill is one of the most active places I have been to. Some of the results I got were intense! Here we go! I must say this was not the typical investigation. I asked some questions but not too many. Since I was wanting to visit each grave and trying to beat the heat I didn't stay long at any particular grave. I was reading a bunch of the tomb stones and getting EVPs in response.

Results and evidence collected
Session one

I read a tombstone, "3 Fingered Jack Dunlop Shot by Jeff Milton." Right after that an unexplained moan is recorded. An EVP of a man asking, "Hey, see it?" I say aloud to myself, "Interesting." Then what sounds like the same man says, "Look." Followed by an unexplained exhale. Right after I ask, "Are you mad that Jeff Milton killed you?" A disembodied voice says, "What happened?" Followed by unintelligible words.

I ask, "Why did he kill you?" Unexplained sounds are recorded. What sounds like horse hooves clunking down on the ground. An EVP of a man is recorded, "He robbed." I believe this to possibly be Jeff Milton himself explaining his deadly actions towards Three fingered Jack Dunlop. I want to talk a little about this Old West outlaw. Dunlop was a train robber. So, the fact that I got an EVP of a man saying, "He robbed" is quite accurate!

February 15, 1900 proved to be a fatal day for Three Fingered Jeff Dunlop. He and his gang of train robbers targeted The Fairbank train. Lawman Jeff Milton was on the train as the guard. A gunfight took place which resulted in Dunlop being shot. Even though Milton was hurt he fought hard. The gang of robbers fled. Dunlop was seriously wounded, being hit by eleven pellets. While trying to get away from authorities, he fell from his horse, where he laid there bleeding from his wounds for fourteen hours! He died from those wounds on February 24, 1900.

Session two

I say, "Jim Riley was murdered." An EVP of a man is caught on recorder screaming in pain. I ask, "Was it a cowboy fight?" A screech like noise is recorded. A couple with a small loud child come in the area I am at, so I end this session. Very mini session if you will.

Session three

I ask, "Charley Storms, how do you feel about being shot by Luke Short?" An EVP of a man is recorded saying, "Hate it." An unexplained purr like noise is recorded.

Session four

Shortly after I start this session, an unexplained loud heavy breathing is recorded, followed by, "Ohh." I read, "He was right." I get an EVP of a man saying, "Hung." I ask, "What did you die for?" A man breathing is recorded.

I read, "Seymour Dye, killed by Indians." I pause, then ask, "Were you doing something," as I pause unexplained static is recorded. I continue, "that they thought they had to kill you?" An EVP is recorded of what sounds like a possible Indian man saying, "Shot him. Seymour." (r is silent when spoken - Seymo) SEE-MO.

Seymour Dye and Harry Curry were driving their wagon and were in the middle of transporting hay when he and his companion were ambushed by Indians. They were shot, and when they fell from their wagon they were dragged more than 150 feet. "Shot him. Seymour." Was this an Indian who possibly murdered Seymour and Curry? This is chilling to say the least. The tombstone doesn't say how he was killed, just that he indeed was murdered by Indians. After doing research about him online it was revealed that he was indeed shot.

Session five

I am now at the final resting place of the outlaws who were killed at the gun fight at the O.K Corral. I say, "Billy Clanton." I pause and an EVP whisper of a man, "Yes." I say, "Frank McLaury." Another EVP by possibly the same man, "Yes." I continue, "Tom McLaury." Yet another EVP, "Yes." Wait … what?

I say, "Doc Holliday was hurt but didn't die." An EVP from the same man says, "Yes." This is followed by an unexplained noise, followed by a pop. Unexplained sounds are recorded, what sounds like unseen hands grasping for the recorder followed by two additional pops. I say, "You hurt several people including law men." A sigh from a man is caught on the recorder.

I ask, "Can you tell me why you did this? Please?" I get an EVP of a man saying what sounds like, "Fuck you." Immediately after the F bomb is thrown my way, an unexplained loud labored breathing is recorded, followed by a pop sound.

Session six

I continue walking and stop and I read, "Eva Waters, died at three months old from Scarlett Fever." Child-like noises are recorded, unintelligible. I walk over to a headstone, stop and say, "Florentino Cruz." I receive an EVP from a man saying, "Yes." I ask, "Florentino, also known as Indian Charlie, what do you have to say for yourself?" A few seconds later an EVP of a man is recorded saying, "Go to hell." As I start to walk to another grave, an EVP of the man who just told me to go to hell, is recorded saying, "Come back."

Let's talk a little about Indian Charlie, shall we? The body of Indian Charlie was found with several bullet wounds. He had met a grisly end. It is thought that Wyatt Earp and his men had something to do with this death. No, Earp wasn't looking for people to shoot down, it is believed that this man is responsible for the death and murder of Wyatt's younger brother Morgan.

Morgan's death was a heart wrenching one. After a long day all he wanted to do was have a drink and play a game of pool. As he took his turn and his friends and brother Wyatt watched, the door flew open and he was shot. Wyatt witnessed this happen. Can you imagine? No wonder he wanted to take out the people responsible for his brother's death.

I move along, remember it was very hot there, but I certainly wanted to visit each grave, so I continued on, I read, "Van Houten, beaten in the face with a stone until he died." A few seconds later a creepy thump-like noise followed by a man moaning is recorded. I step in front of another headstone, I read, "Two hot tempered ranchers, who disagreed over the best way to drive cattle. Fast or slow. Causing Chas Helms to be shot and killed." Two unexplained pops followed by unintelligible whispered words by a man. My recorder captures pop sounds from time to time as you all have read, but there are times I get them after mentioning someone has been shot. It might not be a connection, if it's not, the timing is very interesting.

I walk by a grave and say, "Louis Daves." An EVP from a man is recorded saying, "Tell em, tell em, tell em, die, tell em, tell em." This is then followed by an unexplained pop. A few seconds later, I am standing next to Thos Gregory and his small son. As I stand there looking at father and sons graves, a labored breathing from what sounds like a child is recorded. An EVP from a child saying what sounds like, "Five."

Session seven

I read, "Peter Smith, age 23, a native of Germany, was struck on the back of the head with a poker and killed by Thos Doland during a fight." An EVP of a man is recorded whispering, "Dollars." Seconds later an exhale from a man is recorded. I was unsuccessful in the research to find out if the reason Thos and murder victim Peter had this fight due to money, hence the EVP, "Dollars." Loud labored breathing is recorded.

I continue to another headstone, I say, "Sorry you were shot Jasper Von." Another labored breath is recorded. This goes on for a few seconds. I walk then stop at some unknown graves. I sadly shake my head and say, "A few unknowns." I walk away and as I walk a sad EVP is recorded, "I know." As I keep walking, the same voice repeats, "I know." How sad is that?

As I walk, my footsteps are recorded and a second set of footsteps are recorded, as if running after me. I just want to note, that if I am in an area where people are present, in any investigation, I stop the session and go elsewhere, I also say what the noises are and debunk things immediately. Thankfully, the heat was intense so much so that not many people were out at this time and when they were it wasn't for long.

Unexplained man breathing, with a slight wheeze noise as well. I say, "Row two." An EVP from a man is recorded saying, "Come." Then the same man is recorded saying, "Come back!" Amazingly he repeats this seconds later saying, "Come back!"

Session eight

After completing the first row, I now am standing in front of the first graves of the second row. I say, "I am at row two of the cemetery now. Dan Kelly hanged. Bill DeLaney hanged." A creepy panic-stricken gasping sound is recorded. I continue, "Tex Howard hanged." Another gasping sound is recorded. I go on, "Red Sample hanged." Again, more gasping for air is recorded. You will hear more about Comer Red Sample later in this book. I walk to the last headstone of the Bisbee murderers and say, "Dan Dowd, hanged." One more labored short breath.

To me this is absolutely amazing. No, I did not hear the gasping for air as it was taking place. These men were robbers, and murderers. They were the first to be legally hanged in Tombstone, Arizona. You will hear more about them and their crimes later.

Can this be residual? These people, hanged for robbery and multiple murders, including a pregnant woman, as the noose tightens around their necks, know they are doomed. No way out. Death, a painful one will come soon. Can these horrible sounds my recorder caught, be gasps escaping from the condemned lips?

The Bisbee five were legally hanged. However, there were six men involved in this massacre not five. The mastermind John Heath was handed a life sentence for some bizarre reason. An angry mob of townspeople disagreed with the verdict and took it upon themselves to break him out of jail on Friday, February the 22nd in 1884 and lynched him. The five other men were legally hanged a little over a month later, on Friday, March the 28th in 1884.

I am reading about the crime they committed, "Hanged for a bank robbery in Bisbee that resulted in numerous peoples' deaths." An unexplained pop is recorded. This is where I open my big mouth and am disrespectful—for the first time and last time of my investigations. It is unlike me and I really don't know why I did it. This is an eerie place for me because this is where I got my attachment. Lesson learned Red Sample. Lesson learned.

I say, "You guys deserved to die. You murdered innocent people." Unintelligible words are spoken and recorded from a man. I continue, "How dare you? You thought it was okay to do so?" An EVP from the same man saying, "Yes." An EVP of a different man is recorded saying, what sounds like, "Sarah." Now, during my research I thought maybe one of the victim's names, the pregnant woman, might be Sarah.

Nope, her name was Annie. However, I did find that the mastermind, John Heath's mother's name was Sarah. Can this be the Sarah? Maybe. It's a possibility. Maybe one of these men had a wife or girlfriend named Sarah, but the only Sarah I found was connected to the mastermind, who is buried a row over.

I say to the murdering group of five, "That's not cool. Taking a human life". An EVP of a man saying, "Romas" or "Romans" cannot tell which one, and I am unsure of what this means.

I say, "You took it all, including their lives." A struggling gasp for breath is recorded. This is followed by an unexplained pop. Again, a creepy struggle for breath, gasping for air. What sounds like suffocation. Very eerie to hear. This is repeated several seconds later.

Did these men deserve to die? Yes. Absolutely. They took several lives. Innocent lives. Those lives were law enforcement, a pregnant woman, and hard-working people. It still is eerie to hear someone desperately trying to catch a breath. Killer or not.

Session nine

I am still with the killer five. It was weird. Due to the heat, I had been moving at a more rapid pace, faster then I usually would be. It was almost like I couldn't leave them. I ask, "Gentlemen, do you have anything to say for yourselves?" As I pause, that all too familiar gasping for air sound is recorded. Again, I must ask, residual? Stuck in time. Reliving their deaths. I say, "You murdering group of five!" An EVP of a man is caught on recorder, saying, "I'll pass." This is followed by unexplained breathing from a man. As I walk away, "Come back" is recorded.

I walk on and stop and read, "Jerry Sullivan died in 1881." I get this amazing EVP from a man saying, what sounds like, "Pull 'em up boys, pull 'em up!" I was still really close to where the five men who were hanged are buried so I believe this might have to do with them possibly. Perhaps, "Pull 'em up boys." Means to pull up their dead bodies. Just a guess.

As I talk to a suicide victim, Verone Gray, an unexplained loud pop is recorded. I read, "W.M Clayborne shot by Frank Leslie. Clayborne sought to settle real or fancied wrong with Leslie. This took place in front of the Oriental Saloon, where Leslie tended bar." I stop reading and ask, "Were you just really confrontational?" I receive an EVP from a man saying, "Yes." Another EVP from the same man is recorded a few seconds later saying, "Hey."

An unexplained loud thump-like noise while I am talking in front of Joseph Wetsell's grave. I read, "He was stoned to death by Apaches." I shake my head in disapproval and say, "Ridiculous." Another loud thump noise is recorded. Then something amazing is recorded, what sounds like numerous people chanting, unknown words, and at the same time, drum like sounds, using hands as part of the instrument. Did my recorder just catch Indians?

Joseph was not alone, friends were in the same area he was in, he was just a short distance away. It is thought that the Indians did not want to attract attention so they stoned poor Joseph Wetsell to death. I'm sorry, call me stupid, but wouldn't that just attract the very attention that you are trying to avoid?

I'm reading about Frank Bowles who was killed in a freak accident. It is rather unfortunate what happened to Frank Bowles. He was riding his horse, and he was thrown off, this caused his gun to go off, hitting him right in the leg. He sadly didn't seek the medical attention he so desperately needed soon enough and died due to his injuries.

As I was reading about Frank, unexplained static is recorded. This is then followed by a metal on metal sound. I take a picture of Frank Bowles' grave, he died August 26, 1880. Carved into his wooden grave, "As you pass by, remember that as you are, so once was I, and as I am, you soon will be. Remember me." A man gives this EVP, "Hey." Then a few seconds later, he repeats himself, "Hey."

Session ten

I read, "Old man Clanton. He, along with several other men were ambushed on a cattle drive by Mexicans. All but one man was killed." An EVP of a man is recorded as he says, "So what?"

I am going back and forth from row to row. I am back in the area where the outlaws who died as a result of the infamous O.K Corral gun fight. I see two men, I believe father and son, taking each other's pictures in front of the three graves. I offer to take a picture of the two of them together. They accept. I leave the recorder going and put it on a rock by a nearby grave. As I am taking the pictures a creepy EVP is recorded by a man, "I hanged." This is followed by a man breathing, very close to my recorder.

Session eleven

I am in the area where John Beather, a man who was hanged, is buried. I take a picture then start walking to the next grave. An unexplained loud drag-like sound is recorded. I then start talking to a miner who was found murdered in his cabin. His partner is thought to have murdered him. I say, "I am so sorry that you had to die Ernest Brodines. What pure hate!" A sigh from a man is recorded.

A bird starts chirping in the background. I laugh at the bird. An EVP of a man is recorded whispering, "Did you hear it?" I look over, and say, "J.D McDermott killed, his spinal column fractured when his horse fell with him while crossing the San Pedro River." A disembodied sound, what sounds like a horse in distress. Sad, yet unbelievable!

I read about Judge Lindley and walk on. An unexplained very loud noise is recorded. Like something or somebody falling hard to the ground. Very loud. I am taking a picture, I receive an EVP, "Who?" Then another EVP, "Tighten it." I am standing by two unknown graves and sadly say, "A couple unknowns." My recorder catches yet another sad EVP regarding unknown graves, "Too bad for us!"

I walk past the unknowns. A disembodied voice is recorded saying, "Go ahead … do it." This is followed by three unexplained pop sounds. I am walking from Row 3 to Row 4 and as I am doing this, a man is recorded breathing heavily as if right by my side. I am reading about Mrs. Stump who died during child birth from an overdose of chloroform which was given to her by her doctor. I say, "Aw poor mama." A woman is recorded saying, "Pulling out hairs." Whatever that means.

I say, "In row 4 now." An EVP whisper, "Come on." Several seconds later the same voice speaks again, "Now." I stop in front of Mrs. Campbell's grave. She died in 1882, she was the wife of a restaurant owner and it is strongly believed that she was poisoned. I ask her, "Were you poisoned, Mrs. Campbell?" An unexplained thump like sound. Then a knock sound is recorded. An EVP is recorded, "I'm okay." Followed by a wheezing sound.

I read, "Thos Kearney, blown up in a blast." A man is recorded saying, "Yes." As I am walking, an unexplained pop is recorded. Right after the pop there's a loud gasp followed by a very loud thump. As I am paying respects to an eleven-month old child, Thos Cowan, who sadly died of Diphtheria, an EVP is recorded saying, "Go home."

Session twelve

Before I can even speak, an EVP from a disembodied voice is recorded, "Enjoy their cuts." I read, "John Gillespie was one of the officers sent to arrest Billy Grounds and Zwing Hunt, suspected murderers of M.R. Peel. He died when Hunt shot him in the head ... John Gillespie," as I pause an EVP, "Hello." I continue, "A hero" An unexplained pop is recorded. I say, "who died because a murderous coward shot him." Buried right next to Officer John Gillespie is murder victim M.R. Peel. John was murdered by the same people who murdered M.R Peel, while out on duty trying to find the killers of Peel. May both these murder victims rest in peace. An unexplained pop is recorded.

I ask murder victim M.R. Peel, "Hi M.R. do you have anything to say?" An EVP of a man is recorded, "Yes." I continue, "The man who's buried next to you died trying to bring your murderers to justice. I'm sorry that you both died. That's horrible." An EVP of the same man who spoke last saying, "Hold me."

Session thirteen, final session

An EVP of a woman saying, "Pray for us ... pray." I am paying my respects to suicide victim, Delia William. A colored proprietress who killed herself by taking arsenic. As I finish talking a very loud noise is recorded, that sounds like numerous heavy objects falling onto one another.

Boot Hill definitely did not disappoint. I will absolutely be back here some day and when I do, I will bring a flower for the man who attached himself to me, a promise I made to him the day he finally left me. Best day ever.

Chapter seventeen

The Bird Cage Theatre, Tombstone, Arizona

The Bird Cage Theatre is a historic landmark that I have wanted to visit for a long time. I have seen documentaries about this old saloon/brothel/gambling hall. Every time I see the Moriah, the gorgeous horse carriage hearse, made in 1881, I am simply mesmerized by its beauty. They sure don't make hearses like this anymore. This Moriah resides here at the Bird Cage.

A little history about The Bird Cage Theatre; it opened the day after Christmas in 1881 and closed its doors in 1889. Still on the wall today is a beautiful large painting of belly dancer, Fatima. It has several bullet holes and a knife slash in it as well. Back in its heyday there were over a dozen cages where the ladies of the night would entertain the patrons. The ladies, while not with their patrons would be on the floor serving half dollar beers.

Downstairs in the basement sits a poker room, famous for the longest poker game in history. Doc Holliday, and Bat Masterson were among the players in this eight-year, five-month and three-day game.

More than 100 bullet holes are found throughout this historical building. After exploring Boot Hill, my next stop was Bird Cage. I walked up just in time. Two women in period dresses were inviting people in so they could listen to the history of the theatre, then after that, you could shop around in their sweet gift shop (there is also a gift shop with more things in the basement past the poker room) and pay a small fee to check out the brothel, the Moriah, museum, poker room and more.

The first session is not me investigating just a brush up on the history. Now while people were quiet and listening for the most part, there were a couple times where I couldn't make out what the woman was saying, so I apologize for that. Even just standing there and not asking any questions, this front room that used to be the bar, definitely had paranormal activity, even finishing the sentences for the women a couple times as she spoke.

If you ever find yourself in Tombstone, please, if you enjoy history, do yourself a favor and head over to The Bird Cage Theatre. If you are like me, you will fall in love with the haunting beauty, the Moriah.

June 18, 2016
The investigation

This investigation was conducted by Tessa Mauro. Like I said in the Boot Hill chapter, when I came to Arizona I was unaware that I'd be doing any investigations at all, let alone Tombstone! The only equipment used here was my Mel EMF meter and my trusty recorder.

I met with a woman who approached me while at the Moriah. She looked slightly familiar to me, but I couldn't figure out why. If you ever watch Ghost Adventures she was on the Bird Cage episodes (two). She shares her experience with me. Her name is Darba Jo Butler, and she was super friendly and so knowledgeable when it came to the Bird Cage Theatre. We talked for a little while and even sang Happy Birthday together to try to get the spirits to speak to us.

Results and evidence collected
Session one, The bar room

I walk in just as a woman, whom I will call Martha, in a beautiful period dress, starts to talk about the haunting history of the Bird Cage Theatre.

Martha says, "If the ladies of the night had to walk across this bridge from side to side, it was called the cat walk." As Martha ends that sentence and pauses an EVP is recorded of an aggravated female saying, "And for what did it _____ _____?" The last two words are unintelligible.

Martha starts speaking again, "We had sixteen gunfights here, twenty-six people have died here." A man speaks unintelligible words. Martha continues, "We have 104," an EVP is recorded, really close, "Hey." Martha ends her sentence, "bullet holes throughout the building." A man gives this EVP, "Bullet hole."

As Martha is speaking, a female starts to talk over her. "I'm a witness." Martha is still talking when a woman gives this EVP, "Das Busch."

Immediately after this EVP Martha ends her sentence and says, "Busch Brewery."

Martha is talking about the famous poker game and my recorder gets this EVP of a woman saying, "Holliday." Martha says, "And of course, Doc Holliday and Wyatt Earp." An EVP of a man, "Yes." As Martha starts to talk about Wyatt Earp the same man whispers this EVP, "Watch this."

Martha starts to share the history about the fifteen-foot Fatima painting, how it has been on the wall in the same spot since 1880. She is riddled with bullet holes but she still stands proudly on that wall to this day. As she is describing where the bullet holes are on this famous painting, an EVP of a man, "Ow."

What happens next is utterly amazing to me. Remember that whole finishing sentence thing I mentioned earlier? Well we saw this earlier with Busch Brewery, now check this out. Martha says, "This was a busy place back in the day," She pauses for only a second, the same man who just said "ow" is recorded saying this EVP, "It was hoppin." She ends, "It was hoppin."

Session two, museum, brothel

After buying some postcards and other small items, I stay talking to a couple of the ladies who were so friendly. I paid the small museum fee and walked through the door. I was the only person (for a good twenty minutes) in there. No disruptions. No debunks. Nothing. Just me. I walk in and I look around and cannot believe I am finally here.

I start off by saying, "I am in the famous Bird Cage Theatre in Arizona. It is absolutely amazing in here!" A disembodied whisper gives this EVP, "Yeah." An EVP of a woman, "Help me out." I ask, "Is there anyone here with me?" Unexplained footsteps are recorded. These footsteps sound as if they are very close, and remember, as for now, I am the only one here.

I ask if there are any ladies here with me and an unexplained whoosh-like sound is recorded. A man speaks an unintelligible word. This is followed by an unexplained sound. As I am walking around trying to soak in all the history this old building holds, an EVP is whispered, "Get out." I repeat my question, "Any ladies have anything to say at all?" A woman is recorded saying, "Yes."

An unexplained deep breath from a man is recorded, this is repeated several seconds later. It reminds me of a machine that would help someone to breathe, like it's forced or with help.

I continue to look around. Even when I am not speaking, they are speaking to me. The Bird Cage is full of spirits. An EVP is whispered, "Doc." Do you ever get the feeling that you are not alone and that someone is watching you? This happens to me all the time, including while alone at the Bird Cage Theatre. I ask, "Is there anybody here with me?" A sound that goes unheard by me is recorded. A loud clang-like noise, like a door opening, but I was the only one there. (Again, if it were a door that I heard I would have debunked it) An EVP is recorded, "Yes."

Off to the right up above are little open rooms with a curtain for each, where the ladies of the night would entertain the patrons. To the left are antique type things, including a small table. I walk over to the table and read, "This is the famous table where Doc Holliday played and dealt Faro." A loud bang-like noise is recorded. Again, I find myself just blown away with all the history that is here, not only in The Bird Cage Theatre, but in Tombstone itself. Really? Doc Holliday, here? Just a few feet from where I'm standing. Blown away.

You can tell I was still kind of delirious from spending hours outside at Boot Hill cemetery when I say, "Bird Cage Theatre at Tucson, Arizona." An EVP is recorded of a man, correcting me, "No. Wrong."

Session three, The Moriah

An EVP is caught of a woman saying, "Come." I am just taking it all in—the Moriah, my surroundings. I excitedly say, "This blows my mind." An unexplained breathing of a man is recorded and he is really close. At this point I am still the only person here. I read aloud about the Moriah:

"This is the original Boot Hill hearse. Trimmed in 24 carat gold and sterling silver. Owned by Watt and Tarbel undertaking parlor (I investigate at this mortuary later the same evening, this is in a different chapter) of Tombstone used from 1881 through 1917 with the exception of six people, they buried everyone in Boot Hill Cemetery. (As I end that sentence an EVP whisper, "Yes" is recorded) It was built by Cunningham Bros in Rochester New York for $8,000.00 original 8. 1881 model, there were only 8 of these models built that year. (I pause looking the Moriah up and down. Another EVP, repeats,

"Yes.") It is the only one left of the original eight. The trim on the hearse is all sterling silver, 24-carat-gold leaf, the curved glass is the first ever manufactured on a vehicle."

I ask, "Was anybody taken away in the Moriah to be buried?" An unexplained loud exhale from a man is recorded, still alone folks! The exhale is repeated a few seconds later, this is followed by an EVP from what sounds like either a woman or a child saying, "Yes."

I ask, "Anybody here with me? What's your name? Are you buried at Boot Hill? Were you taken in this hearse?" A man speaks, saying what sounds like, "Bandit." Suddenly, there's a beep sound, and I debunk it as being my phone and as this happens unexplained static pours through the recorder. Then a man is recorded breathing heavily. I say, "This is a creepy hearse." At 6.39 an EVP of a woman disagreeing with me, "Not creepy." She's right. It is not creepy, it is beautiful. In fact, it's hauntingly beautiful. A woman in a white period dress walks in and starts talking to me. Enter Darba Jo Butler.

Session four, the Moriah

After talking for a minute or so, before recording, Darba lets me know that the spirits at the Bird Cage like it when it's someone's birthday. I suggest we pretend that it's mine. Darba cheerfully says, "It's Tessa's birthday today!" Then an EVP is recorded mumbling, what sounds like, "No it's not." Darba and I sing Happy Birthday, we cheer after singing. Then I give out a short laugh and immediately after that a man is recorded laughing, very close as if he is standing right there with us.

Darba starts to speak and a man is recorded saying an unintelligible word. She starts to talk about the Moriah, "This is the original coach." A man gives this amazing EVP, "Was in that hearse." Darba continues, "It cost $8,000.00 back in 1881." A man is recorded saying, "Oh man." Darba says, "It shipped from New York City. Ford Museum estimated the value well over a million dollars."

She tells me, "I just cleaned it up pretty good, so it's looking pretty spiffy. The crosses are shiny now. 24 carat gold." As Darba continues to speak, an unexplained static is recorded. Darba says, "I start polishing the silver," an EVP from a man is recorded as he says, "Rub." Darba was just sharing with me how she was busy polishing the Moriah, maybe this spirit was watching her do so.

Darba looks over to the left of the Moriah where a viewing casket leans against the wall. (The viewing casket was used for funeral services of those who couldn't afford to buy a casket. After the funeral was over, the body was removed and placed in a plain pine box for burial.) Darba asks me, "It looks tilted. Does it look tilted to you?" It was indeed tilted. She goes under the rope to fix it. As she does this unexplained static is caught on recording. I ask, "Did any of the spirits here move this casket?" An EVP is recorded of a man whispering under his breath, "Yes." Darba told me some interesting information about the viewing casket, where you would lay there for ten days with someone with you just in case you wake up.

Darba explains to me what the break in the middle of the casket is for, take it apart, it folds in half, and goes below the Moriah. She mentions, "This is the area where people get attachments and residuals. There is an intelligent spirit here who tries to talk to people. There are many spirits in this building. We have the stage manager, Charlie Keen, we have the lady in white," a disembodied exhale is recorded. Darba says, "Some kids, not necessarily died here, but are drawn here. You can really tell the difference in their footsteps because kids are pink-pink-pink, adults are boom-boom-boom, then ladies with their high heels.

I tell Darba about my book, this book, and as I do this an unexplained pop is recorded. A man is recorded breathing. I pause and look to the left, something moved, I cannot put my finger on what it was, but something moved. Peripheral view. Darba asks me, "Have you ever watched Ghost Adventures? Have you seen the one about The Bird Cage?" They came through twice. She relives her experience, "I'm the girl that fell down the stairs. Did you see the girl fall?" An EVP is recorded, "I did." She says, "That was me. I fell all the way down the stairs. My manager was up at the top, they were doing a scene, an excerpt, kind of."

An unexplained pop sound is recorded. She continues, "An excerpt of something that happened in the building, and they were using me. So, the first step I took, I endowed [sic]. I have been going up and down these stairs for over nine years, I don't know what happened that time. Zak asked me, 'Did somebody push you?' I told him, 'No but somebody caught me.' So, when you watch the episode, you see me bouncing off the bottom of the stairs. It was really weird. I'm a tour guide, I'm not some special sensitive, but I have many experiences here. Watch that episode. The Bird Cage Theatre. It happened the first time they were here and aired it the second time."

Session 5, the Moriah / Poker room

Darba is still telling me about her experience when Ghost Adventures was on-site filming the episode. She says, "You can see I'm like this, boing-boing-boing." An unexplained sound, what sounds like a woman weeping is recorded, going unheard by us. She continues, "Not a scratch on me!" She pauses and continues, "Zak asks, 'Why did they catch you?' and I said to him, 'Cause I have a lot of friends in this building Zak.'" I laugh and say, "Oh Zak!" An EVP from a woman is caught saying, "Forget him." Darba says, "He's at the bottom of the stairs saying, 'What are you doing?' and I'm like, 'Well … help, help me out of here!'" A man is recorded saying what sounds like, "Go home." I tell Darba how Aaron is my favorite and how he is so funny, an EVP from a man saying, "Fun."

I ask Darba if her experience can be in one of the chapters and she said yes! A man gives this EVP, "Ask her." I already did! I ask Darba if the morticians table that is hanging above the Moriah is an original. She replies that yes indeed it is an original mortician table that they used back in the 1880s. She points out to me that it is moving by itself. I look up and see it also. We stand there in silence watching this. As this is happening a woman is recorded speaking unintelligible words. We are still the only two people in there at this time.

While the mortician table did move by itself in front of us, it was slight and soft. Darba says, "The mortician table moves so hard sometimes, you can hear a click-click-click, loudly." I ask the Bird Cage spirits, "Did you spend your last moments on that morticians table?" An eerie EVP is recorded saying, what sounds like, "Watch the body."

Darba says goodbye and starts to head downstairs where the poker room is, I didn't even see that earlier, so I follow her downstairs. The longest poker game ever played took place right here, downstairs of the Bird Cage. For twenty-four hours a day, seven days a week, this game lasted an amazing eight years, five months and three days. Quite impressive! Walking downstairs you see two old poker tables standing proudly on a dirt floor with cards, poker chips, money and change strewn about on the tables. I ask Darba, "Is this all original?" She replies yes. An EVP of a man also verifies the originality, "Original."

It is believed that during this long, seemingly everlasting game, $10,000,000 changed hands. Besides Holliday and Masterson, another participant was Adolphus Busch. Remember in the first session, while Martha was giving history about the Bird Cage, she mentioned Busch, and I also received an EVP of a man saying, "Das Busch."

Session 6, Poker room

Unexplained static along with what sounds like a wheel turning, followed by more static, this goes on for several seconds. I ask if there is anybody in here with me, and more static is recorded, then an EVP from a man, "Don't know. Quiet." The static stays for about ten more seconds. I ask, "If there is anybody in here with me can you please tell me your name and how you died?" An EVP is recorded, "Cheated."

The unexplained pop sounds are recorded. Then a concerned EVP from a man asking, "What's wrong?" I take a picture, and as I do this an unexplained exhale of a man is recorded. An EVP is recorded of a child saying what sounds like, "Raise your arms."

Session seven, the Moriah

I say, "I'm just about to leave." An EVP from a man is recorded, telling me to, "Leave." I go back upstairs, stopping to take a picture and "Stop" is recorded. As I head towards the Moriah, my recorder catches static, then a pop is recorded. This is then followed by an exhale from a woman or a child.

You can hear people in the distance, I debunk them. No one is around me and as for these people, they are at the beginning of the museum, on the other side of the door. An EVP is recorded of a woman, "Pardon me." Very close, as if she is standing right next to me. A not so friendly EVP from a man saying, "Wench." I am unsure if this was directed to me, or the friendly spirit of the woman who just said, 'Pardon me.'

As I stand in front of the Moriah, I look up and ask, "Can anyone move that mortician table?" While the table remains still, I do get an EVP of a woman saying, "Or what?" My phone rings, as I go to answer it, a man's exasperated breath is recorded. I am flustered, as I am on the phone trying to end the conversation quickly, I say into the phone, "I have no idea ... ugh!" A woman whispers, as if right in my ear, saying, "Come with me."

A couple walk up to the Moriah as I stand there. I tell them what Darba told me earlier, about the mortician table moving by itself, and how we both witnessed it just a few minutes earlier, as I speak an EVP of a woman is recorded, "Shh!" Two unexplained click-like sounds are recorded. Followed by an EVP of a child, sounds like a boy, saying, "Come off."

I am still at the Moriah but now talking to a different couple. I have the EMF in my hand and am talking to the couple about the tools I use for investigations, as I am talking, an unintelligible EVP is recorded. Then an EVP of a woman is recorded of her saying, "Hurry up." Followed by a moan.

Session eight, the final session

I say, "I am leaving now, off to the next place. If anybody wants to come and show themselves to me in these pictures I am taking or need to say something, please do so now." A few days later, I am looking through my camera, and I see what looks like a large man with what I think is a blacksmith's apron. There's the Moriah, then next to it, to the left, is the viewing casket, then to the left of that is a glass case. The man's reflection was in that glass case.

An unexplained sound followed by an exhale of what sounds like a child. As I take a picture an unexplained pop is recorded. An EVP of a woman is recorded, "Ghosts." As I am leaving I say, "The show must go on." An unexplained exhale from a man, very close, as if right in my ear. This is repeated again several seconds later by the same man. As I walk downstairs towards the exit, again the man exhales.

The Birdcage was a beautiful place, the people there were friendly and happy to spend time with their guests and answered questions. I can't wait to go back there some day, and be in the Moriah's hauntingly beautiful presence once again.

Chapter eighteen

Big Nose Kate's Saloon, Tombstone, Arizona

Through my teen years, when I attended school in Ojo Caliente, New Mexico, I was a target for the bullies for multiple years. These people were so mean and had so much hate towards me I was flabbergasted. Every day these pathetic losers taunted me, hurting me by calling me immature and painful names.

What I did to make these monsters treat me like I had the plague, I will never know. I was called witch, bruja (witch in Spanish) white trash, and many other names. I won't go further than that because the pain is still there, my self-esteem will never be what it was before New Mexico. I often wonder what my life would be like if I was able to magically erase those years, what I would have been. Since I was a 'witch' you'd think I would have been able to do it. Jokes on me I guess!

When I saw the saloon and the name, it reminded me of the horrible names those kids called me all those years back. I knew it was a place I had to check out, so I called ahead of time and asked if I would be able to go in for lunch and a drink and bring my equipment as well.

A little history about the lady behind the saloon's name:

> Kate, whose real name was Mary, was born in 1850 in Hungary. She was a prostitute, and a boarding house owner. She also happened to be the common law wife of Doc Holliday! They met in 1877 in Fort Griffin, Texas. Kate lived a long life, dying due to health problems, just a few short days before her 90th birthday.
>
> The saloon itself, started life as a hotel dating back to 1880. The Grand Hotel, sixteen rooms, one of Arizona's finest back then. Some of this hotel's well-known guests included brothers Virgil and Wyatt Earp, Doc Holliday, and when in town, the notorious Clanton's. The hotel met a fiery end—not even two full years later when it found itself

engulfed in flames of the May 25 fire back in 1882. In the basement you can wander down and find a sweet little gift shop. Besides the gift shop, the tunnel that leads to the mine shaft can still be found there.

While this was a functioning hotel, there was a man who went by the nickname, 'The Swamper' he was the hotel's trusty janitor and did other odd jobs around the premises. He lived in the basement area, as part of his pay. There he had his privacy, where the hotel guests were unable to venture. It was here that, not being too far from the mines, he spent a large unknown number of hours tunneling an entrance to the mine. To this day nobody knows if the Swamper spent the silver he extracted from the mines or if he buried it in or around this building. People have seen a spirit here and believe it to be the Swamper himself.

June 18, 2016
The investigation

The day before I went to Tombstone I called the Saloon and introduced myself as a paranormal investigator and asked if it would be okay if, while I was there visiting and having lunch, I could use my equipment there as well.

The woman on the phone was very friendly and said there wouldn't be a problem with doing that. She unfortunately forgot to mention that the day I was coming had live music, so it was quite loud. I was able to conduct a couple short sessions, but due to all the noise I basically debunked the session. I will have to go back sometime when there is no music going on, nothing against the guy, he was really good, very friendly, and quite the comedian as well.

Results and evidence collected
Session one

I am enjoying an ice-cold drink and the live music, I am not speaking but I do have my recorder on to see if it can catch anything. I had been sitting there for about ten minutes until the table next to me emptied. At that point, I was the only person in that area so then I started to record. For a while there's nothing but music and chitter chatter in the distance from the other guests, then unexplained static is recorded.

The Mel Meter spikes at 0.6 and stays there for several seconds. Some sounds and voices are recorded, but I am debunking these things as being typical bar noise. The Mel Meter which I have positioned in front of me is now at 2.7. Unexplained breathing from a man is recorded, remember nobody is sitting near me at this time. As I am listening to the music the same man is recorded exhaling. The music temporarily stops, cheering and applause from the audience, then music starts up again. An EVP is recorded saying what sounds like, "I itch." Again, this is close, as if speaking right in to the recorder.

Session two, final session

After eating lunch and re-hydrating myself, I make my way to the spiral staircase that leads to the basement where the gift shop is and where the Swamper lived and is still thought to haunt this section to this day. I mention the Swamper, the man who lived below the hotel and was stealing silver from the mine, he was murdered. I say, "The Swamper stole silver down here." I receive an EVP whisper, what sounds like, "I didn't."

I make my way down the stairs. I enter the basement where the Swamper lived and died. I say, "I'm in the area where the Swamper died." An unexplained inhale from a man is recorded. When I was going down there the only people there were the cashier, a woman and two customers, also ladies who were just leaving. I say, "So this man lived here, he was on call twenty-four-seven for everything." An EVP from a man saying, "A lot." Followed by, "Ahh" like a sigh of relief, what sounds like the same man. After this, unexplained static is recorded.

As I stand there looking into the area where The Swamper lived and died, I close my eyes and try to picture being here back when this occurred. This man was brutally murdered. This was the place where he lived, his safe haven if you will. He found peace here, it was his home. Then someone came and destroyed that home, that safe haven.

I am quiet. Music is heard from upstairs, very faint. I get this neat EVP whispered, "Wyatt Earp." After this incredible EVP is recorded, unexplained static is also recorded. Amazingly, I receive another EVP from the same man, repeating himself, "Wyatt Earp." Followed yet again by static.

Remember, Wyatt and his brother Virgil Earp were among the guests that would frequently visit this hotel. While I am trying to communicate with The Swamper, can this man who is speaking and giving me these clear EVPs be

Wyatt Earp himself? Who knows? But talk about amazing! Here is a place where the man himself, Wyatt Earp and his brothers would spend a lot of time. It wouldn't be surprising if he spent time here as a spirit since he was here often when he was alive.

I am still in the same area and I start talking to somebody. For a good twelve seconds, very loud obnoxious, static is recorded.

I am now talking to the woman who is the cashier, and is the only employee for this gift shop, super friendly by the way. A few seconds later, what sounds like the same man who has been talking this whole time is recorded again making a sound, "Ahh." Followed yet again by a recording of unexplained static. My time in Tombstone was very limited and I most definitely plan to come back to this amazing town.

Chapter nineteen

Watt and Tarbell Mortuary, (Sisters Paranormal Investigations) Tombstone, Arizona

When I saw the sign 'Sisters Paranormal Investigations' I knew I had to check it out! The name alone meant a lot to me, my sister and I have our own paranormal investigating team so, it was close to home. These two sisters conduct investigations at this old mortuary. I knew I had to do this. One of the sisters, Stacy and I talked for quite a few minutes. I prepaid for the investigation and I went on my way to explore more of Tombstone.

The investigation
June 18, 2016

After a whole day of investigating some of Tombstone's most haunted historic landmarks, it was time for the Watt and Tarbell investigation. Like I said earlier, I can really relate to these sisters. One of the sisters was unable to make it on this investigation. Stacy, the woman I met earlier, was there along with another woman, her friend, who is also part of her investigating team named Tressa.

Besides Stacy, Tressa and myself there were also two couples who were there as well. Before the investigation even starts I have my recorder on. Check out these results!

Results and evidence collected
Session one (before the investigation started)

Two unexplained pops are recorded. The Mel EMF reads at 0.8. Everyone is getting situated, heading to the front of the building. The investigation hasn't even started yet and I get an EVP of a child either breathing or speaking an unintelligible word. One of my tools (they are awesome and let people use their own equipment) is malfunctioning and I say, "Sorry, stupid thing." The same child is recorded sighing, this is followed by another pop sound.

Stacy greets the group and gives us some history about the mortuary. She says, "By now all of you know this building was the morgue. In its heyday there were three morgues here in Tombstone. All three of them with full time morticians. At the very same time, New York City, St. Louis and San Francisco," an unexplained whistle is recorded. Stacy continues, "they had one morgue," Another whistle is recorded. Stacy finishes that sentence, "with a part-time mortician. So that tells you a little about the town's history. This building started being built in 1878 and it was completed in early 1879." As she finishes that sentence an unexplained pop is recorded.

Stacy says, "It opened up as Tarbell Undertakers." A woman gives this encouraging EVP, "Go on." Stacy does just that, "About the time it opened, the town was still known as Goose Flats. So, when the silver rush hit, people started coming in and the town became Tombstone." A woman whispers this EVP, "What." Stacy continues, "Mr. Tarbell took on a partner and it then became, 'Watt and Tarbell.' It was Watt and Tarbell until 1887, when they then dissolved their partnership." Unintelligible words are spoken and recorded.

Stacy says, "It went back to being Tarbell Undertakers." A moan is recorded. Stacy continues, "We know this was the morgue at least up until 1909, this was the latest record we were able to locate." Another moan is recorded. Stacy continues on, "The original building goes all the way from here till Doc Holliday's Saloon. Our gift shop and saloon part were the family parlors, the viewing area, the chapel and there was a living space by the far back of our building. For a short period of time the front portion of the saloon, was also the Wells Fargo at that time. This area of the building that we are standing in was where the horse drawn hearse called the Moriah sat."

As Stacy talks about the Birdcage Theatre, where the Moriah is and where I was earlier in the day, disembodied loud footsteps are recorded. Stacy says, "Mr. Tarbell purchased two of the Moriah's from upstate New York. He paid $8,000.00 a piece for them. That is the purpose for these little doors in the front of the building. That's where they would pull the Moriah in and out from." An unintelligible word is whispered and recorded. Stacy continues, "If a body was brought in here that was unidentified the morticians would go ahead and do the embalming." An EVP is recorded asking, "Why?"

Stacy continues, "And prepare the body for burial. They would then put them in what's called the 'Viewing Coffin' which is," as she pauses an EVP of a man is recorded saying, "I've had enough." Stacy continues on, "A viewing coffin that has a glass front on it. They would roll your body right to that door there, open the door, and prop you up. They would leave the body there for as long as ten days hoping that someone walking down Allen Street would recognize you and come in and identify you. Unfortunately, most of the people that sat in that door were buried as unknowns. There are a ton of unknowns here."

We start to make our way to where the morticians worked. As we make our way into the small room, Stacy speaks, "This is the portable morticians table. You can see on the top here it's dated April 12, 1881." An unexplained pop is recorded. Stacy goes on, "The reason why they had the portable tables like this, a lot of the time back then, you didn't take your family member to the morgue, they'd process the body right in your own home." Another unexplained pop is recorded.

Stacy goes on, "The mortician would come right to you to do the embalming. You can tell by looking at it. It folds up and looks like a big wooden suitcase. Do any of you know what these holes on the table were used for?" Silence. I guess, "Fluids?"

Stacy replies, "They did embalm, but the main reason for the holes are that they would put blocks of ice underneath the table and that would allow the cold air to seep up and keep the bodies cold. Another term for the table was, 'the cooling table.' A sad sound, what sounds like a woman weeping is caught on the recorder.

The group starts to walk to the far back part of the building. An EVP of a man is caught saying, "Touch the hair." (Remember this EVP, several different things happen later during the investigation.)

Stacy says, "This area had actually been an outside yard, it would have been fenced in. It is where the second hearse, would have sat, along with all the building materials for the coffins. You can see where there is a window there and there used to be a door on the other side of that wall was the area of the building that was a living space. The morticians and their families lived there." As she pauses, what sounds like a disembodied, labored deep breath is recorded. Stacy continues, "The metal on the wall is the original roof to our building." An EVP of a man saying, "Yes" is recorded.

Stacy continues, "When it had to be replaced the owners didn't have the heart to put it in the dump, so that was their way of keeping it in the building itself. If you look in this direction, you can see that's the exterior to the building, so in the 1800s that's what this entire building would have looked like pretty much inside and out. Because of the age of the adobe, it's become very brittle."

Stacy continues, "So anything exposed to the weather and most of the inside has been covered just to preserve it." An EVP is recorded, "You're right." Followed by a metal-on-metal sound. Stacy points out, "The doorway that Tressa is under is original to the building and everything on this window over here including the bullet hole that we have on the top left pane is also original." A disembodied voice is recorded saying, "Wow."

Stacy continues, "We do have it stabilized with a washer and a screw, just so we can keep the original glass in there for as long as possible. We have no idea why someone was shooting towards the morgue. We do know there was a livery stable that sat directly behind the building." Three unexplained small pop sounds are recorded. Stacy says, "We have found this morgue in the newspapers advertising that they can make mud-drops at the livery behind the building so you can just take a body back there, drop it off and go about your business."

We start to make our way toward another room. Stacy speaks, "This is original to the building, can anyone tell me what this item is used for?" Silence, one of the ladies in the group guesses, "Draining?"

Stacy smiles and says, "Exactly. It's the morticians sink where they'd do embalming. Where you guys are standing … that's where the morticians table that sat right here would have been. It would have been slightly bigger then the portable one, with a little bit of a tilt." An unexplained loud clank like sound, followed by an unexplained excited sound, "Whoo-whoo."

Stacy says, "They'd use the gravity method. The window over here would hold it straight above and there's a window on the other side of the wall, that's what they used for the ventilation back here. Not only did they have dead bodies back here, but at that time, they used cyanide in the embalming fluids. So those were there for the health of the living."

An EVP of a woman saying what sounds like, "Whoever rocked it." Followed by a gasp for air. Stacy continues, "It was common for morticians to die at young ages. Ours lived to be 85 and 89 years old. Now the next place," she warns us, "is the basement. It's very short, so you do have to be bent over. Not everybody chooses to go down, but everyone is welcome."

Session two
The Basement

We head down to the basement, walking down the stairs. As we are walking, Tressa says, "I don't even hit 5 foot and I have to bend down." An EVP is recorded, what sounds like, "Pull it." Possibly a woman or a child.

We are all now in the basement and situated. Stacy speaks, "So during the time that this was the morgue, this is where the sulfur, the cyanide—everything that was used in the embalming—this is where it was stored. If you have time before you leave check out the display case up at the front. Most of the items were found right here in the basement." Unfortunately, I forgot about this case by the time we were done, and I forgot to check it out. Next time for sure. A man is recorded moaning. There is no one else here but us—there are two men with us, and they sure as hell didn't moan.

Stacy continues, "I showed you guys the morticians sink," an unexplained pop is recorded. Stacy goes on, "so, if you look on that back wall, you see that piece of pipe coming through that's no longer connected to anything? That's the original clay plumbing that connected to the mortician sink. It simply drained out from behind the building and down into the wash. The wall that's collapsed in here, that wall was collapsed down on purpose. It leads down to the tunnel systems that run below the town. They ran to the different businesses, to the mines and to the opium dens." As she finishes that sentence an unintelligible EVP is recorded.

Stacy continues, "You can see we have the original adobe down here as well." An unexplained loud breathing coming from a man is recorded. Stacy shares a special moment that happened down here in the basement, "Actually, one of my favorite EVPs we got was recorded down here. We had an all-female private group down here. One of the ladies who was here for an EVP session was squatted down. She didn't want to get her clothing dirty. On her recorder she got a man's voice that said, 'Make it easy on your butt. Sit down on the dirt.' If you want to hear this amazing EVP for yourself, go to our Facebook page, it's our very first post that we ever posted."

My Mel Meter starts making sounds, and spikes to a 1.1, then seconds later, to a 1.3. An EVP of a woman is recorded saying, "Ahh."

We are upstairs again and go into the first area we started. We get situated into the chairs which were put together in a big circle with a table in the center with equipment on it.

Session three

Stacy starts to explain the equipment to the group. "The theory is that spirits use electro-magnetic energy. These are EMF pumps that just found some energy up in the air for us." She points to the wall, "This is another EM pump plugged right into the wall. The red light is a static detector. The theory is that spirits throw off negative ions. The red is negative, the yellow is positive." A disembodied sound is recorded.

She continues, "When you turn it on, you should get no lights on, if it detects spirits you will see red, motion is yellow, if it detects both, then both the lights come on." She holds another item, even though I had my equipment with me, they let me use their tools as well, so I picked this next item she talks about. "The Parascope, they read energy. The tubes up here are fiber optic tubes, so if they come near them, the tubes light up. If it's a weaker energy you might only see one or two lighting up, where if it's a nice strong energy they'll pull the lights all the way across. I take control of the Parascope and I must say I enjoyed this tool very much and I plan on purchasing one very soon.

As Stacy is explaining the equipment, the teddy bear, which has an EMF in it, starts to talk, "I like holding hands." Stacy says, "This is Boo Buddy. He's my favorite thing in here. The green light means he is on, he's got KII meters in his paws, if it's a weaker energy, one paw will light up, if it's a nice strong energy both will light up. He will talk about every forty seconds."

"Mostly he is trying to get a child to react to him and come up to him, but there are a few things he says that tells you something is actually happening. He also has a temp gauge in him, so if we get a good drop in the temperature, he'll ask, 'Did you just make it cooler?' A rise, 'Did you just make it warmer in here?' If he's touched in the mid-section, he giggles and says, 'That tickles.' If his paw is touched, he says, 'I like holding hands too.'

We all laugh as one of the guys calls dibs on Boo. We are laughing when a disembodied deep laugh joins in, unheard by us but recorded. The Ovilus is turned on, another tool that I have been dying to try, I didn't get to use it for this investigation, but after the investigation Stacy and Tressa were amazing and let me stay a while longer and use it in the basement! While Stacy is explaining what the Ovilus does, it gets two hits, 'ACTION' and 'POEM' The Ovilus also has an EMF on top, so the stronger the energy, the more bubbles light up.

At the time of this investigation I had never used the Ovilus. Then a little over a year later my amazing family gifted me with my very own Ovilus, I am so lucky and so grateful to have a family who support me in my para-adventures! They are totally awesome!

One of the ladies of the group picks the Ovilus, and it immediately gets a hit, 'PULL', Tressa warns the girl, who happens to have much longer hair, "Watch your hair." I get an EVP of a man saying, "Gloss." Tressa says, "It said, 'pull' she better watch her hair."

Stacy explains the flashlight method, then she starts talking about the SCD1, "Designed by Steve Huff of Huff Paranormal, along with Anthony Sanchez. It's very clear, it sweeps through internet radio, so when it sweeps through the radio you are not getting the regular spirit box noise. Listen for full words and full sentences. It cannot connect to a station long enough for an entire word." After the tools are all explained, Stacy says, "Some of you are sensitive, you feel them or see them, if you experience anything, feel free to share with the group." A child is recorded giving this EVP, "Ready?"

Stacy starts speaking to the morgue spirits, "Hello ladies and gentlemen of the building. We brought a few friends to come and visit you." An unexplained sound is recorded, that sounds like a woman crying.

Session four

We all say hi to the spirits. Old music—that sounds like old circus music—comes through the SCD1. A man's voice comes through the SCD1 saying, "We can hear you." Stacy replies, "I can hear you." A man speaks through the SCD1 saying an unintelligible word. A child comes through saying, "I'm a baby, baby." Then a man says, "You." A boy comes through the SCD1 saying these creepy words, "Surround them." Then a few seconds later a man says, "Doc."

The flashlight, that has been off this whole time, turns on by itself. Stacy asks, "Doc, is that you? Can you please turn the flashlight off? Only if its Doc. If it's not Doc please leave it on." A few seconds later, I notice the two ladies that are part of the couples in the group whispering to each other, so I debunk that right away, whispering into my recorder, "Whispering debunked." This is then followed by unexplained static.

The KII meter in Boo Buddy spikes. Stacy asks, "Whoever is playing with Boo Buddy, can you please back off the hands for a minute, make the hands go off." The flashlight goes off. Stacy asks, "If you're a little girl, can you make the paws light up again?" An unintelligible EVP of a child is recorded. Stacy adds, "Only if it's a girl." Boo Buddy speaks, "Ah, thanks. I like holding hands too!" Stacy asks, "If you are a little boy can you touch Boo Buddy again and make his paws light up?" Stacy encourages the man holding the bear to ask questions.

Boo Buddy says, "Thanks for making it warmer." The man says, "You're welcome. Are you a boy?" Immediately after he asks this question a paw lights up. An EVP of a child is recorded asking, "Hello?" The man asks, "Are you a kid? Light up both paws if you are a kid." Boo Buddy giggles, "That tickles." Stacy asks, "Can you tell us your name through the SCD1 please? Who's playing with Boo Buddy?" The SCD1 immediately comes to life. What sounds like a child comes through saying, "A ghost." A man comes through saying, what sounds like, "You damn kids!" Stacy and I say in unison, "That was a kid." A woman comes through saying, "Dishes." Unsure what that means.

Stacy asks, "What's your name hun?" A woman comes through saying, "Ingrid." A few seconds later the Parascope that is sitting on my lap suddenly lights up. Tressa asks, "Did you say Drew?" A man comes through saying, "Fuck you Louis." The guy who's holding the Boo Buddy asks, "Is your name Drew?" My recorder catches an EVP of a man replying, "Yes."

Again, one of the people—a guy this time—is whispering, a big no-no while investigating, again I whisper, "Whispering debunked." Stacy says, "If this is Paul, which I'm positive it is," she pauses, and as she does I get this EVP on my recorder of a man confirming what Stacy just said, "It is." Stacy warns the group, "Watch your shoes. He likes to untie shoes." I laugh and say, "I don't have shoe-laces, so the joke is on Paul."

The man with the bear asks, "Are you Paul? If your name is Paul light up the paws." Boo Buddy speaks, "Did you say something? Can you please say it again?" Stacy starts to name off resident spirits who happen to be children, "Seth. Quinn. Zach." The guy with the bear asks, "Is your name Zach?"

Immediately after asking this, an EVP growl is recorded—on the deeper side—this is definitely not from a child.

Stacy asks, "How many of you are here with us right now? Can you give us a number?" The SCD1 goes off again, a man comes through saying, "Three" another voice, "Eighteen." Tressa explains what it feels like when a spirit touches you, "You can feel anything from a tingle like feeling …" as she says this, Boo Buddy is recorded as he giggles and says, "It tickles."

Session five

Stacy describes being touched by a spirit as walking through a spider web, as she is talking, a man gives an unintelligible EVP. Tressa says, "You could all of a sudden feel very warm or really cool for no reason there are many different signs and it's different for each person." As she finishes that sentence, an unexplained pop is recorded.

Tressa goes on, "For me, I always know when somebody is around," as she pauses, I get an EVP of a child taking a deep breath. Tressa continues, "because I instantly get cold." Another unexplained pop is recorded. The flashlight just goes off by itself. Stacy thanks the spirits, "Thank you for turning that off, we appreciate it." A few seconds go by when suddenly the lady with the long hair says, "My back just got really cold." I suggest they take pictures.

Stacy asks the lady who just got cold, "Do you want to ask if somebody is behind you?" A woman gives this eerie EVP saying, "Behind you." The lady asks, "Is anybody standing behind me?" Unexplained loud thump-like noises are recorded. Suddenly the SCD1 goes off and a voice says, "There are people." Another voice says, "Multiple." They are confirming that yes, there are people behind us.

Stacy asks, "Can you tell us the names of the people standing behind her?" SCD1 goes off, a woman says, "Please say ____" Last word unintelligible. Then a child says, "Behind you, go in here?" A few seconds later the same child, who I believe to be a boy says an unintelligible word. A man comes through saying, "Good call." Another man says, "Victor, I am."

Tressa reminds us, "When you first had the Ovilus remember it said, pull hair." A child gives this EVP, "Go ahead." Stacy asks, "Do you guys like her hair?" Tressa asks, "Do you like her hair?" The SCD1 goes off again, a man says, "I like her hair." Another man comes through saying, "It's very smooth." Stacy asks, "Do you want to play with her hair?" Unintelligible words come through the SCD1. Stacy asks, "Do you want to run your fingers through her hair?" A man whispers this EVP, super close as if he is sitting right next to me whispering in my ear, "Sorry." An EVP of a man whispering, "I just did." Then the same words pour through the SCD1, "I just did." The girl confirms, "I just felt something!"

Stacy asks, "What's the name of the person you said she just felt it?" Tressa asks, "Who just ran their fingers through her hair?" The SCD1 blurts out the name, "Chris." A name that Stacy and Tressa are all too familiar with, they tell us about Chris, a young boy who is here often. I feel something and say, "Woah!" As this happens an unexplained breath of a child is recorded.

Stacy looks at me and asks, "Oh-oh! What did you get?" I explain how I just felt something tap my shoe. Tressa points at my lap, "The Parascope is going off!" She explains to me that nothing can make the Parascope go off, the only thing that can make it go off is spirits. Amazing. I am touched and the equipment I am holding goes off right after that! Can this be the spirit they warned us about earlier, who likes to tie peoples shoe laces together? Paul? I guess the jokes on me.

I ask, "What's your name? Can you," as I am speaking a child is recorded giving an unintelligible EVP. I end, "tell me why you just did that?" Boo Buddy says, "I like holding hands." A voice comes through the SCD1, answering my question, "I wanted to." Amazing! My Mel Meter spikes at 0.5. An EVP is recorded speaking unintelligible words. I offer my Mel Meter to the girl whose boyfriend is holding the bear, to see if they get any spikes or alerts. An EVP of a man is recorded saying, "Oh no." Then a child is recorded making an excited noise.

As I explain the tool to the girl, we get this creepy EVP of what sounds like a young boy, in an annoyed voice saying, "Get rid of it." Tressa takes note, "You have a few behind you." I get an EVP of a woman whispering, "Won't you run with me?" An EVP of a man, possibly responding to the woman who just spoke says, "Yes."

Unexplained sounds are recorded. What sounds like a child making click noises through mouth. The Mel Meter fluctuates between 0.3 and 0.4. Stacy checks hers to see if she is getting any hits and replies, "Mine is at 0. I'm not getting anything. I'm getting temp fluctuations but nothing else." I ask the spirits, "Why don't you give her some love over there, give her a spike please!" Seconds later unexplained footsteps are recorded. We are all sitting down and have been the entire time. Stacy says, "Wow! As soon as you said that it went to 1.3, but only for a quick second." We laugh. I say, "Thank you for doing that." A man is recorded giving this EVP, "Kiss or hug?" Is that supposed to be a sort of payment? No thanks!

After Stacy is done saying Happy Fathers' day to all the dads out there, not only does the SCD1 come back on but the flashlight turns on as well. A man comes through saying an unintelligible word. Then what sounds like a little girl comes through cheerfully saying, "Hi."

The Ovilus gets three hits, "REACH" "DUG" and "RELIGION" Stacy asks, "Is this the man that has been telling me to have *Jason find you down in the mine?" A man comes through the SCD1 saying, "Yes." Stacy encourages the lost spirit to tell them where he is located so they can find him. A man speaks through the SCD1 saying, "To the right." Tressa says to us, "I just saw a light go left to right." Stacy says, "So Jason wants to find you, but we need more then 'to the right' please." A man comes through saying an unintelligible word. Then an unexplained loud thump is recorded.

Stacy says, "Let me rephrase the question, when Jason was down there today, did you see him? Did he pass your body?" The SCD1 reacts, a man speaks unintelligible words, a little boy comes through saying in this sweet little voice, "I'm scared." Stacy explains to us the situation about this spirit, "For the mine tour down there, they do this longer tour and about a week and a half ago we started getting this man telling us that his body is down in the Tough Nut Mine." The flashlight turns on. Stacy asks, "If this is the man who is down in the mine, can you please turn it off?" The flashlight turns off.

Boo Buddy says, "Thanks for making it warmer." Stacy encourages the spirits to make noise, so we know they're here. Seconds after she requests a sound, footsteps are recorded, unheard by us and remember we are still sitting at this time. Stacy suggests that one of us should hold the flashlight. I offer. I put my equipment down, and keep the recorder running. As I stand there with the flashlight, Stacy asks, "If someone holds it, will you walk over to them?" A man is recorded exhaling, "Ahh."

Stacy says, "They're following you." The same man repeats himself, "Ahh." As I stand there, I say, "Hello. I am a paranormal investigator as well and I welcome you." A loud footstep is recorded. I continue, "I respect you fully. If you would like to come to me, my name is Tessa. Can you tell me your name?" A few seconds go by when suddenly the SCD1 roars to life, a man says what sounds like, "Peyton" then a little boy comes through saying, "Billy" then a man comes through saying, "Boots." Then another man comes through saying, "Hello." Lastly, a voice comes through asking, "Paranormal investigator?"

I laugh and say, "Yes, I am a paranormal investigator. Can you tell me what you used to do for a living?" Voices start pouring through the SCD1 speaking unintelligible words, a man comes through saying, "Disrobe." I laugh and say, "No thank you." Tressa says, "Guys, be respectful." An EVP from a man asking, "Why?" I offer the spirits, "Please go ahead and touch me, shake my hand, pull my hair if you want." The flashlight goes off.

Stacy points at the man holding Boo Bear and says, "For the man who said disrobe, this guy over here said he would be happy to disrobe. You want him to take his clothing off for you?" The SCD1 comes on, a man says, "Keep them on please." We all laugh. I say, "Here, I'll disrobe. I'll take my hat off for you, is that good enough for you?" A man comes through, possibly the same man who just spoke and says, "Thank you, madam." Right after that a child is recording breathing loudly, going unheard by us.

Unexplained static is recorded and as this happens, the flashlight turns back on. Tressa notes, "I see someone standing there in the doorway." Stacy asks, "Who's back there?" I get an EVP of a man responding, "All of us." A loud unexplained thump is recorded, followed by a man coming through the SCD1 saying, "Jared." A child comes through asking, "Are you truly?" A man also comes through saying, "Albert."

Tressa asks, "Can you repeat your name for us?" A voice comes through the SCD1 saying, what sounds like, "Axe." The flashlight turns on and a few seconds later turns back off. Stacy asks, "Thank you for turning that back on for us." An EVP of a man is recorded, repeating, "All of us." Stacy starts to speak, I interrupt, "I just heard a whisper." An unexplained loud deep breath from a man. Stacy asks, "Did you?" I reply, "Like a man whispering." Stacy asks, "Can you do it again please?" Then a man gives this EVP, "Yes."

Just to clarify when this happened the guy who was holding the bear said the bear recently talked, we just left it at that, but as soon as the man whispered I responded so I am taking the debunk back, it was indeed not the Boo Bear that I heard. Stacy says, "For the person using the flashlight, are you a man? If so turn it off so we know whose using it." Seconds later, the flashlight starts to dim. The Ovilus gets a hit, "UNHOLY"

Stacy talks to us about a man who is there many times, who is believed to be autistic, who goes by the name Oscar. He likes to watch them. Stacy goes on, "We had two adults with minor forms of autism and he came right up to them saying, 'I'm the same.' When he was seen in the door the Ovilus would always say, DEVIL or UNHOLY." Earlier Tressa told us that they use words that are familiar to them. It may mean something completely different in this day and age. Unholy - disabled.

As Tressa speaks, "I've actually had first hand," what sounds like a female is recorded giving this EVP, "Sike." Tressa continues, "communication with him. I actually work with people who have developmental disabilities. He knows that. He is comfortable with me because he knows that I understand." Stacy asks, "With what the Ovilus said, does that mean that Oscar is here?" The SCD1 comes on and a man comes through saying, "Potentially." Another voice comes through saying, "Safe."

Stacy offers Oscar a chair and ensures him that he is safe with us. Tressa says, "Oscar, are you the one I keep seeing standing back there, like right now, staring at us." Stacy starts to take pictures. The voices come through the SCD1, a man says, "Butter balls." An unexplained sound, like something medium sized falling.

Tressa is positive that she sees a large shadow staring back at us. Stacy says we should take pictures and video tape if we want as she encourages Oscar to let his presence be known. An EVP of a man is recorded, "Matthew." Followed by two unexplained thumps. Stacy gets a drop in the temperature from her Mel Meter. Both Stacy and Tressa feel someone keep walking behind them.

Stacy asks, "Who keeps pacing around? I keep feeling," An EVP of a man asks, "So what?" Stacy continues, "the air as you pass over here." A man comes through saying, "Mischief." An EVP of a man, "Say it." The same man repeats it, "Say it." A woman comes through saying, "Megan." Stacy excitedly says, "Megan welcome back!" Tressa equally excited says, "Hey Megan, we missed you!" An EVP is whispered, "Hey." Stacy explains who this special child is, Tressa, Stacy and her sister helped this little girl pass over. Stacy says, "I'll tell Nora we heard from you." An EVP is recorded, "Go on."

Stacy explains, "We had some mediums help her cross over one night. They told us that she'd probably come back and visit with us." I ask Megan, "Sweetie can you turn this light on for us?" Stacy says it's a little girl, so I bend down. Boo Buddy says, "Did you say something? Can you please say it again?" An EVP is recorded, "No." Stacy asks, "Megan, can I ask you a question? When you crossed over, did you meet back up with your parents?" A man's voice comes through the SCD1 saying, "There is something."

Stacy suggests Tressa sit down with the Parascope. Tressa sits and says, "Hi Megan." Boo Buddy says, "That tickles." Tressa asks Megan to play with one of the 'toys' and immediately Boo Buddy lights up. Tressa says, "Thank you." Stacy says, "Good job."

What happens next is amazing. Boo Buddy says, "Count with me. One-two-three-four." An EVP is recorded, "Five." Amazing! Stacy encourages Megan, that if she is too shy to talk that she can maybe tap somebody on the hand. Stacy says, "Megan, since you are here with us again, is there something you want to tell us?" A little girl gives this EVP, "Weeee." The SCD1 comes on, a man says, "Beth." My Mel Meter spikes at 0.5.

Stacy asks, "Megan are you with your mom and dad?" A man comes through the SCD1 saying, "Negative." Stacy asks, "Are you guys happy to see her again, you all loved her too." A man comes through and says, "I have her." Another man comes through asking, "What?" One of the girls in the group feels tingling around her fingers and asks Stacy and Tressa, "Does Megan like nail polish?" Stacy asks, "Megan, do you like nail polish? Can you make the numbers go up?" An EVP is recorded saying, "Yes." The Mel Meter reads at 0.6. Boo Buddy says, "Did you make it cold in here?" I ask, "What year did you die?" An EVP whisper of a child, "Seven." This is then followed by an unexplained pop.

Session six

I ended the last session too early, as I did this an inappropriate man comes through the SCD1 saying, "Cunt." We try to figure out if he is talking about one of us or a spirit. One of the guys in the group says, "I said that word earlier ... did you hear me say that word at lunch?" The SCD1 turns on, a man says, "Yes."

Stacy tells us about the vulgar spirit of a man who usually curses, 'bullshit' 'fuck you' etc. An unexplained thump sound is recorded, followed by an EVP, "Tressa."

I notice something in the back, by the bar. I say, "There's something back there." We all walk over to the bar and Stacy asks if any spirits would like to go to the bar with us to have a drink. Our footsteps are recorded as we make our way to the bar. Stacy says, "There are pretty girls standing at the bar." A man comes through the SCD1 saying, "You all look great."

I say, "Hey, I'm holding a poker chip," as I pause an EVP is recorded asking, "Why?" I continue, "does that mean anything to anybody?" A loud unexplained thump is recorded. Right after the thump, the Mel spikes to 3.7, seconds later an EVP is recorded, "Merry out." Stacy asks, "Do you want to take pictures with my friends?" An EVP is recorded, "No." Stacy says, "This is your chance to touch them, or to make some noise." Tressa says, "Shake the bar." At this point two spirits start speaking at the same time. One EVP is of a man saying what sounds like, "Already did." The second EVP is that of a woman saying, "So crazy, hair."

Stacy instructs us to put our hands on the bar and she asks if it can be moved. She encourages the spirits to move the bar. The girl standing next to me says, "Oh! My hair is moving!" I turn my camera and take pictures trying to catch the hair touching culprit. The SCD1 comes to life, a man comes through saying, "I was just curious." A woman also comes through, "I love you." A man replies to the woman, kindly saying, "I love you too." Ahh!

Stacy asks, "Are you having fun with my friends? Is there anything you can do for them?" An unexplained loud exhale of a man is recorded. A few seconds later an unexplained pop is then recorded. An EVP of a man, "So give me a hug then." Amazingly, right after this EVP, Boo Buddy says, "I like hugs." Stacy saw someone pass the mirror, "Who was that? What's your name?" A man comes through the SCD1 saying, "Bill." Followed by what sounds like a growl.

I hear a man exhale with my own ears. So close it's like he's exhaling right by my ear. Stacy speaks, "My friend Tessa is also holding a recorder." An unexplained pop is recorded. Stacy continues, "She has her recorder in her hand, can one of you say something in her recorder? Anything you'd like to tell her about Tombstone or yourself?" Very faintly, an EVP is recorded of a disembodied saying, "I'm a lost ghost."

Boo Buddy says, "Did you say something? Can you please say it again?" Stacy goes on, "She's actually writing a book about paranormal experiences. Is there anything you'd like her to put in her book?" Another exhale of a man is recorded. The Mel Meter makes an alert sound. Then an EVP of a woman is recorded, "Yes." The EMF spikes to 2.1.

An unexplained sound, a possible footstep is caught on the recorder, followed by an encouraging EVP, "Calm down. It's all right." Stacy tells the spirits, "Thank you for allowing us into your building." A man gives this EVP, "Tired." Stacy reminds the spirits about the recorders that are still on. An EVP of a young girl speaking unintelligible words is recorded. Followed by five light footsteps.

It's around this time that I take pictures of the bar area and what I see blows my mind. Above, a noose is visible with a blue outline of a figure below. Remember that countless people who died from hanging have come through these Mortuary doors!

Figure 12 Picture of noose with blue figure below

Stacy says, "Last chance on the SCD1, thirty-seconds, then I am turning it off. A man comes through the SCD1 saying, "Goodbye." I get an EMF spike at 0.6 and shortly after the spike, a man comes through saying, "You're safe." This is then followed by several unexplained pops. I start to talk about the Ovilus and the EMF spikes at 5.9. Stacy replies, "Good job guys, that's a great way to say goodbye." The session ends with one more pop.

Session seven
The final session

After the investigation was over, I asked Stacy for a favor, if I could try out the Ovilus. It's a tool that for years I have been wanting to buy, but it's been unavailable. She had to get ready for the next group coming in, but she asked

Tressa if she could hang back with me for a while and she kindly said yes. Tressa and I make our way down to the basement armed with the Ovilus, EMF and the recorder.

The Ovilus gets several hits, "EMPATH" "PUSHED" "LAMP" "GATEWAY" "REACH" "HOLY" and "DUTY" I ask, "How did you die?" An unexplained labored breathing is recorded. The Ovilus gets hits again, "BELL" "FRANCE." Tressa says, "Did you happen to build the Liberty Bell? Because, if I remember correctly, we have gotten a few things from France back in the day." The Ovilus lights up, detecting a presence. A faint EVP is recorded that sounds like, "Right."

The Ovilus gets another response, "ROLLED" and Tressa says, "That is …" an EVP of a man is recorded, "A wolf." I am impressed with what happens next, the Ovilus says, "WOLF" Tressa asks, "What about the wolf?" The Ovilus says, "CELLAR" Tressa replies, "Yes. We are in the cellar." I ask, "Can you tell us any of your names?" An EVP from a man is recorded, saying what sounds like, "Come."

I ask, "What was your occupation when you were alive?" A very faint unintelligible EVP from a man is recorded. A loud unexplained thump is recorded. Tressa looks to her side and says, "Back off a little please." The Ovilus gets some more results, "GLOVES" and "CROPS." I repeat a question, "Can you tell us how you died? Oops, I already asked that question … can you tell us what year you died?" An EVP is whispered, "Smooth" amazingly the next word that comes on the Ovilus is also, "SMOOTH"

I ask, "What's your name?" For several seconds unexplained heavy breathing is recorded. Very close, as if right in front of the recorder. Tressa again warns the spirits, "Back up now. Quit pulling at me … thank you." A woman is recorded giving this EVP, saying, "Cut it out." Tressa reveals to me that she is an empath. Remember, earlier the Ovilus said EMPATH. She feels them in different ways.

I share that my sister and I are both sensitives. I tell Tressa, "I see them sometimes, I get phantom smells, and I hear them at times." An EVP from a woman saying, "Really."

Tressa shares more, "Sometimes I feel how they passed. They will push it on to me. I physically can feel," An EVP of a man is caught on the recorder breathing loudly. Tressa continues, "sometimes how they passed. In this building I've been hung, shot, stabbed," A disembodied sound is recorded.

Tressa goes on, "drowned, buried, I have felt each and every one. It doesn't hurt me, but I have the pressure. Not the pain that they went through, but physically feel it. I can feel when that one miner was buried alive. I could feel like I had dirt on me, I could taste the dirt in my mouth. Being hung, I could feel the noose—the pressure of it there. Not enough to hurt me, but enough to know." She pauses. "I have been touched, prodded, and goosed."

I ask Tressa, "Has anybody ever died down here?" She replies, "In the tunnels. There were several murders in the tunnels." A man is recorded loudly breathing. Tressa points to the left of us, "That's one of the entrances, the rubble."

An unexplained pop is recorded. Tressa says, "You would have to wear a hazmat suit to go into the tunnels under Tombstone because of the opium. The opium," an unexplained knock-like-sound is recorded. She continues, "is so strong, you would last maybe five minutes before having an opium overdose and die. That's how strong it is now. Its concentrated the smells, miles under Tombstone."

I ask Tressa, "Are there bodies still down there?" Tressa replies, "Oh, I'm sure there are." An unexplained disembodied screech is recorded. I ask, "Were you one of the people who died here in the tunnels? Were you murdered?" A faint EVP of a man is recorded as he says, "Yes."

This is followed by the Mel Meter spiking at 0.3. A few seconds later, a disgruntled grunt is recorded. I say, "We know you are here because the Ovilus is lighting up a lot sensing a presence." As I am talking what sounds like a child is recorded letting out a deep breath, "Ahh."
Tressa lets me know that she is feeling the presences, several of them.

I ask the spirits if they can let Tressa go, and give her a break. An EVP of a man is recorded, "Ugh." Tressa tells me, "When I am in the building, these men stay right behind me to make sure nothing happens to me. They are protectors. We start walking back up the stairs. An unexplained pop is recorded. Then an EVP of a child is recorded saying, "Come here." This is followed by static.

I forgot to mention, after the investigation was over, when I followed Stacy into the gift shop, that is next door to the morgue, we both noticed a very lemony clean smell. When we were in here earlier there was no such smell.

No one was in here when we were next door investigating. We both smelled that strong lemon smell.

I just want to do a quick re-cap of the whole hair situation. Throughout this whole investigation, the hair came up several times. My recorder caught several EVPs regarding the hair, such as, "Touch the hair" "So crazy hair" and when asked if anybody wanted to touch the woman's hair, a man gave this EVP, "I just did."

The SCD1 had quite a few responses to when it came down to the almighty hair, "I like her hair." "It's very smooth." When her hair was moving by itself, a man came through saying, "I was just curious." Insane!

I really enjoyed investigating with Stacy and Tressa, I hope to do it again sometime! This old mortuary did not disappoint.

Chapter twenty

Sheila's Copper Penny, Jerome, Arizona

When my mom and I went to Arizona, we went to several places, Tucson, Sedona, Cottonwood, Jerome, and my solo day trip to Tombstone. Honestly, I have never stopped and spent time in Arizona, I always just drive through and on into the next state. I enjoyed it immensely. I got to spend time with my Grandma who I don't get to see nearly enough!

You already know about my exciting time in Tombstone. My mom and I got to spend time at her best friend Joan Sedita's lovely home. It is here, in Cottonwood that we spent a few days. Being so close to the old historic mining town of Jerome, we went there quite a few times.

It was one of these trips that I met Sheila. My mom wanted to go shopping and it was a really hot, typical Arizona summer day. Joan and I didn't feel like running around all over town, so we hung out in the car enjoying the AC. Joan mentions that since I do all this investigating that I need something to protect myself—like a crystal.

Since we have about thirty minutes until my mom meets back with us, we go to check out a couple nearby stores. The first one we stop at is where I met Sheila. She was very friendly. Joan and I mention that we are looking for a crystal for protection against negative spirits. She begins to tell me about some of her experiences that she had dating back to her childhood. We end up finding a sweet pair of crystal earrings and Joan insists on buying them for me. Now every time I wear them I think about her and the fun times we had while I was there visiting.

Sheila mentions to me that she has her own store and would like if I could come by and investigate there sometime. She shares with me that very odd things have been happening there and has been wanting somebody to come with their equipment to see if they could get any answers. I told her I was going to Tucson but would let her know when I was on my way back. I will not go into detail about the building in which is now Sheila's Copper Penny. The history behind it reveals itself in the investigation.

June 21, 2016
The investigation

Two days after getting back from Tucson, the day has come for the investigation at Sheila's Copper Penny. I am hoping to get some answers for Sheila. We wait until later in the evening, as she is closing up shop for the day. Joan and my mom drive me up to Jerome for the investigation. While I am with Sheila at her store my mom and Joan are on a mission as well. A couple weeks ago, before Tucson and Tombstone, we had come to Jerome, and went up the hill where Jerome Grand Hotel is and where we found out they had haunted tours happening.

The next upcoming tour happened to be when we were coming back through and when we went to talk to them the man at the desk, Chris, said the tour was booked. We put my name and number down if something was to open up. We never heard back from them unfortunately, so my mom and Joan planned to go up and see if they could talk to Chris again.

Thankfully I was able to get in. They were still booked, but since it was only me, they said it would be okay. I am so appreciative to my mother and to her best friend, Joan, who went out of their way to make this happen. I am also appreciative to Chris, who ended up being the tour guide, and who is very knowledgeable about the hotel, he should be because his family owns it! Altogether it was a successful night all the way around.

Results and evidence collected
Session one

I arrive as Sheila is closing her store. She turns off the fans and the air conditioning unit so not to taint any evidence we may receive. The investigation hasn't really started yet, but I am recording because Sheila is telling me a little about the store. Throughout the investigation more is revealed. She points out, "In that corner, there's something there, I used to have my sewing machine in that area. I couldn't stay awake to save my life. I kept falling asleep. My energy completely drained."

I speak to the spirits, "Sheila says there are some things happening here, it's been affecting her personally because she gets really tired and fatigued very quickly when that wasn't the case before. Sheila also mentioned to me about a rumor of an old man and his cat that haunt this place, which I think is really neat." An EVP of a man is recorded saying what sounds like, "Go for a ride."

I say, "This also used to be where mechanics worked." An unexplained deep breath of a woman is recorded. I continue, "This was the Studebaker showroom upstairs and was owned by the Dicus family." Sheila shows me an old picture of Dicus as a young man at school and gives it to me. The Mel Meter spikes up to 1.0.

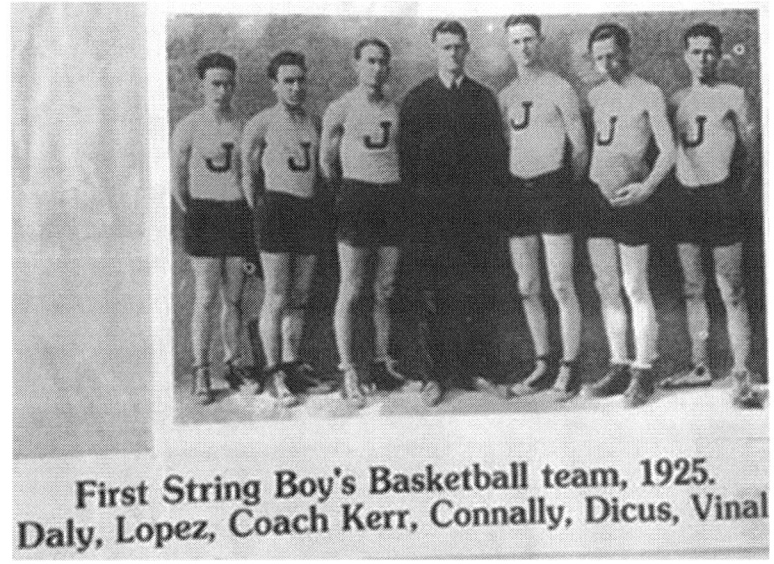

Figure 13 Sheila's picture of Dicus as a young man

I walk around the shop to take it all in. The area that Sheila pointed out to me earlier is an area with clothing, a sewing machine and other random things. Why is it that every time she spends time there the energy is drained from her? Just this space—everywhere else in the store is fine. I make my way to the side room where Sheila is affected the most.

As I walk into the room an exasperated breath is recorded. I stand in the area where the sewing machine once stood and say, "Sheila was so tired, she even took a nap, which has never happened before." An unexplained snicker is recorded. I go to the counter and grab the Mel Meter and walk into the affected area, the EMF rises to 1.5. Seconds later it's at 1.9.

I continue exploring more, I am at the wall that she shares with her neighbor, the store next door, so I am limited to how far I can go, but at the wall the EMF rises to 1.2. An EVP is recorded, whispering, "Join us."

Session two, Opening prayer

After I'm done checking things out, we start the investigation off with an opening protection prayer. I usually start each investigation with one. I don't add them on here but listening to it, there is definitely something going on here. We are doing the opening protection prayer. An unexplained sound is recorded, that sounds like the beating of a heart.

I say, "This prayer is for Sheila, myself and her store." Another unexplained beat sound is recorded. Then an EVP is whispered, "Go inside." I continue, "We come with absolute respect and honor, we mean you no harm or disrespect. Please protect our bodies, our souls, equipment, all personal and business possessions from any harm." Yet again the mysterious beat-like noise is back and recorded.

Session three

As we start this session the EMF spikes to 0.6. I ask a couple questions with no responses. I encourage Sheila to join in, she's silent for a few seconds, then she asks, "Do you ever," she pauses, at the same time an EVP is recorded asking, "What?" Sheila continues, "sense me getting frustrated when there's no one here and I'm swearing to myself uncontrollably?"

She is quiet for a couple seconds, thinking, and adds, "Can you sense me getting frustrated?" An EVP of a man is recorded shushing her, "Shh." I say, "Okay I am putting the EMF down." An EVP of a man whispers under his breath, "Why?" I continue, "It's getting something." Unintelligible words are spoken. An EVP is recorded of what sounds like a young girl saying, "Lie."

I ask, "Can you tell us the name of this establishment?" The same girl who just spoke gives us another EVP, "Come picks." Whatever that means. An unexplained sound is recorded, what sounds like a coin dropping or flipping a coin in the air. As we end this session a loud static is caught on the recorder, this is followed by a heavy breathing, I believe this to be a child.

Session four

I introduce myself, "You know my name, but I don't know your name. What's your name?" A loud static is recorded. I situate my phone on the counter, so it can record a video. As I press record on the phone the Mel Meter makes an alert sound and at the same exact time static is also recorded. Again, a child is recorded breathing. A loud thump is also recorded.

I ask, "How many people and animals are here with Sheila and me?" A very faint voice of a man is recorded speaking unintelligible words. I ask, "Can you make a sound for us, so we know you are here and where you're at?" It takes a lot of energy to do this, so we stay quiet for a while. Two loud thumps are recorded. It was quite an uneventful session.

Session five

A child is recorded breathing. This has happened a couple times already. Sheila definitely has at least one child who is in her shop. I ask for the spirits again to make a sound for us. A hum-like sound is recorded, followed by a purr-like sound. The purr is then followed by an unexplained sound which I can only describe as an anxious eater, eating food very quickly. I just want to note that I have a cat and have had many cats growing up and this sounds like, at least to me, a cat excitedly scarfing down wet food. The Mel Meter spikes to 1.0.

I ask, "Why are you here?" In response what sounds like a woman whispering under her breath is recorded. She is very faint and very distant. It's a whole sentence, but unfortunately all of it is unintelligible, the only word I was able to pick up was the first word, "Because" she keeps talking but it gets more faint. The purr-like sound is caught on the recorder again.

I say, "There is word that an older man and his cat are here. Well … I love cats. Can you tell me what your cat's name is?" Seconds later, two light footsteps are recorded. I ask, "Were you a mechanic here at one point? Is that why you're so comfortable with this place—because it's familiar to you?" Unexplained breathing is recorded followed by a metal clink-like noise. The purring is recorded once again. We never hear the purring with our ears. The Mel Meter spikes up to 1.0.

I say, "Are there any spirits here? If so, feel free to let us know you are here. Tap my shoulder, touch my hair, my shoe, anything." An EVP of a woman saying what sounds like, "I can't." This is then followed by an unexplained loud exhale from a man. Another purr is recorded. Sheila, you have definitely got a phantom cat! I say, "All right, you might be shy. That's okay! It's not a bad thing when it comes to spirits I suppose!" A man is recorded giving this EVP, "Walk around the room."

An unexplained raspy meow is recorded. Mind blowing!

When I hear these kind of results after the fact, it's like Christmas morning for me. The excitement that runs through my body, the goose bumps I receive, I think, 'Did that really just happen?' I rewind probably a dozen times, listen to it in a slower mode, listen to it in regular mode, then in fast mode as well. Christmas time!

I look around and say, "A ton of neat local things in this store. What's your favorite thing about this store? Can you tell us?" A loud thump like sound is recorded, followed by a man speaking an unintelligible word. The Mel Meter once again reads at 1.0, as I am reading the results a child is recorded breathing. Then more cat sounds. I truly believe that there is a spirit of a cat that resides here at Sheila's Copper Penny. I am not sure about the older man, but I'm positive that the cat is here.

I walk to the area where Sheila is most affected. I ask, "Why does Sheila get so tired in this particular spot?" A thump that goes unheard by us is caught on the recorder. I ask Sheila, "Do you still get tired?" Immediately after an EVP of a snicker is recorded, "Heh heh." Sheila wearily responds, "Sometimes."

Session six

Sheila feels really cold where she is standing. I don't feel it, and the AC is off, I saw her turn it off at the very beginning. The Mel Meter spikes to 0.7. Then shortly after, an EVP, "What?" What happens next is quite amazing. As I look at Sheila, she has a very strange look on her face—the look of shock. She literally looks like she saw a ghost. She looked slightly frightened.

She says to me, "I just saw ... and I'm not shitting you," as she pauses an unexplained exhale of a man is recorded, Sheila continues, "the corner of the display case, it looked like ..." she pauses to think of an accurate description, "when someone blows a dandelion." Shocked, I say, "What?" She says, "It went from left to right." As she speaks, a man is recorded speaking an unintelligible word. Very distant. I ask her, "Like an orb?" She looks at me and with shock still on her face, she replies, "It was something ..."

As Sheila continues to describe what she had just seen, a man is recorded breathing. Sheila continues, "From the corner of the jewelry case to the book area." The Mel spikes yet again to 1.0. I ask Sheila to repeat what just happened. Sheila starts, "Well I … I'm not moving and there's nothing here in the store, it looked like a white thing, a floating thing. It moved from my left to my right. It looked like someone had blown a dandelion head." An EVP of a man making a whoosh-like noise. "Whooooosh."

I say, "Don't be afraid. Please, we don't want you to be afraid of us." A man is recorded saying what sounds like, "All of us." The Mel meter makes an alert sound. I walk to the book shelves which are located on the right side of the store, (if your standing at the register, facing the front door) I start to talk about my love for books, since the dandelion like form was seen moving toward the book area, I ask, "Do you like books too?" A disembodied voice speaks an unintelligible word.

The Mel EMF spikes to 0.9, right after the spike, a loud thump is recorded. I am holding a Jerome jailer inmate shirt that I recently purchased from the jail. I ask, "Can you tell me what I am holding in my hand? The jail wasn't too far from here. Did you spend time in the jail?" Sheila shares some interesting history about the building we are in, "This building actually housed some of the prisoners at one point when the jail was sliding down the hill. This was an interim jail back in the day." A very faint EVP is recorded, "Me." Is this spirit admitting they did time here when it served as a jail? The Mel Meter spikes to 1.0, it seems to really like that number as it keeps going to 1.0.

Sheila asks, "How old were you when you died?" An EVP of a man is recorded, "Seven … seventeen." Sheila asks, "Where in Jerome did you live?" A man speaks an unintelligible word, possibly the same man who just spoke. Sheila, who I'm starting to think is also a fellow sensitive, warns me that she just saw a shadow in the sewing machine room. A spike on the EMF, 0.8.

Session seven

I walk back to the room where Sheila had just seen a shadow. The Mel Meter still is at 0.8. I ask, "What's your name?" An EVP of what I believe to be a woman is recorded saying, "I can't." An unexplained thump-like sound is recorded. Again, I must add that I am a debunker. I will verbally debunk things in a heartbeat, so all these thumps, purrs, and other sounds are unheard by us at the moment of investigation and remain undetected until I listen to it.

Sheila and I start to make our way to the hall that her neighbor, another store, and she share. As we are walking, we both notice a roly-poly. She puts it somewhere, so we won't step on it. I kid around saying, "Stay safe dude. Stay safe. Keep living the dream." Apparently one of the spirits, a man thought that was funny and is recorded laughing. "Ha ha ha ha." As we are standing in the hall unexplained loud static is recorded, and it continues on for several seconds.

Session eight, final session

So maybe hallway is not the best word to describe where we are at, just a few short feet, then a sheet, we look past the sheet and off to the left is her neighbors store. She told me about this store and it sounded neat, I will have to go check it out sometime. The Mel EMF spikes to 0.5, this is followed by two unexplained clink-like sounds. I ask, "How did you die?" An EVP is recorded. It is very faint, and very distant. Multiple unintelligible words are spoken. I did understand one word, "Axe."

Sheila says, "This store that is next to us, 'Scooters Trash', he has signs that say, 'Welcome to the Dark Side.' The store is almost all skulls and dark angels." She pauses and asks the spirits, "Do you feel comfortable and at home here?" An EVP of a man is recorded as he says, "Comfortable."

I tell Sheila, "Good question." I then ask, "She has a good point, I'd be really comfy in a place like that. How about you?" A man whispers this EVP, "Go home." Then a few seconds later, another EVP from possibly the same man, three words, the first word, "Ask" the other two are unintelligible.

I feel an unexplained pressure on my foot. I stand still and ask Sheila to put the EMF by my left foot to see if we get a spike. A disembodied sound is recorded. I tell Sheila, "I feel like a hand just clamped my foot." The Mel Meter makes an alert sound. Remember earlier in the evening when I asked the spirits to let me know if they are there by touching me, I even mentioned my foot.

We head back into Sheila's Copper Penny. As Sheila is closing her door, an EVP is recorded, greeting us, "Hey." I ask Sheila, "Do you know of any documented deaths linked to this building?" Sheila responds, "Well, behind," as she pauses for a second an EVP of a woman, or a child is recorded saying, "Listen." Sheila continues, "out my front door to the left," again another EVP, this time from a man, whispering, "Go outside."

Sheila goes on, "The Cuban Queen Bordello, which is currently abandoned, is there. Behind that was a barn where they would transport the deceased in the carriage hearse. They would pass right by this building. They would go right behind the building almost every weekend because there were so many deaths." A woman's moan is recorded. Sheila continues, "That carriage hearse, led by horses would come around this building constantly." I ask Sheila, "Is this like the Moriah?" A woman gives this EVP, whispering "Horse."

Sheila replies, "Yeah. It would come around this building, up along this wall for every single funeral. Thousands of funerals." I ask Sheila if she can show me where the Bordello is and everything else she mentioned. She kindly agrees to it. Sheila says to me, "There might have been a man," as she pauses, an EVP is whispered, "Hurry up."

Sheila continues on, "that was killed. What started the jail to slide down the hill, was a dynamite explosion." An eerie EVP of a man saying, "Dynamite." Sheila adds, "It exploded. There used to be a building across the street to the right." Sheila unlocks the front door, and we walk outside. The EMF spikes to 1.2. A creaking sound is recorded as Sheila closes the door, which I debunk immediately.

Sheila points out the Bordello to me, relatively close, just across a dirt road. She says to me, "The Cuban Queen Bordello was run by Jelly Roll Morton, the lead founder of Louisiana jazz music. Him and his Milano wife, she was Milano, so she passed herself off as Cuban or Mexican back in the day. Hence the name Cuban Queen Bordello, which is right over there." An EVP of a man is recorded saying, "Right there."

Sheila gives more history, "That prostitution house was known for its famous fried chicken back in the day. Behind that was the barn, where they would store the horses along with the hearse. A loud static is recorded. I start taking pictures of the area we are in. I look at the last picture I just took and say, "Oh. That's creepy." I show Sheila the picture. An unexplained deep breath of a man is recorded. A white mist is revealed in the picture. I take more pictures and it is no longer there.

As Sheila starts to speak, an EVP of a woman is recorded saying, what sounds like, "Stop." Sheila tells me, "Right where we are standing is the Dicus family warehouse." We are outside and are standing on what can easily be mistaken as a parking lot. I only say that because it's like a concrete area, by the dirt road, lifted. Sheila says, "This is where the Studebaker's used to be, where they would work on the cars, beneath our feet." As I continue to take pictures an EVP of a man is recorded saying, "Hoes." Remember we are in an area where the prostitutes were active and lived. I notice that as I'm taking pictures, I see a white thing fly past. This happens a few times.

As we stand there looking at the old Bordello, I look to my right, and there stands a slightly collapsed old building. I ask Sheila what that building used to be, "I'm not really sure, but there was an earthquake and under our feet it did sink twenty-two feet. They had to fill it with old cars and junk, under our feet." I take a few steps forward and take a few more pictures of the bordello. Sheila excitedly says, "To the right of you, I just saw a blue speck, near the ground. A bright blue light."

She shares something about herself with me, "I do see pinpoints because I can sometimes pick up on spirits. Not a light blue, more a dark blue." When I ask her what the difference between colors, she replies that she is uncertain, but would like to learn more about this gift she has. She says, "I see different colors, a rosy red, green ..." she stops and says fast, "I just saw it again! This time next to your feet!" Remember my left foot was touched earlier by an unknown presence. I am unsure if this is an aura thing or what but if anybody reads this and knows more about this subject, please let us know.

Sheila and I both witness a flash up in the trees. No one else is around and it was dark there the whole time till the flash happened. At the same time this is happening, an unexplained static is recorded. As we start to walk back to our store, I learn more about Jerome's history. Sheila speaks, "This town had an Asian community, as well as a Mexican community. In the 1920s there was a pool that only the Mexicans could swim in. Segregated from the white swimming pool. There were reports of people finding opium dens under different renovations of buildings in this area."

She pauses, and continues, "The Jerome Grand Hotel has had 9,000 people die in that building alone. It used to be a hospital, there was cancer, unchecked diabetes, murders, suicides and more. There was also a psych ward in that hospital. People were being committed for the smallest things."

As we approach her store, we are both confused as to why the door is open. Not only did the recorder record the sound of the door closing as we left, but I saw with my own eyes Sheila closing the door. Even as we stood outside talking, she kept turning back to make sure the door was closed, (it was unlocked so she kept just checking to make sure no one was opening it) and there it stands before us, door wide open. I slowly walk in the shop and say, "Is anybody in here?" Immediately after I ask this an EVP is recorded, which sounds like, "I am." I search every corner of the store and nobody is there at all. The Mel Meter spikes to 1.0.

I put my phone on the jewelry case where she saw the dandelion floating earlier. We decide to go back outside for a few minutes to see if the door opens again. It does not open this time however, I leave my phone on, recording video in the area where the dandelion was. I record a time-lapse video. While the door did not close, we did catch something on the time-lapse video, close to the end. All is still until the ending when an unexplained black thing is recorded floating from the corner off to the left. You can see it through the glass case. It does a sharp turn at the end of the jewelry case and comes straight in the direction of the phone, suddenly disappearing.

As the time-lapse recorder is set and we leave the door for the second time, an EVP is whispered, "Come here." As we are outside for the second time, Sheila shares some personal experiences she had as a child, and more recent years. She has had quite some intense paranormal experiences. You can read about Sheila's paranormal experiences in Chapter four of this book, along with many other peoples' true tales as well.

Chapter twenty-one

Jerome Grand Hotel, Jerome, Arizona

In the small mining town of Jerome, up the hill stands a building with quite the history. This building opened its doors in January of 1927, first as United Verde Hospital, and then later on as Phelps Dodge Hospital. In 1930 the hospital was listed as the most well-equipped hospital in Arizona, very impressive and quite the achievement! Unfortunately, the hospital days were short lived and it closed its doors in 1950 due to the mining operations shutting down. After the closing of the hospital, the building sat abandoned for over four decades

Fast forward, a family purchased the old hospital from the mining company. There are many spirits that call the historic hotel home—even a feline spirit—caught on camera more than a couple times by lucky hotel guests. Another spirit who roams the halls of the hotel is a man named Claude Harvey. He is believed to have been murdered, but his untimely death was made to look like a freak accident. His head was squashed by the Otis elevator, the same elevator that still is in operation today.

Manoah Hoffpauir (Hoff-power) is another restless spirit. He was hired as a caretaker after the hospital closed down and resided in a room by the boiler room. He hung himself in his room and is thought to be around as well. I first came to the Jerome Grand Hotel about seventeen or so years ago, for a beautiful Thanksgiving dinner. Joan introduced this place to my mom and me. I'm glad she did.

Besides eating a turkey feast there for the holiday, I have seen the hotel featured on one TV show, Ghost Adventures. They have been to the hotel two times. One of those times, Chris, whose family owns the hotel, (he was only a child when his family purchased it) actually saved Ghost Adventure's, Zak's life. You will hear more about that incident later on in this chapter.

June 23, 2016
The investigation

The night before this investigation I was violently ill. I was up the whole night throwing up and dry heaving. It was absolutely horrible. My mom woke up and stayed with me and tried to calm my nerves. I hyperventilate when I throw up, always have. I knew it wasn't an option for me to cancel on Jerome Grand Hotel, not after they squeezed me into an already booked tour.

The next day we tried to pinpoint what it was exactly what could have made me sick. Joan, my mom and myself all had the same thing the last couple of days and neither of them was sick. It was weeks later that I found out that what made me sick was an attachment from Tombstone. I hadn't felt right since leaving, but that night in Joan's bathroom was completely different. While that was the only night of throwing up, thankfully, that wasn't the end of my attachment issue. It lasted for quite some time. That is a chapter all in itself.

The tour started at 7:00 p.m. so around 5:00 p.m. Joan and my mom took me to Jerome where we had a nice dinner at the Haunted Hamburger which happens to be pretty close to the hotel. I finished early, so I could walk up the hill to the hotel and read some of their books. They have numerous notebooks of peoples' paranormal experiences at the hotel. As I am walking up the hill, I stop to take some pictures and run into a group of people. They were very friendly. I stayed and chatted with them for a while about my book and the equipment I use for investigations. They seemed to be very interested in the subject.

I walk into the lobby thinking I have an hour to kill. The friendly man at the desk, *Corey, asked how he could help me, I told him, "I'm here for the paranormal tour but came early to look at the books." What he said next shocked me, the tour started at 6 p.m. not 7 p.m. Oops! He was very understanding about the situation and he knew I was already a few minutes late, so he showed me to where the tour was and said I could pay after the tour. I know they usually don't do that, so I am very appreciative.

The tour started in the boiler room area just left off the lobby. I grab a chair and sit down. I turn my Mel EMF on and set it down on the counter, I also turn on the recorder. There are a few times, that an EVP is recorded at the same time as Chris is speaking so I miss some of what it said, on both parts.

Results and evidence collected
Session one, Boiler room

As we all sit in the boiler room, Chris talks to us about some of the history behind this former hospital. Chris has been doing tours here since 2008 and since then there have been many reported sightings and other experiences.

While this is mostly about the history Chris shares with us, there are some results that are recorded. A few months back, I believe they cancelled the haunted tours, not by Chris's choice. Reading these words, the words we heard, it's almost like going and being there for one final tour. I am so glad that I went and got to enjoy the tour and do some investigating while Chris was still doing these awesome tours.

Chris says:

> When we first opened up twenty years ago, we had several people come down to the lobby to check-out and ask us if people were in the rooms next to them. Doors open and close on their own. Twenty years ago, we only had six rooms for rent when it was much slower. Now it's a lot busier and now we have twenty-five rooms. We still have seven left that are under renovation. I remember as a kid hanging out in the lobby, hearing stories. In 2008 we started tours, really reluctant at first.

When Chris is asked if he has had any paranormal experiences himself he answers,

> Yeah, I have had a few personal experiences. One of them happened on a tour. The family and myself, we never believed in this kind of stuff. When we first came out here, we never bought the building …

I get an eerie not-so-friendly EVP from a man that sounds like, "I'm gonna murder you." Really creepy.

Chris continues,

> thinking one day we would be doing tours like this. I really do believe something is here!

Chris laughs,

> The funny one we hear about all the time makes me laugh, it's a cat. People will feel a cat jump on the edge of their bed when they are laying there going to sleep at night. They will hear it or feel it. People will tell us, "It seemed like there was a cat in my room." I've been told this a thousand times!

If you ever get to go to this hotel, even it's not to stay the night but for a tour or a meal, go to the lobby and ask to see the cat picture! This cat has been photographed!

Chris begins to talk about a surgeon, amputations and more. The boiler room was kind of loud, so I was unable to get much of what he was saying, but I did get a crystal-clear EVP of what I believe to be a child saying, "Run, run, run!"

Chris continues:

> Two years after we started the tours, it was 2010 and the Travel Channel came up here with Ghost Adventures and we filmed an episode where they investigate the building. They also went to the building right next door which was the hospital before the mining company owned this land.

(An EVP of a man is recorded, sounding like he is trying to get my attention, "Hey!" Very close as if he is sitting right next to me.)

> I was the host that took them through. It wasn't scripted or staged, everything was shot in one take. It was really low budget. They came through for the weekend, for that one-night investigation. They really were locked in here all night. We didn't rent out any of the rooms while they were here, and even the restaurant was shut down.

(What sounds like the same man who repeats himself yet again, "Hey.")

> There was something that happened in the elevator when they were filming it. There's a story about somebody that died back there. We went back and filmed. Okay … let me tell you the first story.

(He sits down in a chair that he reveals was there when his family bought the building.)

> The building sat for over four decades. It shut down in 1953, my family bought it in 1994.

(Yet again another EVP from the same man, "Hey!")

> The bench in the hotel lobby is a pew from a church. This bench was on the third floor where they had a psych ward. They didn't have AC back then so all the patients, even the psych patients, got to sit outside on the balcony or sun porch. They'd open the doors and let the air come through. It was good for getting better and well, but it was also dangerous. Especially for a mentally ill person sitting on the third-floor balcony when there is just a railing. You can easily fall over. So, you can sit in the chair

(the chair that he was just sitting in)

> and they'd have some sort of straps around here that came through.

(A woman is recorded, a painful yelp-like-sound.)

> They wouldn't leave them unattended out here because it's not stable, but they would put them in the chairs, open up the doors so the air is flowing through. Some of these hotel rooms have access to these balconies, porches. A ton of this stuff we didn't add, it's the same from when it was a hospital. The last death, it was many years after they shut this place down. It was in 1983, eleven years before we bought the building.
>
> The chief of police told us this story. The man was a caretaker for the building. The Phelps Dodge mining company owned the hospital. That's who we bought it from. The mining company hired on a caretaker or a night watchman to come and live inside the building. His room is down the hall. His job was to keep everyone out of the hospital. There were many liabilities, people getting hurt, some people could fall down the elevator shaft, lawsuits.
>
> So, they pay this man to live in that back room. He was only here for six or seven months. His name was Manoah Hoffpauir. He would make sure no one was breaking in. With the doors locked up, sometimes he'd walk down the roads going to the bars down on Main Street. He often went to The Spirit Room. Everybody got to know the

guy, even the Chief of Police. He split with his wife before coming and taking this job. So that made it worse, and he drank all the time.

He didn't like being in the building all the time, but it was his job, so he had no option. One night he stopped showing up at the bars. The Chief of Police said he waited three nights before he came up to the old hospital and find out why he's been missing. On the third night, at 5:00 am,

(as Chris pauses, an EVP of a woman is recorded saying, "Ah" as if she was right in front of me and speaking into the recorder. Very close.)

they shut the bar down. The Chief of Police said, "That's when I got in my car and I drove over, parked in the front, came in through the doors and started walking and calling his name, 'Hoff! Hoff!'

I couldn't find him. I waited for a response, I walked around the building a couple of times." Well, he ended up walking down the hallway, opened his bedroom door and sees his bed back there. He sees some of his belongings. He realized that was his room. He was standing in his bedroom. It's almost two in the morning, so he turns his flashlight off, thinking maybe he is passed out drunk or something.

The Chief of Police tells us, he turned the light off and yelled in the room one more time, "Hoff! I'm here looking for Hoff." The Chief of Police says, "He was regularly in that room, and I was getting no response, around the corner someone was standing in the back. It scared me so bad. I jumped up and almost fell over, mumbled a few words as I caught myself on the wall and said, I can't believe your just standing here in this room! I've been looking for you for thirty minutes! What's going on?

The guy didn't say anything, so I ask him, 'Do you see? I'm standing right in front of you.'" He turns his flashlight on. The guy had tied a rope around his neck, stood on a little stool and hung himself from the steam pipe. That was the last death, which was eleven years before we had bought the building. That's the first real creepy story I had heard as a kid.

(Can you imagine? Thinking you see someone standing there? It's dark, you don't see much but just a figure, then to find out this person is dead, and just hanging there. That is pretty creepy.)

> One more story before we head out. The elevator back there ... someone perished back there.

Before he shares this death with us, he turns around and on the counter are different investigating tools. He starts to explain the equipment and what they do and lets people pick what they want to use for the tour. As he talks about electromagnetic fields an unexplained static is recorded which continues on for quite a few seconds. This is immediately followed by an EVP of the same man saying once again, "Hey." Before sharing the Otis elevator death with us, he talks more about the Ghost Adventures visit, which was quite interesting all in itself.

> They even walked up and down the stairwells because it goes around the elevator shaft, to see what had to be debunked. When they filmed the building and investigated it we turned the power off on the whole place. They wired everything to their van out front. That's how serious they were about not wanting any false readings going off. It was neat getting to see what they were doing. They spent like two days just wiring the whole building.

Everybody in the group, excluding me, were hotel guests. So, Chris tells them they can feel free to use the equipment over night. He shares with us an experience two past guests experienced. They got an EVP around three in the morning of a man saying, "Come on!" As Chris is still explaining the tools to people, yet another EVP is recorded from the same man, "Hey!"

Session two

We are still in the boiler room, so I still can't hear everything that is being said. Even though I was recording, it not only got Chris, but all the background noise as well. Chris shares another experience from former hotel guests:

> There were a couple of ladies, like three years ago now. They were doing their own audio, they had their things lying on their night-stand and they're going to sleep. So, they get into bed and the last thing you hear is them saying good night to each other. That was it. Minus them breathing and snoring. Well, the next morning they're down getting coffee and listening to their audio. You should have been there, they

> were screaming and jumping around the lobby. You could tell it wasn't fake, it wasn't a charade.
>
> I ask, "What's going on? What did you guys get?" So, they play it back for me. As soon as they both say goodnight to each other, there was this third voice that was captured. It sounded like a little girl. Definitely female and didn't sound like either of them. The voice is recorded saying, "Goodnight sweethearts." It heard them say goodnight to each other and responded back to them without them knowing it until they replayed the recording.

Chris shares with us that in the past, hotel guests have seen apparitions. As equipment is getting passed around to people, static is recorded. As Chris comes to the back where a couple and myself are, unexplained static is recorded again. As Chris is getting our equipment, I get an EVP of a man whispering, "Get her."

Unexplained static is recorded. Then the same man who's been recorded saying, 'hey' several of times gives this EVP, "Earrings." He was very close. I was wearing crystal earrings, many believe, crystal is supposed to be one of many things that can help protect you from negative spirits. I am unsure if that EVP was directed to that or something else but it's a possibility.

Chris tells us:

> I'm going to tell you guys real quickly about the elevator, then we'll start looking around. Listen up for this last story. I'll tell you what happened in the back of the elevator and why the Travel Channel was interested in going back there.

(Unfortunately, there was static at the end of this sentence, so I couldn't understand what Chris was saying. A not-so-friendly EVP from a man is recorded, "Get the fuck outta here.")

Chris starts to tell us how he and his family first heard about the elevator story among other incidents that happened at this old building:

> So, we all get quiet for a minute. No one is saying anything, and Larry makes a joke. "I guess what I'm saying is that in a couple months when we open up this building, we'll be Arizona's most haunted hotel." (As he says this an EVP is recorded by the same man, "Hey.") Larry starts laughing, he thinks it's funny. He's joking about it. Here I

am eleven years old and I remember looking at the nurses and not one of them laughed at his joke. You know that was his intention, to get a laugh out of them. One of them responds to him in a real serious tone, "Yeah. This building is haunted." She didn't think it was humorous at all. No smirk, no smile. In fact, I think it pissed her off a little bit, the way he was making this sarcastic joke about it.

Larry responds, "The reason it's going to be haunted, is because of all the people looking for ghosts after it was abandoned and shut down in the 1950s. So, for over forty years this place was a hot spot." I remember the way she looked at him, she says to him, "This building has been known to be haunted since back in the 1930s, before you were even born."

She warns him, "If you're really the owner of this building and bought it from the mining company and you've got permission from Jerome to turn this hospital into a hotel, starting today you better get your story straight." His smirk went away and he wasn't laughing any more after that.

Chris then tells us about the gruesome event that took place that is connected to the Otis elevator:

Larry asks, "What happened in the 30s?" The nurse replies, "You haven't heard what happened with the elevator? With a man named Claude Harvey?" After Larry replies no, the nurse walks down the stairs and into the elevator room, what she tells us next is bone chilling. She told us she will never forget that day. The elevator had broken down. So, the nurses, including the one who told us all this, were in the lobby trying to get the elevator working. They were pushing buttons. It comes down and stops four feet short. It wouldn't go down the rest of the way. So, they went to the first floor and tried to make it go up and it wouldn't go up. The elevator, as far as they knew, was broken.

There was one guy here who could've fixed it and his name was Claude Harvey. He was one of the guys that was trained by Otis, the company who'd built it. He would fix it if it breaks down, otherwise it would be weeks before Otis could come out from Chicago to fix it. So, Claude Harvey is in the back taking a look, and the nurses are waiting out there for him. It was about forty-five minutes later, that nurse, who was telling us this story twenty years ago says, "I walked into that back room, came through the copper door, walk around the tank and I look back to find him, he's lying on the floor with his arms and legs swelled up from underneath him. He's face down with the elevator all the way on the back of his neck. Unbeknownst to everybody else, it came down on him, and he was lying there!

You could tell this man was dead before going further than that. I ran through the lobby, grabbed the strips and checked for a pulse. I tried to pull him out from where he was working on it and get him out from underneath, but he was stuck, and he was dead, no pulse. I couldn't get his body out, so I ran back out and to the emergency room. We all went back, before the body could be removed, they had to get the elevator off him. We had to get the elevator to go to the next floor. It would still not operate. It took an additional hour for somebody else to come to get the elevator going and off the body.

He grabbed him and pulled him out. He had damage to the back of his head. Which would make sense since it came down on him—no decapitation. There wasn't that much damage. The damage was on the front of his face and his throat. It looked like blunt force trauma. There is no way it could have gotten that way from the elevator. Right away we thought, there would be x-rays, an autopsy, and we figure it out. That's when the Mining company owned it, they said, 'No. We're taking him to the morgue.' Instead of going to the x-ray room, the operating room, they took him straight out of here and down to the morgue, which was in the mortician's house.

Within a week they had gone to court and did a coroner's inquest. The only reason for the inquest was so they can get a legal verdict that stated it was an accidental death caused by an elevator. So, there was no liability to be suffered by the mining company because it was an accident. People were asking, 'Why was the damage on the forehead?' They never did an x-ray. Never x-rayed his body or autopsied him. Buried him in Phoenix next to his wife who died six years earlier."

This was the first ghost people used to stalk in the building back when it was a hospital. The guy wore a black suit, real short, about 5'2. A long beard, he always wore a black suit since his job was working on the elevator and everybody else who was working in the hospital were wearing white coats, nursing outfits. Even the cooks working in the restaurant wore white coats. He was the only guy with a black suit. People would see him all the time. He's the first known ghost.

When Ghost Adventures came up here, that was the first room we took them to. They walk to the lobby. I'm out there waiting for them. When these guys walk in they have cameras on you and are filming as we're going around. So, the first place we went was the boiler room. We walk through here, go back there and I'm telling them about the elevator.

(An EVP is recorded, a gruff-like voice saying, "Up.")

Zak asks me, "Can we film the elevator moving down the elevator shaft with me laying right here where the body was found?" We've put an outline of where the body was, so you can see it, so obviously he sees that. Right away Zak wants to lay on that outline and he wants to film this elevator as it comes down the shaft. Zak asks, "Is this possible?" It seemed like he knew what he was doing, he had it all figured out. So, I told him, "Sure. Let's go for it." I open the gate and he lays on the floor right where Claude Harvey was found back in 1935. Zak says, "Make the cart come down."

So, I used the wooden dowels that I attached and made the cart come down. Now I was thinking that this guy is going to get up and out of the way after five, maybe ten seconds. We hadn't gone over this at all. This was not staged at all! I walk to the back of the room, the cart's coming down and he's lying there on the floor, under the elevator, camera on his face and he's filming the cart coming down.

I walk in the back behind Nick and Aaron who are standing there filming him. I'm still thinking at some point he's going to get out of the way. He gets lost in the moment. I should have realized it was too long. You can see the elevator visibly now, he's still lying there filming it. He's got an elevator six feet above him and still making its way down. I'm not there where I can shut it down. It was funny, but so serious.

So, his investigating buddies Nick and Aaron are screaming at this point as they are still standing there and filming. They're not moving but yelling, "Get outta the way! The elevators coming down!" He's not prepared to move. He's focused and looking through his camera. Confused, he says, "What!" I just jump down and grab his feet and pull him out. If I didn't do that, it would have killed him.

I would have watched the elevator come down and crush the camera right into his chest, he would have been killed. It was his idea of filming where the guy was killed and it could have happened to him as well. He cleared the bottom of the elevator with less than an inch!

(If you haven't seen this GAC episode, you can find it on YouTube)

Chris laughs, I'm sure some people have seen it on TV and go, "No way, they had to of set that up!" It happened.

We all get up and start to explore the boiler room, the room where Manoah hung himself and the Harvey death scene. My Mel Meter spikes to 1.7. A few seconds later, an EVP is recorded saying, "Go to my house." A couple minutes later, the meter goes to 3.2.

My camera malfunctions, annoyed, I say, "No" seconds later, an EVP whisper, a small voice, "Yeah." As this is being recorded the Mel Meter goes to 4.6. After waiting for Manoah's room to empty a little, I slowly make my way in there. Good timing because a large amount of people are passing me and going down the short hall toward the elevator where Harvey was killed.

Session three

As I fumble for my equipment in Manoah's room an EVP of a woman is recorded saying, "Stop." The Mel EMF, still in my hand spikes to 1.8. An unexplained pop is then recorded. Then an unexplained loud shuffling sound, like numerous dishes being quickly moved. I accidentally touch the antenna to my Mel making it go off. I debunk it, immediately after I do this, an EVP is recorded, "Stop it." This is followed by another pop sound.

I am standing below the area where Manoah took his life by hanging himself. There are a few others around but most of the people are by the Otis elevator. Suddenly my Mel Meter spikes to 5.2 and starts making alert beeps and sounds, this goes on for almost a full minute. Chris walks in and joins those of us who are in Hoff's room. He points to the ceiling, "I trust you have all seen the spot." Chris says, "That's his name." He points to the pipe where his name is written in marker.

I ask Chris, "How do you pronounce his last name? Poy-ah?" Chris pronounces it, "Hoff-power." An EVP of a man verifying what Chris just said, "Power." Chris tells us, "He lived here. He had a kitchen over there." An

EVP of the man who just spoke says, "Yes." Chris continues, "This was the bedroom, over there was his bathroom." The Mel Meter makes a quick alert beep. Chris says, "This was all Manoah had while he was here for six/seven months. He wasn't here for a long time. He was just living by himself, keeping people from breaking into the building. Loud beeping comes from the Mel again.

I tell Chris, "I keep getting hits on my EMF. It keeps going crazy." I walk back into the area where I was getting spikes and alerts. The EMF alerts me again, a short series of unexplained pops is recorded. Chris checks his EMF and brings it to the same area with no results. He says, "I don't know … maybe it's you."

Chris recaps, "So, it is in this room the caretaker that was living here in the early 1980s hung himself on that large steam pipe. It was around here where the Chief of Police was." My Mel Meter once again makes an alert beep sound and continues doing so for several seconds. "He still doesn't see him at this point. He's just standing at this wall and asking if anybody is in there. No response." An EVP is recorded from a man whispering, "Knock, knock."

My Mel alerts me again. Chris says, "Nothing really right now on mine but you sure are getting something on yours." The first time it keeps alerting us for about 15 seconds. Then silence, seconds later it alerts us again, this time for about ten seconds. This is then followed by static. Now, at this point, it turned out that I had an attachment from when I was in Tombstone just days earlier. Could this be my attachment messing with my equipment or since we are in the death room of Manoah, perhaps it's Manoah trying to get our attention. Just pure speculation.

Mel once again starts making alert sounds, this is then followed by static, and ends with several pop sounds. A woman points to my EMF saying, "There's something." I reply saying, "There is something, it's crazy!" An EVP is recorded, "I know." I walk out of Manoah's room and head over to the Otis elevator. I'm now in the area where Claude Harvey was killed, believed to be murdered. He is thought to be one of the hotels resident spirits. The Mel spikes up to 5.1. A few seconds later, a man gives this EVP, "Aids."

Chris announces to the group that we are about to head up to the next floor. One of the people in the group says that his EMF meter spiked up to 6.0. Chris lets us know that as we go up the floors we can scatter around but move up to each floor as a group. As we walk into the lobby Chris speaks, "This was the ambulatory entrance. This is where they would bring you through and get you on that elevator and take you up to wherever you needed to go. So, this is where we decided to do the lobby, check-in and gift shop."

He looks around and tells us, "Okay, let's go to the first floor. You can walk the stairs or use the elevator." A couple of the kids, Chris and myself wait for the elevator. The elevator doors shut behind us. Since we're in the elevator I try to see if I can get an EVP or some other type of result. As my recorder is on, I ask, "Is there anybody in here with us? Can you say something, anything?" While I didn't receive an EVP, an unexplained breath was recorded. It was very loud, as if someone's mouth was on the recorder. The Mel then spikes to 1.2.

The elevator doors open. As we all gather on the first floor Chris warns us, "Be careful for restaurant staff going up and down the hallway. The restaurant is down there. That would have been the main entrance to the hospital back then. The cafeteria kitchen was down here, the restaurant still uses the same kitchen. The bathrooms that they have, used to be in the area where the minor surgeries were performed." He points out a few rooms to us, "Room 10 was a physical therapy room. Room 11 was the coat room, and Room 12 was Claude Harvey's room—the man who was killed at the elevator." An unexplained wheeze-like sound is recorded.

Chris says, "The nurses didn't think it was an elevator accident. They believed it was a set-up. Somebody killed Claude Harvey. They think it was the guy who got Claude's job position. He killed him, so he can get that job." Chris starts to check if there are any vacant rooms we can explore. I ask Chris about Room 10 and he replies, "It was a physical therapy. They got therapy in here. I don't know if it's the same spot but at some point they were doing electroshock therapy." As Chris is speaking, an unexplained labored breathing is recorded. Then what sounds like either a woman or a child is recorded giving this EVP saying, "Grab on."

Chris explains, "In this level here, it's got the original door with the frosted glass. For some reason they didn't want you seeing in or seeing out of here." A woman in the group shares, "We're staying in here, and we heard some weird noises." She then goes on to share a little paranormal experience that they had and actually recorded. "We got an EVP. We asked, 'How many people are here with us?' and the EVP said, 'Twenty-seven.'" Chris talks more about the area we are in, "The set up that it was, with the windows, now back then you could have probably opened up these doors and stepped out just a foot. The only balconies now that you walk out onto are on the third floor.

These doors don't open anymore, but when they had these doors, the idea was probably to give them fresh air and some sun while out on the patio."

He continues, "Hydro-therapy for sure was in here. Electroshock might have been in a different spot in the building but for sure hydro was here. They had some heated whirlpool baths for people who were hurt back then." The Mel spikes to 0.8. A server walks past us with a tray of food. I sniff the air and say, "Yum. Smells good." An EVP of a man is recorded whispering, "It's good."

We start up to the second floor and the Mel spikes and an unexplained static is recorded. The Mel EMF spikes up to 0.9 and once again, loud static is caught on the recorder. As we are in the stair well heading up to the second floor I tell Chris thank you for allowing me to be a part of the already booked tour. I tell him his hotel will have a chapter in the book and he mentioned maybe it can be sold in their gift shop in the lobby. As we walk past the elevator my EMF spikes to 8.3. Chris and I are able to debunk that because of the elevators wiring. Chris tells the group, "Let's stop here for just a moment, I'll run through a few things."

Session four

Chris starts to give us some history about the hotels second floor as we stand in the hall and listen intently. He says:

> The second floor, this is where they kept quite a few of the patients that were in the hospital. Most people did not have a private room. Down there behind that door, that's where they kept all their male patients. There were sixteen beds altogether in that one room. They had bathrooms, showers and a patio where you can go outside and get some fresh air. That's where I lived as a little kid for six months, when I was nine years old.
>
> My brothers and me, my mom and dad were down here. Then Larry was somewhere else in the building. One thing that didn't seem like much, but creeped me out as a kid, was that there wasn't a bathroom back there. So, to use the bathroom, you had to come down this hallway late at night if you had to use to the bathroom. You had to go down the hallway, down the stairs and go to room 12 which was Claude Harvey's old room. Just doing that … there were times where I'm the last one to go to sleep and everybody's asleep. I would have to

> go to the bathroom, it's like, I'm not going to go down there by myself! I'd just wait until the morning. I'll wet the bed if I have to.
>
> Down on this end is where they kept all the children and female patients. So, sixteen people here, and sixteen people there. That's thirty-two beds there and fifty-two beds in the entire building. Most people did not get a private room. Room 26 was the x-ray room. It's the only room that had double doors like that.

(He points to the wall, above us)

> Notice that there's a call-light on the wall above the door. That's the original hospital call-light. So, they can flip the switch in there and I think for the x-ray room, the way that they used it was they didn't want people opening up that door when they're shooting x-rays in there. The whole room was painted out with this black paint.
>
> The windows, the ceilings, the doors, the walls—it was all painted black. Then they had to go into this little back room to develop their pictures, their x-rays. All these other rooms, 22, 25, and other rooms, those might have had patients in there and they had the call-switch, so you flip the switch if you wanted to call the nurse. The nurses' station was room 27. So that one does not have a call-light above the door because it was the call-station. The nurses were constantly in and out of there. If you look above the ceiling, there are five lights there. That's all original. Over forty years abandoned, and not one of these lights were broken."

(As Chris pauses, an EVP of a man is recorded saying, "Get out of here.")

> The doors were all in good shape—it's the original doors. The tubs in the bathrooms, we kept those as well. Room 24 was the chief surgeon's office. Room 22 was the consultation room. Room 20 at the end of the hall used to be the treatment room. The creepy one … Is anyone in room 25?"

(An unexplained static is recorded. Then what sounds like a young child breathing rapidly and loudly is recorded.)

A woman replies to Chris saying that she is staying there. Chris nods and says:

Okay guys. The story about rooms 23 and 25. Rooms 23 and 25—it was vague what it said on the blue prints, we didn't really know. So, the nurses came up here and they gave us some history behind these rooms. If they had a patient that was in one of these wards—sixteen people here, sixteen people there—not everybody is going to get better. Somebody is dying in the ward. They would realize this and they would not let the person die in the ward with sixteen witnesses. They wanted to give the person who was passing away some privacy.

(He looks at the lady staying in room 25)

So, they would put them in your room, and 23. So, we asked the nurses, "So, it was the hospice?" They replied, "Yeah, but we didn't call it hospice back in the 1920s and 30s." I remember we asked, "Well what did you call it?" They told us, "Most of the people called them the death rooms." Kind of eerie.

Chris is unlocking the area where they kept the male patients—where he temporarily lived as a young boy with his family. He reminds us to be careful and to watch our step because the area is under renovation. We, as a group, split up and wander around the large space. Kind of like a mini-maze so there is plenty of room for us all to have our own space and explore. As I am walking around, recording and taking pictures, an unexplained pop is recorded.

I take a picture and immediately afterwards an EVP of a man is recorded, "Hey." Another EVP is recorded. This time it's a child, "Hold my hands." Very close. At this point, I have walked away from everyone, and no one is by me.

Chris had also unlocked and opened the doors to the female and children's ward, so I head that way. As I enter the ward, I look around and say, "It's a little more fancy in here." An EVP is whispered, "My house." I ask a woman who I spoke to earlier, "Catch any more orbs?" In which she replies, "Yeah a couple." A little girl who has caught a few orbs of her own on camera, excitedly walks over to me and proudly shows me another orb picture. Cutest little investigator ever!

An EVP of a man is recorded, "_____ _____ as is." First two words are unfortunately unintelligible. I hear this with my own ears, and I say aloud, "I just heard a man talk." Sometimes I hear them talk, this is happening increasingly more often. Then a man is recorded breathing real loudly. Another EVP from possibly the same man saying, "No. Get out. Get out."

I am talking to a married couple who are also paranormal investigators, the man being a former police officer, on the force for over thirty years! How awesome! The former police officer who I'll call George says to me, "We're in Preston Castle in California. There were four of us doing an investigation, we're not getting anything, we're using the spirit box and we are getting nothing. I say, 'I used to be a police officer.' We get a really clear, 'Fuck you.' It was very clear. It used to be a reformatory so there were a ton of troubled kids there. Many murders happened there.' I share with him some of my Tombstone adventures.

Chris summons us all, we start making our way out of the female and male wards and gather. He wants to talk about the Psych Ward.

Session five

We head over to where the old psych ward is located and gather around Chris. He says:

> Okay, I'm going to tell you guys some stories that will creep some of you guys out, because I know some of you have these rooms. These ones down here, 37A, 37B, 39A and 39B were all part of the old psych ward. For a while, I believe this was also the sanatorium. They added the fourth floor for babies. This happened in 1929, two years after this hospital was built. There was no fourth floor. They added the babies, later on they used the fourth floor for the sanatorium for the people who had tuberculosis.
>
> There is a patio and sun porch on the other side of this wall. There used to be some doors right there. Now there's only doors from 39A and 37A, you have to go through those rooms to get out there. This was a sunporch where they could go outside for fresh air. When they made this a psych ward they were still taking the patients out there but now they are sitting in restraint chairs. You open those doors and risk somebody falling over this railing and hurt themselves or even worse.
>
> Even with the doctors and nurses that were here and the safety precautions they took, there were some accidents that happened. There was something that happened in this room, 37A.

(At this point a woman in the group laughs nervously. Chris looks at her)

> Is this your room?

(It was.)

> All right. This is something we heard from the nurses before we opened, it's a little bit of a sad, creepy story. It's about somebody who passed away when it was a hospital.
>
> It happened December 22, 1945. So, three days before Christmas. This mother and daughter had come to the small mining town of Jerome from Nebraska. I don't know how long they were here in Jerome, but the daughter was mentally ill. I think she was schizophrenic. She was twenty-four years old and her mom had brought her to the hospital.

(An unexplained sound, like that of a baby breathing loudly. While there were kids in the group, like 11 and up, there were no babies.)

> They had the daughter in the psych ward in this room, 37B. She was only here for about five nights. Each night when they had her in the hospital, they'd put her in this room to go to sleep because she was mentally ill and she was a new patient. We're also going back sixty to seventy years, they didn't understand her very well. They were putting the girl in her room, in a bed, with restraints. She was being restrained while she sleeps. They're sedating her with Thorazine."
>
> They were leaving her alone restrained and on anti-psychotic medications. On the fifth night she was there, the nurse tells us, "I think we forgot to give her the Thorazine." She was not given the medication, so she's left in the room by herself, thinking everything is okay. Well, she hasn't been sedated. At some point she starts to, probably, and we're guessing about this, freak out. She doesn't know where she is. "What's going on? Why am I stuck in this room? I can't get up!" Since she's restrained to the bed, she's probably struggling against these restraints.
>
> She gets the restraints off. So, the medicine was missed, the restraints failed and she is loose in that room. She probably just was desperate to get out. She goes to the window and jumps, she fell three stories. She survived for thirty-six hours in the hospital after it happened. I don't

know how long it took for them to realize she was gone, but they found her and brought her back in and a day and a half later she died from her injury due to the fall.

We heard about this death back in 1996. About ten years later, we get a letter in the mail. It was from a lady who lives in Canada. In the letter she tells us that she's doing some research on her family ancestry and that she came across a person that died in this building, which happens to be the girl I was just talking about. The woman says, "This was my great grandmas first cousin." She didn't know that we had talked to the nurse about this girl. She did her own research and she felt she had to send us the information she found out. She sent us the death certificate, it's down in the lobby. She told us through the letter that she was sending the death certificate to us because she knew it's our building now and it's a hotel and it's said to be haunted."

My back is to 37A and I'm leaning on the wall. I keep hearing a knock-like sound coming from the room. This happens a few times. Chris says:

Her name was Gurthie May, she died at twenty-four-years old. On a tour about three years ago, I was over here coming out of room 39 and it was before we took the old French doors out, that is now a wall (at the end of the hallway) so, the hospital had doors there. I think to them, it didn't matter, if they wanted to take someone out and open up the doors at the end of the hall and take you out on the porch, then they could do that.

When we bought the building, we left the doors there for a long time and they were closed and locked. You couldn't go through them. That table's always been sitting there, it's because 37A and 39A are hotel rooms that have doors that go out to that porch. So, we can't let other people go out there, but three years ago, those doors were still up we hadn't removed them yet. You couldn't go through them, but they were there. They had white curtains over them so that the guests renting the room could have their privacy.

Which is why we eventually took the doors out and built that wall. I remember one time I was walking out of this bedroom, I'm shutting this door, everybody else in the tour had already come back in and was walking toward the suite. As I'm coming out of room 39, there's one lady waiting for me. She's standing with her back against the wall as she waits for me. We're heading to the Grand Suite which used to be the Operating Room. So, I'm shutting the door and I notice this lady. I look at her and look over at these doors. This was in the middle of the summer. You could still see through those white curtains that we had over the doors.

I look over and see this man walk right past these doors. I haven't had any experiences like this. I saw him walk out and he goes right by to the other side. He is walking from this side of the porch to the other side. I saw a perfect side image as he walked by. I can see that it was a man. As he goes behind that wall this lady asks me, "Did you just see that man?" I'm still looking at the doors, I forgot she was even there. I look over at this woman. She points to the doors and repeats the question. She saw what I had seen and she identified through the curtains that it was a man. I told her I did and asked her, "What did you see?"

Before I told her what I saw she said, "A man walked out from the left and he went by the doors." She tells me, "I think he's trying to get back inside. You've lost somebody who's still out there." She thought it was a lone man from the tour trying to get back in the building. Well I open up that door and I crawled out on that porch and there was nobody out there. I come back in and look in the other side of the room because it's connected and there's nobody out there. I look at this lady and kind of give her a look that confirms nobody is out there. I also look in the room, it's empty.

We put two and two together, she comes right up to me, she kind of took me off-guard with this, she puts her hand in the air to give me a high five. This experience totally creeped me out. Sure, I do this five nights a week, but I've never seen anything like this on a tour before. As she gives me a high five she says, "This was worth the $30.00 for the ghost tour." I think if it were just me who saw it, I would have checked and after not seeing anyone, probably would have dismissed it.

We are exploring some of the rooms Chris had opened up for us. A woman walks up to Chris and tells him that she opened up her room and that we are welcome to go inside and check it out. Chris asks her, "Are you in room 37B?" She confirms that is the room. This is the room where the mentally ill woman Gurthie May fell from the window, later dying.

An EVP of a man is recorded saying, "Yes." Very close, as if whispering in my ear. A little girl who I dubbed the Orb Queen caught yet another orb in a photo. Chris suggests we head to the other end of the floor. Chris says, "Room 33 is the most requested room. There's five rooms that have a balcony. Starts with room 30, then 32, 34, 36 and 38. Four of those rooms were used for patients that had a little higher rank in the company, maybe an executive or one of the bosses."

Session six

Chris continues but unfortunately a man not too far from us is whispering for some unknown annoying reason, so I miss the beginning of what Chris is saying. I whisper into the recorder debunking the rude whisperer. Chris says:

> The first room is 30, which was the nursery. It used to connect to the labor and delivery room, which is now part of the Grand Suite. They end up adding the fourth floor for more maternity space because they didn't have enough space. 32 was the first room where you could actually have your own private room.
>
> They made the exception for this miner who was hurt really bad. He's in the hospital longer than anybody else and he's most likely never going to walk again. This guy has been hurt to the point where he is paralyzed. He is a paraplegic and is confined to a wheelchair. He's downstairs on the second floor with all the other male patients. He's got a bed down there, they put him outside on the porch for a little bit, he asked to come back in. His main thing is he's stuck with all these other people. He's got no privacy and he's been there longer then everyone else.
>
> He keeps asking the staff, "Can I get a room where I can have my own space? A place where I can sit outside and enjoy the scenery. Since I'm stuck in this hospital and not being able to walk anymore, at least I can be out on the balcony, enjoy the view, lift my spirits." He convinced them it would help his recovery. They felt bad for him. This however, was not sincere on his part.
>
> He wants the room for a different reason. So, they bring him up here to the third floor. They put him in room 32, he's there for a few days. He's out on the balcony sitting in his chair. He comes back in at night to go to bed. He seems to be happier. It's not one hundred percent

private, the balcony wasn't a private balcony back then. It was one long compound so there could be a nurse out there with a baby, he can see the nurse.

He can see down there and see somebody in rooms 34, 36, and 38. It was four days of him being here that he was outside. He had a two to three-minute window, it wouldn't have been very long where he's by himself. The nurse leaves to go grab something. There's nobody out there. He rolls up to the railing. He's down sitting in his wheelchair and he somehow pulls his body weight up out of the wheelchair with just using his upper body strength. He goes straight over those bars and falls to his death. He played them. This is what he wanted to do from the beginning.

He didn't want the view. He didn't care about the scenery. He didn't want to be in the wheelchair any more. The nurses said, "We fell for it, he fooled us. It's our fault. We put him in this room and we left him there by himself." So, they had to enclose the railing before they could use the rooms again. It looked like a jail, so when we were turning it in to a hotel, we cut them to an average height. It took a couple of months to do the enclosure.

The next patient that came up was put in the same room as the miner in the wheelchair. This guy was a little bit older. He was supposed to retire in a few months. He had gotten really sick and they told him, "You're probably looking at a few months to live." It was a respiratory type, he had cancer. Working in the mines for forty years and now he's supposed to retire and he's not very healthy now and he's going to pass away. He was given a few short months left to live.

He is in his room and later that night they hear a gun go off. The nurses go down to that floor and check out that room first. The guy, he had his gun there and he shot himself with it. My family ask the nurse, "Why did you give this guy his gun after you told him he only had a short amount of time to live?" They replied, "Back then, this town, that's just the way it was." You had your gun wherever you went.

(An EVP whisper is recorded, "No.")

That's the most requested room because of stories like that. It's the most active room. Over all, the third floor is the best floor to get results. Because the hospital was privately owned and then closed for almost forty-two years it was hard to get all the information.

The couple who are staying in the Grand Suite (if I remember correctly, I believe it was the paranormal investigator husband and wife who had this room) open up the room for us to check it out. As soon as I walk into the suite unexplained static is recorded.

Chris gives us some history about the former Operating room turned Grand Suite:

> The windows actually go up and past the ceiling then come back down. We thought it was for sunlight and the nurses came up here and told us, "No. Ether and cyclopropane were used to put the patients to sleep. If we were going to do a surgery and amputation, we're pumping with ether or this type of propane. It was so dangerous to use this stuff, that the reason they put this glass window was in case there was an explosion in here and you blew up those tanks. The explosion would have nowhere to go, with the glass windows it would break the glass out." So here we thought it was for sunlight.
>
> They said, "No. We did surgery real late at night because it got very hot and we didn't have the cooling, so we tried to avoid hot temperatures." The sterilization room is now the kitchen.

Chris shows us the drain where all the blood and other bodily fluids went down. Chris recommends the group to take pictures in this room because this is where people had surgeries. Chris goes on, "The door was always here, this would open up to the sterilization room, which is now the kitchen. That door was always there. These are the operating room doors that swing in and out. We carpeted all the tile, the old hospital tile. Down that hallway was labor delivery. We didn't change it too terribly much."

Session seven

Chris leads us up to the fourth floor. We lucked out tonight because the fourth floor is completely vacant. It is here on the fourth floor that a spirit touches me. Chris begins to open some rooms up for us to check out. Before we venture off to check out the rooms Chris gives us some history about the floor:

Okay, so this would have at one time been the roof. It was a roof that was accessible. It had a patio up here. In fact, the elevator came right up to the roof. They said that back in 1929 when they decided to make a fourth floor for maternity the elevator was already coming up here. They added five extra rooms. Three down that way and two right here. There's a door at the end of the hallway that still takes you out to a portion of the roof.

One of the big things people have experienced here is hearing a baby cry. Being a former maternity, that makes sense. We'll get people asking us in the morning if there was anybody up there with a baby. So, many times I would check, and there wouldn't be any guests registered up there with a child. That's a regular occurrence.

What Chris says next proves that even if there was a baby upstairs, it could have screamed and cried all night but would go unheard because of this,

> These floors are so thick. They poured concrete, so you wouldn't hear people from below or above.

We start to walk around the fourth floor. I spend a few minutes talking to the paranormal investigator couple.

I enter a room where there are a few teens hanging out on the bed. One girl asks me, "Do you have a lot of stories?" I tell her that I do but obviously now was not the time to talk about them, so I told her, later. I stay in the room a couple more minutes and talk to the young-ins. An EVP is recorded saying, "Go ahead."

At this point everyone has left the room and I stand alone and take several pictures. As I'm doing this a loud static is recorded. I then walk into room 40. I walk through the first doorway and walk down a mini-hallway that leads to the room itself. I am standing in the doorway and looking into the bedroom. The lights are off, it's dark and I'm alone.

Suddenly I feel, what I can only describe as a hand, gently grasp the top of my head, gently squeezing my head three times. I excitedly say, "What the!" I look above me, behind me and into the room, and there is nobody there with me. I know what I felt. An EVP of a man is recorded speaking an unintelligible word. I walk out of the room and tell the people nearest to room 40 what happened. They follow me in the room to the doorway where I was touched, and I show them what I felt. After I share my experience someone shares something that just happened to them, "I was over here, and I take a picture of the bed, and there is an orb in this area. So, I take another picture and the orb was still there!"

I am back in room 40 along with a couple other people now. I say, "We're in room 40. Somebody grabbed my head while I was standing right here in the doorway. Who touched me?" An unexplained thump-like sound is recorded. Then an EVP is recorded saying, "Pull the head." Amazing! A woman in the background asks, "Is there somebody else in here?" An EVP is recorded, "I don't want to."

I ask, "Can you tell us how you died?" A few seconds later an EVP is recorded saying quite clearly, "On the lawn." Then the Mel Meter spikes to 0.5. I talk to someone, telling them how I was recently touched by a spirit. The guy I'm talking to says, "That room has something very powerful in it." An unexplained pop is recorded, then yet another EVP is caught on recorder, "Come alone."

Session eight

As I start this session the Mel Meter spikes up to 2.2 and starts making alert sounds. Chris joins me and the woman I was talking to. Chris tells me, "The spirits are messing with you. They know you're looking for them." An EVP is recorded of a man saying, "Go home." I say, "I was looking in there and," as I pause an EVP is recorded, "At last." I finish, "they know I can sense them." I'm leaving the room and an EVP is recorded, "Get out."

I'm standing outside the room talking to someone, they were asking me about what happened in room 40, as I explain to them what happened, a male gives this EVP, "It was me." This is followed by a loud unexplained breath. Several seconds later a man is recorded whispering this EVP, "Check the bouquet." A long pause and then the same voice gives another EVP, "Check the b …"

Session nine

I walk in room 41. As I am walking around, checking the room out and taking pictures, unexplained static is recorded. It continues for several seconds. Chris starts to shut the doors. The tour is over, and people start to head downstairs. The couple I have been talking to and myself wait for Chris. As we walk down the stairs with Chris, more static is caught on recorder.

We are back in the lobby now, first things first, I pay Corey for the tour, he was so friendly and knew since I was late I should pay later so not to miss more of the tour. After that, Chris shows us some interesting things, "This is a couple cool things. This is the newspaper article that came out after Claude Harvey was killed by the elevator. A little hard to read but there's some information about it." He makes copies for the couple and myself. He grabs another paper and says, "This one is Gurthie May's death certificate, the girl who fell out the window and died." He makes copies of that as well.

Chris finds another paper and says, "This one here, I don't think this has the names of the two jumpers, this is just miscellaneous. Some names we were able to get, the year they died and what they died of." Chris makes copies and continues to look for more information. Chris looks at the paper in his hand and shares another experience:

> This was the guy that they called the Butcher. It tells you his real name here. This is kind of funny. I was doing a ghost tour a few years back and I stopped doing this since, now I just call him the Butcher. Before I would use his real name and say, 'This Doctor was known as the Butcher.' There was this old timer in there and it happened to be his family doctor when he was a kid.
>
> He kind of got upset. He defended the doctor saying, "He was a really good doctor. He was my family's doctor." I told him, "Sorry! I just heard that from many people that his nickname was the Butcher." He was all offended. Now I don't say his name anymore, now I just refer to him as the Butcher. What a small world!

Chris and I chat for a while about different things. He talks about his experiences of when the Ghost Adventures crew were there. Chris says, "So Claude Harvey, the elevator guy, he lived in room 12. He had a couple of nicknames. His name was Claude, but they called him Scottie because he was a Scotsman. He was from Scotland. Scottie or Dad. My guess of why they called him Dad, he was in his fifties, so he wasn't very old, but the nurses might have been much younger here and he was maybe a surrogate-type father. He joked around with much of the staff. He was a very friendly man."

Chris shows us the picture of the phantom cat, that has been seen or felt countless times throughout the hotel. Very impressive. Chris talks about a photograph, it's a group of hospital employees. In the picture there is one face that you cannot see. Chris thinks it's Claude Harvey. This is creepy because his head, you can't see his head. This picture was taken a year prior to Claude being killed. Chris says, "I am sure Claude has to be in that picture." He explains the picture, "These are restaurant people, he might have been in there, these are nurses obviously, then the doctors. He's the only one wearing a different type of shirt. He would have been there."

Session ten, final session

The couple, Chris and myself go back to the room where Manoah Hoffpauir hung himself. As we enter, an unexplained pop is recorded and as I walk to where Hoffpauir's body was found hanging, my Mel once again starts going crazy with alert sounds. This is then followed by static. There's definitely something in this room. Manoah's death room.

Chris points to my Mel and says, "I need to get me one of those. I like the story that went along with this one. The man's daughter died, she was still coming to him at night. I think her name was Melanie. He's never heard of this stuff and he kept feeling the presence of his daughter after she died. It was driving him nuts, so he got into it and came up with a ton of things." I ask Chris, "How did Melanie die?" He replied, "I don't know. I think it was a bad accident."

As Chris is talking about Melanie the person my Mel Meter is named after, once again static is recorded, as this is happening a very loud gasping like sound is also caught on recorder, of course going unheard by all of us. Then an EVP of a man is recorded, what sounds like, "Everyone."

Chapter twenty-two

Old Jerome Jail, Jerome, Arizona

Joan, my mom and myself went to Jerome for the day. Joan's friends are in a band and were performing at the Spirit Room so we thought we'd go have some drinks and listen to some good music. The place was packed. We managed to get some seats at the bar and decently close to where they were playing the music. Joan and my mom danced along with other patrons and I sat at the bar and watched them. They met a man called Wreckless Rick. After a quick discussion about Jerome's spirits, my mom and Joan knew they had to introduce Wreckless Rick to me.

June 11, 2016
The investigation

Wreckless Rick is a local tour guide who happens to be very knowledgeable when it comes to the paranormal world that Jerome offers. He was so sweet and said that after the band takes a break he will take me for a walk and give me a dose of haunted history. So, after five or so more songs, the band announced they were taking a little break. Joan decided to stay in the bar and talk to her friends (the band) and my mom and I went with Wreckless Rick outside.

We started outside the Spirit Room, and then checked out an old jail where the prostitutes would be locked up if things got out of hand. When we went to Jerome that day, I had no idea we would be doing this, it was a very nice surprise.

Results and evidence collected
Session one

As Wreckless Rick, my mom and I walk outside, Wreckless Rick starts giving us some history, "The Spirit Room burnt down twice. David Connor was the first business to have insurance." We continue to walk. Wreckless Rick takes us to an area where people are known to get readings. We are in a part of the former Red Light District. Wreckless Rick speaks:

> Just before I got to Jerome, a man was wanting to tear down some of the historic buildings because he wanted to erase his father's and grandfather's association with prostitution. So unfortunately, we lost a whole bunch of historic buildings. Some of the guys, that got here a year or two before me, took in the demolition. Strictly because *Jon Struthers wanted to erase the cribs.

(An unexplained static is recorded.)

> Arizona is the forty-eighth state. We have fewer laws than anybody else. As far as toxic waste, environmental pollution, we are way behind civil rights.

(We are now standing in front of a building that used to be the Historic Ladies Jail, which was a holding tank/ chill out chamber for the ladies who got violent and unruly, not just the ladies in the cribs, the street walkers as well.)

> This building is two stories tall, all the rooms were eight by ten. The Struthers rented them out, many Struthers around America and here in Jerome. These buildings were all taken down by one family.

(He points to a building on the corner)

> If you're up on Main Street, that's the Hotel Conner. When we were in the Spirit Room, we were in part of David Conner's building. The bar used to be a café. The other three places, he had his own bar, billiard hall and his own gambling parlor which was mostly card playing back then.
>
> The hotel up above there used to be a building that was built right up against it. I remember seeing the doorway; there was a plaque commemorating the doorway. It was called, 'Husband's Alley' because it was a secret passage way. It looked like a Lawyer's office or somebody's business. Men would come through the door, go down the hall, down a flight of stairs and they would be right here in the midst of the cribs. Which was mid-range prostitution because the Struthers would rent these rooms out. Otherwise, we have the street walkers who would do it in the bushes. Generally, women claim their space and the street walkers would do it in the bushes or in shacks.

Wreckless Rick asks us, "See all the doors?" We nod. He goes on:

> These were private rooms for the high- class places. See, they couldn't be on Main Street. This was one of Belgium Jenny's daughter's places. One of four locations she had in Jerome. Why four? All those fires, you rebuild, rebuild, and if you have the money, you can relocate, kick out the person that used to be there.

(He pulls a key out of his pocket and shows it to us)

> I have a key to the Historic Ladies Jail.

(A loud static is captured on the recorder.)

> People will sometimes get orbs. I don't attract many, once in a while a spirit will follow me home. When that happens, I have to sage my house and do some talking to the spirits. With illness, because that's why they hang around hospitals so much. When the ailments are in a weakened state, drunk, or a drug addict, that's when their defenses, their aura,

(an unintelligible EVP from a man is recorded)

> is diminished and it's easy for a tag along. At any rate, so, we have the street walkers, the mid-range, ladies in the cribs, and also Jenny's place.

> In the Brothels, the evenings' entertainment could go on for hours. More like the great-date situation, rather than rapid turnover. It cost more to be there, and the Madams would distribute the work load

(an unexplained pop is recorded)

> therefore the pay, so there wasn't competition amongst the ladies in the brothels because you had someone in charge that understood the business. Meanwhile, the ladies in the cribs and the ladies on the streets were in competition for the working-class men. So, they'd be more prone to violence and or drug use, alcoholism, because there was no manager.

> That's why there was a police ... well sheriffs. Back then it was the sheriffs. Down here was a sheriff sub-station. It wasn't the deputies' job. This was entry level, or if you're into merits, I mean breakup's and horse fighting. There was no citing and no tickets, no judge and jury. They just wanted to keep this business off Main Street. So, the ladies would be locked up for a day or two and fined $5 or $10, that was four or five times higher than any other jail in town.

(An unexplained static is recorded.)

My mom, who was on a business phone call, is now off the phone and back with Wreckless Rick and me. We point out the building to her and she says, "Woah, those are itty-bitty rooms." I tell her, "Well they were there just for that one thing." An EVP of a woman is recorded saying what sounds like, "Serious." This is followed by unexplained static.

Session two

Wreckless Rick continues:

> Mid-level prostitutes would get in fights, they would just lock them up for a day, or a day and a night. They'd pay a few bucks and then they'd release them, and the ladies would get back to work. They didn't want them to clog the courts and walk these ladies across Main Street to a judge then back across Main Street to the jail.

(An unexplained pop is recorded. Wreckless Rick then unlocks the historic ladies jail.)

As we walk in to the old building my mom points cats out to me. An EVP of a woman is recorded, saying, "Cats." My mom tells me, "Go ahead. I'm going to take a picture." Another EVP from the same woman whispering, "Better not." This is then followed by more static. Wreckless Rick walks through a small doorway, looks back and says, "This is the jail." I reply excitedly, "The jail? Oh my gosh, how cool!" As I walk through the doorway, an EVP is recorded, a disembodied whisper of what sounds like a man saying, "Hide the gold!" Followed by an unexplained pop.

Jerome, Arizona, like Tombstone, back in the day was a total booming mining town. One mine dubbed 'Little Daisy Mine' proved to be very profitable. In 1916 alone, this mine produced over $10 million worth of gold, copper, and silver. So, this EVP, "Hide the gold" can easily be from one of the miners or maybe someone who planned to steal some of the miners' findings.

Wreckless Rick says, "These floors are eight inches thick and there were vehicles here and the mechanics. They drilled through the ceiling in a couple places so they can spy on the ladies. They'd also get cigarettes and drop them through the drilled holes down to the ladies."

I ask Wreckless Rick if I can go into the jail cell, A few seconds later, I get an EVP of a man saying, "Sheriff." Followed by unexplained static, then an unexplained pop. Wreckless Rick gives me the go ahead to go check out the cell, I say, "Cool. I'm hoping to get an EVP or two." An EVP from a woman is recorded, so close it sounds like she is standing right by my side, "It hurts." Then an unexplained pop is recorded. An unexplained loud static is recorded and it continues on for ten seconds. Very loud, it actually hurt my ears when I listened to it.

Wreckless Rick says, "This is a 1918 building, and before that, other things had been here like housing, prostitution, mechanics etc. In Jerome there could be layers of hauntings. What you see now and what you get on recording may not be associated with this jail." As I tell Wreckless Rick about my book a loud unexplained static is recorded and this goes on for several seconds.

For almost the whole time there's static, a woman is recorded breathing and moaning. I take a picture and an EVP is recorded of a woman saying what sounds like, "Should get out." An unexplained pop is then recorded. This is then followed by an unexplained recorded sound that sounds like a kissing sound.

Session three, mini session

I say, "I know a bunch of prostitutes were in here." A few seconds after I say this, an unexplained sound, that sounds like to me a woman groaning, is recorded. As I stand silently in the jail cell, I get an EVP whispered to me, "Go." Very close. A disembodied voice is recorded saying, "Yes." The Mel spikes to 2.0. This is followed by a pop sound.

Session four, final session

Immediately as I start this session, an EVP of a woman is recorded, saying, "Come." Static follows, then the Mel spikes to 1.0. Wreckless Rick says, "The Chinese restaurant would bring food to the jail." He pauses then says to me, "Maybe you got some EVPs, maybe you didn't." An EVP is recorded saying, "You know." About thirty seconds later another EVP is recorded, this one is unintelligible.

Wreckless Rick says something, and I laugh, an EVP is whispered, "Hurry up." As I am thanking Wreckless Rick for his time, another EVP—same voice—is recorded saying, "Get out." The Mel spikes to 0.8. Another EVP, same voice, "Get out!" As Wreckless Rick is locking the door an unexplained pop is recorded.

Look at these EVP's we've collected:

Should get out…Go…Come… Hurry up... Get out… Then, a more excited, Get out! Clearly someone doesn't want us there, again, 'Hide the gold' comes to mind.

I wish I could have spent more time in Jerome. I got to tour the Jerome Grand Hotel, investigate at Sheila's Copper Penny, and a private tour of the ladies' jail, but I feel this old mining town hides much more sinister history.

Wreckless Rick was great, and I hope to come and see him again some time in Jerome. Same with Sheila and Chris.

Chapter twenty-three

Sedona Community Cemetery, Sedona, Arizona

This cemetery is very close to Oak Creek Canyon, famous for the breathtaking gorgeous red rocks, more like boulders. Unlike the other cemeteries I have investigated, this cemetery is much newer. Established in the 1970s. The cemetery, though smaller, is absolutely beautiful. The red rock mountains are a short distance away, beautiful green trees grow throughout the cemetery and red clay covers the ground.

I very much enjoyed this place and I will be back. My favorite character on the TV show Cheers, his mother and father are buried here as well.

June 12, 2016
The investigation

This investigation was conducted by Joan Sedita and myself, with my mother there not wanting to join in, but just to watch. An observer, a witness if you will. We had just come back to Joan's home in Cottonwood after spending some time in Jerome.

It was still early in the day and Joan knew just the place for us to go. Sedona is a short, lovely drive from Cottonwood. She told me how there is a grave she had to show me—one of the most popular graves at that cemetery.

We pull up to the cemetery and nobody else is there. I love when that happens! As we pull up and park I am admiring the beauty this cemetery holds. Due to the rising Arizona heat, we don't spend too much time at this cemetery, but I am able to get a few mini sessions in.

Session one

Joan leads us to the headstone she was telling us about. Being the most popular sometimes isn't always a good thing. The headstone reads:

***TO OUR MOTHER
MONA HEROLD VANNI
OCTOBER 14, 1912 TO APRIL 11, 1996
YOU SPENT YOUR LIFE EXPRESSING ANIMOSITY
FOR NEARLY EVERY PERSON YOU ENCOUNTERED.
INCLUDING YOUR CHILDREN. WITHIN HOURS OF
HIS DEATH YOU EVEN MANAGED TO DECLARE
YOUR HUSBAND OF FIFTY-SEVEN YEARS
UNSUITED TO BEING EITHER A SPOUSE OR A
FATHER. HOPEFULLY YOU ARE NOW INSULATED
FROM ALL THE DISSATISFACTION YOU FOUND
IN HUMAN RELATIONS.
BUDDY, JACKIE AND MIKE***

We are standing in front of Mona and her husband Guido's headstones. I say into the recorder, "Okay, today is June 12th," as I pause, an EVP of a woman is recorded, saying, "Come on." I continue, "2016. We are in Sedona Community Cemetery and are here with Mona Harold Vanni." Another EVP of what sounds like the same woman is recorded saying, "Come here." I ask, "Mona, is there anything you'd like to tell us?" For several seconds, an unexplained static is recorded. This is then followed by a pop.

Session two

We walk over to a Doctor's grave, he had recently passed away and Joan had known him very well. Joan says, "Hi Dr. Masters. You got yourself quite a nice plot here. How's the other side? I'm wondering why you were so miserable to *Joshua when he was doing fine work for you and in turn you became not very nice to me." Joan pauses, shakes her head, then continues, "You never thanked me for the Holy Soup that I made and dropped off for you." An EVP from a man is recorded speaking an unintelligible word.

Joan goes on, "I'm kind of wondering what that was about. That really hurt. I was always there for you." Joan says a few more things, speaking from the heart. Unfinished business. I've been there too. Someone in your life dies and things go unsaid, issues that are never worked out. Problems, issues, or arguments that are never solved or settled. I get that. I've been there. Joan lets him have it and you'll read about the result of that in a while.

Joan asks, "Is there anything you'd like to respond to about that?" A man is recorded whispering an unintelligible word. His voice is very light and distant. The Mel spikes to 0.9 and shows the temperature being at 95.8 degrees. Much warmer over here then it was at Mona's grave, which is not too far away. (The temp at Mona's site was 88.0)

Joan continues to talk to Doctor Masters, "I had liked you Doctor Masters. I took really good care of you after your heart surgery." I ask, "Can you tell us why you changed with Joshua and Joan?" As I pause, an EVP of a man is recorded, "Yes." The temperature went from 95.8 to 88, a slight cold spot here on a hot Arizona summer day! This is followed by three loud unexplained pops.

Joan says, "Well, you have a beautiful plot, that's for sure. I'm sure you'll have a tombstone every bit as grand. You will be remembered." A man is recorded breathing, as if right by the recorder. Right after that the Mel spikes to 1.0. Joan continues to speak to her old friend, "I was delighted to hear that you appeared to have gone peacefully in your sleep. I'm sure your education is continuing where you are. I hear that they're still busy at the University that you created." An EVP of a man is recorded as he says, "Better." She continues, "Doing well with enrollments." Another EVP by the same man, just a little fainter, "Okay."

Joan says, "I hope you blessed *Rachel with all that she did for you and gave to you over many years of her life." The Mel rises to 1.1. After we finished this session I turn off the recorder and the EMF. Joan walks to the car, where my mom is standing in the shade under a tree. A few seconds later the Mel roars back to life and makes a sound I have never heard before, it does it nonstop. Remember I had just turned this off. This piece of equipment is trustworthy. I have never had any problems or malfunctions before, or since, and I hope it stays that way! While I got spikes throughout this investigation, the EMF itself has remained silent. I call Joan back over telling her, "Whatever you said to him pissed him off." She comes back over and I start recording again.

Session three

I ask, "Okay, I turned off my EMF and a few seconds later it went crazy with weird sounds. Are you doing something to my equipment?" As I ask this question the Mel is still making the mysterious loud sounds. I just want to say that before each investigation I make sure the batteries are good and make sure that the equipment works.

With the EMF still crying, I ask, "Can you stop the noise?" A man is recorded, faintly saying, "Yes."

Joan speaks, "Doctor Masters, please don't take anything I said as derogatory. I was just speaking factually about our experience. I'm sorry." Amazingly, as she says sorry my EMF stops making sounds and it is now eerily silent. I say, "Thank you for stopping." An EVP is recorded of a man amazingly saying, "Welcome." Then an unexplained pop is recorded. This is followed by a man breathing heavily.

Session four, final session

We are about to leave the cemetery, we are in the car driving, still in the cemetery, I look to my left and ask Joan to pull over. I jump out of the car and see an unmarked grave. I don't know why I was drawn to it, unknowns are so sad to me. How can one be at peace? We are just about to leave so I didn't stay too long. In fact, this may be one of the shortest sessions I have ever conducted, however, the results are mind-blowing.

As my mom and Joan wait in the car I stand in front of this unmarked grave and say, "I'm standing in front of an unmarked grave. No name. No dates. No nothing. Just a rock. Can you tell me what your name is?" First, there's unexplained static. Then a few seconds later an EVP of a man, very faint, very distant, "Somebody killed me." How horrifying! I ask, "Can you tell me how or where you died?" The same man gives yet another eerie EVP, "I would ask Carl." It's sad because there are no dates, this man claims he was murdered and that a man named Carl either was responsible for his untimely death or witnessed it.

I wanted to look more into this but, without any dates, it is almost impossible to even try to find out anything at all. I sincerely hope this man can be at peace one day and maybe his murder will someday be solved.

Chapter twenty-four

Waverly Hills Sanatorium, Louisville, Kentucky

Waverly Hills Sanatorium. When I hear those words, I think death, tuberculosis, sadness, desperation and much more. I have seen this old tuberculosis sanatorium on TV several times. One time, I was driving cross country from North Carolina to Colorado, my two homes. I happened to be staying the night in Louisville that one particular night. A few days earlier I had checked Waverly Hill's operating hours online. According to that they were open.

As I drive up the dirt road towards the driveway, Waverly comes in to view. Such a beautiful building. I had seen it on TV several times and now here it sits just a hundred feet or so away from me. There is one thing holding me back, a gate. They are closed. I was very disappointed to say the least. I call their office and talk to a not-so-friendly person basically saying the hours online are hours they are allowed to answer the phone and made it seem like how dare I not know that. What the … So, folks if you plan on going, please don't look hours up online. Please call ahead. It's a lesson I learned and hope you don't go through the same thing.

A few months later while in Colorado, I become friends with a man named David. He happened to live in Louisville and has been to Waverly several times. We plan to go there together in a couple months when I head back that way to go back to North Carolina. Once I found out exactly when I was going to be there David did an awesome job and found some tours going on at the same time. There were two-hour tours and six-hour tours. Of course, we went with the six-hour tour and good thing too, because I heard from a Waverly employee that the short tours you aren't even allowed to use your recorder. That's my main tool. I totally would not have been okay with that!

Waverly Hills Sanatorium was a place people would bring their family members to, that had tuberculosis, or if they thought they had it. If you were sent to this sanatorium it was thought to be a death sentence. Many people went in, not very many ever came back out, not alive anyway.

The investigation
August 12, 2016

Since David and I weren't going to Waverly until 11 a.m. and knowing that by the time the overnight investigation was over we'd be exhausted, we tried to get some shut eye during the day. David went to his room and passed out, as for me, I wasn't so lucky. I sat in the guest room just thinking about Waverly and the results I might get. I finally turned the lights out and forced myself to lie down and close my eyes.

I think I got a couple hours of sleep, which is better than nothing. We are anxious and arrive at Waverly much earlier than expected. The gates won't open until twenty or so minutes before the tour, so we wait in the car and go for a drive. We go to a nearby restaurant and hang out there for a while. Now, the email that I received from Waverly was basically just a list of things you are not allowed to bring; booze, drugs, common sense things. The list of things you could bring was reasonably smaller, your phone and a flashlight.

I was bummed out that it didn't say anything about equipment for investigations. To be honest since the last time I called, and the experience wasn't that great, I was intimidated to call and ask if I could bring equipment. Also, I figured if I could bring it, the email would have said so. In the end I brought my recorder and my phone. Sadly, I left the Mel EMF, the spirit box, my 38 zoom camera, and the other tools behind.

While at Waverly, an employee asked us all, "Are there any paranormal investigators here? If so what kind of equipment do you have?" She was asking because she was curious. Hands go up in the air. Confused, I raise my hand and ask the woman, "I thought we could only bring our phone and flashlight." So that's not true. If you're doing a short tour, then yes, it is very limited to what you can bring. However, if you pay for the six-hour tour then you are free to bring your equipment. Information I seriously wish I knew. They were selling 'Ghost Meters' (EMF) and I was desperate, so I bought one. Boy, I sure missed my equipment.

I am saying this so that people who are interested in going to this old sanatorium are not caught off guard. While I got many results here, I'm sure I would have gotten much more if I had all my equipment with me.

Results and evidence collected
Session one

There were several people there the night David and I went, so I was super relieved when they separated us into two groups. So, while the group I was in got to explore the third, fourth and fifth floors, the other group explores the first and second floors. The tour guide opens the door and leads us up the stairs. David is holding the EMF and immediately he gets a spike at 1.5.

We are still walking and an unexplained pop is recorded. An EVP is recorded, very close, as if right next to the recorder, "Hat." I just bought a Waverly Hills hat from the gift shop and was wearing it. I have no clue if that EVP was about that or something else, but it's a possibility. An unexplained hiss is also recorded.

We get to the desired floor and we all gather around the tour guide, *Lexi. She goes over the rules with us:

> First and foremost, no taunting, no being disrespectful. You know what I mean by that. If you want to communicate with the spirits and this building, the way I always do it is talk to them like they are a person, because they're people. They just don't have their physical body anymore. Talk to them as if they are a family member or a friend. That's what I do.

(She tells us that sadly sometimes people come here and tear things up and are just destructive and rude and they are trying to preserve this building.)

> This spot here is a place of unnatural deaths that occurred in the building. What I mean by that is it wasn't caused by Tuberculosis. When one of the previous owners had the building, they kept a couple of security guards to watch over the property. They would see a man, an elderly man, up here from time to time. They didn't know him by name, just by the way he looked. The owner of the building knew about it. He figured the old man wasn't bothering anybody, might as well just let him stay up there.
>
> They would see him occasionally, knowing he was up there. They started kind of missing him, it had been a while since they had seen the old man. They start to look around. They smelled an odor that led

them to the third floor and straight to this elevator shaft. When they looked inside they found the man and his pet dog. They had been murdered and thrown down the elevator shaft. There were no charges pressed because the murderers were juvenile. They think it was a ritualistic or gang-related murder. We do get some activity in this L shaped room.

Lexi then goes on about how the spirits will communicate through flashlight. As a paranormal investigator I do not use this method. The mag lights are temperamental and easy to manipulate. I had only done this one time and that was in Tombstone. In Tombstone the light wasn't used prior and it was all the way off, so I do believe that was possibly paranormal, here at Waverly a little later on, you'll read about how the light goes on and off by itself in front of me and a fellow paranormal investigator. I do not believe this to be paranormal, so I am debunking it. While I debunked this, Waverly and its spirits did not disappoint me. Armed with just my phone and spirit box I caught white mists in my photographs and several EVPs on my recorder.

As the guide talks to us about how sometimes peoples' equipment malfunctions for no reason, my recorder catches a hiss. Very close to me, as if right next to me. Lexi shares a past guest's experience:

> We had a couple on the two-hour tour that were here. The girlfriend was listening to the tour guide telling the story. The boyfriend wandered off into this room. He said when he turned the corner back there, he saw a tall thin man standing there. He described him as having long greasy hair and he had a long trench coat on. His back was facing him. He said the man turned to look at him, over his shoulder and when he did the boyfriend said that the tall man didn't have any eyes.
>
> There is a man who has been seen in the building, the dog also has been seen. A white German Shepard. Dog barks have been heard inside the building as well. Yes, we do have houses nearby, but this occurs within the building. You'll know the difference. I've heard it myself a couple times. You may have heard of a little boy named Timmy, who likes to wander around the hall. How that came about; the current owner bought the building, there was about a foot and a half of garbage in here. The owner had some people help clean it up and one of them found a bouncy ball.

(Unexplained static is recorded)

> They start kicking it around playing with it, and afterwards went and stuck it in a closet. They go a couple rooms down and start cleaning up, when they find the ball in another room in another closet. They start to play hide-and-go-seek with the ball. It shows up in different rooms, then on different floors. They thought it was childlike in nature, so they gave it the name Timmy. Now we don't know if there was a child here with the name Timmy but it's possible. A ton of kids came through Waverly Hills, some came as patients themselves, some were born with it, some were brought in with their parents because their parents had no other place to put them while they were at Waverly.

Lexi shows us where a bouncy ball is and encourages anyone who wants to experiment with it. She then leads us to another area. We walk up the stairs and gather around her. She shares more history with us:

> Okay, so this was an operating room. There were two surgery bays, one right here and the other right there. There were two windows in the wall, those were the windows they'd use for x-rays. They'd put up the x-rays to see what they were working with. They did the surgeries in a last-ditch effort to save the lives of the patients.

(As close as I am to the guide, as to catch her voice on my recorder, at times her voice seemed distant so unfortunately, I missed some of what she was saying.)

> Thorax is where they would build in a little cast cabin, put the air in and collapse the lung because they thought the rest of the lung would try to heal itself. It was quite successful because tuberculosis thrived on oxygen. So, when they would collapse that lung, it would deprive that lung of oxygen supply. It was decently successful. The other one, 5% chance of survival; the removal of ribs.

What she is referring to is Thoracoplasty, which is a surgical removal of several ribs in order to collapse a lung. On average the required ribs removed were 7-8 ribs. Most surgeons would only remove 2-3 ribs at a time, making the patient have to endure numerous painful surgeries of rib removal. Can someone say ouch?

Lexi continues:

The thought behind this was to free up some air so that the lung could expand and make it easier for the patient to breath. They would make an incision at the base of the neck and go down along the spine and then around the front to the valve. Like I said, the surgery had a low success rate, it was very painful and very bloody. Doctors had good intentions to help the patient survive. The small room in the corner was the nurses prep station. The room across the hall was a recovery room where they put the patients that actually survived the Thoracoplasty treatments. There is an elevator that opened right outside in the hall. So, if you didn't make it out of the operation, you'd take a ride on the elevator down to the first floor to the morgue, which is right below us on the first floor.

We leave this room and follow Lexi to the next destination. As we walk, an unexplained pop is recorded. We head to the fourth floor. The recorder capturing all the clanging of our shoes and shuffling as we walk. People talking to one another. I am just so thrilled and honored to be here, so I am staying silent and just taking in my surroundings. I am stoked to be here, but I cannot imagine calling this place my home.

We get to where we need to be and listen to what Lexi has to say:

> The fourth floor is famous for two shadow-like entities. One is a very large black shadow. When it gets dark, the mass grows larger and larger and will come towards you very fast. If you get stuck in this mass, it's almost like a vacuum. People have screamed, and they go unheard. The other thing is called Creeper.

As she continues to a talk, I receive two EVPs, the first is a man asking, "Can you hear me?" Then a more lower voice replies, "I know." Lexi continues:

> Creeper is very small and very fast, and it has been seen crawling across the floors, across the walls, on the ceiling and going through the walls. If you're going to watch for shadow people, this is the floor to do it! Make sure that you have no lights on and let your eyes adjust. When you are up here tonight, and you let your eyes adjust, you realize just how much light is in here. You'll see shadows on the floors in some rooms, as if they're just walking around and casting shadows on the floor. Stand and watch.

We start walking to another area. As we walk I make small talk with a couple who is celebrating the man's birthday. They have never done anything like this before and are excited to see what the night brings them. We all gather around Lexi as she speaks:

> Okay everyone, this is the fifth floor. Part of this floor is outside. A patio is on either side of these wards. This floor is probably most famously known for room 502, which is right here.

She looks up and points,

> There was a nurse that was found hanging up there. She was not found in the room but found hanging from a light fixture right here.
>
> This was around 1935-1940. We know this because the owner talked to a man who lived in a nearby cabin. His uncle and dad worked up here. He spent plenty of time up here as a child. To his best knowledge, between 1935 and 1940. His uncle was called in, they used the elevator and when it opened they saw her hanging there. She had been pregnant, she was no longer pregnant. The baby was found about a week later in the sewer wash out system. We know she was tuberculosis positive, which meant her child would have had it as well.
>
> She wasn't married. Around that time, if you were pregnant and not married ... that's just something you would not do. There was a rumor that she had an affair with a married Doctor who worked here.

(My recorder picks up an EVP of a woman, possibly confirming the rumor saying, "Yes.")

> Affairs, that's another thing you didn't do back then. She would have probably been shunned by her family, friends and co-workers. What we don't know is how she got to be hung here. It's possible that she committed suicide and hung herself. She couldn't find a way out of her situation and maybe miscarried or aborted the baby. The other theory is the Doctor helped her perform the abortion, which back then was new—it hadn't been perfected yet. Something may have gone wrong, perhaps she died by accident and the Doctor hung her here to make it look like a suicide so that his reputation wouldn't be ruined. Back then it would have been really easy for them to write her death off as tuberculosis.

Lexi goes on to tell us that the woman is up here and will communicate with us through flashlight and to be kind and gentle with her. This is where I experience the flashlight going on and off by itself, this is where I debunk that. I would rather get EVPs then a flashlight turning on and off. EVPs are real. I got an EVP from the woman earlier in this area.

> This ward to my right housed three patients. They got tuberculosis of the brain. Not only could it effect your lungs, but it could get to your brain, your bones, your skin, your blood, your organs. They were here and on the opposite side was a ward for children. Being in the sunshine would create a vitamin.

(Unfortunately, some of the other guests are being rude and talking at the same time as Lexi, so I miss what she is saying.)

> You are able to go outside on either side. She then talks about where the smokers can go and enjoy a cigarette. She goes on:

> We will take a break around 3 a.m. If everyone agrees, I can let you free roam floors three through five until 3 a.m.

That sounds awesome obviously we all agree to that. I am curious about the flashlight and a debunker of flashlights, so I walk over to where the flashlight is positioned, in front of room 502. I ask, "Are you here? Can you make the flashlight turn on?" I receive an EVP from what I believe to be the same woman who spoke earlier saying, "Yes."

About forty seconds later the flashlight turns on. I ask, "Can you turn the light off now?" An EVP from the same woman, "K." The flashlight turns off. A man walks up and joins in, "Hi there, the device I'm holding lets me hear you. Is there anything you'd like to say?" An EVP of a man is recorded, "Get out while you can." Very eerie. This isn't the only EVP I get warning us to get out.

A series of unexplained pops are recorded, followed by a disembodied voice saying, "Stop." I just want to say that all the voices I caught on my recorder are EVPs since I left my spirit box at David's house.

Session two

I'm still in the area by room 502 where the nurse was found hanging. David comes over and lets me know that the EMF got a few spikes. A woman nearby asks me if I just saw what happened with the ball. I had not. She tells me that the ball was moving by itself in circles. David saw this too. I'm bummed out that I missed this! David is bummed out because he wanted to record this event but his phone was dead, so he was unable to.

As David and I are about to go off and explore a different floor, a man walks up to where we are, by the ball and says, "If I had candy, I'd give you some. I know I'm a bigger guy, don't be afraid." An EVP of a man is recorded saying, "Ball." As we start to walk I dodge a bat. They are here and are definitely not shy. They definitely don't mind invading someone's personal space. As this is happening a series of unexplained pops are recorded.

We continue to walk around. Graffiti on the walls. When you came here with the dreaded disease tuberculosis, it was like being handed a death sentence. On our right are several rooms, on the left are the sun patios, where the patients spent most of their time. I say, "We're on the fourth floor right now. Does anybody want to talk with us?" When I say us, I mean David and I, as we are now free roaming and have the area to ourselves. An EVP in a hiss-like-voice, "Me!" Then another EVP, a whisper, "Yes." A woman's disembodied voice is recorded singing unintelligible words.

The convenient thing about free roaming in a huge building like Waverly is that we were able to be alone almost the entire time. Once we saw and heard people around, we could either wait until they left or venture of to a place that was vacant. It was easy to go somewhere free of people.

David wanders off. I say to the spirits, "So my friend left, I'm here by myself, does anybody want to talk to me?" David calls out to me in the distance. I call out to let him know where I am. I continue speaking to the spirits, "Please talk to us. We aren't here to hurt you or disrespect you or anything." I am interrupted mid-sentence by a bat that almost flies right into me. David calls for me again, I find him, he says, "There's something right here. I feel it. I know there's something here." An unexplained sound is recorded, what reminds me of an air ventilator that you would hear at a hospital. Then an EVP of a man saying what sounds like, "It's me." Amazing! Is this man verifying that what David is feeling is this man's energy?

I take several pictures trying to capture what David is feeling. Again, I grow frustrated that I do not have any of my equipment with me, including my 38 zoom camera. I ask, "Is somebody here with us? David feels some type of energy here, who's here with us?" Several seconds later an unexplained sound is recorded—a possible voice—but David starts talking at the same time, so I will debunk this sound. David shows me where the feeling starts and the area where it ends.

I ask, "Is someone here? Can you tell us your name?" A disembodied voice is recorded saying what sounds like, "Seth … come on." I receive more EVPs from the same voice, "Come. Come." Then about twenty seconds later, "Come on." I ask, "How long have you been here?" The same voice, "No … come on!" Then, the same voice is recorded, but more anxious now, "Come on out!" This last EVP is closer, as if right by my side.

David calls out to me from a room. I search for him in the dark. He tells me he felt a tug. I told him to be careful about the bats. The room that David and I are in has a weird feeling to it. We both feel it. An unexplained pop is recorded. As I start to leave to go to another room, I see a bat quite close to David, I warn him. I ask, "Is anybody here with me right now? Would you like to talk to me? My name is Tessa. Can you say Tessa?" An EVP of what sounds like a woman or a child, "Huh?" Then a very distant, "Essa" I cannot hear the T but it is possible the spirit did as I asked and said my name! This is followed by unexplained rapid breathing.

Unexplained movement sounds are recorded. That sounds like as if something heavy is being dragged. Again, we are in an area free of other guests. I suddenly feel weird and run a short distance. I tell David, "How creepy. It sounded like something was chasing me." As I pause my recorder catches this eerie EVP from a man, "Gonna getchu." I continue, "I thought someone was behind me, I heard footsteps coming up quick behind me, I just looked and there was nobody there." The man who just spoke says, "Oh yes I was." So creepy!

We continue to walk around. Fellow investigators are heard in the background in the distance, I debunk them, and walk away so we are away from the other investigators. I say, "If anyone wants to talk to me, please speak up. When I listen to the recording later, I will hear you, so if you have anything to say, do so now." An EVP is recorded, "Don't, go home." I say, "I feel something here … is anybody here?" I wait a few seconds, "Are you a victim of tuberculosis? Can you tell me what your name is?" An EVP of a man saying, "Come on." A few seconds later, another EVP is recorded, this one has a more raspy voice, "Come on."

David comes to me with excitement in his voice. He was in a room and when he turned his flashlight off he felt something move around him. As he tells me this experience an unexplained pop is recorded followed by unexplained heavy breathing.

David asks, "Is there anybody in here?" An EVP is recorded, "Yeah." The EMF starts making alert beeps in David's hand. David asks me, "Do you want to go down a floor?" A couple seconds later a man is recorded giving this EVP, "Down." This EVP is immediately followed by static. The couple I spoke to earlier comes through the area we are in. We talk for a minute and then go our own ways. David had already left, so I go off to search for him. As I go to the stairwell I find him. I'm talking to David and stop mid-sentence, excitedly I say, "Something keeps moving my hair!" In which David replies, "I know what you mean ... I'm feeling something too." An EVP is recorded, "Coward." Very close, as if standing right next to us. Several pop sounds are recorded.

I ask, "Anybody here with us?" A disembodied voice is recorded saying, "Yes." I realize that David has left me alone again. I say, "Am I alone right now? Who's with me?" An unexplained beat-like sound is recorded. What sounded to me like a beating heart. "Thump-thump-thump-thump" Then an EVP of a man is captured whispering, as if very close to me, "Come on." I say aloud to myself, "I thought I just heard somebody." When this happens I always say it loudly because many times I hear something, it ends up being an EVP that no one else hears. It's awesome when it happens. Of course, I don't know it happens until well after the fact, while listening to the recordings.

I ask, "How many of you are here with me right now?" An unexplained pop followed by deep breathing coming from a man are recorded. David is nowhere in sight, I am completely alone. I ask, "Can you show yourself to me?" Unexplained static is recorded, followed by an unexplained pop. Both of course go unheard by me. As I walk around by myself I walk past a small group of fellow investigators. We make small talk and go on our separate ways. I receive an EVP from a man whispering, "Go." Before leaving, the group shares with me that on the fourth floor they had earlier encountered shadow people. As I find David an EVP is recorded, "Come on, come on."

I ask, "Is someone here with us?" Immediately an EVP is recorded, that sounds like a child, "Yes." I ask, "How did you die?" The same little voice gives this sad EVP, "I don't know." I turn to say something to David, to find out he wandered off again. I call for him a couple times with no reply. I am still by myself as I walk the never-ending hallways of Waverly Hills Sanatorium. I'm walking in silence and a man is recorded exhaling, so close, as if right in front of me. I finally find David. We start to make our way to the fifth floor for some pictures. The time is 1:41 a.m. As we are walking an unexplained sound is recorded, that sounds like a bounce-like sound, followed by an EVP of what sounds like a woman saying, "No."

I say, "Flash" to warn David and anybody else who might be in the near area that I am taking a picture. A disembodied "No" is recorded. Then an EVP from a woman whispering, "Don't do anything." Again, I say, "Flash." The same woman says, "Don't" I am unsure if this woman is speaking to another spirit or to me, either way she was caught on recording.

I ask a lady, "Where did Lexi say the woman was hanging? Right here?" The same woman who spoke earlier gives me yet another EVP as she says, "Yes." The woman I actually asked answers seconds later, "Yeah, right above on the light fixture." An EVP of a man, "Shh." The woman shares something with me, "There's a man with a recorder that can go and you hear it before you play it back and over here we were talking about a baby that I had lost and she said, 'Fell' and we went over here and the monitor started beeping." David asks, "What did the EVP say?" The woman replies, "Fell." Right after the woman says fell an EVP of a woman is recorded, "Fall."

Session three

I'm still in the area where the nurse was found hanging. I call out for David, "Hello?" An EVP is whispered, "Hello" Then unexplained scratch-like sounds are recorded, no one is around me. Then an EVP whisper is recorded, "Hear it." As I continue to search for David a woman gives me this EVP, "Hurry." The search continues to find David, as I keep walking the same voice repeats the last EVP, "Hurry." A bat flies past and screeches. David calls out to me, and once again we find each other.

I ask, "Is there anybody here with us right now?" An EVP, "I am here." Another EVP is recorded, "Help me." As we continue to walk around, an unexplained thump-like sound is recorded. I ask, "How did you die?" An EVP is recorded saying what sounds like, "You know." I receive yet another EVP of a man saying, "Wench." This is followed by a series of pops.

A couple of people walk by us and ask if we had gotten anything yet. The woman shares with me something that just happened to her, "I stay away from the phone apps usually, but it said 'game' and 'through' and it led us to one of the games. I had it recorded. I played with this app when a death in the family occurred, I brought it into the funeral parlor. I wish I recorded it, the phone app got all my families names." As we end our conversation I notice David has walked off again. Sheesh!

An EVP is recorded saying, "It's out." His voice sounds like what would come out of a spirit box, but I didn't have my spirit box with me. I must've given up looking for David, as I continue to just walk and explore in silence. As I wander around alone in the dark, I cannot help but feel a very strong presence that's with me. I feel this is my friend Michael, this happens from time to time. As I say this aloud that I feel this presence, an unexplained breathing from a man is recorded followed by an unexplained pop.

I ask, "Is there anybody here with me? I'm by myself again right now. I lost my friend again! If you're here with me can you talk to me? My name is Tessa ... What's your name?" After seconds of silence a voice is recorded giving this EVP, "Hold me in your a___ ... hold me." I assume that word is arms but didn't hear it all. I say, "Now just because this was a tuberculosis ward doesn't mean you died from tuberculosis. How did you die?" Unexplained footsteps are recorded (seven total) followed by an EVP of a man saying, "Death." I hear this and I say aloud to myself, "I thought I just heard a man."

David finds me and we continue to walk around. As we are exploring an unexplained pop is recorded. Followed by a raspy voice, saying, "Tess" or "Test" unsure which. An EVP of a woman is recorded, "Come on." The woman repeats this except more anxious, "Come on!" David and I are talking, I ask, "Can you come here real quick?" An EVP of a man is recorded, "Yes." Followed by David saying, "Yeah."

What happens next freaked me out. To this day I cannot explain what the hell it was. David excitedly calls me over from one of the rooms. "Turn off that flashlight, I'm seeing the craziest shit I've ever seen!" He points to the sky, at two distinct hovering lights. "They were moving towards each other, now they just stopped ... now they're just sitting there. It moved up, it moved down, now they are just hovering there." We stand there in silence just watching these unexplained hovering objects in the sky. Perplexed David says, "Those aren't airplanes, not helicopters, they aren't stars."

I gasp. He points out, "See! They're fading out." I observe and say, "That one's moving up a little." One of them is moving back and forth. I admit to David, "Ghosts don't scare me, aliens and UFO's scare the daylights out of me." He agrees, "Me too!" They remind me orbs, lit up in the sky. David says, "Okay, now look! That one is moving this way now." We continue to stand there staring in awe. David says, "Wow! There's a little light under it!" We now witness the unknown light move upwards.

I start to get nervous. So, apparently besides spirits and shadow people there seems to also be unidentified objects in the Louisville skies as well. Explaining this does not give this experience justice. In the recording you can hear the excitement and disbelief in our voices. It was something we experienced together, and I know I will never forget it and while I cannot speak for David, I don't think he'll forget it either. David says, "That's weird." As he pauses an EVP of a man is recorded saying, "Yeah." David makes an observation, "Now look! There's a beak there, like a pine, and that wasn't there before. Now look, the other one is barely moving. Now the beak is gone! There's one … two …" An EVP whisper, "Three." We notice that the other light now has a beak as well. I gasp as a bat flies past us. David asks for the time, it's 2:19 a.m. We start walking around and an EVP of a man is recorded, "Come here."

Session four

As I start this new session, a series of loud pops are recorded. After hanging out on the roof with Lexi for a while we go off and start to explore again before we have to all meet up with the rest of the group to take our half-way break. As David and I continue to walk, an EVP of a disembodied voice is recorded saying, "Pull it. Pull it." Another EVP is recorded, this one was a woman's disembodied voice saying, "This kid."

What happens next is awesome. David starts asking several questions, and a spirit starts talking to him answering David's questions. These are EVPs, so David doesn't hear the responses. I am unsure if this is a man or a woman, but the voice is the same. David would ask a question and would wait about thirty seconds or more before asking another, so this session took a little while. Here is that conversation:

David: Are there any spirits here with us?"

EVP: Yes.

David: My name is David, this is Tessa and we're not going to hurt you. We just want to talk, see what you're up to. Why are you here? How long have you been here? I know there's someone here with us."

EVP: No.

David: We just want to see what's going on.

EVP: Hey … hey.

David: Did you die here?

EVP: Yes. (What sounds like talking under your breath.)

David: Do you have any friends here?

EVP: No.

David: What month did you die?

EVP: April.

David: What year?

EVP: Help … You don't want to know.

David: Were one of these your room?"

EVP: No.

David: Do you remember what room you died in?

EVP: No … no.

David: Were you scared?

EVP: Yes.

Not knowing David is having an EVP session (and a full-on conversation) with a spirit, I call him over to the next bedroom that I am currently in. I let him know that I am feeling something over here. When I call him, my voice is in the distance, he's holding the recorder as he asks the questions. The spirit's voice is close, as if right next to David, my voice was distant.

Ever since Tombstone I have panic attacks and times where I cannot breathe. I am having a hard time breathing at the moment. As quickly as the breathing issue comes, it leaves just as quickly. After catching my breath, I feel a presence again. I ask, "Who's here with us? I feel something." A few seconds later an EVP is recorded, "Roger … Roger."

David calls me into a room that is noticeably warmer. If only I had my Mel EMF so I can see exactly how much warmer it was. A disembodied voice is recorded giving this EVP, "Help me." I check the time, it's 2:42 a.m. meaning we have eighteen more minutes until we take a break from investigating. A bat flies past us. Out of nowhere David starts to feel sick to the stomach. We sit down and take a breather out on the sun patio.

I ask, "Can you make the EMF spike for us?" A disembodied voice is recorded saying, "I don't want to … I don't." David and I start to make our way to the meet-up point we all agreed on. As we walk in silence an EVP from a woman is recorded, "Ten." As we stop walking another EVP is recorded, "Help." We are out on the roof on the fifth floor where part of the group has already gathered.

As we sit there waiting for the rest of the group to get there my EMF makes an alert beep. The tour guide comes back with some stragglers and we all make our way down the stairs and through the halls to take a break before we're allowed to investigate floors one and two. After walking for a couple minutes, somehow this guy and I get separated from the rest of the group. Both of our EMFs spike up and make alert sounds, next thing we know the rest of the group is nowhere to be seen. David calls out to me, and we are able to find the group.

I stand in a particular area and the EMF starts spiking again. It's a strong spike going all the way to 5 milliGauss. The man who was lost with me turns on his spirit box and asks, "Is there anybody here tonight?" A woman comes through the spirit box and says, "No." A man then comes through saying, "Move it." The EMF goes off again. An EVP of what sounds like a child to me is recorded saying, "Yes." Someone else's EMF starts making noises as well. An EVP of a woman speaking two unintelligible words.

Session five

After a couple of minutes of small talk amongst ourselves, *Lexi comes over and speaks, "Okay, I'm going to show you guys some of the hot spots, then you can free roam and investigate." An EVP from a woman, so close, as if she's whispering in my ear, sending me a warning, "Do. Not. Go. In. There." This is then followed by a childlike EVP, "Get out." As this happens wheezing is caught on the recorder. I just want to note that symptoms of Pulmonary Tuberculosis are chest pains, difficulty in breathing, chest pains, and WHEEZING, just to name a few.

Lexi speaks:

> First floor, everybody always wants to know about the body chute (AKA the death tunnel). The body chute is down this hall here where it says exit. I'm not going to walk us all down there because it's probably too toasty and it would be cramped. So, the body chute is down there, you can walk down it if you want. There is a set of stairs on one side and a ramp on the other. It's not a giant slide. That's where they slid the bodies down. It's about five hundred feet down with a forty-five-degree angle, it's a long way down. Going down is easy, coming up is another story. Be careful if you go there tonight.

She warns us that if any of us have any health issues, like knee or leg problems, asthma or any other medical type complications to take extra caution or not go at all. I had recently gotten rid of a spiritual attachment and had still been slightly feeling the effects of a hard time breathing, but you can't go to Waverly Hills to investigate and not go to the body chute, right?

Lexi continues:

> It is partially underground so the farther down you go, the concrete tends to get wet and slick. The body chute was not built with the intention of being a body chute. It was built as a service tunnel to bring goods into the building. It was a way for the staff to get into the building during the harsh winter months. They'd park at the bottom and walk up to work. It was also a way to heat the building. There was a steam plant at the bottom and they would use the steam to heat the building.

> At the height of tuberculosis in the 1930s when there was a patient dying, one of the medical Doctors thought it would be a good idea to find a discreet way to get the dying patients out without the other patients—who were trying to get well—seeing it, sitting up in their rooms seeing ambulances, hearses and stuff like that. If they'd seen that they would have absolutely no hope of getting better and would lose their will to survive. One of the head medical Doctors thought of the idea of taking them out of what is now known as the body chute. They had a cart system on a set of rails that ran by cables, pulled by a small motor. It would load the deceased and lower them down the hill.
>
> Family could arrange to pick them up if they wanted to, if they could afford it. Many were afraid of contracting the disease themselves, so they didn't want to be near the bodies. For those who did not get picked up by family, they were taken over to the University of Louisville Medical Department to be studied.

(An EVP of what sounds like a child is recorded saying, "Yeah.")

> When the students were finished, they were brought back here and buried in mass graves. So that could account for some of the activity for the property and the building. Some of the paranormal stuff that goes on down there; you may hear people talking,

(An EVP is recorded, "Yes.")

> you might see strange lights. People have seen blue lights, green lights and white lights. At the bottom of the body chute you will see a light, the outside area, which is part of the property, a light on the lamp post. What's been going on there the past couple of weekends is that light gets blocked as if a shadow apparition is walking back and forth. Keep an eye out for that. Keep your eyes and ears open while in the body chute. The majority of the patients that left the building, left through the body chute. It was their last ride.

We start to walk, following Lexi. An EVP is recorded, "You. Hey!" We stop and gather around Lexi. She speaks:

> This doorway that I'm standing in, this large room here was once used for an auxiliary ward, it was basically a holding room to place the bodies.

An unexplained wheezing sound is recorded.

> Before they can get them out through the body chute, although that was an efficient way, it was a little bit slow and the actual ward, which is down the hall here to the left, was not large enough to hold the bodies so they used this room. We know this because the owner of the building, his father used to work here in the kitchen when he was a teenager. The kitchen is up on the second floor. They sent him downstairs one day to the loading dock to pick something up.
>
> The loading dock is one floor down from this one. He didn't go to that door, he went to this one instead. He said when it opened, the room was lined wall to wall with bodies, it's something he wished he had never seen. Quite an interesting room. People get a ton of strange pictures in this room.

(An EVP from a child, "Yeah.")

> It goes all the way down until you see the construction going on. This whole building gets paranormal activity, even the stairwells. People have gotten activity there.

(We walk to another area. As we walk, something gets my attention, I say, "Woah!" An EVP from a child, "Hey.")

> Some of the patients would get tuberculosis of the brain and one of the treatments for that was electroshock therapy. This is the electroshock therapy room. There would have been a half-wall up where this large black wall is now. The Doctor would have been on one side watching the patient. The other side over here is a panel that would have held the lightbulbs that lit up when they were administering treatments.

As Lexi pauses, my recorder catches an eerie EVP of a man, "I was here." Lexi continues:

> There are two doorways going into this room, it's a fairly large room, we've had different things happen in this room. People have been touched. Anyone who has a spirit box, this is a good room to try to get EVPs. For me personally, it's more a feeling. Very compressed tight feeling in here. I always get hit with static. Every time.
> Sometimes it's hard to breath in here. I don't know if it's left over energy from all that's happened here … you've got to keep in mind,

what were these people thinking, the way they were being treated, how they felt. It wasn't a torture treatment, at the time they thought electroshock therapy would help. Many times, if you're in here and trying to communicate, keep an ear open for what's going on. You may hear sounds.

We start to walk and a couple minutes later, we are now in the morgue. This was one of my favorite places. Every dead body came through here at Waverly. This room has a ton of history right here. Gurneys on one side against the wall and then body trays. Lexi shares some more interesting history with us:

> The tables are not original, but they are similar to what would have been here. We ask that you do not lean, touch, tap, or jump on them. They are very heavy and quite old. There is an elevator that opens up into the morgue and opens on each floor, so they could discreetly cart patients down the hall as they were passing away. Go down to the elevator then right here to the morgue. They didn't do autopsies on everyone, just if they thought the person had something besides tuberculosis. The morgue is a real active room. Keep in mind that everyone that passed would come through here first, then down the hall to the body chute. There is a camera in here and we see many weird things on the camera. Strange light anomalies will come out of the elevator, kind of stop and hover, then go back in. Also, listen for the elevator, people have heard it before. You can crawl into the body-riding tray if you want.

She warns us that the top tray is no longer there because people abused it and broke it, so she asks that we be respectful of the equipment. Some people are so destructive and ignorant and it's sad to see them destroying a part of history. Lexi says, "I recommend going in, I wouldn't recommend anything that I haven't done myself." We start to walk off to another area. An EVP from a man is recorded, "Look out!" He repeats this several seconds later, "Look out!"

Lexi says:

> Okay, so this is the lobby. It's quite a large room but you wouldn't know it because haunted house fake walls are up [Halloween attraction]. No matter how it ended for people, this is how it began. Coming in, being admitted to the hospital, or even coming in for x-rays if they thought they were sick. First floor would contain the

pharmacy, a gift shop, the x-ray room, a records' room ... they had a barber shop, a radio station. They had their own radio station that would broadcast up here in the hospital where they would talk about goings on, what was happening during the week, different activities and things like that.

The patients were allowed to plug in headphones out there on the porches; put their head phones on and listen to the local radio station, which was kind of neat for them. We get a bunch of strange photos in this room, so if anyone is taking pictures tonight, this is a good room to try that out in. It's usually active. We do have a resident spirit here, he likes to hang out in the lobby here, and he is not very friendly. So, if you're down here investigating and you hear something like a growl, or you feel funny like you shouldn't be in this area, I would leave the area if I were you!

His name is Tim. If you have a spirit box, Tim will usually come across the spirit box. He's got a very deep voice. He is really unfriendly. He likes to call people dirty words, he usually hangs out down here, but there are other people down here as well. In addition, people have seen strange lights down here. Like a firefly, the lights are very bright. They light themselves real bright then fizz out really quick. White lights and red lights have been seen in the area. It's a good area to come, sit down and just listen. You might hear footsteps, one person heard what sounded like a mop bucket being rolled around.

Lexi points to a stairwell and says:

This main stairwell here, people believe it to be a portal, or vortex doorway, down at the bottom. It's a way for the spirits to kind of cross over into our world and their world.

We start to make our way up the stairs toward the second floor. As we are walking I hiccup, I debunk myself and say hiccup in the recorder, A disembodied man's voice is recorded saying, "Hiccup ... go away!" A childlike EVP is recorded, "Go." Then another EVP, "Go away! Right now!" Followed by another EVP, "Come on!"

An EVP from the voice who just said, 'come on' seconds earlier, "Hey ... come." Then a scary hiss-like sound. Remember, we are still in the main stairwell, where it is believed by many people that a portal to the spirit world is thought to be. As we walk, we are deep in thought and taking the old Sanatorium in. These EVPs all sounded quite close to me on the recorder.

We stop at an area and once again gather around Lexi as she talks:

> So, this is a patients' room. It was two patients per room for rooms this size. There's larger ones upstairs, those may have had four patients in them. They were like small wards. For the most part, it was two patients to a room. They spent the majority of the time here on the bed porch. No less then thirteen hours a day with that fresh air and sunshine. At the time, Doctors thought that, combined with good nutritional food was going to help cure them. There was never glass in those large openings, it was copper screens with wooden shutters. The patients were out there in their beds regardless what the weather conditions were like, rain, snow, sunshine, even nights like this. [Hot and muggy]
>
> They invented electric blankets to be used in tuberculosis hospitals, that's why they were invented. If you look on the wall there are outlets and headphone jacks so they could plug their headphones in. Sort of like the first iPod if you will. This room here is neat because we know who belonged here. We have a description about her in the closet. Many of these rooms we don't know who stayed in them. We had a ton of patients coming through, then they'd either die, or get better and go home. We know this woman was in this room because one of her family members was on one of our tours. The woman said as a child she would go to the doors on the breeze-way to get to her Aunt's room. This is her Aunt *Louise Briggs room.
>
> Now Louise was sick for eight years, spending six years here at the hospital. Sadly, she did not beat her battle with tuberculosis and ended up dying here. She had a sister who was here as well. She got better and, believe it or not, she beat tuberculosis, not once but twice! She got better and went home. Her sister Louise got worse so she came back to Waverly to stay with her sister. While there, she caught tuberculosis again then beat it again. She lived to be in her nineties. She recently passed away. People have gotten EVPs with Louise's voice in them. It's a woman's voice saying her sister's name. We get investigators from all over the world who will get that same recording. We think she's waiting for, looking for her sister. She loves to communicate with people; she enjoys people coming to visit her in her

> room. She likes gifts, you'll see in her closet things left for her by other guests.
>
> Across the hall you might notice that these rooms are smaller. They were terminal rooms, private rooms. If your conditions were worse, you'd be here. They'd move you across the hall. They did not have access to the fresh air or sunshine like the patients over here did. If someone were to die, the patient could be discreetly carted to the elevator, down to the morgue and to the body chute without the other patients knowing what's going on. All in very discreet fashion.

We start to make our way to another area. Lexi points and says:

> To the left is the cafeteria and from the cafeteria you can see the front of the building. Across the hall is the kitchen and bakery. Sometimes people get phantom smells in here, pay attention to that. The light at the end of the hall is a loading dock light and that's outside, it is not paranormal. People have seen shadows down that way though ... does everyone agree on free roam again?

(We all agree because it worked out great the last time, no crowding or anything)

> Okay let's do free roam again. You guys have the first floor and the second floor. Does everyone know how to get to the lower area? You'll pass it on the way to the body chute, let's all meet down there at 6 a.m.

We all go our separate way. An EVP is recorded, "Care care care careful." Then about half a minute later, a more disembodied EVP is recorded saying, "Careful!" We are currently in the cafeteria, unexplained chew-like sounds are recorded. Again, if I heard something like that I would have debunked it. The same voice who said careful gives me another EVP saying, "Look at her ... trouble!"

We walk around in silence and I receive an EVP from a child asking, "Really?" Followed by another child's voice replying, "Yeah." It's interesting because even when we're not asking questions and just walking quietly we get so many results.

David and I haven't spoken a word for a couple minutes now, just taking in the new surrounding and exploring. I always keep the recorder running to see if it catches any EVPs. An EVP from a man is recorded saying the same thing over and over again, "Carol ... Carol ... care ... Carol ... Carol ... care ... Carol." This is followed by static. Interesting.

We walk around, slowly making our way to the morgue. As we walk in silence an EVP is recorded of a woman crying, "Please help." This voice reminds me of a spirit box voice, but again, I don't have mine with me and no other people are around. An EVP is recorded, "Get the fuck out." Not in a threatening tone but more like a warning. Another EVP of a man is recorded saying, "Take care." Yet another EVP is recorded, several seconds later saying, "Kill." This EVP was in a growl-like voice.

Session six, Final session

As I start the final session, an EVP from a man, "Get out." I ask, "So what do you think of them remodeling this place?" An EVP of a man is recorded of him saying, "Hold hand." Unsure of what this means. I ask, "Is there anybody here with us?" An EVP is whispered, "Yes. Yes." I repeat myself, "What do you think of all this remodeling?" An EVP from a child says, "Hate it."

The EMF meter makes an alert sound. David and I are now in the morgue, I carefully get into the body tray, not so gracefully, grunting as I get situated. As I lay there, an unexplained child's breathing is recorded.

As I get out of the body-riding tray, I start to take pictures with my phone and receive this EVP, "Gimme it." We are now in the room where electroshock therapy took place. I am standing by an antique wheelchair that is by the bed. Unexplained childlike breathing is recorded again! The EMF meter makes another alert beep. As we make our way toward the body chute, this EVP is recorded, "Come on, get out."

We are now in the tunnel. David goes on ahead and I take my time walking down and taking in the dark, damp atmosphere. Crickets chirping in the background. Remember, every body came through this tunnel. A man is recorded whispering this EVP, "Get out of here." Very close, as if whispering right in the recorder. Again, not in a threatening way but more like a warning like, "Hey don't let what happened to me happen to you." Another EVP is recorded from who I believe to be the same man who just spoke, "Get out." Another EVP is recorded, telling us to, "Get out."

I ask, "Can you tell me what your name is?" A child is recorded breathing heavily. I take a picture and an unexplained sound is recorded, that sounds like a man groaning. Very close. Remember David is much further down the tunnel then myself. I finally make it to the bottom where David is waiting for me. We start to make the long walk back up the stairs. A woman gives this EVP, "Get out. Get out."

As we continue to climb up the stairs, I start to struggle. Since I am still feeling the results from my Tombstone attachment, I am much weaker then I usually would be. I cannot wait to come back here once I have fully regained my strength. Attachment or not, I went down that body chute, all the way down and all the way up, so take that! I am breathing, groaning and moaning quite loudly. I never breathe loud in investigations but right now I have no choice, so I debunk it and continue walking. David, whose further ahead than me, calls back to make sure I'm okay, in reply I groan. As we leave the tunnel the EMF makes an alert beep sound.

We run into a woman who said she got a bunch of results in the kitchen area. As we walk away an EVP is recorded, "Come back." David asks for the time, it is 5:09 a.m. giving us fifty-one more minutes until the investigation comes to a close. Bummer! An unexplained pop is recorded. We find ourselves back in the morgue and we receive an EVP, what sounds like, "Get in."

A bat flies past us so closely that the fluttering of its wings are caught on the recorder. Due to the Southern humidity, both David and I are sweating profusely. David suggests we take a break and go back to where the sun patios are to catch some fresh air. Remember, patients spent at least thirteen hours a day out on those patios. As David and I are walking in the stairwell, my recorder catches two spirits, both men, in what sounds like a conversation. One saying, "What." The other saying, "Okay." Then, "Tell me, okay?"

We are now back at the bed patio area. We are both really exhausted. We've been here since close to 11 p.m. it's now past 5 a.m. An EVP of a woman is recorded, "Harder." Another EVP, from who I believe to be the same woman who just spoke, is recorded saying, what sounds like, "I love." Unexplained foreign beep-like sound is recorded.

A very loud and constant static is recorded. The static reminds me of an old school record skipping continuously. A man gives us this EVP, "Go home." We slowly start to make our way back to the first floor where we all are supposed to meet up, making this investigation at the old tuberculosis hospital complete. Waverly you've been kind to me, I'll be back!

They are short on staff, so my group and the other group are all standing around in the meeting spot and getting more grumpy by the minute. We are all sweating and dead tired, with no Waverly Hills staff in sight. People are starting to get very irritated. I understand that the staff have to make sure there are no looters, stragglers, people trying to hide, people who are lost, etc. but it was unfortunate they didn't have an extra person to release us from the locked building.

We make our way to David's house in silence. I speak and say something like, "I don't care … it's weird I have like a I don't care attitude. Like we can crash the car and I wouldn't care what happened." It's weird because even though I'm not particularly the happiest person in the world, I never have felt this way.

Here we are, pulled an overnight investigation at one of the most haunted locations in the country, thousands of deaths linked to this place, a sanatorium where people died every day, all that energy still in the halls and I feel like I don't care. David is quiet for a second then says, "I feel the exact same way. I have since we left."

So, it's interesting that both David and I are feeling this awkward, depressing feeling, silence for moments just not saying anything but feeling the same way, then share with each other our thoughts. Another experience I will not forget. Thankfully when we got back to his house, I went in to the guest room, fell asleep and woke up with that negative feeling going away. I'm glad it wasn't an attachment. I don't need more of those.

Chapter twenty-five

The Ouija Board sessions, Louisville, Kentucky

I have never been part of a seance before. I knew of Ouija boards but my childhood experience with one turned me away from them. I never thought I would use one again after my experience and what I've heard from other people and their experiences. I just wasn't interested. Ouija boards were off the table for me, that's until the evening of August 11, 2016.

I was staying at my friend David's house for a few nights, we were doing an all-nighter at Waverly Hills the next day so we were both really pumped about it. David has this old Ouija board that has been in his family since the 1930s, I believe. David made this seance happen. We conducted the seance in his office which is located separate from the house in the backyard. May I add it's the coolest office I have ever seen. He invited two friends over, one of them being MariAnne, you read about her experience in Chapter four.

Since I have never done this before, I decided to sit out for a while and be the one to write down the results from the Ouija board sessions. I recorded the whole session as well. We ended up channeling numerous spirits. My friend Michael, who I feel his presence with me often, came through. The results confused the others, but it would make sense to me, so I would explain to them what it meant and then it made sense for them as well. I had no control of the planchette and besides David, his two friends had only met me moments earlier. The results were real.

I left that night feeling good about what happened. It was a good experience for me. I am now open, as an adult to Ouija boards. Never taunt the spirits. As a child, I was in way over my head. They are not for kids, even if you see them with other kid games at the toy store. Even adults can get hurt by the Ouija board. We all sit in a circle and wait for his second friend *Cassie to arrive. David wants to show Cassie the beginning ritual of the Ouija board session.

Session one

David, with a small bottle in his hand says, "Okay, so put on some of this." As we are putting on this oil we are talking and MariAnne says, "I have orbs around me all the time. One time me and my boyfriend were hanging out and I touched a woman who was overdosing on heroin. I was at 'Down Town Grooming' and she was hunched over in the car. That night we felt like something was watching us, mocking us. It wasn't good. I have pictures with orbs all around us. There was something there." David mentions to Cassie that she needs to pay attention to him, so she can learn how to do this.

David asks me to pass him the red candle that is sitting on an alter behind me. As this is happening, an EVP of a whisper is recorded. Multiple words, all unintelligible. David then asks MariAnne to hand him the shot glass that is next to her. When MariAnne and Cassie ask David if the shot is an offering for the spirits, David smiles and says happily, "I've got this, girl." He then looks at me and points in the corner, "Please, can you hand me the skull that's up there?" An EVP is recorded whispering, "Right there."

David speaks, "On top of the alter I need my Bourbon, the skull, and the little bottle of Holy Water. I'm getting out a cigarette too. So, one of the very first things you do, I always use permanently this cable as my protection cable. It's specifically made for this. So, the first thing I do was take a shot of this and I spit the Bourbon on this candle as a blessing. Now you will take sage or anything like that and Shaka it on to the candle. It's what they use in Voodoo, Sangria, HooDoo, everything. Some people use sage if you are unable to use Cannabis. Since the beginning of times Cannabis has been preferred."

They pass a cigarette around. David instructs Cassie, "Instead of making a ring of salt around the circle, make a ring of salt around the candle holder. This really helps to protect us from any sort of possessions or attachments." Cassie asks how to get rid of possible attachments. David asks for me to explain. I tell her my experience and how after a month of the attachment I was able to rid of the spirit we know as Red Sample.

With a shot of Bourbon in each of our hands, we take the shot and David says, "As above, so below." We are ready to begin. I have paper and a pen in front of me. David, Cassie and MariAnne gently put their fingers on the Planchette that is sitting on the Ouija board. The silence is deafening. David starts off by asking, "Are there any spirits here? If you are here let the planchette glide like the sun and the wind. We want the spirits to talk to us. Let us hear you. If you are here, give us a sign."

An unexplained loud thump is caught on the recorder followed by what sounds like chanting, unintelligible. The planchette starts to move. Cassie's eyes start twitching, she says to us that she can make her eyes twitch on their own. The planchette glides to 'Yes.'

David asks, "Is your purpose here, evil?" An EVP of a man is recorded saying, "No." At the same time of the EVP, the planchette glides to, 'No.' David asks, "Would you like a drink?" The planchette starts gliding over several letters, stopping on certain letters, 'R-A-C-H-E-L.' I ask, "Rachel?" A small unexplained cry is recorded followed by an EVP of a woman saying, "Yes."

MariAnne asks, "Are you Rachel?" The planchette glides to 'Yes.' Then spells, 'W-E-I-S' David notices that as the planchette glides, at points it tilts ever so slightly. David explains that after each word, depending on the spirit, they'll either circle the board or tilt. Also, words spelt, might be jumbled or misspelled. Sometimes they are totally random letters thrown together. That happens a few times at this seance. MariAnne asks, "We're sorry Rachel. Can you still talk to us?" The planchette spells, 'P-J-P' (Unsure if that's initials or something else.) MariAnne asks, "JP? Is that a person?" The planchette glides to 'Yes.'

I ask a few questions while we are communicating with this spirit, but my hands stay away from the planchette and I continue writing the results. I ask, "How old are you?" The planchette glides over the numbers, '7-5' MariAnne asks, "You're seventy-five years old?" The planchette makes it way to 'Yes.' I say, "Okay Rachel is seventy-five. How old is JP?" The planchette stops on '4.' MariAnne, "Awe. Only four years old?" The planchette glides to 'Yes.' Then spells out, 'D-A-V-I-D.'

We all look at each other stunned. Is this spirit trying to communicate with David? MariAnne asks, "Are you talking about our David?" The planchette glides to 'Yes.' MariAnne asks, "What about David?" The planchette stops on 'J' then moves a short distance and without stopping moves back to and stops on 'J.' Cassie asks, "JJ?" The planchette goes to, 'Yes.'

Perplexed, David says to us, "I've never heard the name J.J before in my whole life. So, let me first say that … so lately I've been binge watching this British show for no fucking reason, just because I've been sick, and it's a really bad show. There's a character on the show whose name is J.J, and that is the only J.J I have ever heard." I ask, "What does JJ stand for?" A disembodied voice is recorded saying, "Oh-oh."

The planchette starts moving across the board spelling, 'J-U-S-T-C-U-T-E.' We laugh, MariAnne asks, "Do you think David's cute?" An EVP of a woman is recorded saying, "Yes ... yes, yes!" The planchette glides to 'Yes.' Then spells out, 'T-R-Y.'

Suddenly we all hear something in the corner. My spirit box turned on all by itself. None of us were near the spirit box and it had been silent and off this whole time. It turned on by itself and was sweeping through channels. That has never happened before. With the spirit box I have, you have to press the power button to turn it on and it takes a few seconds of holding the power button on until it turns on, then you have to hit the sweep button. The spirit box turning on all by itself, is very unexplained.

Session two

MariAnne and Cassie are talking about the results we have gotten so far. Cassie says, "I can feel the letters that had the energy." MariAnne asks, "What did you want David to try?" The planchette stays still. They continue to talk amongst themselves.

David speaks, "Listen, as a witch, as a long time practicing witch, you're supposed to do what's right for you. Right?" An EVP whisper is recorded, "Yes." The whisper was very close, as if sitting right in the circle with us. David continues, "L and F are the most powerful. It feels cold over here." David feels hot and cold, while Cassie feels more magnetic. David explains, "The planchette, that is the medium for what is happening right here. So, we are the ones that are moving the planchette in the same sense of the words that collectively ... "

Cassie asks David, "How do we know what letters it will go to?" David shakes his head, "We don't. Notice the tip. None of us could have made it tip there without putting pressure. The idea is that all of us, as a collective group, us as a Covent is collectively letting go of the skepticism ... We as a group, as a tribe, this planchette is our connection to the spirit world." As they speak about the board, I sit in silence and listen.

Besides the one time as a child, I have never dealt with the Ouija. It is foreign to me, so it was neat listening to these people who have had a ton of experience with the board, talk and discuss it. We start the session again. MariAnne repeats herself, "You spelt T-R-Y earlier. What do you want David to try?" The planchette glides to, 'M.' The Mel meter makes an alert sound. David notices that the planchette is moving differently. He senses a different energy. We all feel that this is a different spirit and not Rachel anymore.

MariAnne asks, "Are you somebody else?" The planchette starts moving across the board stopping at its designated letters, 'M-A-L-I-C' An EVP whispering an unintelligible word is recorded. I ask the others, "I just heard something. Did you guys hear that? I thought I just heard a man." I want to remind you that the spirit box is off, the only thing on is my recorder. The planchette continues to move, 'H-E.' Then it stays still. Remember that sometimes the letters are mixed, and you have to unscramble them. We all stare at the paper, 'M-A-L-I-C-H-E'

MariAnne asks, "Michael?" The planchette slides to 'Yes.' MariAnne asks, "Are you Michael? Can you move it back to yes?" The planchette moves, but it doesn't move to 'Yes' it moves to the bottom of the board where the Zodiac signs are at. It stops on 'Scorpio'. Cassie asks, "Michael, are you a Scorpio?" The planchette slides to 'Yes.' I ask, "Michael, what year did you die?" The planchette glides to '2' and stays. MariAnne asks, "Two?" A disembodied man's voice is recorded saying, "Yes." David asks for a time out.

Session three

David asks us, "Who is Michael? Does anybody know a Michael?" None of them knew a Michael who has passed away. They look at me, I tell them that I did. What's interesting is that Michael, as you know by now is an alias for one of my friends who passed away a few years ago. This isn't the first time he has approached me using his known alias. Remember in Chapter two when I am talking about my experiences with Mediums? He came to me as Michael then, and he has come to me again now with the Ouija board session, knowing I would put the pieces together, and yes, he was a Scorpio!

I say, "He passed away awhile back ... too much alcohol." An EVP of a man is recorded whispering, "Drink." We pause for a moment and David gives more helpful tips to Cassie. I re-ask my question, "What year did you die?" The planchette runs across the numbers, stopping at, '2-0-1-3.' Again, this is accurate when it comes to my friend Michael, he passed away in September in the year 2013. The planchette then moves to the letters, 'Y-O-U-E.' David comments, "This is so smooth, do you notice that? Feel it? Much smoother than earlier with Rachel." An EVP of a man is recorded saying, "Course."

The planchette continues to move, I add to the words 'Y-O-U-E-V-E-R-F-E-E-L-L-I-K-E-Y-O-U-D-I-D-N-T-K-N-O-W-M-E.' This planchette was all over the board, stopping at its target letters. 'You ever feel like you didn't know me?'

MariAnne asks, "What are you wanting to tell Tessa?" The planchette starts to glide, 'T-H-A-T-S-H-E-I-S.' as the planchette is still moving, an EVP is recorded from a man, 'Yes.' The planchette goes on, 'N-O-T-A-B-U-R-D-A-N.' As David, MariAnne and Cassie start to talk an EVP of a man saying, "Come on word." Unexplained static is recorded. So, what we got from the last burst of letters was, that 'she is not a burden.'

The planchette continues to move, 'S-H-E' The next few letters are random and jumbled and I am unsure of their meaning. 'T-H-I-Q-L-J-E-Y-F-M-S.' We decide to take a quick break, MariAnne goes to the house to use the restroom and David asks if I can go outside so he can privately speak with Cassie.

Session four

MariAnne asks, "Do you have a message for Tessa?" Immediately after she asks that question two unexplained thumps are recorded, this goes unheard by us. The planchette once again starts moving all over the board. The first few letters are words, but it doesn't make sense to me. 'N-O-E-V-E-R-Y-O-N-E' then it spells out, 'S-H-E-T-H-I-N-K-S-N-O-O-N-E-L-O-V-E-S-H-E-R.' The planchette stops. As we read the letters we put the words together, "No everyone. She thinks no one loves her.'

An EVP is recorded by a man, "Get it right." The planchette starts to glide again, 'I-D-O' pauses then continues, 'T-B-G-O-K.' I understand the 'I do' part but the last five letters are a jumbled mess to me. David notices that the Ouija board itself starts moving and turning all by itself. An EVP from the man is recorded, "No. Ever." MariAnne looks at me and asks me, "You think nobody loves you?" David says, "Wait girl, let's talk about this shit!"

I laugh, and a disembodied laugh of a man is recorded. David asks, "Did you think nobody loved you? Does this make sense to you?" Uncomfortably, I explain to them my bully days in Ojo Caliente, New Mexico and how I was bullied so much by several students that I wanted to die. Every day for years I dealt with the pain. Then how in Colorado I had a group of people who I thought were friends but were not friends. (Not the group Michael was in, but an earlier group of 'friends')

The burden thing makes sense to me because that's how I was treated by so many for a long time. Just a burden to people. I have talked to Michael about my bully days and he knew my self-esteem was shitty.

MariAnne asks, "Michael, you're her friend. Do you love her?" The planchette moves to, 'Yes.' Cassie and MariAnne start to make ooh and aah sounds, I explain to them that back in the day he was one of my best friends, that type of love, not the other kind. The planchette continues to move. 'W-H-A-T-I-W-A-S-S-A-Y-I-N-G-W-A-S-B-A-D-T-O.' When I put the words together it made sense, as all of this has to me. 'What I was saying was bad to.'

We were good friends a long time ago and then I stopped talking to him and the rest of the group of friends we hung out with. It was over something so stupid I honestly don't even remember what it was about. I just remember that I felt betrayed and was devastated that I lost so many friends. Years later, and after he died, I found out by mutual friends that he was upset with me and spread a nasty rumor about me that wasn't even close to being true, to the group of mutual friends.

I was so sad when I was told about it, I just stood there and cried as my friends consoled me. One of them even admitted he asked Michael if the rumor was true and he said, 'No not at all.' I decided to forgive him for that and get over it, but the pain was still there. I hope he wasn't mad for a long time. MariAnne asks, "Are you feeling guilty?" We all notice that the board itself starts to move all on its on again. I ask, "What are you guilty about?" The planchette moves, spelling, 'D-I-D-N-T-S-A-Y' then it glides to and stops at 'Goodbye.' MariAnne asks, "Did you kill yourself?" The planchette glides to, 'No.' David looks at me and asks, "Was it accurate? Did he say goodbye to you?" I shook my head. He was right, he did not. In fact, we hadn't spoken for a few years.

The planchette glides, 'W-A-S-I-N-S-P-E-A-K.' I explain how we hadn't spoken to each other for years. I think what he meant to spell was 'Wasn't speaking.' As I am talking and explaining this to them the planchette glides to 'Yes.' Then spells out, 'W-H-Y-I-C-A-N-T-S-A-Y-S-H-E-K-N-E-W-M-E.'

When we put the letters into words it says, 'Yes, why I can't say she knew me.'

When we stopped being friends, we stopped all communication. I would even go on Facebook and see social media trying to suggest I add him as a friend, and I would get angry when I saw his face. When we were friends though we were close. He was a very private person and he would tell me things that he wouldn't tell others that were in our friend group, he trusted me with many of his secrets. He had a crummy childhood and I did too. In different ways. I had a wonderful loving family but bullying from the children made my life hell. He had a poor childhood due to his family.

Unexplained footsteps are recorded, unheard by us. The spirit box once again turns on by itself. This has never happened before, or since, that incident. I am happy we are communicating with Michael, but I feel guilty that nobody else is coming through for David, Cassie or MariAnne. Always feeling guilty. Always a burden. I ask, "Besides Michael, is there anybody else here with us?" The planchette moves to 'Yes.' Then glides to 'No.' Then quickly back to 'Yes.'

Then the planchette goes all over the board, 'O-M-M.' MariAnne asks, "Was that three M's?" An EVP from a woman is recorded, "That's me." MariAnne notes that all of her initials are M. Perhaps someone is trying to reach out to her. I ask, "What's your name?" The planchette glides, 'Y-J-K-H-M-Y-H.' Clearly Michael is gone and this is another spirit, based on the EVP, a female. While Michael, for the most part, was using words, this spirit is all over the board.

David requests that the spirit box be turned on. We turn it on and it starts sweeping through channels. I explain to them that when using the spirit box, to ask a question and wait twenty or so seconds for any responses because sometimes it can take a while for spirits to respond. A disembodied voice comes through the spirit box saying, "Help." The planchette then spells, 'M-E'. A man comes through the spirit box saying what sounds like, "Tess." The planchette continues to glide, 'M-O-R-Y' altogether spelling 'Memory.'

I ask, "What memory are you talking about?" The planchette glides, 'L' a woman cries through the spirit box. The planchette continues, 'U-I-A' a man comes through the spirit box saying, "Take." The planchette goes on, 'Z-H-M.' A man comes through the spirit box saying, "Read." The planchette continues to move, stopping on random letters. 'I-6-H-A.' Making no sense at all. The same man who spoke earlier on the spirit box comes through again saying, 'Love me.' The planchette ends with, 'D-S-A-M.'

Definitely not real words like Michael was giving us earlier. So, try to solve this puzzle 'L-U-I-A-Z-H-M-I-6-H-A-D-S-A-M' I cannot figure it out. While none of these letters and numbers make sense to us, the last three letters SAM ring hard for MariAnne. She shares with us how a friend of hers passed away a few months ago, her name was Sam.

Excitedly, MariAnne asks, "Sam what are you trying to say?" The planchette spells, 'M-E.' "Do you have a message?" A man comes through the spirit box saying, "No. No." MariAnne asks, "Sam ... do you have a message?" A woman comes through the spirit box and says what sounds like, "Want." The planchette slides and once again spells, 'M-E.' Possibly the same woman comes through the spirit box saying, "Hit." David says, "Give us a really clear message." The planchette slides to and stops on 'H.' MariAnne asks, "Do you have a message for *Rick?" An EVP from a woman is recorded, "Yes."

The planchette then glides to 'Yes.' MariAnne asks, "What do you want to say to him?" The planchette glides, 'F-O', a disembodied voice comes through the spirit box saying, "Free." The planchette continues to move and stops at 'P.' David says, "Fraternal Order of Police ... F.O.P.' MariAnne asks, "Was the guy who hit you a police officer?" A sad woman's voice comes through the spirit box in an echoey voice saying, "Yes." The planchette glides to 'Yes.' MariAnne asks, "Can you give us a name, Sam? Did you know him?" A man's voice comes through the spirit box saying, "Hate."

An EVP is recorded, "It's alright." We feel a cold spot. I feel very cold, we are in the south in the summer and it's been average in the office this whole time. I am also closest to the office door that leads outside, where it's hot. MariAnne asks, "Sam, do you have a message for Rick?" The planchette starts moving all over the board, 'O-R-I-O-S' then it lands in the middle of C and D. I am unsure which one it meant. Then it stops at 'S." The Mel meter EMF makes an alert beep sound. MariAnne again asks, "Sam, was the guy who hit you a police officer?" The planchette glides to 'Yes.'

The planchette goes to the numbers, '2-6-5.' MariAnne sadly says, "Maybe it's not my Sam." MariAnne says, "If this is Sam, please give me a message for Rick." An EVP of a woman is recorded, "Yes." The planchette glides and for the first time in a while spells out words, 'D-O-N-T-S-E-L-L.' A man comes through the spirit box saying, "Rich." MariAnne reads the paper, "Don't sell?" The planchette lands on 'Yes.' MariAnne asks, "Don't sell what. Sam?" The planchette glides and spells, "H-E-W-I-L-L-I-N-T-I-M-E-K-N-O-W' Then lands on 'Yes' the planchette then stops on 'Goodbye.' He will know in time. Sort of cryptic.

David asks MariAnne, "Who's Sam and who's Rick?" She replies, "I told you before, *Tammy's brother had a wreck and Sam and the baby died. His girlfriend and child. Sam and *Lance died in a fire. Somebody hit them, killed her sister too. Nobody knows who hit them. He cannot find out who killed them. It said FOP. That makes sense to me."

She pauses and angrily shakes her head, "Of course they would cover up a police officer being drunk and hitting people. The boyfriend has a whole bunch of her shit. He kind of took it spitefully from her family. He is fucked in the head. He survived Iraq, and he witnessed three of his battle buddies being blown up right in front of him. Then he comes home and his baby, girlfriend and her sister die in front of him in a fucking fire. He is so fucked."

MariAnne stares at the board, "Don't sell what? What's the message? Rick needs to know." No answers. The planchette remains still. We just stay there talking, something funny is said and we all laugh, an unexplained deep growl-like laugh joins in.

Session five, final session

MariAnne asks, "Sam … Is there anything you need to tell Rick?" No answer. "Sam are you still here with us?" No answer. David and Cassie are in their own small conversation as MariAnne talks to me about her friend Sam. Her death has really affected MariAnne, not knowing what really happened to her friend that night is not sitting well with her at all. She desperately wants answers. "There was people that came and helped him, they actually pulled Rick out." An EVP of a woman is recorded saying, "Yeah." The Mel meter spikes at 0.3 and starts making alert sounds. The Mel then spikes to 0.9. Immediately after the spike, a woman comes through the spirit box saying, "Now." An EVP comes through, "Ha ha ha ha Hawk."

So, to re-cap, we communicated with a Rachel, who seemed very interested in David, spelling out his name and saying how he was cute. We then communicated with my friend Michael, every single thing he said via planchette made sense to me, then, we possibly communicated with MariAnne's friend Sam. It was a pretty successful seance through the Ouija board.

Chapter twenty-six

Bernard's Mining Cabin, La Veta Pass, Colorado

Some of my cousins have a little slice of property right off one of the exits in La Veta Pass, Colorado. I went there one time with my cousin Nick and his girlfriend, Laurie. Nicely hidden in the woods, and close to a creek. On the property is an old mining cabin long since abandoned. Parts of it are slightly collapsed. Just looking at it, you know it's old. Nick told me a little about the mining cabin and I had my equipment with me, most of it anyways, so I thought why not see what we can get. A miner named Bernard used to live in this cabin and he actually sold the property to my cousins several years ago.

July 1, 2016
The investigation

Nick, Laurie and I conducted this investigation. It was a beautiful summer's day with a slight breeze and after our investigation it rained, perfect timing. We investigated Bernard's mining cabin and then afterwards, something caught my eye up a small hill behind the cabin. Not sure what it was but something was moving around up there. We walk up there, and Nick shows me things that he had dug up from the ground.

Something that resembled a small bed, maybe for an animal, just the skeleton of it remained. Along with wood planks. What else is buried down there? Was there a secret bunker or something? We dug a little, and it would be neat to go back some day and dig more and see what else stays hidden under the ground. The ground by the way was super soft, very easy to dig. It was almost spongy. Not natural.

Session one

Nick gives a little history of this old mining cabin where Bernard lived and died.

So, this is an old mining cabin that belonged to Bernard Stone in the early 1900s. He passed away right in this very cabin in the 1940s. My Grandpa bought this property from him. He died in the far room on his bed. The frame is still here. He was a veteran, he was in his mid-fifties, I believe. Cause of death unknown.

We are walking around the cabin, which is completely open, roof, door frame, windows, etc. There are small trees and weeds growing in the house. It's quite the site! We stop and Nick points, "I think this room was … the kitchen was off to the left and I assume the dining room and living room was to the right." I say, "Bernard Stone, we come with respect. Can you let us know you're here by making a noise, or say something to us?" As I pause an unexplained muffled sound is recorded. Then an unexplained pop is recorded.

I ask, "We have an animal with us, can you tell us what that animal is?" An unexplained pop is recorded. I say, "My name's Tessa. Can you say Tessa … or any of our names or your name?" An EVP of a man, "Gold … gold." Remember Bernard Stone was a Miner! Then unexplained loud deep breaths of a man are recorded. As we talk about Bernard and the area where he died a pop is recorded. I ask, "Bernard, where did you die?" An EVP of a man whispering what sounds like, "Right over the tank." Followed by static and a pop, both unexplained.

I ask, "Can you tell us the name of the people you sold this house to?" An EVP of the same man who spoke earlier saying, "Yes." Then he repeats himself several seconds later, "Yes." Several pops are recorded. Nick says, "You have a pretty nice view here from your cabin Bernard." Another pop is recorded.

Session two

I ask, "The person across from me must look familiar to you because he is up here often. Can you tell us his name?" An unexplained thump is recorded then an EVP is recorded of a man saying, "Nick." Amazing! Nick says to Laurie, "Laurie get Lilly (the dog) out of here please. Lilly, go!" An EVP of the same man is recorded saying, "Get out!" Nick says, "Bernard, what did you use this section of the cabin for?" An unexplained thump-like sound is recorded. This is then followed by a disembodied snicker. Then three pops are recorded.

Nick asks, "How long did you live here?" A loud unexplained static is recorded. So loud that if there were any EVPs they went unnoticed. Nick asks,

"Bernard, did you live in this cabin by yourself?" Laurie asks, "What made you decide to live here?" Again, static is recorded, very fast like, then what sounds like a slow-motion static, after that a man's voice is recorded giving this EVP, "Sound's good."

Session three

We are standing right in front of the bed that Bernard Stone slept in, and died in. As we stand there in silence, static and a quick pop is recorded. I ask, "Bernard, are you here with us right now?" A disembodied voice is recorded giving this EVP, "Yeah." This is followed by static. Nick asks, "Do you like that we come to camp here every summer?" Yet another pop is recorded. I am standing in front of the bed and Laurie and Nick are behind me a few feet. Nick warns me, "There's a rat right by your foot." An EVP of a man is recorded, saying, "My pet." Followed by an unexplained pop.

Nick puts the Mel meter on the bed frame. I say, "Bernard, we have this tool on your bed. I know you don't know what this is, but if you come over to it, it will make noises and light up with different colors just letting us know you are here. It doesn't hurt, I promise." A loud thud sound is recorded. Something falling hard, we all hear it. We were just standing there in silence not moving at all. We investigate the area, just feet away from us to see if we can figure out if something fell or got thrown. Earlier we did ask if he could make a sound for us.

I say, "So, even if you don't want to make this tool (EMF) go off, you can still make the temp change. Right now, it's 61.6 degrees. Can you make it go higher or lower? The EMF is at 0 … Can you make it go up at all?" Laurie, who's holding the EMF says, "The temperature changed right after you told it to change." We thank Bernard.

I say, "Now the temp is 61.2. Can you make it go up?" An unexplained static is recorded. A very loud static. The temp slightly goes up, 61.4. I say, "Can you make it go to 62 degrees? It's too chilly for me right now …" Nick notes that it went lower, 61.0. Nick asks, "Okay, how about lower? Bernard can you lower the temp to 60 degrees?" The temp does just that and goes to 60 degrees. We thank him. A loud static is recorded, then it gets a lot lighter, as if someone has a volume control.

Nick says, "Right now, it's 60.8 degrees, can you make it go lower … perhaps to 60.6. The temp starts to rise, Nick says, "Can you make it go lower?" An unexplained fumble-like sound is recorded, followed by two unexplained pops.

An unexplained sound is recorded, what I describe as popcorn in the microwave starting to pop. Nick asks, "Bernard, did your winter stove keep you nice and warm in here during those cold winter days? If so let's see you raise that temperature a little bit." No responses. Nick asks, "Did you ever have visitors here?" Unexplained shuffling sounds are recorded. We are all just standing there surrounding his bed, not moving. No motion at all. Then unexplained heavy breathing coming from a man is recorded.

After asking Nick if he tried looking up how Bernard died he shares that he did look him up but was unsuccessful. I say, "So, it's pretty much a mystery how you died Bernard. How did you die?" The whole time I am talking, loud heavy footsteps are recorded, going unheard by us, as if circling us. I counted sixteen footsteps total! I ask, "Were you a miner Bernard?" An unexplained sound is recorded, that sounds like a hinge being tampered with, then an EVP from a man is recorded whispering, "Yes, with a beard." I ask, "What did you mine for?" The same gives us this EVP, "Who cared?"

Nick asks, "What was your favorite season out here?" The same man's voice is recorded whispering, this time the words are unintelligible. I read the EMF, "It says the temperature is 60.9 degrees." Nick adds, "Can you bring it down any lower? Maybe 60.5?" Unexplained static is recorded, the temp lowers to 60.7. I thank Bernard letting him know that we know it takes plenty of energy to do this. The same man whispers this EVP, "Yes."

The EMF temp fluctuates between 60.7 - 60.9. Nick says, "Let's try one more time, one more big push, get us to 60.5." Unexplained shuffle-like sounds are recorded. The temp keeps going to .7, we ask if seven was his favorite number and we get an EVP of the man saying, "Uh huh." It is now at 60.9 I ask, "Can you bring it back to seven?" It immediately changes to 60.7. Then a few seconds later it changes to 60.5, the number Nick originally asked it to go to. Laurie asks, "Bernard can you change it to 60.0?" While it doesn't change, the recorder caught two unexplained pops.

Nick and I kneel down by the death-bed, while keeping an eye out for the rat. Laurie starts taking pictures of us. As this is happening unexplained heavy breathing from a man is recorded. Very close to us. Then two loud footsteps are recorded. I say, "Let's check out those pictures." Static is recorded followed by an EVP of the man saying, "Got it."

Session four

We turn the spirit box on. Nick asks, "Bernard, was that you making the temperature fluctuate like that?" An EVP of a man whispering, "Yes." Followed by an unexplained thump. Nick asks, "Are you in here with us, Bernard?" Two unexplained pops are recorded. I say, "They mentioned their dog's name earlier, can you tell us what that name is?" A man's voice comes through the spirit box saying, "Lily." Amazing! This is followed by unexplained fumble-like sounds, that sounds as if hands are grasping at the recorder.

Nick asks, "What color is she?" A disembodied laugh is recorded, "Heh heh heh heh heh heh." Followed by more static. Nick reads the temp at 60.1. "Can you bring it down to 59.0 please?" A series of pops are recorded, five counted. I ask if the temp can go to 60.0. No results, I then say, "Please …" Immediately after saying please it goes to the requested degree, 60.0. We all cheer him on and say thank you. I ask, "I know this is asking a lot, but can you get out of the sixties and dive into the fifties?" As soon as I end that question the temp goes to 59.8, only for a second then back to the sixties. We thank Bernard again. After asking a few questions and no answers, I suddenly get very cold. Nick and Laurie come to where I am standing and feel the difference as well. As we talk about the cold spot an echo-like sound is recorded followed by an EVP of a man saying, "Shush."

Session five

I ask, "It's 59.6, can you bring the temp to 59.7?" I kid around saying, "It's been at 59.6 for a while, stop dilly dallying." Right away it goes to 59.4. Then static is recorded, the static gets louder and faster. I say, "Bernard?" A few seconds later an EVP of a man is recorded asking, "What?" We're quiet for a moment and an EVP of the man is recorded saying what sounds like, "Take it." We notice the temperature is at 59.3. We ask if the temp can change to 58.9. It rises, I say, "No!" Seconds later an EVP of the man says, "Yes."

Session six

We start session six but Nick's neighbor comes up to ask for a favor, so we stop the session short, no results.

Session seven

As Nick talks, bursts of static come through and are recorded going unheard by us. Nick says, "Last summer I was digging down there. There was a … I don't know if it was a cellar or some kind of structure but I," in the middle of his sentence, what sounds like a woman is recorded exhaling loudly, very close to the recorder. (When deep breathers are around I always debunk them so not to manipulate evidence.) Nick ends, "I dug but never could find anything."

Behind the old mining cabin is a small hill in a wooded area. I keep seeing something move quickly in that area. First, I thought I saw a man, then a shadow. We make our way over to the hill. I ask if someone is there with us and an unexplained moan is recorded. We reach the area where Nick had dug in the past and where I saw the man and shadow. I look around and there's dug up dirt. I see a small skeleton frame of what I can only imagine was a bed for a dog, or an infant, along with other objects. Nick dug all these up, who knows what else is buried here. It is very possible a hidden bunker or cellar is located here without anyone even knowing it.

I ask, "If someone is here with us can you make a knocking sound or something?" An EVP is recorded whispering, "No." Sounded like a child to me. I look around, Nick looks at me and asks, "What? Did you hear something?" I reply, "Yes, like a huff or something, over here somewhere." An EVP of a man is recorded saying, "Too close." Followed by static. The sound reminds me of an old school Nintendo video game, squashing bad guys on Mario Brothers but it's static. Very weird. An EVP is recorded in the middle of the static but it's unintelligible. The Mel meter spikes at 0.6.

Laurie was talking with the neighbor while Nick and I were up the hill. She finally is able to break away and join us. She shares some interesting things the neighbor just told her. Laurie says, "He said there's a ton of history. Evil history in this area, from the Spaniards. He said that he's talked to a few people in the area, but that most of them have passed away. He told me that back in the 1700s and 1800s there was a bunch of evil history that people don't like to talk about. He said it's hard for him to find people that lived here long enough to know what has gone on here."

I suddenly feel very cold. The temp shows 57.1 but it feels much cooler than that. I start shaking. Nick comes over and feels the coldness as well. An unexplained pop is recorded.

As we stand there on the hill staring at the loose dirt, Nick talks about the Westcliffe cemetery that is located just outside Walsenburg. The small town my dad grew up in. Nick says, "If you go on overcast nights like this, you can see blue lights dancing from tombstone to tombstone." As he finishes speaking, static is recorded, followed by Nick and Laurie's dog Lily whimpering.

Laurie asks, "Bernard, did you hike up here at all?" As we stand on the soft ground we notice how unnaturally mushy it seems. Note that it's dry ground, not muddy at all, but it's almost like it's been disturbed at one point and it still is just soft. I kick at the dirt in one spot and keep kicking, and eventually ash comes up with the dirt. Interesting. I ask Bernard if he burnt stuff up here and the recorder is overcome with loud bursts of static followed by an unexplained sound that sounds like a child breathing rapidly. First the EVP of the child, now the breathing. Makes me wonder if something with a child happened here.

Session eight

The spirit box is turned on and sweeping channels. I say, "Nick, a while back dug up this small spring cushion mattress. What else is buried here?" No voices come through the spirit box, no EVPs. Nothing. We continue to notice just how unnaturally soft the ground is, so Nick goes down the hill to grab his shovel. While Nick is gone Laurie and I stand there and are talking, as we talk, an EVP of a man breathing loudly is recorded. The breathing reminds me of either someone being helped to breathe through a respirator or on oxygen.

Laurie asks, "Bernard, what did you use this space for?" Unexplained static is recorded. I record a short video on my phone just to show how soft the ground is just in that particular area. Everywhere else is rock solid. As I step on the tender ground, a man is recorded panting, quite unexplainable seeing that Laurie and I are the only ones there and Nick is down below fetching the shovel. I say, "Nick is getting the shovel, he's going to dig something up, hopefully." A crunch-like sound is recorded, that sounds like footsteps on gravel. An EVP whisper is recorded, "Hey." A man is recorded breathing again, followed by static.

I say to myself, "Look at this." An unexplained thump is recorded followed by an EVP of a woman saying, "Twinkle." A woman's voice comes through the spirit box and says what sounds like, "Help." Nick is back with shovel in hand and starts to dig. As he does this, static and a pop are recorded. Nick digs up large pieces of wood planks. He continues to dig, and more things come to the surface. We are unsure if things were buried here to hide, or for safe keeping or if there is an underground space, but something is here. Several minutes into Nick's digging, wood is unearthed. Laurie notices the neighbor approaching the property once again. She recently, moments earlier, had dealt with him. This time it's Nicks turn to go see what he wants. As Nick walks down the hill to talk to the neighbor, a man gives us this interesting EVP, "Place to hide." Sort of creepy.

Session nine

The Mel meter spikes to 2.2. For the longest time the temp was in the fifties. I look down and I see 58.6, a moment later the temp changes to 65.9. That's a 7.3 degree jump. We start to make our way down the hill, back to where the mining cabin and the camp is at. Nick is holding the Mel meter and notices it spiking at 4.4. He asks me, "Did you see that?" Before I can reply an EVP from a man is recorded, "Yes." Laurie, who went down just a few minutes earlier greets us and lets us know that the shadow detector, which we had left on earlier before we left, had gone off. She was nowhere close to it.

Session ten

We walked over to another collapsed cabin nearby. Exploring in silence and recording as well. A man is recorded breathing very heavily, Nick is nowhere near by. Unexplained. Static is recorded, and an unexplained pop is recorded. I walk up to a decaying old chest and nudge it gently with my foot and ask, "Is somebody out here with us? Is this your chest?" An EVP is recorded, a disembodied voice says what sounds like, "Hide it." Followed by an unexplained pop.

I ask, "What did you put in this chest?" The same disembodied voice speaks, unintelligible words. Laurie says, "It looks like it's handmade." A hushed voice gives this EVP, "Yeah." Lilly the dog starts to enter the cabin. We are all paranoid there might be something she could step on that would hurt her, so she is directed out of the cabin. An EVP is recorded, "No … below." Nick and Laurie are talking in the background as this EVP is recorded. Nick says, "This must have been the roof." Loud noises are recorded as Nick walks on tin among other things, debunked. The same hushed voice gives this EVP, "Oh no."

Laurie asks, "Did you live here alone?" A disembodied voice is recorded saying what sounds like, "Alone."

The Mel EMF spikes to 2.7. I tell Nick and Laurie about the spike and the hushed voice gives this EVP, "Yes." I say, "It's 57.5 degrees." The hushed voice says, "Cold." I ask, "What happened to this house?" An EVP of a man says, "Party." I say to Laurie, "I wonder if it would be easier to go around this way." An EVP from the man saying, "No, no."

We are tripping out because there is a large tire in the house and a skeleton of what was once a bed outside the house. I say, "Bernard, do you know the person," before I can finish my sentence an EVP of the hushed voice saying, "No." I finish, "who lived here?" Laurie who is holding the Mel meter says, "It just spiked to 2.9." We are walking back to Bernard's mining cabin and I point off to the left, "Look at that! Is that a mine cart?" The hushed voice is recorded saying, "Yes." The EMF spikes to 4.0. The nosey neighbor is back, we decide it's time to end the investigation due to all the interruptions.

Chapter twenty-seven

Hose Company No. 3 Fire Museum, Pueblo, Colorado

This historic firehouse was designed by a local architect named John Bishop. Sadly, Bishop was killed, along with his sister, later on in the "Eden Train Wreck" that occurred north of Pueblo. That wreck was considered one of the worst railroad disasters of the time, when it comes to fatalities, it is the worst. Over one hundred people were killed.

The firehouse horses and cart were housed at the firehouse. In 1989, a fire buff and business man opened a museum in the old firehouse, he mixed his personal collection along with city owned property and ran the museum for a few years. In 1992, the fire buff took his collection and closed the museum's doors. It stayed closed for ten years until several firefighters started to get involved in the old museum.

Fire Inspector Gary Micheli made it a priority to preserve the artifacts. He also started to give tours to people and soon other firefighters got involved. My Aunt Bridgett is friends with Gary, and as I learned later after meeting Gary the night of the investigation, he is also a childhood friend of my dad. Gary was so kind to have met us there and gave us a private tour, and even though he was probably tired after a long day of work, he allowed us to stick around and do some investigating. If anybody reading this lives in Pueblo, Colorado or comes to visit Pueblo, I recommend calling Gary and requesting a private tour.

Donations small and large are appreciated; the money goes to helping preserve this old 1895 building. Fire Station No.3 has been thought to have hauntings since the 1930s. The famous handprint on the upstairs window has been cleaned off several times, only to appear in the same exact spot every time. I have witnessed this handprint myself. An old fire-truck, Seagraves truck started and drove all by itself as well. There are many other experiences and haunts here. I definitely plan on coming back here someday.

August 9, 2016
The investigation

For years I have wanted to come to this museum. Timing was always bad; if I wasn't out of town, then my Aunt Bridgett was out of town, or Gary was gone. Finally, we were all in town at the same time and we all met up one night to go on a tour and investigate. It was August in Pueblo. It was a beautiful day and in the eighties. Armed with my equipment, and the curiosity of what treasures were hidden in this old building, I got there early and checked out the outside of the building, which is next door neighbors with one of Pueblo's mortuaries.

The front fire-door slides up and Gary walks outside to greet me, at the same time my Aunt pulls up. First walking into the firehouse I am amazed at all the artifacts and antiques that are housed here. The collection is absolutely amazing, any fire-fighter, fire buff or anyone who loves museums must come here! Call first and set up a tour! So just a note, this investigation is of Gary telling us things that have happened here, and some history here and there. As this happens EVPs are recorded. Later on we ask some questions and use the Mel meter and spirit box.

Session one

After spending a few moments talking with Gary, my Aunt's phone, which was fully charged, starts to malfunction and doesn't allow her to take pictures or videos. Bridgett says, "My phone just went dead!" Gary shares with us that his phone has suddenly died as well. Paranoid, I check mine and it still has full battery life. Thank goodness!

Gary shares some interesting history with us, "This is the second oldest building that the city owns. It was built in 1895 by the Stroyers next door." As Gary pauses an unexplained hiss is recorded. Gary goes on, "Given to the city." An EVP is recorded, "Yes." Gary continues, "There was a building here before this, but then they tore that one down and built this one. It's the second oldest building … The oldest building that the city owns is what?"

Bridgett guesses, "Central High School?" An EVP from the same voice who spoke earlier, "Yes." (Wrong) Gary replies, "No, it's owned by the city. Actually, it's the Goodnight Barn out on the west part of town. The train station is old, but as far as what the city owns this is the second oldest, it's also one of the two buildings left that the horses ran out of. There were two horses here and it's the only station now that has the brass door." Unexplained shuffle-like sounds are recorded. Like unseen hands grasping at the recorder.

Gary speaks, "The Engine Station Four is the new one on Lake Avenue." An EVP is recorded that sounds like, "Hand me the pads." Gary continues, "Has a brass pole but it's not functioning anymore." I tell Gary, "Besides my Aunt and watching the TV show 'The Haunted Collector,' I have never heard of this place." We talk a little about the show, and in the middle of our conversation an EVP is recorded, "Hold."

Gary says, "They were here the whole weekend." A disembodied voice of a woman says, "Yes." Gary points at something, "These … you see the black with the white on it? Those are different events that have occurred in this building. *Max, the other guy who works this with me on this, his father was actually a fire-fighter here and Max is presently a fire-fighter. He's the one who did most of the display work. I do the finding and most of the tours. Then he does the display and historical aspect. We've had some pretty major paranormal groups from Boulder come down. They were here at 7 pm and stayed until 7 am."

As we move on to another area my aunt asks if she should grab the equipment and a disembodied voice is recorded saying what sounds like, "The net, your head." I point at an antique truck and ask Gary what it is, he replies, "This here? This is a 1924 Johnny Cash car. A bunch of car parts put together. The guy who used to run the museum was an antique car buff and he built this himself. Then he was going to take it to Denver to sell it and I got Dave to donate it to us. Do you want to hear the scary part?"

Um, yes. We definitely want to hear the scary part. After we excitedly say yes, he starts to give us a little history. "Okay we got two vehicles in this building start up and take off driving by themselves. One was a 1960 Seagrave Pupper that we have down at our other building. It was an active truck, this was an active station. Sometime in 1977, the guys were upstairs sleeping. There were four of them. Around 2:00-2:30 they hear a big noise, they come down the stairs."

He points at an old firetruck that sits in front of us. "This truck right here started up by itself and went through the doors." A disembodied, unexplained laugh is recorded, "Heh." Gary continues, "It stopped at the curb. A policeman walking the beat, because back then in 1977 they used to walk the neighborhood, he came up to the truck and started writing a report when suddenly it started up again and went across the street! The 1960 Seagrave. So that's a documented story."

He pauses for a second, thinking, "This was an active station from 1895 to 1979." As he speaks, an unexplained pop is recorded. He continues, "March of 1979 was the last run out of here." Unexplained panting sounds are recorded, followed by an EVP, "March." Gary says:

> In 2005, four of us came over here on a Sunday morning. We were going to have an awards dinner at the firefighter, police train station and so we were going to bring a bunch of stuff from here to put on display. So, we came up here, the four of us. We start up this car, we drove it around and brought it to the back parking-lot and parked it, facing Evans street. We came back around and backed a trailer in here. No sooner, I was standing right over here for some reason, there was a guy on the east side of the trailer

(An unexplained mumble like sound from what sounds like a child)

> on the sidewalk and the guy was just getting out of the truck when we hear this really loud noise. BANG! We look out, there's pallets of fire extinguishers, headlights rolling down the streets. This car ran into the tongue of the trailer. We were worried thinking, 'Okay did a little kid get in there and drive it around?' We couldn't find a driver, there was nobody there. So, we're out here baffled, a young couple from the apartment complex comes through the back door and tells us that they saw it drive through the parking lot all by itself.

(An EVP is recorded, "Ride up.")

> Here's where it gets interesting. It went in between the tombstones that are on display out there, at the corner of the mortuary. How we know that is that it left skid marks on the sidewalk. Went up to Evans, came up the driveway, took a ninety-degree turn, came down Broadway before it got to the station. It turned forty-five degrees into the trailer. The lady across the street, the bartender, she saw it. What she thought happened, when you park a vehicle on the trailer, if you don't tie it down and the trailer moves but the vehicle stays. We had three eye witnesses that saw it happen.

(He tells us that they named the car, 'Chiefs car.' Then he honked the horn for us!)

> It cost $30,000 worth of damage. Only one person could explain what happened. One of the guys that was here,' as Gary pauses, an EVP is recorded, "Go ahead." Gary continues, he dies at the age of 54 of a heart attack. He's the only one that knows. We can't explain what happened.

Bridgett asks, "What do you think happened?" He replies, "You know what? We were so dumbfounded we didn't even take any pictures. It was our trailer, our car, it didn't hit anybody, it didn't damage anybody else's property. It was decided not to write a report. There's all kind of stories in here."

Session two

We walk over to an antique extinguisher. Gary picks it up and gives Bridgett and myself a neat firefighter tip:

> When you want to use it, you turn everything upside-down so the lid comes out. Everything that is in the jar and extinguisher mixes, it creates pressure and pushes the water out.

(He then reaches for another old extinguisher)

> This is mine. It's a fire extinguisher. This is the type that was on Titanic. When you watch the movie, and she is in the hallway looking for the ax and the water is up to her waist. [He demonstrates] The way it works … this is the handle you use to carry it, you turn it upside down again, your chemicals are going to mix.

I look at the extinguisher and read aloud, "Tested with 350 pounds, 2 gallons water level … Wow!" So then," An EVP whisper is recorded, "The handle." Gary continues, "This is the handle." Amazing! Is this the spirit of a former firefighter?

Bridgett points at the wall and asks, "What's this Gary?" He responds:

> That's the communication systems that they had. Back then all the wires and telephone wires you see in all the old pictures, that was the great minister computer. The story behind that is, in the 1921 flood, this was downtown, that was taken down stream about fifteen miles. Went back and cleaned it up. See this, when you pull this station …

you pull this box right here, it intersects, there's a list from 1912. All special intersections. Pull box number 5, it's going to send a message to this thing here. It sends a message back to this thing. Each station had a ticker tape.

So, the way it worked was the bell at the station would ring in sessions of three. Five rings, pause, five rings, pause, five rings. So, when they guys heard it, they knew it was number five. But it would also punch five holes, pause, five holes, space, five holes. So, they could see it and hear it and they knew where to go.

Bridgett says, "That is brilliant." An EVP is recorded, "Yeah." Gary walks towards a display case and opens the door to it. "This right here is Pueblo's first motorized fire apparatus. We have that down at our other building. We have two buildings. This one is owned by the city, the other is owned by us firefighters." I am admiring the old gas masks on display. Gary opens the case, so we can get a better look. Bridgett points, "What's that?" Gary replies, "A fire grenade or a fire bomb. It's full of carbon tetrachloride." Bridgett asks, "Did it put out fires?"

Gary explains:

> In a special way yeah. These are all carbon tetrachloride. What happens is, you throw this in the fire, it breaks, when the carbon tetrachloride liquid heats up to 150-155 degrees.

(A disembodied voice gives this EVP, "Yeah." It seems like a spirit is there and gives us EVPs usually agreeing with what is being said about the history in the museum, making me think that this is possibly a spirit of a firefighter.)

> It turns into a gas which dissipates oxygen. That's what they used in WWII to kill people. When it heats up, it changes as a chemical reaction. You don't want to drink it or spill it on yourself. In some cases, it has a little heat sensing device on it and it'll actually pop and burn.

> This is our most prized area right here. This is our oldest apparatus. JB Hose Company. He becomes governor of the state. That's a hand-pulled hose cart. It's not horse-pulled, it's hand-pulled.

(Looking at this thing, I try to picture people pulling this with their bare hands, it's a huge cart and boy does it look heavy! He show's where you would pull it.)

> Four people would pull. If they were going uphill, they'd use the rope so more could pull uphill. These black things right here is a fire book, but it's made out of leather, they go with the cart. Leather is tough to take care of.

My aunt is admiring a presentation trumpet. She says aloud to herself, "Wow, a presentation trumpet!" A disembodied EVP is record saying what sounds like, "Trumpet."

Gary says:

> Bugles are used to designate rank.

(He closes a case and hands me a horn-like item.)

> The story is after they got through all the structures when the fire was out, they would actually plug this with a piece of wood, turn it over and they would fill it up with beer or ale and would drink it. If they got in to a fight they would use it to hit each other over the head. One bugle on the collar would make you a Lieutenant, two side-by-side a Captain, three Assistant Chief, four is a Deputy Chief, and the big boss, number one, has five bugles.

> About two years ago, a girl from Central High School came for her fiftieth high school reunion, her great grandfather used to work here. She brought us his foot locker. Now in the olden days, the petite people were firefighters, the big brawny guys were police officers. To show you how petite they were, this is her great grandfather's foot locker right here.

I am shocked, it's the size of a small backpack. Gary kneels and carefully picks up the footlocker and looks at it and says, "What's interesting is that it somewhere on here it says, 'South Pueblo' which makes it older than 1895." An unexplained wheeze-like gasp is recorded.

Session three

Gary shares with us a story of when the firefighters were gathering to take a picture and the paper boy photobombs the picture, that little photobombing paper boy would become a firefighter years later. Great story! He shows us the picture. There's a small smile plastered on the paper boy's face. What a great picture, a little piece of history. Gary tells us, "Look over your head." We look up and in unison say, "Wow." Unexplained static is recorded. Gary explains:

> Elephant hose. Even today the hose has to drop. So, once you go to a fire, you bring it back to the station, you roll it out, you wash it off and fold it in half. Each section is roughly fifty feet.

(An EVP is recorded, once again agreeing with Gary, "Yes.")

> Then you hang it in the tower. So, the youngest guy goes to the top, two of the guys pull it up by the rope. [He points] This is what they'd pull it up with.

(A disembodied voice is recorded saying, "Help me." Gary tells us to look up the tower, it is so high up, unbelievable!)

> Get ready to go up the stairs, but first … do you want to see the shadow? [We excitedly reply yes.] About two years ago my daughter calls me up. The boys, my two grandchildren were five and seven at the time and wanted to go to the station and see the ghosts. I had something else I had to do so I gave my daughter the keys and they came here around 5:00 in the evening. They had some food with them and were going to go upstairs and eat in the kitchen which is really kind of a neat thing to do. She calls me and excitedly says, 'Pops!' I say, 'What?' She says, 'We saw a shadow!' I ask her, 'What do you mean you saw a shadow?' She says, 'The boys saw it too papa. The shadow.' I did some investigating later on. They really did see a shadow, but it was a silhouette.

Figure 14 Fire-fighter ghost silhouette

Gary points at a spot and asks Bridgett and I to stand there. He runs upstairs to turn a light on, so we can see it. As we are left alone an unexplained pop is recorded. We stand here waiting to catch a glimpse of the famed silhouette. Gary says, "Look between the yellow helmet and the white helmet on the wall." We see it and gasp, it truly looks like a man sitting there on the stairs. Creepy, and amazing! It looks like the silhouette of a fire fighter!

Gary explains, "What you are seeing is just the paint peeling off the wall. What we tell the kids is that the ghost is doing a self-portrait of himself." Bridgett comments, "It looks like an artist's drawing, how wonderful!" He tells us to come closer, so we can get a better view. Gary tells us that they did something to preserve the paint silhouette. It's amazing that his daughter and grandkids saw it. Who knows how long it had been there just waiting to be discovered.

As we make our way closer to the silhouette an unexplained pop is recorded. Gary tells us about a fire museum in Manitou Springs that has a ton of orb activity. As he is telling us this an unexplained chuckle is recorded.

We walk up the stairs and Gary kids with us, "You know you girls are making me miss the Olympics. Missing Michael Phelps." He tells us to stop at the top stair and to look at a mysterious hand print on the window. No matter how many times the window is cleaned, and that area is scrubbed, the hand print always reappears.

There's a plaque about it, I read it aloud:

> To the left is the window with the mysterious handprint on it. Stories come down from the 1930s or 1940s of a handprint on the glass of the

window. The firemen would wash the window, within hours the handprint would reappear when no one was looking. At first the firemen thought it was a prank, but after several months of this happening with the handprint always being in the exact same place no matter who was working, the firemen thought it was a defect in the glass. Within a day the handprint would reappear.

As Gary points out the handprint, unexplained static is recorded. Bridgett, who's holding the Mel meter notices it spiking to 2.5. As I am taking a picture of the window with the handprint, the face recognition goes on and forms a yellow box around the handprint. Creepy! The EMF starts to make alert sounds. I ask, "Is anybody here with us right now?" The EMF goes off again. Gary mentions, "Most of the activity happens upstairs." We are now in the kitchen where the Mel is going crazy. The EMF spikes to 2.8. The shadow detector, motion sensor goes off, making an alert sound. I debunk it as catching our shadows, and as I debunk this aloud an EVP is recorded, "Yeah." Then unexplained static is recorded.

Session four

Gary talks to us about the hay loft. "They would bring the hay up in a big net and store it up here. So, the hay was up here, and the horses were down below usually with one dog and one goat. Goats are very soothing to horses." Bridgett asks, "So when this was a fire house how much of Pueblo was here yet?" Gary answers, "There was a pretty good portion of Pueblo here. In 1914 we became fully motorized. Once they brought in a motorized fire truck in here then they turned it into a kitchen."

Gary points out, "Now here's the upper part of the hose. Turn this black knob clockwise." Bridgett does as requested and as she does this you can hear the click sounds. Gary says, "One more time." Another click. Gary explains, "That's the light switch. Now look up and over to your right, there's a ladder so you could go even higher if need be.

We see this old stove and Bridgett gets excited and says, "My grandmother, my mother's mother, she saved a baby's life by putting the baby in a shoebox then in the oven." Gary nods, "They did that to my sister. My little sister, they used it as an incubator!" Bridgett smiles and says about the person her grandmother saved, "The woman is still alive. She was from Walsencamp." (A coal-mining camp my Grandma and Great Aunt grew up in—their father was a miner) An unexplained pop is recorded.

We walk over to some old pictures that are on the wall, this is a dedication to the fallen fire fighters. Gary says, "These are our three lights of duty, this was our first chief." The EMF makes a spike alert sound. Gary continues, "He was killed in a buggy accident over by Dutch Clark. Robert and these two were killed in the forties in separate accidents. They were responding to calls and someone ran into their emergency response vehicle."

I read, "Auto smashes in ambulance." Gary points and says, "His son is still alive. His son and his wife gave us this guy's spaghetti recipe from 1937." Gary points to several pictures on the wall, "These were all Chiefs of Pueblo Fire Department. Now if you notice, the upper row has a little bit more difference in physical feature. The mustaches. Look at the two with mustaches. They can't have them. The breathing apparatus that is over their face, they'd throw water on their mustache, shove it in their mouth and go fight the fire. When the fire was out they would take the mustache out, reshape it, light a cigarette and go on their way."

He points at one picture, "This guy is still alive ... this guy is alive." He continues to show us the firefighters fortunate to still be alive. I look down and, on the desk, lies a drawing of a handsome man in uniform. The drawing is so detailed, someone put a lot of hard work into this masterpiece. Gary says about the drawing, "We don't know who this man is ... Do me a favor and come over here and take pictures of this right here." I do so with my phone, I take several pictures. I take some with the flash, then without. Gary says, "You will have to look through your pictures later on."

We walk into a room where there are some cots and on the wall are hundreds of fire patches from fire stations all over the world. It was quite an amazing impressive sight to see all of these patches! Each different, and proudly representing a town. Both my Aunt and I are very impressed, the collection is impressive.

When we ask Gary how many patches are here, there are so many of them he is unsure. Gary points to one small but noticeable bare spot on the wall. "Guess which one goes right here that somebody stole?" After a few guesses, he replies, "Roswell, New Mexico." I just need to say how sad and disappointing that someone would steal something. These people go out of their way and are so generous with their private tours and someone disrespects them like this.

Gary says, "See this ping pong ball? A group came in with high end equipment. They set a pad and pencil, they record all night. Enticing the ghost." A disembodied voice, almost radio-like of a man is recorded saying what sounds like, "Right now." Gary says, "So what I do when I bring like the Cub Scouts up here, I tell them what they do and as we're getting ready to leave, I will 'accidentally' throw the ping pong on the floor and you should see how big their eyes get!" As we laugh at his joke an unexplained pop is recorded.

We are still standing in front of the patches. Gary points some out to us, Warner Brothers, Baghdad, and several more. Bridgett asks Gary how they are able to get so many patches. He responds, "Every week there's about thirty guys that go to the test center for hazmat training. I open up the other building. They come in and look at the trucks and then that's when we can do some trading." The Mel spikes to 3.2. We walk to the bed on the left side of the room where the brass pole is located. Gary points at the pole and says to us, "Now there was young boy, he was twelve years old he fell through the opening when Max's dad was here. He was a friend of the family. The boy was seriously hurt but not killed."

Gary points to an area, "Okay here is what happens. Most of the paranormal readings they get in this area, is here in the corner." An EVP of a man is recorded whispering, "Hey." Gary says, "One of the groups asked, thought it would be interesting to do a study on the firefighters that spent most of their life here. Because they are surrounded by the electrical wires. One of the big groups that come down from Boulder, they had a girl sleeping over there on the floor, and she could hear somebody breathing over here." Unexplained static is recorded.

Gary goes on, "Then that picture that I had you take of the card, one of the guys was married to a psychic. She was in North Phoenix. He was talking to her on the phone, and she picked up a name on that card, and picked up other stuff that isn't in any of our books or website. Just picked up on some weird stuff. She picked up on something very angry, very upset. Short in stature. Didn't know if he was Harry or Larry, didn't know if he was a wanna-be firefighter, but he was very upset." Gary points to a picture, "His name is Larry but he's still alive."

Gary shows us an old game, the firefighters version of, 'Shoots and Ladders.' Gary says, "This is from 1922 from the District of Columbia, presented to this guy's uncle in 1922, police and fire games. What's unique about it is, the pen that was used to sign it, President Harvey actually signed it." He points out his signature to us. "We're trying to get it back to the museum back east but we haven't had much luck. Now there was a girl from Phoenix."

A disembodied yelp is recorded. Gary continues, "This girl was dating a police officer, she came here with a brand new 45 mm digital camera. She took pictures upstairs and downstairs. She went downstairs to download them onto the computer. Every picture that she took upstairs did not come out. We had a paranormal group come with brand new equipment, brand new batteries and nothing would work up here." In my peripheral vision, I thought I saw something move from my left to the right. A light. Gary says, "See, there is no air conditioning up here. Can you imagine in the olden days? You had hay, horses, a dog, a goat and all the by-products downstairs … Imagine the smell!" I hand my Aunt the Mel meter and have her walk around to see if she gets any readings. About a minute or so later it spikes to 3.0, shortly afterwards it goes to 3.7.

Session five

We turn the spirit box on. As this happens the Mel, which my aunt is still holding spikes to 3.2. A woman comes through the spirit box saying, "Booze." Followed by an unexplained pop. The Mel EMF spikes up to 3.7. Another unexplained pop is recorded. I ask, "Is somebody here with us right now?" A man's voice comes through the spirit box saying what sounds like, "Peanuts." Maybe a nickname? I ask, "What's your name?" The same man's voice comes through the spirit box again and says, "Ryan." Another man comes through and says, "Hayes." I ask, "Can you say that again?" A man comes through the spirit box saying, "Yes."

I ask, "Did you used to be a firefighter?" Bridgett lets us know that the Mel meter just spiked to 3.4. A man's voice comes through the spirit box, very faint, saying, what sounds like, "Away." I ask, "What year did you die?" A man comes through the spirit box and says what sounds like, 'oh-eight.' Can this be 2008 or maybe the year 1908?

Then a man comes through the spirit box saying either 'Doug' (or 'dug') or 'Dog.' I turn up the spirit box and debunk the clicking sounds I'm making. I say, "That's me turning it up. My bad, thought it was up all the way." A man comes through the spirit box saying, "Up." An unexplained pop is recorded.

I ask, "Is there a Harry or Larry here with us right now?" Another unexplained pop is recorded. Besides that, no EVPs or no spirit box voices.

Bridgett asks, "How are the fallen firefighters?" As she pauses a woman gives this EVP, "Go." Bridgett asks, "Are they doing okay?" A man comes through the spirit box saying, "Yeah." I ask, "Are any of you gentlemen with us?" A man's voice coming through the spirit box saying, "Me."

After we asked a few questions with no results, I ask, "Do you miss not being a firefighter?" An EVP is recorded, "Yeah." I ask, "How old were you when you died?" A disembodied voice gives this EVP, "Stop." After a few more minutes we start to make our way downstairs.

Session six

The spirit box is still on. An unexplained sound is recorded, that sounds like as if I'm in the middle of a tunnel or whirlpool. When Gary speaks at the end, it's very echoey. As fast as this weird sound came, it leaves. Gary says, "There's some light coming through the windows. When the Haunted Collectors were here they taped up all areas where the light came through, so it was pitch black. They taped up all the doors once they were inside."

Gary finds a gas mask that I am able to try on. He instructs me what to do and Bridgett videotapes the process. I laugh a muffled laugh due to the mask. Gary points, "Normally this would be tied in the back and sealed. That's why firemen couldn't have beards." As we talk to each other a disembodied voice gives this EVP, "Come on." Gary starts to speak, then the same voice repeats himself but more impatient, "Come on!" As we continue to talk, I put the recorder down but still have it recording. We are a few feet away from the recorder. The same voice asks, "Ready?"

Bridgett starts to take pictures as I pose in front of the pole, I still have the gas mask on, so we are having some fun joking around. A woman gives this EVP, "What a mess." Well! Gary hints that it's time for us to leave soon so he can close up and go home.

Gary takes us outside to show us something. He wants to show us a spot where the horses licked the wall raw. You can see the markings. Amazing! While he is showing us this, I left my recorder in the fire house still recording. You can hear our voices very faintly outside. Our laughter is recorded, what sounds like a woman or even a child saying what sounds like, "Wow … let me wait." Followed by an unexplained exhale.

We open the door and walk back in the firehouse. Gary in the middle of a sentence, " ... but there was a harness that was on the ceiling, and when the bells rang once the harness would automatically drop. When the bells rang twice the horses were trained to step in to the harness and when the bell rang three times the guys would get on the rig and take off and go. So, what happened one time, according to the books upstairs, the guys were on the rig and the horses went on without them. So, they took off looking for them. Guess where they found them? In the baseball field, Starter field. That's where they would graze. So, they figured, we're out in town, let's go eat!"

Gary rings the bell for us. Then he rings another bell, this one more chime-like then the other. Several unexplained pops are recorded. He points to a black and white photo of a firefighter. He says, "This guy here, his daughter showed up in an open house and she talked about him, on and on and on. She never once spoke about her husband or children. Just about her dad, she was so proud of him.

Bridgett and I gather our purses and all my equipment and get ready to leave. Before leaving Gary points to a hydrant. "See that hydrant? Those were at the dog track. They were urinated on for sixty years! We washed them off. They would drug test the dogs, they would put a test strip where the dog was urinating on the hydrant." We are thanking Gary for his time and the generous tour and allowing us to investigate a little. An unexplained static is recorded.

Sadly, this building is in need of help. If you are ever in Pueblo, please call for your own private tour, donations are welcome! It's worth it, you won't be disappointed.

Chapter twenty-eight

Teller County Jail
AKA
'Outlaws & Lawmen Jail Museum'
Cripple Creek Colorado

The Teller County Jail opened its doors in 1901 and closed them in 1992. A brick building on a corner street, located not too far from the court house. Back then, Cripple Creek was a booming mining town and they had their fair share of trouble-makers. They housed men, women and juveniles here. From grand larceny to murder, the crimes were various.

I have been lucky to come here two times. The first time Jourdan and I came to investigate was earlier in the summer of 2016. The second time my cousin Nick, his girlfriend Laurie and I, went to meet Michelle, who you can catch on the Ghost Adventures Cripple Creek episode. Thanks to Michelle, we were able to investigate the old jail after hours. We investigated and explored the jail, the area where the men were housed, upstairs where the women and juveniles were housed, then the basement. I was unaware there was a basement, but there is one, and it's creepy. I loved it! If you are in the area, go check it out! The tour is only a few bucks and so worth it.

August 6, 2016
The investigation

I have lived in Colorado for more than half of my life and I have never been to Cripple Creek. This being the first time, I wanted to go everywhere. First stop was the old Teller County Jail which is now known as Outlaws and Law Men Jail Museum. I have been told about this place by others and have seen it on TV watching Ghost Adventures.

I have always had a special interest in old jails, prisons, penitentiaries, asylums and hospitals. The history behind these places, the death they have seen, the emotions the people felt while there. When Jourdan and I went on this August day, it started out as sunny, later on it was a bit windy and drizzling rain. We walk in just in time for the tour that was about to start. A woman who works there gave us a little history and then lets us explore the jail on our own. We were lucky, besides Jourdan and I there were only two other people and we got to go our separate ways.

Session one

The history given by our guide:

> Cripple Creek, the largest of the Gold Rush. They were larger then California and Alaska combined, and still bringing in millions! Up the wooden staircase is where the women and children were held. Then here is where the men were held. This was a working jail from 1901 until 1992.

We walk into where the men were held and, on the wall, hung up are inmates' clothing that guests are able to wear while exploring. She continues speaking, "You can walk through here and look where they slept, six to a cell. They would roll up their hammocks during the day time and use the chamber pockets. As the gold rush left town, the population went down." The guide then lets us go off on our own.

Jourdan and I start to search for inmate garb and what we should wear. What to wear, what to wear, casual black and white stripes or classic orange jump suit. I chose the stripes when Jourdan went the classic orange route. (My second visit I wore the orange suit.) As Jourdan and I are changing into the inmate uniforms we strike up a conversation with the tour guide. We make our way to where the men were housed. An unexplained static is recorded.

I say, "We are in a jail cell right now. Any former inmates in here with us right now?" An EVP of a man is recorded, "Hey." Immediately after that is recorded I say to Jourdan, "I thought I just heard a man." I stand there in a jail cell that six men shared, I'm staring at the walls. Scrawling and scratch-writing is all over the walls by men that had nothing to do but do their time. I ask, "Whose jail cell was this?" Immediately after I ask this question, an EVP of a man is recorded whispering, "Jeremy." This is followed by static.

As we head to another cell, two voices are recorded whispering these EVPs, "I can't." Then the other voice says, "Tell her." We are at the last two cells on the bottom floor of the men's housing area when an EVP of a woman is recorded telling us to, "Stay." Three unexplained pops are recorded. Jourdan took a picture of herself and joked saying she looked all gangster. We both laugh at the picture. When we stop laughing a man whispers this EVP to us, "Get out!" This is followed by static.

I calmly try to get Jourdan's attention as she starts to speak saying, "Hey." I go unheard and she continues to talk. A little more excitedly I say, "Hey! Someone just grabbed me." We go silent. I show her, "Right here." An EVP is recorded, "I did." This has been the fourth time in one month that I have been touched while conducting an investigation. I ask, "Did somebody just grab me?" An unexplained sound is recorded, to me it sounds like hands grasping for my recorder. I take a picture and right after that an EVP of a man is recorded, saying what sounds like, "Got her."

As we walk down the hall, surrounded by jail cells, a disembodied voice calls out, "Patsy." This can mean several things. This can be an inmate calling out to his wife, this can be a woman calling out her own name, or patsy can also mean a person who is easily taken advantage of, being cheated on, or blamed and accused of doing something. An EVP of a man who is so close it sounds like he is speaking right into the recorder says, "Hell." Right before this session ends a woman is recorded giving this EVP, "Don't tell her."

Session two

An EVP of a disembodied voice is recorded saying, "Hold." Then a series of unexplained pops are caught on the recorder. Jourdan asks, "Is there anyone here with us right now?" A distant and faint voice of a man are recorded, "Yeah. Here." Jourdan asks, "If so, what was your name?" The same faint voice, it is kind of hard to understand, gives this EVP, saying what sounds like, "Ed Burr." A few seconds later, a man is recorded whispering this EVP, "Hey." The same voice repeats, "Hey." The Mel meter makes an alert sound.

Update: I emailed Michelle and asked her if there were any jail staff or inmates with the name Ed Burr or something similar to that, she was unsure of inmates, but she did mention that in the early 1900's they had a Sheriff there named Edward Bell. As many Edwards, he was usually called Ed. Did I get an EVP from the sheriff himself? It's very possible!

Jourdan and I make our way up the stairs—still where the men were housed. A man gives this EVP, "Let's go look it." I ask, "Is there anybody here with us?" A disembodied laugh is recorded, "Ha ha ha." Jourdan reads part of a wall, someone wrote, 'Do you ever get the feeling you're in Mexico?' Someone answered, 'No, I've been there. It's a lot nicer than this.' She points her flashlight at another part of the wall and finds a pentagram. Written next to it, "No whining. Welcome to Hell." Remember earlier in the investigation an EVP of a man was recorded saying, "Hell." It might not be connected but still worthy of mentioning.

That feeling that we are not alone creeps in, we ask again if someone is with us and immediately after asking this an EVP whisper, "No, no."

Session three

I'm reading some of the history that is displayed on the walls. "Murders were regular occurrences, and murderers who were caught spent time here before they were taken to jail in Colorado Springs and the penitentiary in Canon City. Some of the men died with their boots on in the dance halls."

The other two people who were there when we went in are now in the gift shop and talking to the guide, so we continue to not ask questions and keep reading more on the history of this old mining town. Here's a little prostitution history for you. "Prostitutes, bawdy women, women of the half world, soiled doves ... that's how residents of the Red Light District of Cripple Creek were described. Town Fathers' handled the situation carefully, requiring prostitutes to remain in one location away from the Main Street."

This very much reminded me of the old mining town of Jerome in Arizona. Jerome even had a jail away from Main Street just for the prostitutes. Cripple Creek had a city ordinance but was ignored by many. A series of unexplained pops are recorded, which is then followed by static. We walk around looking at more displays waiting for it to quiet down. We walk around the gift shop and talk to the guide for a while before heading upstairs where the women and juveniles were held, and later on, men also stayed there. We look out the window and see a donkey.

Now I didn't know this, but Cripple Creek is famous for its sweet donkeys. They even have their own special vet that checks up on them. They all sell donkey cookies that people can feed them and every store I went to, there were money jars that went toward their resident donkeys. It was awesome to see how the community cares for their animals. We buy cookies and plan to feed the donkey when we leave.

Session four

We head up the stairs to where the women and children were housed. The Mel meter is turned on. Jourdan, who is holding the Mel meter notes that it just spiked to 6.5. Current temperature is 74.5 degrees.

I ask, "Are there any ladies in here with us right now? If so, what's your name?" Unexplained click-like sounds are recorded. The sounds are close as if they are coming from the cell we are currently in, going unheard by us. Nobody else is around. Jourdan reads something disturbing, "A cat was murdered here. The case is taken to court. This is the story of a cat that then would come back … It is understood that the boy will be given steady employment killing cats on Eaton Avenue … Trying to avoid reformatory." An EVP whisper is recorded saying what sounds like, "Don't share."

I ask, "Is anybody here with us?" A disembodied voice is recorded saying, "Yes." Then a few seconds later, the same voice says, "With me." The Mel meter, which has a fresh battery in it, starts to malfunction and shows a low battery. We turn it off for now. I say, "So there's information about a lady here on the wall, I don't see her name … Not sure what your name is … oh wow, your crime was murder." An EVP whisper, "Yeah." I continue, "You came here in 1914 to serve time and you were discharged January 15, 1958." The same voice is recorded, "Yeah."

I do a short video on my phone and start talking, and again the same voice is recorded giving the same EVP, "Yeah." Amazing! I say, "In the old jail, women were here in this ward for murder, larceny, prostitution and much more." Another EVP is recorded, this time saying, "Free." I repeat my question in a different cell, "Is there anybody in here with us right now?" No responses. I ask, "What were you arrested for?" A very faint voice of a woman says what sounds like, "Money." About ten seconds later, the same EVP is recorded, "Money." Many were doing time for larceny.

I read some carvings in the wall. "Freedom is a big fat joke." I say to Jourdan as I point to the wall, "Look. You can tell they were counting down the years." An EVP is recorded, "Yes." I go back to the wall in the hall that has some information on some of their inmates. I read, "Crime: Burglary." An EVP of the same voice that said, 'yes' is recorded saying, 'Hey ___ch." either bitch or wench. I couldn't figure out which one, hard to make out. Either way, not nice.

I continue to read, "Larceny, murder." I call out the ladies by name, "Alice, Cora, Sarah, are any of you ladies here with us right now?" An EVP whisper from a woman is recorded, "Yes. Yes. I am … Yes."

Session five

I ask, "Sarah, was it worth the two to three years of jail time for burglary? It says you were a subject of parole. Seven months to three years." I walk on to the next lady, "Cora, you were in for larceny." I continue to walk and stop, "Alice, you were a real, bad one, you were a murderer. Jenny Dwyer, in for grand larceny." An EVP whisper, what sounds like, "Ever." We continue to walk around and explore.

We had other places to go to, so we didn't stay as long as I would have liked to here. As we were buying some things in the gift shop we notice the donkey still in the alleyway. The guide shows concern that the donkey is on the wrong side of the road and can possibly get hurt, she encourages us to try to relocate the donkey across the street where a park is at. Jourdan and I, with cookies in hand, walk over to the lone donkey and pet him and feed him cookies.

He is so adorable. You can tell this donkey is older and has eye problems. (Before we left I let the Jail guide know he looked sick and she said she'd let the local donkey vet know so he can be given the proper medication.) So, with some reluctance we lead the donkey, one of us is in front the other is behind him, across the street. He walks past a donkey memorial plaque and makes himself at home in the park. So that's our Cripple Creek donkey experience.

End of investigation.

January 6, 2017
The investigation

When Jourdan and I were here last time in August, I was told by the woman in the gift shop to get in touch with Michelle. There was a picture in a frame with Aaron, Zak and Nick from the TV show Ghost Adventures, with them is a woman and man. They look familiar because they were in the Cripple Creek episode. I e-mailed Michelle a few days later and she responded and we have been exchanging e-mails ever since.

Fast forward to January the following year, Nick, Laurie and I plan to come to Cripple Creek and investigate the Jail. I am beyond excited. I knew of the results Jourdan and I had gathered last time and was anxious to see what we would get this time. There was one big difference. The first time we went during open hours, this time we are going to investigate after hours and have the whole building to ourselves, including the basement, which is off limits during normal hours.

Michelle made this happen. We are very grateful to Michelle and her generosity. She was supposed to join us in the investigation, but she was unfortunately feeling ill and was unable to partake but she stayed in the gift shop area and was there if we had additional questions or needed help with anything.

We were actually unsure if we would be able to make it because Colorado got hit with snow blizzards all over. To our amazement the roads were in perfect condition and we made it to Cripple Creek, checked into Hotel Saint Nicholas, which happens to also be haunted, and we had the whole place to ourselves that night. After dropping off our things at the hotel, we make our way to the Jail.

Session one,
History and walk-through with Michelle

We follow Michelle into the men's cell block and stop. Before we start the investigation, Michelle shares some history with us:

> From 1901 to 1992 this was used as a facility. Ninety-one years as an operational facility. This is the original building and the original cells. This is the real deal. So, this part of the facility has fourteen cells, ten on the lower floor and four on the upper, that's including solitary. Solitary is a good place to hang out, usually have some energy in there. This was designed to house one hundred men. That's an average of six men per cell. The cells were six and a half feet by nine feet. In the early 1900s, the average daily count was fifty men incarcerated. It was a hopping busy joint.

(Unexplained disembodied footsteps are recorded but go unheard by us.)

> You'll notice the cells with the hammocks. Those were the beds we used for the first thirty years. Three on the top, three on the bottom. Back in the 1930s we lost a ton of the population. That's when we

went to the bunks. There's only two toilets to this part of the facility, those were shared.

(We ask Michelle where Nick should put his motion sensor camera)

We've noticed that the energy has shifted in this building. I used to be able to pin point it before, but it has shifted. Now the downstairs seems to have some stuff going on, more than usual. The basement is active.

(She points to the stairs leading to the upper block and confinement)

We still get footsteps on the upper catwalk right here.

I say to Michelle, "We didn't even know that there is a basement here. That's cool!" Michelle responds:

Oh, it's yeah … it's really cool. So, this is the men's facility. We were a county jail, so that means we had to have cells for women and juveniles as well. We covered Divide, Woodland Park, Florence, Cripple Creek and Victor. This is our County Seat to this day … This is the backside of the women's facility. When you go up the wooden stairs, there are three more rooms or cells. Those were for females. There was one room just for the juveniles. Then we had a Matron's Quarter, any time we had females or kids, we had a female jailer on the premises.

That was up until the mid-1970s. They were given a certain amount of time to bond, if they didn't bond, we would ship them out to El Paso County. It became pretty much an all-male facility. We do have people who were incarcerated here coming back to visit. They like to tell their stories. That's how I learned about upstairs because a man told me that his cell was upstairs. I argue with him telling him, 'No it wasn't!' He says, 'No, really … it was!' I tell him how upstairs was for women and juveniles. He was sure, 'No. It was upstairs.' He was in here towards the seventies and eighties.

Keep in mind, we had all offenses, from drunk and disorderly to murderers. We had male murderers, female murderers. We had kids … actually as late as the 1970s … Do you ever watch true crime and jail shows? [Jourdan and I both say yes] Well my dad worked for the

Department of Corrections down in Canon City. There's an inmate named Jacob Ind. He's still in Canon City. He might be in Super Max.

Quick fact: Some other infamous inmates at Colorado's Super Max Prison include Ted Kaczynsnki better known as the Unabomber, a couple of terrorists behind the 1993 World Trade Center attacks, and Oklahoma City bomber accomplice Terry Nichols.

Michelle continues:

> He murdered his mom and stepdad. He was thrown in here while he awaited trial. He was only fifteen or sixteen years old. Wait … it wasn't the 1970s, it was late 1980s or early 1990s. He is still in prison. He got coerced into … the guy screwed up killing the parents. This other guy was supposed to kill the parents but he screwed up and Jacob had to do it himself. The other guy ended up killing himself. The motive, abuse. His step father was very abusive, and his mother knew about it and did nothing to stop it. So, there are mannequins in the building. I want to tell you guys and show you where they are so you don't forget, so come on.

She points them out to us. They indeed are very lifelike and exploring in the dark and seeing one of these in your peripheral vision can really creep you out. As we start to walk up the wooden stairs to where the women and juveniles, and later men stayed, an EVP is recorded whispering "Get out."

Michelle points a room out to us, "This is the kids room. Last time I investigated, which was the end of Fall, there was a ton of activity in these two rooms. It never used to be like that before. Really shifted." She shows us the female mannequins and afterwards we head downstairs. She points out that each cell has a tiny step—a tripping hazard if you don't pay attention. Michelle opens the basement door and, after warning us about the awkward stairs, requests that we use the hand-railing. A few steps in I understand why she warned us. We make our way down to the basement we didn't know existed.

We are now in the basement. I am in awe. It's huge. We are standing in a large, open area. To the left is a doorway that leads to an even larger area. To the right, a dungeon-type doorway. Michelle explains, "This is a full basement. Entire length." An EVP is recorded, "Shh." She looks at us and asks, "Is anyone a sensitive?" I raise my hand and quietly say, "I am." She smiles and points towards the dungeon door way, "Go on … go in there."

I walk into the small room by myself, Michelle, Nick and Laurie stay out by the stairs. As I walk in, I close my eyes, immediately, I see bodies. I have my recorder in my hand. I open my eyes and quietly look around. A disembodied voice of a woman is recorded saying this EVP, "Here … Bridges" or instead of bridges she might be saying Bridgett's. Unsure. Then another EVP is recorded, "Hey … Help her."

Michelle tells Laurie and Nick, "This room … I'll tell you about it when she's done in there." I stay silent, concentrating. I finally turn around, trying to shake the images of bodies out of my head and ask Michelle, "What's going on in here?" She smiles, "What do you sense?" I ask, "Were there bodies in this room?" She nods, "Yes." I ask, "Was it like a little morgue or something?" Another confirmation, "Yes." I'm silent for a few seconds, "Was there a murder down here?" She responds, "We are actually trying to figure that out … possibly." A disembodied disheveled loud breathing takes over the recorder, sounding as if someone's mouth is on the recorder.

Laurie notices the wooden floor is different in a certain area. She points and asks, "Does that have anything to do with anything?" The thought that remains can possibly be buried down here, floods our brains. Michelle responds, "I have been asked that before. I think I'm going to have my paranormal group dig it up. Find out."

She explains the room that I was just in:

> So, this is called the Ice Room, because back in the day they refrigerated with big blocks of ice. [She points] That window is actually a door to the outside of the building. So, in this room they would load the coal in through that chute into the building. Same thing with the ice, right through the chute and into the building, but you were right, in the winter time we would store bodies in several buildings throughout the city because you cannot dig graves in the winter time. Even in the summer time it's mostly granite.
>
> As far as a murder, for years through investigations, we believe there is a young lady down here by the name of Emmy. We are not sure why she is still here. Most people … interestingly enough you didn't, but most people that I put in here, when I ask who's a sensitive, I put them in there and they start crying. Literally crying. It's very heavy.

An unexplained yelp is recorded, unheard by us. Could this be Emma? Remember when I was in the Ice Room by myself just moments earlier an

EVP of a woman was recorded giving this EVP, "Help her." Michelle points toward the large room on the other side:

> You can tell this is where we hang out and investigate, there's always chairs. The activity down here has really changed. It used to be playful, we've had kids down here. We have seen full-body apparitions.

(An EVP is caught, "Come on." This EVP is followed by an unexplained loud thump sound followed by yet another EVP from the same voice, repeating, but more excited, "Come on!")

> Someone took a picture of a child. We've seen a shadow go across back and forth here. My boyfriend who's so funny, at first was like, 'This is all bullshit.' I talked him into coming here. I told him, "Go with a group, you won't be in my group, and you have your own experiences … He was touched upstairs. His shirt was tugged down here in the Ice Room. He felt like someone was behind him. He saw shadows … now he's a member of our group!

I tell her how I can relate to someone close to you not believing. My boyfriend, Justin is like that, things have happened to him and he still refuses to believe, but unlike Michelle's boyfriend who now believes, mine is still a skeptic! I jokingly say to Michelle, "He's the world's biggest debunker." Michelle responds, "We go to great lengths to debunk stuff, you have to." I agree with her. As a team, we debunk things all the time. We hear sounds, we say what they are. We make a sound like sneeze, cough or anything else, we say it, so later on when I am listening to our audio sessions, there is no question whatsoever what those sounds are.

Michelle warns us about the building having no insulation, so for us to be aware of any outside sounds like traffic, dogs barking, etc. She shows us one area.

> The spirits down here have become more … aggravated is a good word to describe it. We don't know who it is, or why he is so pissed off. He is in here, just in here.

After my experience with the attachment from Tombstone I find myself a little on the paranoid side when I hear about hostile spirits. I mention this to Michelle, she responds, "I always encourage before you leave to make sure to let them know that they have to stay here. That they cannot come with you.

We've all taken them home before. Most have been mellow. We had an investigator, it was so funny, we were closing up and she had left early. She comes back in five minutes later saying, 'Tell it to get out of my car!' She goes, 'I'm done! Get it out!' It was funny." Michelle shows us where all the light switches are located. All on the left walls, easy enough to remember!

We talk about the jail episode that was on Ghost Adventures before Michelle leaves to go upstairs. My Mel makes an alert sound, followed by an EVP of a man saying, "Come on." Michelle points out an electrical box and warns us that it can cause our EMFs to have false reads and spikes. It does just that later on. Michelle heads upstairs and leaves us so we can start our investigation.

Session two

I say, "It is January the sixth. We are at the former County Teller Jail in Cripple Creek, Nick, Laurie and myself." While down in the basement, Nick sets up his motion sensor camera. Laurie has my Mel Meter, Nick has his Mel Meter, and I have the spirit box and the recorder. With hopes that the motion camera will capture something, we head upstairs and decide to start our investigation where the men were housed, including the second floor where solitary confinement was located.

We enter the men's block cell. I do a quick walk around on the lower level, turning the spirit box on, I say, "Is anybody here? Just walking around these cells." No response from the spirit box but I do receive an EVP, which is whispered, "Kill." Then another EVP from a different voice is recorded asking, "Who can?" This second EVP sounds like as if speaking under one's breath. I start to walk up the stairs to confinement but then remember about the jail garb and run down the stairs to put an orange jumper on. Laurie puts on a black and white striped shirt. As I am putting the orange jumpsuit on the equipment is sitting on a dresser unattended, the recorder of course is on. An EVP is recorded, so close it sounds as if the spirit is right in front of the recorder speaking, what sounds like either, "Heal" or "Heel."

After changing clothing, I turn off the spirit box and grab the rest of the equipment. Nick points at a light, "That light was off earlier and now it's on." I ask Nick to turn on his infrared camera and to start recording me. I extend my arm with hand open. I say, "Is someone here with us? Can you shake my hand?" I ask a few questions, Nick's camera caught nothing and the recorder recorded nothing but silence. We start to walk up the stairs towards solitary confinement. We start exploring the cells, Laurie whispers something, I debunk the whisper. I ask, "Anybody here with us?" A disembodied voice gives this EVP, what sounds like, "Bad girl."

We walk to one of the two toilets in the area and Laurie asks, "How did you guys like using the toilets?" An EVP of a man is recorded as he says, "Nasty." I imagine that's exactly what it was, nasty. Two toilets shared, I'm sure it wasn't pretty.

A car drives by, Nick debunks the sound. Nick suggests we go and sit in one of the cells. I turn on the spirit box and we choose a cell, the last cell, closest to the toilet, to the right side. We settle in and get situated. I say in a loud voice, "Okay jailers, lockdown starts right now." An EVP of a man is recorded, extremely close saying, "Don't kill them."

As of right now no voices have come through the spirit box so I turn it off. We decide to start a new session and sit in silence to see if the recorder captures anything. An EVP is recorded, "Get out." Two-seconds later the session ends, we could have missed this EVP.

Session three

We are still in the last cell on the upper floor in the men's housing unit. I say, "We're just going to stay here in silence, so please speak to us. Tell us anything." Things stay silent for a couple minutes when suddenly a man is recorded speaking unintelligible words, he sounds angry. The voice sounds like he is in the bottom floor below us, unheard by us. Remember no one is here with us, Michelle is on the other side of the building and we have the door closed down below.

A loud snap-like sound is recorded, sounding like it is in the cell with us. As we sit in silence suddenly footsteps are heard by us and caught on the recorder. Laurie excitedly whispers, "What the …" The footsteps get louder as they get closer. This is followed by two knocks. I counted thirteen steps total. Amazing! Remember Michelle told us that from time to time they get footsteps coming up the catwalk. The catwalk which is just a short distance from us. That's exactly what we heard.

Laurie admits to us that she is nervous. I let her know that I won't let anything happen to her and if she is too uncomfortable she can always hang out in the gift shop where Michelle is. After a few more minutes, we gather our things and leave the cell. We walk down the catwalk where the footsteps were recorded a few minutes earlier. Laurie thinks she saw something in her peripheral vision. We are now on the ground floor of the men's cell block.

On his infrared camera, Nick thinks he see's something peeking around the corner down the hall, leading to all the cells. He starts to videotape and I start to make my way down there. I walk to the very back where the last cells are located. He thinks it's outside the cell block. I head out of the cell block and he directs me to the area of interest. Nick and Laurie stay in front of the cell block as I start to make my way around towards the back where a display case is located.

As I walk, I talk, "I'm wearing an inmate uniform. I am one of the inmates here. Do you want to talk to me? We can bond about being stuck here doing time." I pause and an EVP of a man is recorded, "Get the funds." As I get closer to the display case, Nick notices the object is not moving at all. I stop at the case and extend my arm out and Nick directs me. "No, no, go lower." I kneel down and he says, "Yup. Right there." It turns out that the spot is affected by the heater and that's why it was showing up on the infrared camera. Major debunk!

Laurie calls out, "Nick! The EMF just went to 2.0." I walk back into the cell block and do a quick video on my phone while still recording on the recorder. "Former Teller County Jail in Cripple Creek, Colorado. We are doing an investigation after-hours thanks to Michelle." An EVP is recorded, "Thank you" in a hoarse voice. I continue, "Is anybody here? Please say something in my recorder." I walk back to the last cell, it's like I am drawn to that cell or something.

I walk in and sit down. For the moment, I'm alone … or so I think. I say loudly to nobody in particular, "Maybe I'll sit right here, doing some hard time, thinking about the crimes I have committed." The same voice who gave us the amazing EVP, "Get the funds" is recorded saying another EVP, what sounds like, "Huh … you're like me." I sigh. Shortly after, an unexplained rattle-like sound is recorded. The sound came from very close by, at my left where the bars are located to the cell. I call out to Nick and Laurie and ask them if they are on this side of the jail cells, to which they both reply no. Their replies, distant. This sound was anything but distant.

I ask, "So tell me … what did you do to get in here?" A disembodied voice gives this EVP, "Smoked pot." Nick, who's now made his way to the cell I'm in, asks, "Who's in here?" Unexplained fumble-like sounds are recorded, that sound like as if hands grabbing at the recorder. A few seconds later I say, "Something just flew from left to right." In one of the cells on the wall I see what looks like old rusted blood. I take a picture to show Michelle, so I can ask her about it. Later on, I show her, and it turns out that it's not blood. Thank goodness.

We start to head toward the basement, so we can check out Nick's motion camera and see if it caught anything.

Session four, The basement

We head downstairs to the basement. I walk into the Ice House, "I'm in the Ice House where bodies were stored in the winter." A light, distant EVP is recorded, "Come on." Then several seconds later another EVP is recorded, much closer this time, "Come on!" My Mel meter that Laurie is holding makes an alert sound. She looks down at it and with a look of shock on her face, she looks up and asks, Nick and I, "Guys, is 81.8 ... Is that normal?" Nick asks her, "Temperature?" In which she replies, "Um, no ... the temp is Four-Hundred-Seventy-Two degrees." Shocked Nick and I walk over to Laurie and take a look. I've had malfunctions due to wiring and electrical sources, but nothing like this! We are in the area Michelle warned us about.

I turn off the Mel meter and restart it. Nick grabs his Mel meter and walks to the area that mine malfunctioned to see if his did the same thing, at first nothing happened. He says, "Nothing. I'm not getting anything." Immediately after he says that his Mel spikes up to 140, then seconds later, 194. We were warned by Michelle about the wiring in the basement, but we've never had malfunctions like this. At the time we debunk this. However, later the same night, while in our hotel room at the Hotel Saint Nicholas, which also is haunted, my Mel starts acting up again going back to 81.8 and showing 472 degrees. (It hasn't done this since.)

We start looking through Nick's motion camera pictures. After viewing the pictures, we noticed a black mist in a couple of the pictures. We set the camera in another area in the basement. As we walk up the stairs leaving the basement, a shrill disembodied voice is recording saying what sounds like, "Hurry." As Nick and Laurie head upstairs where the women and juveniles were housed, I go back to the men's cell block and head upstairs where confinement is located. I set up my phone in the perfect spot and set up time-lapse. As I do this an EVP from a man is recorded saying my name, "Tessa."

I head upstairs making my way to the women and juvenile cell block to meet Nick and Laurie. The spirit box is turned on. We are in the room that the juveniles stayed in. Nick explains to the spirits to touch the EMF that it won't hurt them just let us know they are there with us. We ask a few questions with no replies or no answers. Suddenly the spirit box which constantly goes through channels makes a certain sound, what reminds me of a wind-up toy.

Whistling comes through the spirit box. We don't notice. I ask, "What's your name?" An EVP of a man with a very deep voice says what sounds like, "Earl" followed by whistling, a few seconds later, more whistling. After hearing the whistling, we all get excited, happily, I ask, "Can you do that again? I like to whistle too you know." A few seconds go by, then faint whistling comes through.

Nervously, I tell Nick and Laurie, "Hearing that whistle makes me nervous … In Louisville, we caught a whistler on recording at my friend David's house. Yesterday at the Windsor, we had a whistler, now here at the jail we have a whistler. I hope I don't have an attachment … I don't feel sick like last time so maybe not." I then ask, "Are you attached to me?" Thankfully I didn't get any EVPs or spirit box voices coming through answering me.

Laurie asks if the spirit can whistle again. A loud footstep is recorded. To me it sounded like a cowboy boot with a burr on it, had a cling to it, this is followed by more whistling. The whistling lasts a couple seconds sometimes longer each time. The whistler was recorded whistling his tune several times while in that location. A sad disembodied voice of a woman comes through the spirit box saying, "Help." The same woman comes through again, seconds later, saying in a lower tone, "Help me." Sadly, it was too low for us to hear at the time.

Session five

We are still in the juvenile room. We receive an EVP, very close to us, saying, "Bad." We sit in silence with nothing but the recorder and Mel meters on. Unexplained footsteps are recorded. I counted at least twelve, maybe more. This is followed by static. We are sitting on the ground, we are not standing or walking. I ask, "Is there somebody here with us? Can you talk to us?" Nothing but silence then a loud unexplained knock. The knock originated from the room we were in on the wall behind Laurie. We all heard it and it was caught on recorder.

We get out of the juvenile room and head down the hall where the cells are where the women stayed. After reading a specific history sheet, I ask, "Miss O'Connor, who did you murder?" An eerie EVP of a woman is recorded whispering, "Husband." I walk to another sheet on the wall, "Cora was here for larceny. Alice was here for murder. Alice, are you still doing your time?" An EVP of a woman, "Yes."

I was looking for answers about the woman who did time for killing her husband and via email, Michelle sent me an old article, this article talks about on the early morning of February 11, 1909, a woman named Mrs. Bedelia Durham who shot her husband, F.S. Durham in the neck. The death was almost instant. So, I must ask, was it Bedelia Durham who gave me this EVP? Even though I will probably never know, she's a possible good suspect.

Nick and Laurie are in a cell, Nick shares that he feels weird in this room, he says, "Almost like … homey." Laurie on the other hand is feeling something, but opposite from what Nick is feeling, she replies, "Really? I have a headache." Meanwhile Nick is so calm and relaxed he says he can take a nap in there. We walk to a cell where the door will still close. An EVP of a man is recorded, "Hid it."

Nick and Laurie leave the cell and close me in. I stand there alone in the dark. I say, "I'm in here all alone." I debunk some background sounds and turn the spirit box on. I ask, "Is someone here with me right now?" The whistler is back and whistles the now familiar tune. After a while, I turn off the spirit box and leave the cell. I go back to the men's cell block and grab my phone and end the time-lapse video.

Session six

Nothing much happened in session six, I go to the men's cell block to grab my phone and to see if time-lapse caught anything. Besides a couple shadows that I cannot tell are paranormal or not, nothing else is recorded. As Nick and Laurie talk in the background an unexplained deep laugh from a man is recorded. Laurie decides it is time for her to take a break from the investigation. She goes upstairs, leaving Nick and I in the basement.

Session seven

The spirit box is on. Nick and I are still in the basement and doing a session in the Ice House. An EVP is recorded, "Bus blue." I say, "We are in the Ice House where the bodies were stored until they could be buried. How did you feel being stuck in here?" A sound is recorded, we debunk it as being Nick's stomach! I say, "Is somebody here with us? Come talk to us. My name is Tessa and this is my cousin Nick." An EVP is recorded of a man whispering, "Cousin Nick."

I fumble with some coins that are on a shelf nearby, "There's some money here, do you want to take it? Come and take it." A loud thump is recorded followed by an EVP from a disembodied voice, "Yeah." No spirit box voices have come through, so I turn the spirit box off.

I tell Nick it's weird how we didn't get any spirit box action in the ice room. As I am talking, an EVP is recorded saying what sounds like, "Go on to the other side." This voice was very close, as if standing right there with us. Shortly after this EVP, I feel weird and let Nick know by saying, "I got a really weird vibe in here." We leave the ice house and are now in the larger room to the left. As we wander around talking to one another, an EVP from the same voice who just spoke about the other side, is recorded saying, "Where's the lock go?"

I walk up to one of the mannequins, legs sticking out of a barrel, looking so life like. I kid around saying, "Here's your body." Nick laughs, and an EVP of a woman is recorded, "Home." I tell Nick, "Let's go watch the time-lapse." As I'm talking, an EVP of a man is caught saying what sounds like, "All of it." Followed by a child's voice, "Kay." An unexplained beep that goes unheard by us but caught on the recorder. This beep reminds me of what you may hear on a plane or something, followed by static.

We are checking the time-lapse of the video we just did down in the basement. This was done while we were in the ice house, so we weren't near it. In the middle of the video something moves, just a small portion is seen the rest is out of view. We try to recreate the time-lapse to see if we can debunk this, but in the end we are unable to. A cough from a man is recorded, this isn't Nick. The EVP we catch next is crazy. So, Nick excitedly points at the video, "Oh yeah! Right there!" An EVP of a man is recorded, he has a very gruff voice, he says, "Get rid of all the whites." Followed by him laughing, "Ha ha."

What happens next is eerie and to be honest, gave me goose bumps the first time I heard it. Nick is walking around the area we are in. He suddenly stops and calls me over. He has found a hollow spot. He says, "I wonder if something is buried right there." A very faint EVP of a man is recorded saying, "Save me." This is followed by an EVP from the man with the gruff voice, who just a couple minutes earlier said to get rid of all the whites, the gruff voice is recorded making a sound, "Nah-uh."

I say, "I bet there's a body down here." As I say this Laurie is coming down the stairs saying, "What! A body? What happened while I was gone?" An unexplained sound, like a beating sound followed by an EVP, "Go away."

Laurie shares with us that Michelle, who is feeling under the weather does not live in town and has to drive an hour to get home. Our time was coming close to an end, so we decide to close down the investigation. At this point, we were all starving anyway. We take a few pictures and start to gather our equipment. An EVP from a man is recorded, "Hoochie." As we are about to go up the stairs another EVP is recorded, very close as if right in front of the recorder, the voice says, "Get in it and quit it." Hmm very weird. First 'Hoochie', then 'Get in and quit it'? No thanks.

Session eight, the final session

The whistler is on my mind and the possibility of an attachment, so as we join Michelle in the gift shop I mention the whistling to her. She says, "I was recording a new message on the machine and there was like whistling. I was getting distracted. Part of the message I pause because there is whistling." After saying this, it made me feel much better. She goes on, "Usually it comes from the main cell block … but this time it sounded like it came from upstairs, (where we heard it) I was right here and on the phone doing the recording … No, I was actually in the hallway. I stuttered, I was like … there's whistling!"

We make plans to meet back up sometime in the summer. As we talk, static is recorded. "Hopefully next time you can meet the team. *Leroy is a hoot to talk to. If you saw the Ghost Adventure Cripple Creek episode, he was the other one they interviewed for the jail. He saw a fully-body apparition and talked to it. One of the co-founders of the group, he's a sasquatch hunter too!" We walk toward the main cell block to take some pictures with Michelle. I leave the equipment, including the recorder which is still on, in the gift shop.

You can hear us walking and talking, faintly in the background. An EVP is recorded coming from what sounds like a child, "Hey."

We ask Michelle how it was when Ghost Adventures was here. She replies, "They were great to work with, they truly were. They were amazing. I would do it again, it was awesome." She went on to say how for three days they set stuff up, interviewed people, etc. However only investigated for less than two hours. We chat for a few more minutes, then call it a night.

A huge shout out to Michelle for letting us investigate after hours. I cannot wait to come back. It's definitely worth the trip. They are very knowledgeable, are happy to answer your questions and it's a very tiny fee to go check out this neat place!

Chapter twenty-nine

Investigating Sarah's home, Pueblo, Colorado

This chapter is a bit different from the others. Whether it's solo investigations or together as a team, the locations have always been abandoned, cemeteries, hotels, businesses etc. I would go to my friends Sarah and *Adam's house all the time. Sarah always felt that something wasn't quite right with their home. Especially when it came to the basement, she felt something paranormal was happening. We had often talked about possibly conducting an investigation there at some point.

I was always curious about investigating a residential home but I was always nervous about it. What if something happens? What if we conjure some angry spirit? What if things go from good to bad? So many what ifs. Then Michael died and that changed things. You see, Michael was a mutual friend. While I walked away from the friendship, Michael and Sarah and her husband, who was like Michael's brother, stayed friends and close. After Michael died, the energy shifted at Sarah and Adam's home.

Electrical problems would occur among other things that she or her family could not explain. She knew deep down that it was Michael. He actually lived with them for a short time before his passing. I believe he would still be alive if he continued to live with them. His death changed a lot of people, including me. Finally, I put the paranoia aside and we made plans for me to stay the night with my equipment and have an investigation downstairs in the basement. This is where Michael lived when he was staying here.

August 10, 2015
The investigation

This investigation was conducted by Sarah *B and Tessa Mauro. Armed with the equipment we were ready to see if we could get any answers for Sarah and her family. We wanted to wait a little later to start sessions, so I first went downstairs to the room Michael stayed in and put the shadow detector and the recorder there. Throughout the investigation we got EMF spikes, experienced cold spots, got several EVPs and spirit box voices.

We got Michael's voice coming through the spirit box a few times. We also decided to use a couple trigger objects, two things that were important to him when he was alive. We got some results with that as well.

Session one,
The basement, Michael's old room

I am in Michaels old room and situate the equipment. First, we want to just record in there to see if we get anything. As I am leaving, you can hear the door closing and a few seconds later an unexplained choking sound is recorded. A few minutes into the recording, an unexplained sound is recorded, that sounds like as if someone opening their mouth getting ready to speak. Very close as if right next to the recorder.

The air conditioner comes to life and a few moments later it shuts off, that is the only sound recorded that we could hear anyway. If there was anything else, the AC covered it up. Now that the AC is off, the silence is very noticeable, then unexplained rapid breathing is recorded. The door opens and I walk into the room. The shadow detector makes an alert sound, noticing my presence. An unexplained pop is recorded.

Session two

The spirit box is turned on. Before recording the session, we said an opening protection prayer. Usually one opening protection prayer at the beginning and one closing prayer at the end is good enough but because this is a home we thought it couldn't hurt to say a prayer before each session. This was done to also put my friend, whose home we were in, at ease. I ask, "Can you tell us your name?" A man comes through the spirit box saying, "A." Followed by a distant EVP, "*Michael." Unexplained heavy breathing from a man is recorded, then another EVP, "Home." More breathing from a man is recorded.

Again, Michael is not his real name, but his real name was said, followed by the same voice saying, "Home" and remember, he used to live here. This place was more a home to him then his own home!

Sarah suddenly gets cold. Very cold. It is August in Pueblo Colorado, which is usually a lot higher in temps then most areas in Colorado, yet she is freezing. She is shivering in front of me. She then starts to get dizzy and goosebumps take over her skin. As this is happening the KII EMF is fluctuating between 3-4.

As we go further into the investigation, Sarah tells me that her energy is draining away quickly. The KII spikes again. Then an unexplained pop is recorded. I see how Sarah is getting more and more uncomfortable, so I say, "You can't use our bodies to talk through us but you can talk TO us." A disembodied voice comes through the spirit box saying, "Go home." This must be directed towards me, since Sarah is home. Sarah gets cold again. She tells me that she just heard something in her ear. The KII spikes as this is happening. We decide to take a break, so Sarah can regain her strength. After each session we would go upstairs and take breaks.

Session three

We start with the protection prayer. We are still in the middle of the prayer when I start to feel very cold. As I am mentioning to keep us safe from malevolent spirits, unexplained static is recorded. Then the KII meter goes off. Sarah and me both feel very cold at the same time. The Mel Meter spikes to 1.0. We start an EVP session, Sarah asks, "Is there a reason that you are attached to this home?" No answers. I say, "We know you are here because we can feel your presence." Unexplained static is recorded.

I say, "I know it's hard to speak, but we really appreciate the effort. Can you tell us something, like what your name is, or how you died?" An unexplained sound is recorded. This sound, to me reminds me of what an old school record skipping. I say, "Michael can you please come to this device and make it light up?" Seconds later the KII lights up.

Session four

The protection prayer is said by both of us. I say, "I'm going to turn the spirit box on now." An EVP of a man is recorded whispering, "Yes, do it." The spirit box is now on and sweeping channels. I ask, "Okay, is that better? Can you communicate easier this way?" A man's voice comes through the spirit box saying, "Yes." Unexplained rap music is recorded.

Michael always loved rap. Sarah asks, "What is your name?" A few seconds later a man who sounds like Michael comes through the spirit box and asks, "Who would?" I ask, "How many people are here with us in this basement?" A man comes through the spirit box saying, "Four."

Sarah asks, "What's your name?" Immediately after a man comes through the spirit box saying what sounds like, "Ike." I ask, "How did you die?" A woman comes through the spirit box saying what sounds like, "Rape." We try to get the woman to come through again, but the spirit box has no further voices for the time being. I ask, "Michael, are you here with us right now?" An EVP of a man is recorded saying, "I am." A few seconds later, possibly the same man who spoke earlier, comes through the spirit box saying, "Yes."

I tell Michael that if he is here with us if he can keep us safe from any negative spirits, and what sounds like Michael's voice coming through the spirit box saying, "All right." A man comes through the spirit box saying, "Ghosts!" Followed by another man saying a couple seconds later, "True." Sarah and I laugh because it sounds like two spirits are having a conversation with each other. Sarah asks, "I'm sorry are they having an argument or something?" I laugh, "Ha ha ha ha." As I laugh a deep laugh of a man is also recorded laughing, "Ha ha ha!"

A man comes through the spirit box saying, "Beer." I say, "We have something in front of us that was very important to a friend." I kneel down and touch the object, "Can you tell us what this is?" A man comes through the spirit box saying, "Yes." The same man comes through saying, "Pool." The item that I am touching and that we are referring to is a pool cue. Again, rap music is recorded. An EVP of a man is recorded saying, "Tess." This is followed by a cough from a man. At this point, Sarah and I are alone—not only in the area where we are currently investigating—no one else is home. Adam is at work and their son is outside next door playing with his grandparents.

I ask, "Michael, if you are here can you make the lights go to the EMF and make it go off?" A man comes through the spirit box saying, "Yes." Then the same man comes through again, "Hurt." Sarah asks, "Michael, what am I touching?" An unexplained scream is recorded followed by a woman moaning. A minute or so later, an EVP is recorded, "Watch me."

Sarah sighs and debunks herself. A man comes through the spirit box saying, "Sigh." Amazing! I say, "You know we think about you a lot and feel your presence at times. Is there something you want us to know, or send a message to someone?" A voice comes through the spirit box, "Yeah." I ask, "What is the message?" The voice that sounds like Michael comes through the spirit box asking, "See it?"

I say, "There is somebody who lives in this house who was like a brother to you. Can you tell us what his name is?" An EVP of a man exhaling is recorded. Then Michaels voice comes through the spirit box once again saying, "*Adam." That is true, that is Sarah's husbands name, Michael's best friend's name.

Sarah and I are excited to hear that Michael's voice keeps coming through and that he just said her husband's name. I ask, "Is there something you want to say to him?" His voice comes through, "Live." Sarah's husband Adam is very much like my boyfriend Justin in the way that he is a skeptic as well. It's sad because Michael is clearly trying to reach out to him and is unable to. Michael's message for Adam to live his life is an important one. Adam thinks about Michael often and feels like he could have done something to help Michael. It's not Adam's fault. Sarah has told him several times, I have told him several times, but it does no good.

Both Sarah and I get teary-eyed hearing his voice. I ask, "Is there somebody here with us besides Michael?" A woman comes through the spirit box saying an unintelligible word. I ask for a name and then a voice comes through, "Eve." I request that whoever is here with us, approach the KII meter that I am holding. The EMF fluctuates between 2-3. Sarah asks, "Michael, we're going on Tessa's dad's boat tomorrow. Throw out a fishing pole." A man comes through the spirit box saying what sounds like, "Love fish." Sarah asks, "You miss fishing, don't you?" The same voice comes through saying, "Sure."

Session five, final session

The KII meter spikes. I ask, "Michael, are you here with us right now?" As I pause, a man is recorded exhaling. Again, it is just Sarah and I conducting this investigation. I continue, "Let us know you are here." An EVP is recorded of a man whispering, super close, "I'm here."

I ask, "Besides, 'live' is there anything else you want to tell Adam?" A man comes through the spirit box, "Yeah." Then a few seconds later, the same man comes through again, "I'm sorry." In my opinion, Michael is saying sorry to Adam because he knows he has been struggling with his untimely death.

An EVP is recorded, "Cool it." The lights are off, the only lights are coming from the equipment. The shadow detector, which is located in a corner goes off, and at the same time Sarah gasps as she notices a shadow moving against the wall. "I just saw a shadow dart across the room!" A couple minutes later, she sees the shadow again, right after this, two pops are recorded. A man comes through the spirit box and says, "Die."

A woman comes through the spirit box saying, "Chris." The voice that sounds like Michael comes through saying what sounds like, "Worried." Then the woman who just spoke, comes through again and repeats herself, "Chris." I ask, "Can the woman speaking through the spirit box tell us her name?" A man comes through the spirit box saying, "Chris." A man comes through saying, "*Adam." We turn the spirit box off.

We decided to do a cleansing of Sarah's home. I had brought Colorado picked sage with me and we went from room to room repeating a cleansing prayer and a closing prayer as well. It was great communicating with Michael and hearing his voice and his responding to us and even saying Sarah's husband's name. In addition to Michael, a woman came through a couple times, the first time saying she was raped. I think of that woman often and I wish she could have told us more. I hope with the cleansing of the home she was able to move on.

I wish I could say that was the end of the investigation, but it wasn't. Sarah told me a day or so later that the energy in the house shifted and had turned negative. She was even having difficulties with her young son, who usually is very well behaved. I left the sage at her house and she would walk around and use it around the house. She started noticing weird things, hearing things, seeing things and it was affecting the household.

A friend of Sarah's and Adam's who happens to be an EMT shared some information that many different types of sage have Salvia contained in them. Salvia is a psychoactive plant which can induce visual and other spiritual experiences. I would consider it a hallucinogen. Once they were told this, she stopped using the sage and buried it in the back yard and things got better. To date, things still occasionally occur at the home. Things have calmed down though, the negativity vanished along with the sage. Hearing that things went wrong after the investigation made me sad. Those were not my intentions. All we wanted to do was try to communicate with our friend.

I didn't know this before while we were doing the investigation, I had never done an actual cleansing at a residence before. When using sage indoors, each room should have an open window. If a window is open the spirits have a way to leave but if there are no openings, then they just get chased from room to room. To me, this makes sense, and that night we definitely did not do that, and I am sure the following days when Sarah was by herself cleansing the house she did not do it either. I shared this information with her and now we both know.

If you are going to cleanse a home, whether it be your own home, or a friend's like what I did, please do your homework and do it the right way. Like I said before, I had never done an investigation in a private home before nor have I ever done or been part of a cleansing. There are several reasons why one may cleanse a home, whether your moving in to a brand-new home, spiritual or otherwise, that's great, just do it right.

I think often of that investigation and wonder what went wrong. Maybe, some day, I will venture back with my equipment and investigate a private residence. For now, I am quite content on the plantations, cemeteries, mines, hotels and so on.

Chapter thirty

The attachment and dealing with Red Sample

After leaving Tombstone, Arizona, something wasn't right. I couldn't put my finger on it. I was having breathing problems and found myself gasping for air often. Our last stop for the last couple days in Arizona was in Cottonwood at my mom's best friend Joan's house. I had two other investigations in Jerome I was committed to going to—Sheila's Copper Penny and Jerome Grand Hotel. Still feeling ill, I went to Sheila's and conducted the investigation.

A couple days later, it was time to go to Jerome Grand Hotel. The night before I wake up in a panic, run to the bathroom which thankfully was close to the guest room, and make it just in time to the toilet to throw up. I was shocked. It's been years since I last vomited. I fear vomiting so much, I hyperventilate, I cry, I panic, if I can prevent getting sick, I will do anything to do so. Whatever was in me that night didn't give me a chance. After brushing my teeth and rinsing my mouth of the acidic taste I get back in to bed and fall back asleep.

Not too long after dozing off I wake up again and run into the bathroom. After getting sick this time, I stay in the bathroom for some time to ensure I don't have to get sick again. After some time has passed, I get up, go back in the guest room and lay down. My nerves are shot and I am feeling sick. I lay there but cannot sleep. It's coming back up and quick. I quickly run into the bathroom once again and this time I didn't make it to the toilet. I throw up all over the ground. Thankfully it was tile and not carpet!

My mom, who was sleeping on the other side of the house, wakes up to find me half on the ground and half in the toilet. She stayed up with me and comforted me and helped clean up my mess. She slept on the couch so she could help me if I had to get up again. I was able to fall asleep and stay asleep for the rest of the night. The fact that I was sick for a good chunk of the night made me nervous. Later the following evening I was heading to Jerome Grand Hotel to investigate. It was booked and I was almost unable to make it.

That evening I went to the hotel, I still felt pretty sick but there was no way I was missing out on this opportunity. I just prayed that I wouldn't get sick in the middle of the investigation. At the end, I was relieved to have not lost control and went home feeling like we had a successful night.

The next day my mom and I had to wake up quite early to get on the road and drive back to Colorado. As we drove I felt horrible. It felt like an elephant was sitting on my chest. I couldn't breathe at all. We stopped in Durango, Colorado at a little grill to take a break from the road and eat. When I stood I felt as if I was going to faint. I was feeling so funky and I couldn't understand why.

We ate, got back in the car and drove the last couple hours back to my mom's. I shared the pain I was feeling with my mom and it was decided to go to the hospital. We arrive into town and go to the local hospital. By the time I am getting out of the car my legs feel like jello, my body is numb, and my chest is hurting more than ever. I'm in my early thirties, is it possible I am having a heart attack? I never go to the hospital if I can help it, but I thought I was dying. There was no other option.

I am panicking and crying, we walk in the doors and we see someone we know. She sees how distressed I am and runs away then comes back quickly with a wheelchair. She brings my mom and me into a room and I change into a gown. They ran blood tests, took vitals, did a chest x ray, everything they could do, they did. The Doctor even approached me and admitted he was happy to say that everything came back just fine, however he felt bad that he couldn't find any reason why I felt sick. It was very obvious the pain I was feeling was real, yet they had no answer as to why.

After everyone left the room and it was just my mom and I, she said to me, "Maybe you should tell them what you were doing this whole time in Arizona, with the ghosts. Perhaps you have an attachment." I brushed it off and told her that she better not tell the Doctor or anyone else that, joking that they may throw me in the looney bin if they hear that. Later that night, as I lay in bed I thought hard, what if I did have an attachment? Tests came back good, yet I felt like I was being suffocated. My whole body ached.

For a few more weeks I felt just as sick. I went to the cemetery one day and asked my friend Michael that if I was indeed dealing with an attachment if he could help protect me, the next day I woke up feeling slightly better. Now instead of a large elephant on my chest it was a medium sized one. As much as I enjoy elephants, having one of any size on my chest is very unenjoyable. Something had to be done, and quick.

One evening I was at a Mexican restaurant in town and enjoying a nice dinner with my friend Jeanette. We had worked together for a couple years at another Café in town. We don't work together any more but still keep in touch. As we are eating and catching up, I explain to her how sick I have been feeling. Jeanette is a trauma and spiritual healer. She invites me to her house to work on me and to see if she can help out with my situation. I happily accepted her gracious offer. Neither of us knew just what would happen. It is an experience we shared and, though I can't speak for her, I don't think either of us will forget this experience.

I asked Jeanette if I could record this session and she agreed to it. I must say that when she was asking me questions, it's like I was floating above us and watching myself answer these questions, I didn't know what the answers were but here I was speaking. A few times, a man can be heard speaking and breathing. Here is our session word-for-word.

Jeanette suggests I sit on the couch. She sits in front of me on a coffee table. She waits until I get comfortable, handing me a small pillow to use. I end up moving from the couch to a small comfy chair. As I get situated an EVP of a man is recorded, "Fuck." (I just want to note that we are at Jeanette's home, just her, myself and her dog who is in the other room sleeping.)

As I close my eyes and get into a relaxed state, Jeanette lights a candle and says, "I am not really into any type of ritual at this point, but I just invite spirit." As she stops talking, an unexplained exhale from a man is recorded.

Jeanette continues, "Benevolent presence and support guidance for the highest benefit of all beings, including Tessa, myself and sweet Gypsy girl (her dog) and any other beings that may be present. That we'd be open to the highest good for all in whatever way that might present itself. I trust that we're supported in guide and in that we can kind of let ourselves relax a bit and trust that. Well, I am not a Christian biblical at this point in nature but still, there's always that passage of when two or more are gathered with the intention of the highest benefit that the assistance we need is here. So that we can kind of just trust that. We don't actually have to try to figure it out or mentally stream it in anyway."

Jeanette asks me, "So with that, is there anything you would like to add? That's a query, prayer, a comment, or a question? Anything that feels relevant to what we're doing?"

After a few seconds of thinking, I say, "Just to keep us protected. Um, possessions and bodies. I'd just really like to know if there is something with me, an attachment, because I haven't been right since Arizona. You know I am not one to go to the hospital, but it was so bad that I had to go and I got no answers to my illness … making it more mysterious. Even right now, I am having a very hard time breathing."

Jeanette replies, "So notice that." She pauses and grabs her iPod, just in case she needs to put relaxing music on to get me into a deeper state. She explains, "We'll use the music if we need to, but we won't start out with it. The simpler the better. This is very similar, I began to realize that working with clients with trauma, that if they had past life stuff coming up, this seems to have worked. It's amazing."

Right before Jeanette speaks, a man is recorded giving this EVP, "Life now feels."

Jeanette says, "So let me ask you to begin," as she speaks, unexplained loud breathing from a man is recorded. She continues, "by taking three deep breaths and I will do that with you. It's a way for us to join together. It doesn't have to be," she imitates a deep breath, and continues, "but just a slow calming …" as she pauses, a man finishes her sentence in this EVP, "Breath." Very clear, very close.

(A month or so later, Jeanette and I got together and listened to the session and it was interesting to say the least, when we heard this man start to speak and breathe.)

Jeanette says to me, "Long slow exhale. So now, with each breath, each in breath and each out breath, it can be normal. With each exhale, I invite your mind to kind of relax and drop down into your body. Let it drop down into your chest, so that your inner-awareness, your mind's eye and all of the benevolent support you have from the unseen realms. In your own highest wisdom that you begin to get more and more aware of that."

I would like to note that her voice as she is speaking these words to me is like velvet butter. Soft and smooth and dare I say mesmerizing.

Jeanette continues, "With each exhale, relax a little bit more into a trusting, that we are held, supported, guided, and protected. To just discover whatever it is that's here, within your chest, within your heart, within your body vessel, organism and what it has to tell you because there is wisdom in the body itself. To be able to communicate."

An EVP from who I believe to be the same man saying, "No."

She goes on, "What it is that's going on. Trusting in your own highest good and your own highest wisdom. That below, the intellectual problem-solving mind, there is an intuitive awareness, an intuitive wisdom. So, with each breath, just connect with that. Stronger and stronger. Then when you feel ready, I invite you to inquire and ask an inner question of your own wisdom. What is here now that needs our attention, to help you to feel love?"

Nothing but silence while I really think about this.

I say to Jeanette, "Huh … it's weird because this whole time, my eyes have been closed. Now it's white, like bright, as if my eyes aren't closed. Like something dancing in front of me."

Jeanette replies, "I don't know what that means … we don't actually have to analyze it. Right now, we just trust. We just take it at face value and we get to trust that we are guided and supported. So that problem-solving mind can actually kind of drop down and trust whatever you're given right now. I also invite you to check in to your body and see what you notice. How does it feel?"

I take a deep breath and say, "I am able to get some deep breaths in, so that's good. Still tight in my chest but somewhat lifted. No anxiety."

Jeanette replies, "It's good to notice, so just be with that for a moment. So, you are feeling a little bit of relief from what you were feeling before. Trust in yourself, in your mind, in your guidance, in your own support … no rush. Nothing really to do. Just be open, open to whatever wants to come through. Yeah. I'm feeling called to come a little closer, not too close, but my hand might be a foot or two above your chest. Just kind of again as a contour of offering support. So, I am going to invite the release and resolution, anything here that's out of balance."

She continues, "Any distortions that aren't blind in your highest good." An unexplained sound is recorded, what sounds like a drop of water hitting a pool of water. Jeanette goes on, "And that anything that is released is able to return to its source, to cease the benefit and the assistance that it needs as well, in order to be whole and heal, content. Then just feel free to give brief little reports of anything you notice. It can be somatic meaning sensations you feel in your body, it could be emotional, could be mental, visual, it could even be fragments of memories or whatever."

A vision plays through my head and I say, "Right now, what comes to mind is when I was in Tombstone, at Boot Hill Cemetery. I saw a father and son taking a picture and I offered to take one for them. I put my recorder on a rock by a nearby grave, still recording. I listened later, and I got a voice of a man saying that he was hung. He said, 'I hanged.' I've heard that voice off and on."

Jeanette responds, "So let's just trust that, be with that for a moment, not having to figure it out or solve it or fix anything, just trusting with the support and guidance that's needed here, for all being ... I ask now, if this person is present with us here? If it has anything to do with Tessa's chest and her heartbeat.

Again, if anything comes up that you want to report, please feel free to do it. Just let your mind stay in this free state ... What I'm feeling, and sensing, is an awareness of the ... how do I say it? The innocence of your heart. An open innocence that you carry, and a deep compassion."

Jeanette goes on, "However that might be relevant to this or not."

I tell her, "I went to the cemetery to visit my friend Michael and I told him that I might have something with me and if it was something, if he could overpower it and make me feel better, the next day I woke up feeling a little better. I still have something, it's just not as overwhelming."

Jeanette says, "So that's one way you've been assisted with this. So, what I am going to invite is the possibility that we don't have to overpower anything. That all beings here can actually work together for the highest good. Even if it is someone else that came along for the ride."

An EVP of the man is recorded saying, "Okay."

Jeanette says, "I ask if there is any kind of message or a quest of communication from any other being and if there's a role that we actually play in helping that being to cross over or do whatever they need to do so that they're free of their struggle and pain as well."

Two unexplained light tap-like noises are recorded, followed by an unintelligible disembodied EVP.

Jeanette goes on, "I feel an activation in my hands and that's just an energetic thing that I generally feel when an energy is starting to move. Still feeling calm, present and supported."

Silence fills the air, suddenly Jeanette says in an excited voice, "Okay, I've never gotten this before, but I'm getting a strong sense that I need to grab my journal."

She gets up and walks to another room to gather some things.

I ask her, "Is that a good thing or a bad thing?" She replies, "Um, good I think. I mean things come through when I draw, but I never … oh wow, never when I am with someone! So, I'll just trust it."

I am still sitting with my eyes closed, Jeanette's voice gets closer and I hear her footsteps enter the room.

"Are you okay? It's kind of warm in here but I turned the fan off just so we wouldn't have peripheral noise."

She opens a small box that holds several crayons. She continues, "So I'm just going to kind of keep seeing with where we are. For some reason it feels useful for me to have you just calmly and gently speak about this, whatever way feels relevant to you … Any memories or associations or emotions that might come up as well … letting the mind kind of keep dropping in a deeper state."

I reply, "Well ever since this has happened, I have been more aware. I have always known there was always a possibility of getting an attachment but part of me always felt I was jinxing myself," as I pause a man is recorded breathing. I continue, "when I tell people that I've never had an attachment, and I've said that plenty of times." The man whispers this EVP, "Why?" I go on, "I have never been one to provoke because I know that's one way you can get unwelcome visitors."

An image plays in my head. I speak, "At Boot Hill there were the five men that robbed a store and killed several people in Bisbee, Arizona. I call them 'The Murdering Five' four were legally hung."

A man is recorded, saying this EVP, "Well my guess is, ___ ___ ___"
Sadly half of this I cannot understand at all.

I continue, "It was 105 degrees and rising, I think maybe I was getting a little delirious. I started saying stuff like, 'How dare you guys kill all these innocent people.' I kind of got angry and showed my anger to them. I didn't think of it as provoking, but it might have been. That's the only time I have provoked."

Jeanette says, "So let's just be with that for a moment. Take three deep breaths. Letting the mind drop in, into the body, into the heart, seeing what's here right now."

I take deep breaths—or try to.

Jeanette asks, "What do you notice now?"

I reply, "I'm gasping for a breath."

Jeanette says, "So let's be with that for a moment. Be present in your own body, stay aware that you have benevolent loving divine support here with us now. What I'm sensing that's coming through for me is a sense of judgment."

I ask, "On their part or mine?"

Jeanette answers, "That's interesting that you would ask that, because the feeling that I get is, sort of a, 'Who are you to judge us?' you know?"

An unexplained exhale from a man is recorded.

Jeanette continues, "Sort of a, 'he who is without sin cast the first stone' sort of thing. I'm curious what sort of self-judgment that you might also have that would be in any way an opening or a vulnerability or a link between you two. Without digging any more, solving or picking, but again using the breath to sync in the body and realize that there's a way that our response can come through you, without having to think too hard about it."

Again, I go into the past, "I got an EVP of a man as I was leaving the murdering five saying, 'Come back.' I was walking to the next row."

An amazing EVP was recorded, mumbling, whispering, "Yeah, but you didn't listen."

I continue, "I didn't hear it until after the fact."

Jeanette asks me, "What do you notice right now, right here? In your body, in your awareness?"

I reply, "My chest feels sort of heavy."

Jeanette responds, "So just be with that for a moment because sometimes we just have to be present to whatever might be coming up. Have there ever been times when you might have felt judged?"

I answer, "Yes, a lot."

Jeanette says, "Just be with that for a moment … Just see if anything rises."

I say, "I feel that my chest is lighter again."

An eerie EVP of a man is recorded as he says, "So is mine."

Jeanette says, "I seem to be getting some sense of connectedness between empathy and judgment and that could be an opening for connection that could be weighing on you. I'm not feeling a sense that it needs to be an attack as much as a need to be heard,"

As Jeanette pauses, a man is recorded breathing.

She continues, "understood, not judged somehow. What comes out in you when I say that?"

I think for a moment, "I have been judged and bullied most of my younger years. I don't bully but I sometimes judge people when I really shouldn't. I know people who've been murdered."

A disembodied voice of a man gives an unintelligible EVP, two words.

I continue, "I get angry."

The same voice is recorded saying, "Yeah."

Again, the only people in Jeanette's home were her and me.

I continue, "They killed innocent people. I let it out. I shouldn't have because they've been dead for well over a century but it just …"

As I pause an EVP of the man says what sounds like, "Cut them off."

Jeanette speaks, "But let's just assume that what happened is okay and that somehow or other there is a gift and an opportunity right here. Maybe this other being is seeking some kind of forgiveness, some kind of absolution, some kind of empathy. My sense is a level or torment, inner torment necessary. To murder, or to execute some type of violence and how most of the time that's never understood by those that judge us. So, what I'm feeling called now is for you to take some more of these long single breaths into your heart and chest, without the intention of changing it or getting rid of anything, but with the intention of breathing in a sense of light, a sense of love, a sense of deeper compassion that may benefit both of you."

She pauses and goes on, "Just slow. Feel in yourself with the goodness that you are, that is inherent. Maybe even so much that it overflows to anyone else who may need it and that innocent heart, that is your nature, is what can come into the fore front instead of any vulnerability … Check in for a moment what you notice in the rest of your body."

An EVP is recorded of a man saying, under his breath, "No way in Hell." This is followed by unexplained footsteps.

I reply, "Knots. Like butterflies, not necessarily a bad thing, like anxious."

Jeanette asks, "In where?"

I answer, "My stomach."

Jeanette says, "So be with that for a moment. Sometimes that is where tension is held, so whenever there is a shifting, or a clearing or leasing, the gut is a place where it will kind of unwind."

Concerned, I ask, "Since there's five of them I wonder if it's one person or all of them. I'm not angry anymore."

Jeanette says, "Be with that for a moment."

Unexplained footsteps are recorded.

I say, "I have my eyes closed, but again there's this dancing light."

Jeanette tells me to be with that and think about it for a moment. A few seconds later, six unexplained heavy foot steps are recorded, followed by an unexplained breathing from a man.

Jeanette says, "Be with the light … Keeping part of your awareness on your body."

I reply, "Butterflies are gone."

Jeanette says, "So that's just a phase of the kind of energetic release moving. My sense is one person, not multiple, but I don't claim to be psychic. I'm more empathic and joining with you to bring through the guidance and wisdom that you actually have."

I say, "There was the man that said, 'Come back.' Just that one man."

Jeanette asks, "So how does your heart feel? As you think about, 'come back' what do you feel?" I say, "It's hard but I forgive him."

Jeanette requests that I take a full breath. I try but am unable to achieve that simple task. She says, "Don't try to force it. Just take a small breath if you need to. Let the body do whatever it needs or wants to do. Farting, burping, yawning, twitching, giggling, crying, all of that is part of this process."

I make a quick fart joke and Jeanette jokes back saying, "I may open a window."

Jeanette says, "So part of what I seem to be called to do is to help find, what is within you that would be a connection or a resonance with some other being. Not just bad, negative attack, I mean, there might be anger, so anger is a strong magnetic emotion. So is emotion. So is empathy. So is judgment. So is forgiveness. Sometimes there's actually a way that a being can come to you, because they feel that you actually have a way that you can help them." There is silence for a moment or two, then Jeanette continues on, "In the process helping both of you because maybe you get to release something that is in common with them. The word that came out on my journal earlier was 'judged.' The other thing that came through and don't think this, if anything, direct comes from it. A heart, that turned into a balloon, that turned into a mouse head. Don't think, just let it be, it could mean nothing."

Jeanette goes on, "So what do you notice in your body now?"

I breath slowly and say, "Lightness in my chest again. I am able to take a deep breath in."

Jeanette says, "So using your breath, not to force it or change but just to kind of support it. Just gentle calm breaths. The words that feel the most relevant for this, that we've kind of worked through is 'Judged' and 'Forgiven.' I got 'forgiven' and whatever way it's relevant for both of you. Stay aware with what's happening with your body."

More silence fills the air. Moments later, Jeanette says, "So what I heard inside my mind, the word, 'thank you.' So, what do you notice now? Check in with your body."

I answer, "Still see light. My eyes have been closed this whole time, but again I see this weird lightness dancing around … I just took a deep breath, that's nice. It's been so long since my chest has felt like this."

As I pause, a man is recorded saying what sounds like, "Good."

I continue, "It feels a little more free, but not, it's like right here in my chest. A tightness. Almost like—" I stop talking and look at my arm, I tell Jeanette, "I felt someone—a hand—gently grab my left arm. Not being mean but more like an awareness type thing."

Jeanette says, "Wow. I have the sense … I'm getting that one is leaving the gang of five. Okay … now I'm feeling some teary emotions that you actually helped one of them leave."

Shocked I ask, "Really? Wow … geez. I wish I knew which one. That's a good feeling."

Jeanette says, "The sense that things are not always what they seem, and when we jump to conclusions sometimes we don't, we aren't able to perceive that something else might also be going on. So, the words that just came into my mind are, 'Falsely accused.' Not even the sense that, not that one didn't do anything wrong … but not knowing the whole picture. Again, I feel this sense of connection like a link between you—you being able to comprehend how it feels to be falsely accused, judged. Some kind of empathetic connection."

I take a deep breath.

Jeanette speaks, "So I want to ask now if there's anything to be shared with us through our minds, through our senses or through the recording of any other information that is relevant for Tessa to find peace with this, and resolution permanently for herself and in any way, she can benefit for another. Let's give this a little time."

We both stay silent for a short while.

Jeanette says, "Checking in with you to see if there's anything else you need right now, before we close."

I reply, "My chest is the lightest it's been in a long time."

Jeanette replies, "I have an inner request for you, that you could somehow within you extend a thank you. I'm not even sure who it's directed at, but I trust that you will know, who or what that might be to."

After thinking, I say, "Thank you to the man who actually attached to me, for opening my eyes and being more aware and hopefully learn a lesson not to be so judging. I sometimes judge without even knowing I am doing it. I think that is an important lesson maybe from beyond the grave that was taught to me without even knowing it until just now. It was a painful lesson. I thought I was having a heart attack … I thought I was dying."

Jeanette asks, "Is there any way that this experience helps you in healing any of your own feelings for judgment that you felt subjected to?"

I think for a moment and say, "I don't know. I was bullied and tormented in New Mexico while in school for years. I was the minority, and I was hated for being the minority. I learned to hate myself. I never had a suicidal thought, only while at that school, stuck with those bullies. I wanted to die. It sounds like he was a tortured soul himself."

A man is recorded breathing loudly.

Jeanette responds, "Yeah, that's some kind of a link that allowed an opening that connected you. Again, I feel the sense of 'thank you' coming."

I feel a flutter in my chest and say it aloud.

Jeanette says, "I just got the words, 'ready to go.' Can you tell him good bye?"

I say, "I hope that you are at peace now and I forgive you. I will always remember this experience that I had with you. I hope you leave a better person, go somewhere now where you won't be judged and where you can be at peace. Perhaps one night you can visit me in my dreams and tell me your name. Then when I go back to Tombstone, I can put a flower on your grave."

As I stop talking, an EVP is recorded, "Yes."

Jeanette says, "Take in a breath. I'm feeling a sense of gratitude. I'm feeling a sense of departure, I don't know if he can grant your request, but I know that he is grateful. I more feel emotion and energy and that somehow this was a chance meeting that benefitted you both."

I reply, "Yeah. It's interesting to pinpoint, I was at every single grave at that cemetery. I have wanted to go there for so many years. People were visiting and leaving quickly because of the heat."

Jeanette asks, "Why did you visit every grave?" I say, "I wanted to because about fifteen years ago my mom gave me a brochure that talked about every burial, row-by-row. How they died. I must've read that thing a dozen times and I always told myself, 'One day I will go see those graves.' That's exactly what I did."

Jeanette asks, "Let me ask you on a deeper level, what compelled you to do that? Beyond just a fascination? This is a deeper question then your mind. Let that be a lingering question. Maybe the answer will come later in a way you don't even expect … What I'm feeling is some level of compassionate empathy. It had something to do with your innocent heart, I got that in the very beginning of the session."

I say, "There were a lot of unknowns. You know there were a lot of,'

an EVP is recorded of a man whispering, "Pain."

I continue, "Hangings. The old cemeteries interest me. The cowboy days, the outlaws …"

Jeanette responds, "That time period seems important to you."

I tell her how I often try to picture living back in the 1800s, how hard it must have been.

We talk for a few minutes about my investigations I conducted at Tombstone and Jerome. Nervously I say, "My friend warned me about the nasty spirits at Waverly Hills, how there are many attacks and attachments that happen there. Am I more vulnerable to that now since I had an attachment?"

Jeanette is silent for a few seconds and says, "Before we go down that road, it feels like the opportunity here was … to look at that in a different way. The words, again, 'innocent heart' you know?"

She continues, "There's a level of empathy. For me, when I was guided, you know that light you saw in front of your eyes and my sense of you being guided to breathe into your heart. It's the possibility of arming yourself from the outside in, of feeling yourself from the inside out, in a way that gives you deeper wisdom, compassion and guidance. So, you know that you are supported and guided and there's presence within you. Some of this comes from my own teaching of one level of consciousness, there's the awareness of ways to protect ourselves energetically from the outside in. The next level is when we are full, when we're not empty and have wounds and holes ourselves. There isn't anything that can get in."

End of session.

Actually, that is not the end, but I stopped recording. I wish I hadn't stopped recording when I did. I show Jeanette a picture from my phone of a headstone at Boot Hill that bears the names of the five men who were hung, guilty of several peoples' untimely deaths and the robbery of a store. She looks at the picture and immediately she turns pale and looks up and past me. I actually look behind me to see if there's a ghost there or something. I ask her, "What's wrong?"

She hands me the journal and says, "Look at this. What do you see?"

I stare at the paper she wrote on. There I see the words, 'Judged' 'Forgiven' and a drawing of the heart turned balloon turned mouse head. She explains to me, "When I use the crayons I use my left hand, the non-dominant hand and simply pick out a crayon. Well, when I picked out the crayon this time, I had to pick the red. Usually red is blood, gore, violence, death. I don't use it that often, but something told me to use the red. So, I picked the red out."

I still stare at her, not knowing what she is getting at.

She points at the picture. "Look at those names."
I read the names on the tombstone aloud. "Dan Dowd. Red Sample. Tex Howard. Bill DeLaney. Dan Kelly. Legally hanged in 1884 … Red Sample! It's Red Sample!" I wish in addition to recording in audio, I would have video-taped this session.

As soon as she said he was leaving me, my chest was completely free. It had been weeks since I had felt good and it's like those words unlocked that pain and set it free. It worked immediately. I am forever grateful to Jeanette and what she did for me, and what she did for Red Sample as well.

To learn more about my friend Jeanette and what she does please visit her webpage at www.blueearthawakening.com

So, who exactly is Red Sample? After finding out who it was who decided to attach themselves to me and to stay with me as long as they did, I was very curious about him. Who was he? What was his crime? I looked up the Bisbee five. It's hard to find specific information on one single person from this crime. This is what I found.

Bisbee five

December 8, 1883 was just any regular day in Bisbee, Arizona until five outlaw cowboys stormed into a general store with intentions of robbing it and ended the lives of four people—one of them being a pregnant woman—making the death toll five. Now they are considered and called the Bisbee five, but in fact there were six men. The Bisbee five contains Dan Dowd, Red Sample, Tex Howard, Bill DeLaney and Dan Kelly.

They were the first criminals to ever be legally hanged in Tombstone. The sixth man involved in this massacre was the mastermind, John Heath. For some reason the Bisbee five were convicted and sent to the gallows later on however, John Heath the mastermind, was sent to life in prison. The townspeople understandably didn't think that was okay—they thought he should be hung like the rest of them, and rightfully so. On February 22, 1884, about a month before the other men were to be hung, the townspeople broke John Heath out of jail and hanged him in the middle of town.

The victims

J.C. Tappenier was leaving the 'Bon Ton Saloon' which was the neighboring business of the general store being robbed. The robbers standing guard outside tried to force him back into the saloon but J.C. refused. Faced with Winchester repeating rifles, he was shot in the head.

Deputy Sheriff Tom Smith was enjoying a nice dinner at the 'Bisbee House' with his wife across the street from where the robbery, and now shooting, was taking place. He ran towards them and the robbers demanded he go back into the restaurant. Deputy Sheriff Smith refused, yelling at the robbers/murderers, "I am an officer of the law!" One of the cowboys replied, "Then you are the one we want!" Then he shot and killed the Deputy Sheriff.

'Indian Joe' a local man, and only known by this name, was shot in the leg while he tried making his escape. Annie Roberts, who was pregnant, came to the door of the 'Bisbee House' which she and her husband owned. Annie was shot by the cowboy outlaws, with the bullet shattering her spine. Annie and her baby died later on that evening. John A. Nolly, a local freighter, was outside standing with his wagon, he was shot in the chest. Death was not instantaneous, like Annie Roberts, he died later that evening.

As the men left, they got on their horses and started shooting at anybody they saw. Deputy Sheriff William Daniels ran out of the saloon when he heard the shooting and emptied his revolver at the murderous cowboys but ended up missing them. The men got away that day, went to a safe place, divided the money then went their own ways.

There was a $2,000 (Today close to $49,000) reward for the capture or known whereabouts of these dangerous men. The Sheriff Department formed two posses. The first posse quickly left after the bloody incident took place. Unbeknownst to the Sheriff's Department or the townspeople, one of the men in that first posse was none other than the mastermind of the crime itself, John Heath.

Sheriff Deputy William Daniels, who tried shooting at them as they made their getaway made up a second posse. They left at daybreak and quickly caught up with John Heath's posse. While in the middle of searching for the cowboys, Heath noticed prints in the sand. Two sets going one way and three sets going another. He brought this to Sheriff Deputy Daniels attention, but he did not believe the mastermind Heath.

Finally, when Heath was tried for his part in the massacre, Deputy Daniels accused John Heath of trying to mislead the posse. Because Tex Howard was the only man who neglected to wear a mask disguise, he was very quickly identified as one of the robbers. Upon further investigation they were able to name the other four men involved.

Apprehended

Daniel 'York' Kelly was caught somewhere near Deming, New Mexico.

Tex Howard and Red Sample made the most fatal mistake of their lives, next to the massacre of course, by returning to their old haunt in Clifton, Arizona. While in Clifton they went to visit a bartender friend of theirs, who in return called the authorities after they left. A posse was formed and within a couple days Tex Howard and Red Sample were captured.

Dan Dowd was captured by Deputy Daniels across the international border in Corralitos, Sonora. (Mexico)

William DeLaney was also captured by Deputy Daniels with the help of Deputy Sheriff Robert Hatch in the town of Minas Prietas, Sonora (Mexico) where he was being held after being involved in a brawl with a local miner.

John Heath was right about those two sets of prints in the dirt, those were the prints of Dan Dowd and William DeLaney. Obviously being the mastermind of this horrific crime and being one of the head people in a posse to search for the murderous gang, I too would have a hard time trusting him.

Kelly, Howard, Sample, Dowd and DeLaney were sentenced by the Judge to be hanged by the neck until they were dead. Heath, upon his request, was tried separately.

Unfortunately, the prosecutors were unable to produce any witnesses that could connect Mr. John Heath to the incident. The County Attorney found a prisoner to testify against Heath. Sergeant Lawrence was in jail for the killing of two men during a saloon brawl and had been incarcerated with Heath and his murdering cowboy gang.

Sergeant Lawrence swore that he had overheard Heath and the other men talk about the massacre and why their plans had failed. Some think that Lawrence's sentence was exchanged for a lighter sentence due to his testimony. John Heath was convicted and handed down a second-degree murder charge. I am glad the townspeople lynch mob took it upon themselves to bring Heath to justice. Why hang five of the men and let the mastermind LIVE the rest of his days in a jail cell?

George Goodfellow had witnessed Heath's hanging in town. Goodfellow besides being a witness, happened to be the County Coroner who was responsible for determining the exact cause of John Heath's death. In County Coroner George Goodfellow's own words:

"Emphysema of the lungs which might have been, and probably was, caused by strangulation, self-inflicted or otherwise, as in accordance with the medical evidence."

So, there you have it. That is the history behind the Bisbee Massacre. Why Red Sample decided to stay with me, I may never know. It is creepy because there were times during my sickness/attachment when I would feel I wasn't alone and would record mini sessions, and a man could be heard breathing. Never in my investigating days had I ever been rude, disrespectful or provoking, until that one day while at Boot Hill. To this day I blame the heat. I am against provoking and think it's unnecessary and inappropriate.

Jeanette shared with me one of her experiences which blew my mind. It involved this spirit helping paint a self-portrait of the spirit itself. When I asked her if she had the painting in the house, she smiled and said she did. She hasn't shown many people this painting or experience, but since we just shared this prior experience, I think it made our bond stronger. She trusted me and shared the experience and the painting itself. She is allowing me to share that experience with you in the book. You can find it in Chapter Four—Tales from Another. Her painting of this spirit you can find with the other pictures, it won't be hard to miss, it will be the only painting.

Thank you, Jeanette for helping me rid myself of Red Sample. (Full name Omer 'Red' Sample)

I will end with this. Red Sample was hanged. There were so many times when I found myself gasping for air. I couldn't breathe and I would panic. This had never happened to me before. Think about when you are super-congested and you can't breathe through your nose, so you have to breathe through your mouth. Times that by ten, and while this is happening, it feels like your chest is caving in. Not only can you not breathe but you feel like an elephant is stomping on your chest.

While at Boot Hill in the area where Red Sample and the rest of the Bisbee Five are buried, I caught on recording unexplained gasping, that went unheard by me until I listened to the audio afterwards, days later. I caught an eerie EVP of a man saying, "Come back." Again, unheard by me until later on.

It makes sense that this is Red Sample. It's like watching a movie. Heck it should be a movie. Paranormal investigator investigates the historic Boot Hill in the historic town of Tombstone, gets an attachment, thinks she's dying, finds help with a spiritual healer, puts the pieces together and there you have Omer 'Red' Sample.

Please don't do what I did. Learn from my mistake. Never provoke. Be respectful. I beg you. It was the worse feeling in the world. I was terrified, I honestly thought I was dying. I was lucky and only had this attachment for a little over a month. Some people have been known to have attachments for years. I cannot imagine living with that for that long. One month was enough torment to last a lifetime for me.

Respect the spirits.

Figure 15 Red Sample's Grave

One Last Thing

If you enjoyed my book would you please take the time to leave a review on the site from which you purchased it?

I read all reviews personally and use the comments to help me make my book the best it can be.

Thank you,

Tessa Mauro.

Made in the USA
Columbia, SC
10 October 2023